Automation of
Legal Reasoning

Automation of Legal Reasoning

A Study on Artificial Intelligence and Law

P. Wahlgren

Computer Law Series 11

1992
Kluwer Law and Taxation Publishers
Deventer-Boston

Kluwer Law and Taxation Publishers
P.O. Box 23 Tel.: 31-5700-47261
7400 GA Deventer Fax: 31-5700-22244
The Netherlands

Cover design: Bert Arts

ISBN 90 6544 661 3

International Board of Editors

USA | Robert P. Bigelow, Counsel to Warner & Stackpole, Boston, Ma.; Daniel T. Brooks, Cadwalader, Wickersham & Taft, Washington, D.C., Partner in charge of computer law practice; Susan H. Nycum, Managing Partner Kadison Pfaelzer, Woodard, Quinn & Rossi, Palo Alto, Cal.; John T. Soma, Professor of Law, University of Denver, College of Law; James, A. Sprowl, Fitch, Even, Tabin & Flannery; Senior Researcher at the American Bar Association for computer law projects, Chicago, Ill.

USA

Robert P. Bigelow, Counsel to Warner & Stackpole, Boston, Ma.;
Daniel T. Brooks, Cadwalader, Wickersham & Taft, Washington, D.C., Partner in charge of computer law practice;
Susan H. Nycum, Managing Partner Kadison Pfaelzer, Woodard, Quinn & Rossi, Palo Alto, Cal.;
John T. Soma, Professor of Law, University of Denver, College of Law;
James, A. Sprowl, Fitch, Even, Tabin & Flannery; Senior Researcher at the American Bar Association for computer law projects, Chicago, Ill.

Acknowledgements

This book could not have been completed without the assistance and encouragement of many individuals as well as organizations to whom I am greatly indebted.

Most importantly, I would like to thank for the support I received from Professor *Peter Seipel*, Director of *The Swedish Law and Informatics Research Institute* (IRI), who shared with me his unique, in-depth knowledge of many of the addressed issues.

Valuable, critical comments have been also made by Professor emeritus *Jan Hellner, Faculty of Law, Stockholm University* and Professor *Andrew J. I. Jones, Department of Philosophy* and *Norwegian Research Center for Computers and Law, Oslo University*, both of whom read the final manuscript.

The writing of this book was performed during a period of four and a half years and the work was made possible thanks to the financial support from the *Swedish Council for Research in the Humanities and Social Sciences, The Law Faculty at Stockholm University*, and *Karl-Adam Bonnier's Foundation.* Practical and technical facilities were provided by IRI and *The Law Faculty at Stockholm University*. These organizations also made it possible for me to travel. Financial support for travels was also generously provided by *The Wallenberg Jubilee Foundation* and *The Foundation of 28 October 1982.*

I also express my gratitude to *Tomas Stahre*, former head of the organizational department of the Swedish *National Courts Administration*, and *Hans Holmberg*, vice managing director of the *The Swedish Engineering Employers' Association,* who made it possible for me to initiate and complete the system development projects that became the basis for the theoretical analysis submitted in this book. (Both system development projects were initiated in 1987, during the period of my court practice.) Important for the completion of those projects were also my contacts with Professor *Carl Gustaf Jansson*, *Department of Computer and System Science, Stockholm University* and Dr *Andreas Hamfelt*, *Uppsala Programming Methodology and Artificial Intelligence Laboratory, Computing Science Department, Uppsala University.*

Thanks are also due to *Teresa Bjelkhagen* who supervised my use of the English language, demonstrating great skill in this task. (The remaining irregularities in the text are no doubt due to my own final revisions and last-minute changes.)

Valuable support was furthermore provided by *Olof Dahnell* and *Martin Brinnen* at the IRI library who assisted in the retrieval of the sometimes obscure references, and by *Barbro Tengz-Nilsson* who carried out numerous administrative tasks.

Last, but not least, I am forever indebted to *Josefine*, an efficient professional, devoted wife, and loving mother, who showed unfailing good humour and great patience during the whole taxing period of this time-consuming work. Important to mention are also the two vivid sources of inspiration, *Kajsa* and *Maja*.

Stockholm, August 1992

Peter Wahlgren

Table of Contents

Chapter 4 Integration

Part 2 The Legal Reasoning Process

Chapter 5 Legal Reasoning

Part 3 Potentialities of Automation

Chapter 6 Automation of Legal Reasoning

List of Abbreviations

ABA	American Bar Association
ABAJ	American Bar Association Journal
ABF	American Bar Foundation
AC	Law Reports, Appeal Cases, Houses of Lords since 1890 (England)
ACM	The Association for Computing Machinery (U.S.A.)
ADB	Automatisk databehandling (ADP)
ADBJ	Svenska föreningen för ADB och juridik (The Swedish Society for Computers and Law)
ADP	Automatic Data Processing
AI	Artificial Intelligence
ASSYST	Applied Sentencing System
BID	International Bibliography on Computers and Law (Publication of IDG, Italy)
BILETA	British and Irish Legal Education Technology Association
BRÅ	Brottsförebyggande rådet (The National Council for Crime Prevention, Sweden)
C&L	Computers and Law (Periodical publication of the Society for Computers and Law, U.K.)
CEDIJ	Centre de recherche et developpement en informatique juridique (France)
CLIC	Canadian Law Information Council
CRID	Le Centre de Recherche Informatique et Droit (University of Namur)
DARPA	Defence Advanced Research Projects Agency (U.S.A.)
DSS	Decision Support System
DV	*See* NCA
EDB	Elektronisk databenyttelse (EDP)
EDP	Electronic Data Processing
ENIAC	Electronic Numerical Integrator and Computor
ESL-89	Expert Systems in Law: An International Conference on Law & Artificial Intelligence. The Center for Law and Computer Science, University of Bologna, 1989

FOA	National Defence Research Institute (Sweden)
HTLJ	High Technology Law Journal
IBM	International Business Machine Corporation
ICAIL-87	The First International Conference on Artificial Intelligence and Law. Boston, 1987
ICAIL-89	The Second International Conference on Artificial Intelligence and Law. Vancouver, 1989
ICAIL-91	The Third International Conference on Artificial Intelligence and Law. Oxford, 1991
ICLID-81	The International Study Congress on Logica, Informatica, Diritto. Consiglio Nazionale delle Richerche. IDG Florence (1981)
ICLID-85	The II International Conference on Logica, Informatica, Diritto. Consiglio Nazionale delle Richerche. IDG Florence (1985)
ICLID-89	The III International Conference on Logica, Informatica, Diritto. Consiglio Nazionale delle Richerche. IDG Florence (1989)
IDG	Istituto per la documentazione giuridica, Florence
IDR	Institut für Datenverarbeitung im Rechtswesen, Bonn
IFCLA	International Federation of Computer Law Associations
IKBS	Intelligent Knowledge Based Systems
ILITA	International Law & Information Technology Association
IR	Information Retrieval
IRI	The Swedish Law and Informatics Research Institute (Stockholm University)
IRS	Internal Revenue Service (U.S.A.)
JAG	Office of the Judge Advocate General, U.S. Air Force
JI	Judicial Information
JJ	Jurimetrics Journal
JLR	The jurisprudential model of legal reasoning elaborated in chapter 5 of this study
KBS	Knowledge Based System
KBS(A)	KBS reflecting knowledge of legal agent requirements
KBS(C)	Class of KBSs consisting of type (R), (Si), (F), and (E) reflecting knowledge of relevance for control of legal reasoning
KBS(D)	KBS reflecting knowledge of legal sub-domains

KBS(E)	KBS reflecting knowledge for the evaluation of legal decisions
KBS(F)	KBS reflecting formal aspects of legal knowledge
KBS(G)	KBS reflecting knowledge of legal taxonomies at a general level
KBS(Gc)	KBS reflecting general components of legal knowledge
KBS(I)	Class of KBSs consisting of type (G), (D), (A) and (S) designed for the support of legal identification and law search
KBS(R)	KBS reflecting legal knowledge of how agent requirements and/or prerequisites can be combined into legal rules
KBS(S)	KBS reflecting legal knowledge at prerequisite level
KBS(Si)	KBS reflecting legal knowledge of how agent requirements and/or rules can be combined into legal situational descriptions
KEE	Knowledge Engineering Environment
KS	Knowledge System
KWIC	Key Word In Context
KWOC	Key Word Out of Context
LIST	Legal Information Systems & Technologies (Foundation), (Canada)
LITE	Legal Information Through Electronics
LRS	Law Research Service Incorporated
MIT	Massachusetts Institute of Technology
MULL	Modern Uses of Logic in Law (Periodical publication 1959-66, followed 1966 by JJ)
NCA	National Courts Administration (Sweden)
NRCCL	Norwegian Research Center for Computers and Law (Oslo University)
NÅR	Nordisk årsbok i rättsinformatik (Nordic Yearbook of Law and Informatics)
RB	Rättegångsbalken (The Swedish Procedural Act)
RF	Regeringsformen (Part of the Swedish Constitution)
RIRA	Reports and Information Activity (U.S. IRS)
RJ	Ratio Juris: An International Journal of Jurisprudence and Philosophy of Law
RJCL	Rutgers Journal of Computers (Technology) and the Law (periodical publication 1970-80, followed by RCTLJ)
RCTLJ	Rutgers Computer & Technology Law Journal

SAFAD	The Swedish Agency For Administrative Development
SARI	Samarbetsorganet för rättsväsendets informationsssystem (The Joint Committee of the JI System, Sweden)
ScAm	Scientific American
SFS	Svensk författningssamling (The Official Publication of Swedish Statutes)
SIGART	Special Interest Group on Artificial Intelligence
SISL	Stockholm Institute for Scandinavian Law
SvJt	Svensk juristtidning
SYSLAB	System Science Laboratory (Stockholm University)
UBC	University of British Columbia, Vancouver
UCLA	University of California, Los Angeles
UPMAIL	Uppsala Programming Methodology and Artificial Intelligence Laboratory (Uppsala University)
VF	Sveriges Verkstadsförening (The Swedish Engineering Employers' Association)
WIPO	World Intellectual Property Organization
YCL&T	Yearbook of Law, Computers & Technology

Part 1

Background and Related Work

1 Introduction

1.1 Artificial Intelligence and Law

This book is written with the ambition that it should provide a contribution to the field of knowledge most widely known as artificial intelligence (AI) and law. The focus is set on automation of legal reasoning.

AI and law constitute a large area of research in which the activities are induced by different motives. It is also noticeable that the various backgrounds of the people involved affect the outcome of the work. It is therefore important to emphasize that the adopted perspective is basically a jurisprudential one. Thus this is primarily a book on analytical jurisprudence, or, as the discipline is usually referred to in the Scandinavian countries, general theory of law (*allmän rättslära*).

Several things make an investigation of AI from a jurisprudential standpoint reasonable.[1] One general observation shows that for several years now the heralds of AI have been promulgating the idea that their applications are some of the most powerful inventions ever made, affecting both practical work premisses and theoretical foundations for intellectual work. A statement about *knowledge engineering* (a label for construction of AI-systems in which certain tools and methods are employed) may serve as an example:

> We can foresee two beneficial effects. The first and most obvious will be the development of knowledge systems that replicate and autonomously apply human expertise. For these systems, knowledge engineering will provide the technology for converting human knowledge into industrial power. The second benefit may be less obvious. As an inevitable side effect, knowledge engineering will catalyse a global effort to collect, codify, exchange, and exploit applicable forms of human knowledge. In this way, knowledge engineering will accelerate the development, clarification, and expansion of human knowledge itself.[2]

[1] Some of the motives that are submitted in this introduction have been previously outlined in Wahlgren, P. *AI, kunskapsingenjörer och expertsystem inom juridiken* (1988) *and* in Wahlgren, P. *Artificiell intelligens, juridisk metod och nya rättsfrågor* (1990).

[2] Hayes-Roth, F., Waterman, D.A., Lenat, D.B. eds. *Building Expert Systems*, xii (1983) (hereinafter Hayes-Roth).

Statements like the one above may seem over-enthusiastic. It may therefore be defensible to treat them with some scepticism. But, on the other hand, when it comes to methodological issues in law no stone should be left unturned. Especially the claim that AI may assist decision-making and other aspects of intellectual toil – the basic elements of legal work – justifies a jurisprudential investigation; i.e. an investigation in which not only the technical considerations, but also the legal presuppositions and the consequences that may appear on user levels are given attention.

The conclusion that such a study is a worthwhile enterprise is strengthened by the development perceived in other fields, making it obvious that computer technology steadily becomes more integrated into society. In many domains de-computerization would now be inconceivable and although the legal sector has so far been quite conservative in its adoption of the new technology, it is relevant to foresee an increased exploitation of computers also in the legal domain. Computer technology may thereby come to affect many aspects of legal work and it is not unrealistic to predict that things which are today considered to be new technology will soon be meshed with the legal method in a very intricate manner. In the long-time perspective it may even be assumed that an interchange of AI-methods and legal theory may entail that basic jurisprudential concepts, as well as methodological assumptions, will be supplemented and changed.[3] From this perspective the need for jurisprudential investigations is urgent.

The objectives that have guided this study are discussed in some length in section 1.2. However, AI is for several reasons interesting to study in conjunction with law and in this section a number of conceivable motives are briefly mentioned in order to provide a general introduction.

a) Theoretical cross-fertilization. Perhaps the most important reason for the appearance of this interdisciplinary field is the fact that AI and law are two courses of study orientated towards similar issues. The development of methods for decision-making is one of the major research aims in AI as well as in jurisprudence. The parallels are far-reaching. A close investigation reveals that almost every methodological concern (related to decision making) within jurisprudence has a corresponding interpretation

[3] Bing, J. *Rettsutdannelse och rettsdannelse på tyvehundretallet*, 87 (1988) "It is perhaps possible to assert that knowledge technology may create a new paradigm for [the discipline] general theory of law." (original text in Norwegian).

in AI. Moreover, many current problems in AI have been discussed in various forms during the centuries in works of jurisprudence. In consequence, the possibilities of fruitful interchange of ideas are promising. This fact was identified already in the early 1970s[4] and since that time it has served as an important theoretical basis for several projects.[5]

b) Jurisprudential development. Besides the commitment of AI and law specialists it is possible to see a significant jurisprudential interest in the topic. That is to say that in jurisprudence there has always existed a vivid interest in methodological issues and from a historical point of view the impulse to scrutinize AI may be looked upon as the latest expression of a tradition encompassing excursions into logic, decision theory, sociology, and a variety of additional topics.

For a practicing lawyer it is, for instance, interesting to investigate whether AI may provide tools that may facilitate the legal work;[6] for legal administrators it is inviting to see whether the technique may enhance the possibilities to accomplish legal decisions of high quality (in terms of equality, predictability, etc.); and for a legal scholar it is relevant to explore whether the discipline, through theoretical contributions, may provide a means for further development of the legal method, the legal language, etc.[7] In addition, for the legal sector taken as a whole, it is a basic concern to attract employees of high competence. It is therefore also relevant to find out whether AI-applications may induce better working conditions for the legal community.

c) A need for an experimental field. From the opposite side, i.e. from the technical point of view, law is at first sight almost a perfect experimental field for AI ventures. Legal work is to a large extent guided by rules and, since most AI-systems lean on so called rule-based techniques

4 "The effort to create programs to simulate legal reasoning processes should have at least two benefits: It should prompt more systematic study of legal problem-solving, and it should advance knowledge of the problem-solving capabilities of computers." Buchanan, B.G., Headrick, T.E. *Some Speculation About Artificial Intelligence and Legal Reasoning,* 41 (1970).

5 *See, e.g.,* McCarty, L.T., Rissland, E.L. *Series Foreword* in Gardner, A. v.d.L. *An Artificial Intelligence Approach to Legal Reasoning* (1987). "A joint endeavour in artificial intelligence and law will strengthen and inform both disciplines."

6 *Cf.* Grossman, G.S., Solomon, L.D. *Computers and Legal Reasoning,* 66 (1983).

7 *Cf.* Niblett, B. *Expert Systems for Lawyers,* 4 (1981).

(to be explained), the advantages of the legal domain may seem apparent when it comes to the development of pilot projects. This has been noticed by many computer scientists and the need for a suitable domain for technical experiments has sometimes been the only distinct incentive for various projects in the legal sector,[8] where a number of activities have been initiated without, or with only a minor jurisprudential consideration.[9]

d) Aim for efficiency. Applications originating from research in AI depend on computer technology. Computers are intimately associated with rationalization. Many initiatives may be therefore seen as attempts to improve efficiency or as reflections of desires to simplify administration.[10] A recognition of the potentialities of rationalization in legal work may be found in both the private market[11] and the public sector. In Sweden, for example, substantial efforts have been undertaken by *The Swedish Agency for Administrative Development* (SAFAD) – an agency under the Department of Public Administration, responsible for promoting rationalization and efficiency in the Swedish civil service – by means of forming development groups working with AI-technology.[12]

e) Commercial motives. Discussing the overall motives for various endeavours within AI and law it is also relevant to mention the computer industry which, among other things, promotes this line of development in its pursuit of new markets. In several countries major computer firms have initiated research and development activities in the area, or appeared as sponsors.[13] In recent years also several firms specializing in accounting

[8] *Cf.* Gardner *supra* note 5, at 67.

[9] This has been illustrated by Susskind who in a comparison of 19 major projects found that almost 50 per cent of them had no references to jurisprudence, and that in only 2 of them jurisprudence was used explicitly as a source of guidance. Susskind, R.E. *Expert Systems in Law. A Jurisprudential Inquiry,* Appendix I, at 257-59 (1987).

[10] *See generally,* on the potential impact of AI related computer systems, Hayes-Roth *supra* note 2, at xi-xvi.

[11] *See, e.g.,* Pear, C.E. *Expert Systems and the Race for Clients* (1989).

[12] Statskontoret. *Statskontorets projekt Kunskapssystem – "Växthuset"* (1988).

[13] *See, e.g., Proceedings from the Second International Conference on Artificial Intelligence and Law* (1989), (hereinafter ICAIL-89) which announce IBM, Canada as a sponsor. The proceedings include papers from work sponsored by several commercial firms, e.g. IBM, U.S.A. (Ashley, K.D. *Toward a Computational Theory of Arguing with Precedents: Accomodating* [sic] *Multiple Interpretations of Cases) and* Xerox, Palo Alto Research Centre (Marshall, C.C. *Representing the*

and law office automation have presented commercially available systems[14] as well as market analyses.[15]

f) Strategic considerations. Several military and defence organizations have shown interest in the field. In the U.S.A., for example, contributions to research in AI and law have been given by the *Department of Defense.*[16] The support of the military community goes far back. The appearance of electronic computers is in much the result of military research during World War II and one of the first projects with a legal application was actually launched in cooperation with the *U.S. Air Force.*[17] Considerations of this kind have been more or less apparent in a number of projects in several countries[18]

g) Protection of group interests. In order to be able to protect the interests of its members several organizations have shown interest in advanced computer systems. In Sweden, for instance, in several cases, the unions together with the employers have signed agreements on how rationalization should be conducted.[19] In a broader perspective, focusing on office automation in general, national unions have contributed to studies of considerable proportions.[20] Simultaneously, in several countries employers' organizations and management consultants have participated in

Structure of a Legal Argument). See also benefactors in University of British Columbia, Faculty of law. *Law and Computers Project, Law and Artificial Intelligence Research Project and L.I.S.T. Foundation* (1989).

14 *See, e.g.,* Capper, P., Susskind, R.E. *Latent Damage Law – The Expert System* (1988).

15 *See, e.g.,* Morrison, R.W. *Market Realities of Rule-Based Software for Lawyers: Where the Rubber Meets the Road* (1989).

16 *See, e.g.,* Rissland E.L. *Dimension-Based Analysis of Hypotheticals from Supreme Court Oral Argument* (1989) *and* Ashley *supra* note 13.

17 U.S. Air Force JAG Law Review. *Special Issue: LITE, Legal Information Thru Electronics,* 5-51 (1966).

18 *See, e.g.,* for a project engaging *The Institute for Defence Analyses* in the U.S., Navarro, J.A., Taylor, J.G. *Data Analyses and Simulation of a Court System for the Processing of Criminal Cases* (1968) *and,* for a Project engaging *The National Defence Research Institute* (FOA) in Sweden, Löf, S. *The POLYTEXT/ARBIT Demonstration System* (1980).

19 *See, e.g.,* Domstolsverket. *ADB inom domstolsväsendet. Studiematerial,* section 4:28, at 10-11 (1985).

20 *See, e.g.,* Docherty, P., Loman, L. *Personalinflytande och datorisering* (1983).

projects involving AI-systems, where some of them were designed to assist with dismissal of employees.[21]

1.2 Objectives

1.2.1 AI-Applications in Law

One primary concern of this study is to investigate to what extent AI and the related techniques are suitable for the legal domain. What kinds of techniques exist? What aspects of legal reasoning is it possible to support, and how can it be done? From this follows that the most notable subjects to investigate are systems designed for the support of decision processes. In practice, this directs attention to the so called *expert systems*, or *knowledge based systems* (KBS).[22]

A KBS is a computer application from which it is possible to obtain various kinds of decision support. The operative domain of a KBS is determined by the content of the *knowledge base* – a part of the system in which a representation of facts and relations about certain situations, etc. is stored. Several knowledge bases may be combined into complex systems and the issues that are processed are usually specified by the user in a dialogue with the system.[23]

The development of KBSs has been swift. Many applications of today were hardly possible to conceive of only a few years ago. In some cases system implementations have been successful,[24] but on other occasions the

[21] *See, e.g.*, Hamfelt, A., Wahlgren, P. *Datorstödda beslut: Artificiell intelligens och juridik* (1988) *and* Expertech. *Employment Law: Clarifying Dismissal* (1987).

[22] Devices originating from AI-research appear in many different domains and are not limited to decision support and administrative work. Industrial robots, systems for medical diagnosing, systems for natural language processing, and systems for surveillance of complex processes, are examples of other forms of applications. *See generally*, on AI-applications, Barr, A., Feigenbaum, E.A. eds. *The Handbook of Artificial Intelligence*, Vol. 2 (1982), O'Shea, T., Eisenstadt, M. eds. *Artificial Intelligence: Tools, Techniques and Applications*, part III (1984), Quinlan, J.R. ed. *Applications of Expert Systems*, Vol. 1 (1987) & Vol. 2 (1989) *and* Feigenbaum, E.A. McCorduck, P., Nii, H.P. *The Rise of the Expert Company* (1988).

[23] The KBS technique is described in more detail in chapters 3 and 6.

[24] *See, e.g.*, Simon, E., Gaes, G. *ASSYST – Computer Support for Guideline Sentencing*, 195 (1989) "ASSYST has been a success."

introduction of systems has been cumbersome.[25] In spite of many difficulties and the existence of conflicting attitudes as to whether further development is advisable,[26] it is nevertheless possible to foresee considerable changes also in the future. Several factors make such a prediction logical: the accelerating technical development is continuously generating more advanced tools at lower prices, the computer readiness in society is growing, the consciousness about the considerable potentialities for rationalization related to computers is increasing, and the in-built factors of the legal system, e.g. principles of equality and predictability, provide natural motives for further experiments.

This study is not, however, restricted to operative KBSs. The intention with this work is to provide an investigation that is of a practical value. This entails that not only various kinds of KBSs, but also that systems combining AI-methods and functions originating from conventional computer science are given attention.[27] This is simply a reflection of the fact that the import of advanced technology does not always result in the implementation of complete systems of certain well-defined kinds and that the elaboration of a variety of functions, as well as innumerable possibilities of synthesized solutions, entail a slow but steady development in which more advanced functions continuously add support to the existing facilities.[28]

1.2.2 AI-Methods in Law

The techniques that are used in AI are often labelled as *knowledge based methods*, or somewhat shorter, *knowledge methods*. A basic assumption in this study is that several such techniques may be of a general nature and

[25] *See generally*, on difficulties related to implementation of AI-systems in law, Morrison *supra* note 15, at 35.

[26] *See*, for optimistic predictions, Grossman, Solomon *supra* note 6 *and* Freeman, P.R.W. *Expert Systems and the Law* (1986), *compare*, with a doubting forecast, Leith, P. *Legal Expert Systems: Misunderstanding the Legal Process* (1986).

[27] *Cf.* Capper, Susskind *supra* note 14, at 146.

[28] *See e.g.*, Koers, A.W., Pelger, W.D. *Information Technology and Court Administration*, 425-26 (1989) *and* Council of Europe. *Integrated Work Stations in the Legal Sector and Decision Support Systems* (1989).

that knowledge methods may be employed as analytical tools even if no construction of computer systems is involved. Thus, it is also assumed that a study on AI-methods may support and deepen the jurisprudential introspection in a creative way. This belief is a reflection of the fact that jurisprudence may be seen as an activity aiming to develop methods for the legal analysis and for legal reasoning (thereby not suggesting that this is the only objective of jurisprudence). In consequence, further objectives of this study are to indicate methodological potentialities and to contribute to the discussion about the suggested solutions from a jurisprudential point of view (i.e. not only by means of elaborating technical aspects related to computer science and AI).

This approach is motivated by the obvious fact that a set of well-defined legal methods is an essential part of any legal system. Decision processes must not be affected by irrelevant factors or by the eccentricity of individual lawyers; a uniform decision making technique is necessary if the consequences of the legal system are to be predicted. Well-known and widely accepted methods for legal reasoning are also important in order to sustain principles of equality; anyone who comes into contact with a given legal system has the right to objective treatment, regardless where or when the issue is settled.[29]

Standards for decision making are not only important for judges or persons occupied with administrative decision making. Methods for legal reasoning are important in all sorts of legal work, also in the private sector. A practicing lawyer who performs poorly, e.g. in a court proceeding, runs a high risk to lose his case, or, e.g. in a process of negotiating, to be outwitted by an opposing party.

The jurisprudential emphasis on the reasoning processes entails that a lot of methodological attention within the legal domain is orientated towards techniques for determining the basis for a decision, law search, interpretation, evaluation of facts, handling of rules of formality, and evaluation of decisions. Likewise the focus on the legal language is intense.

[29] *See generally,* on the importance of *technical aspects* of legal decision making in relation to fundamental legal principles, Strömholm, S. *Rätt, rättskällor och rättstillämpning,* 441-42 (1988) *and,* on "'Formal Principles of Justice' which are the administrative rules of the practice of law ..." Coval, S.C., Smith, J.C. *Law and its Presuppositions,* 36 (1986).

Simultaneously it is noticeable that within AI much interest focuses on basically the same matters.[30] Major research aims are to describe and amplify the means of reasoning processes. AI-system development must, for instance, include a very delicate analysis of the issue at hand. The facts that are to be embodied in an AI-system must be collected, interpreted, transformed, and finally formalized. Simultaneously, the rules governing the reasoning process must be identified and managed.[31] Considerable efforts are devoted to further development of techniques for this kind of work,[32] but also towards the elaboration of criteria for the evaluation of different methods.[33]

1.2.3 Jurisprudence for AI

The issues concerning the feasibility of AI in legal work may be the most apparent ones, but they do not provide the only conceivable motives for research in this field. From the fact that AI and law form an interdisciplinary area of research follows that it is possible to look upon the topic from the opposite side, i.e. to see whether jurisprudence may contribute to the development of a sound basis for further attempts to construct intelligent machines.

Jurisprudence has been concerned with legal reasoning and methodological questions for several hundred years. The birth of AI, in a practical sense, is often dated to the mid 1950s and this fact is in itself a sufficient motive for a thorough investigation of jurisprudential knowledge, or as *Richard Susskind* writes:

> It would indeed be embarrassing for all concerned with jurisprudence if it transpired that we [in the legal domain] had to admit to computer scientists

30 *See e.g.*, on relations between AI-technology and legal theory, Alexy, R. *Legal Expert Systems and Legal Theory*, 67-68 (1988) commenting on, Bench-Capon, T.J.M. *Logical Models of Legislation and Expert Systems* (1988).

31 The development of KBS is described in more detail in chapters 3 and 6.

32 *See*, generally on system developing methods, Diaper, D. ed. *Knowledge Elicitation: Principles, Techniques and Applications* (1989).

33 *See*, on methods of evaluation for legal KBSs, Kracht, D., de Vey Mestdagh, C.N.J., Svensson, J.S. eds. *Legal Knowledge Based Systems: An Overview of Criteria for Validation and Practical Use* (1990).

> that, though we have been speculating about the nature of law and legal reasoning for well in excess of two thousand years, no matters of controversy have been settled, no agreement attained, in consequence of which legal theory has little to offer to the development of legal knowledge engineering.[34]

The necessity to include an in-depth knowledge of law and legal reasoning in AI and law enterprises has been recognized by several researchers and the fact that "all expert systems in law necessarily make assumptions about the nature of law and legal reasoning" is a crucial argument stressing the importance of jurisprudential considerations.[35] A related consideration is that basic legal principles are often interwoven with the modus operandi of legal organizations. This implies that system development and system implementation in the field of law must be often adjusted to certain frameworks, of which some may be visible only to those who are legally trained.

The urgent need for elaborated models of law and legal reasoning is perhaps best mirrored in the fact that practical advancements in the field of AI and law, despite great efforts, have been surprisingly few. Moreover, it is apparent that some submissions have shown a lack of basic jurisprudential insight or, even worse, have been founded on various misconceptions of the nature of law.[36] At the same time, surprisingly few researchers have paid much attention to the underlying reasons for these difficulties.

These background considerations lead to the hypothesis that several basic principles of a legal system, when made explicit, may provide valuable knowledge for further development of legal AI-systems. Simultaneously it was assumed that the ignorance of such principles to some extent may also explain why so few support systems have become operative within the legal sector. An important objective in this study is therefore to pin-point

34 Susskind *supra* note 9, at 35.

35 Gold, D.I., Susskind, R.E. *Expert Systems in Law: A Jurisprudential and Formal Specification Approach*, 307 (1985).

36 Most outspoken about this fact is perhaps Leith *supra* note 26, at 31: "Professionals should send the AI researchers back to their keyboards, requesting them to study real law, rather than this simplified pseudo-law which they present." *See also*, for a more elaborated discussion, Leith, P. *The Computerised Lawyer*, 181-214 (1991).

some fundamental legal principles, and to explain the theory behind those principles.

It is also necessary to realize that legal work entails activities of great diversity. There are few similarities between, for instance, a commercial contracting situation, a tax debt collecting procedure, a criminal court sentencing act, or a legislative drafting process. One additional objective is therefore to point-out some significant differences that may occur in various kinds of legal work. Hopefully, such a description will increase the understanding of how support functions that can be adjusted to various situations may be developed.

Finally, the law affects all parts of society and a legal system must be able to cope with problems occurring in all the sectors of human activities. It is therefore obvious that legal problem solving must be based to some extent on principles of a general nature. Reflecting over the large bulk of the accumulated jurisprudential knowledge, there are also reasons to believe that jurisprudential models of reasoning may provide some of the most articulated descriptions of reasoning processes that exist.[37] A far reaching objective of this study is therefore to articulate those aspects that may be of value for AI-research in general.[38]

To summarize these background considerations it can be said that the aim of this study is to contribute to the process of clarifying at least two things: (i) the potentialities of supporting legal reasoning with AI (by means of incorporating computer-based applications as well as analytical methods) and (ii) the usefulness of jurisprudential theories for AI (primarily for the process of developing support systems for legal reasoning, but also for AI in general). In this respect the objectives are of an interdisciplinary nature, i.e. the ambition is that the investigation will contribute to the field of AI and law as such, and that both lawyers and technically-oriented researchers working in the field will find some interesting features.

37 *Cf.* Strömholm, S. *Genmäle,* 489 (1970) *and* Berman, D.H., Hafner, C.D. *Indeterminacy: A Challenge to Logic-based Models of Legal Reasoning*, 2 (1987).

38 *Cf.* Kowalski, R., Sergot, M. *The Use of Logical Models in Legal Problem Solving*, 217 (1990). "We expect that second generation [legal reasoning] systems . . . will help to identify extension of the technology which may prove useful also in other application areas."

1.3 Scope

The material concerning the issues included in this book is massive. Jurisprudential literature has been accumulated for several hundred years and it alone fills vast libraries. The literature on AI and on the combined topic of AI and law is for obvious reasons smaller in volume, but nevertheless of considerable size.

In consequence, a study like this must find a level of description that in some respect is general. The strength of an investigation of this kind lies in the way that different details and subjects are integrated – not in an array of novel findings in delicate AI formalization problems, jurisprudential foundations, system design techniques, etc. Considering the number of research areas and sub-problems that are included in this book, such an ambitious approach would be foredoomed to failure.[39] From this follows that a number of selections must be made and that the investigation must be limited.

1.3.1 Jurisprudential Considerations

The need for clear demarcations is most apparent with regard to the jurisprudential material. Not only is the material vast, but there also exist various legal traditions providing conflicting perspectives. The disagreements may thereby concern details,[40] but at times the differences of opinion may also concern basic elements of legal theory.[41] The fact that the material is vast, that it is sometimes ambiguous, and that it originates

[39] Susskind, commenting on the vastness of the material in the field, suggests that "the problem here is rooted not simply in the amount of data, information and knowledge. . . . There is the further question of perspective: the history, styles, and epistemological bases of writings on law and computing are diverse." Susskind also raises the question of "whether academic offering in the field should not best be made in the tradition of one or other but not both disciplines." Susskind, R.E. *Review of Gardner, A. An Artificial Intelligence Approach to Legal Reasoning*, 227-28 (1990).

[40] The differences between legal systems are sometimes huge and it may seem, at a first glance, impossible to find uniform interpretations. *See e.g.*, Strömholm *supra* note 29, at 451 about opposing views on *the principle of lex posterior legi priori derogat* in the the common law system and in the Swedish legal system.

[41] *See e.g.*, for an overview, MacCormick, N., Weinberger, O. *An Institutional Theory of Law*, 1-6 (1986).

from various jurisprudential traditions, makes the process of selection a delicate matter.

The initial selection of jurisprudential material in this study was, however, obvious. Due to the fact that the project included system developing activities conducted in cooperation with Swedish organizations, the primary source had to be Scandinavian legal theory.

The investigation is not, however, limited to Scandinavian jurisprudence only. The ambition throughout this study has been to compare and to make references to works of jurisprudence, disregarding which legal system they may originate from. It may thereby be noted that since many previous studies in AI and law have been initiated in the Anglo-American legal environment, the necessity to make references to that legal system has been frequent. Naturally, however, it was possible to include only fragments of the existing jurisprudential material and in order to keep the description within a reasonable length the investigation of jurisprudence is also concentrated to the development during the nineteenth and twentieth centuries.

1.3.2 AI Considerations

The investigation of technical aspects undertaken in this study focuses primarily on the works that have been presented in the field of AI and law. The basic assumption behind this emphasis is that major, and for this study relevant findings from AI, have been reflected in works on AI and law. In addition, in-depth investigations in "pure" AI material have been conducted, concerning aspects that for various reasons have been found relevant. Many difficult selections have been necessary to decide upon, making that this study is in no way a total inventory of on-going AI activities. Nevertheless, it has not been found practicable to make a general explanation as to how the selections have been made. Instead, when found appropriate, references to the various undertakings within the field of AI that for some reasons have been left out are made throughout the discussion of potentialities of automation.

There also exists a limit to the scope of ambition and the perceived prospects of AI. That is to say that this study has been conducted with the aim of producing results of practical value. In consequence, it is not a science fiction-oriented speculation about autonomous legal reasoning systems which may control and guide societies in a distant future. Reachable goals for contemporary AI in the field of law are less advanced. The knowledge about reasoning processes is still very superficial and truly intelligent computer systems are presently remote objectives. It has been therefore the ambition of this investigation not to speculate, but merely to make an inventory of the on-going research and to provide material for a discussion about potentialities and consequences based on facts. Hopefully also, a more sober investigation of this kind may add new arguments to the debate about future legal work environments and about jurisprudence to come.

1.4 Method

The initial considerations in this study lead to the conclusion that a worthwhile approach would be to scrutinize the potentialities of automation in relation to a step-by-step analysis of legal reasoning, and the main part of this book is devoted to that assignment.

The task is pursued by means of elaborating a model of legal reasoning. The elements of the model – the various phases of legal reasoning – are related to works of jurisprudence, to previous attempts of automation, and to potentialities of AI-techniques and related methods. Thus the model provides not only a framework for jurisprudential descriptions of legal reasoning, but it also forms a structure for investigations of AI enterprises in law.

The description of the legal reasoning process is essentially based on various analyses of jurisprudential literature and to some extent on reported studies in AI and law. The theoretical investigation has been also supplemented with various forms of observations.

The discussion concerning the potentialities of automation is based on analyses of the domain as a whole and, when available, on the documentation from reported system implementations. In addition, technical references that are made throughout the discussion originate from controlled experiments as well as observations of legal decision making from a number of system development projects at *The Swedish Law and Informatics Research Institute* (IRI).

In this study two system development projects have been elaborated and documented. The first one deals with criminal court-decisions. It was carried out in cooperation with the *National Courts Administration* in Sweden (NCA) and the *System Science Laboratory* at *Stockholm University* (SYSLAB). The project was also accompanied by a reference-group consisting of judges. Two minor computer-based prototype systems were developed. The first prototype was based on a *Texas Instrument* workstation (a computer primarily designed in order to facilitate development of KBSs) and the software tool *KEE* (Knowledge Engineering Environment). The second prototype was constructed with the assistance of a IBM-compatible personal computer and a *Prolog* computer programming language. The aim of the sub-project was to illustrate how decision support concerning the choice of an appropriate penalty in cases of criminal assault may be developed. None of the prototypes were put into actual use as the ambition was not so much to complete the formalization of the whole area, but rather to try out different methods. Simultaneously, a sketchy scenario of fully computerized criminal court proceedings was drawn. The scenario comprised interacting administration modules, information retrieval facilities, and a decision-support system. The practical parts of the project have been evaluated and the conclusions that were arrived at in the NCA project are referred to throughout this book. A complete documentation is given in the IRI-report series.[42]

The second sub-project studied decision support in situations of negotiation. It was conducted in cooperation with a major Swedish employers' organization, *Sveriges Verkstadsförening* (VF) and the *Uppsala Programming Methodology and Artificial Intelligence Laboratory* at *Uppsala University* (UPMAIL). One elaborated support system prototype (Prolog system developed on Macintosh computers) dealing with the question of employees' dismissal was completed. In connection with this work, a hypertext[43] application was developed. The hypertext application and the decision support system were later integrated into one system. The project had a reference group attached to it and the work was followed by a study

42 Wahlgren, P. *Beslutstöd för brottmål: En förstudie om kunskapsbaserad systemutveckling* (1987).

43 Hypertext is explained in detail in chapter 6.

on cost-benefit aspects related to the implementation of the system. In the latter study various scenarios and different strategies were evaluated. Also the VF project has been documented in the IRI-report series.[44]

In addition, it should be mentioned that several minor projects on legal decision support prototypes have been completed during the initial stages of this work. During a couple of years students in knowledge-based system developing courses at the EDP department at *Stockholm University* were given law as a domain to work within. Instruction and domain knowledge were given in those projects in cooperation with IRI.[45]

1.4.1 A Terminological Remark

Research findings are of little value if they are not understandable to those who are concerned, and in a broad field like AI and law it may be argued that demands for explicit explanations should be set high. An all too technical or all too abstract approach without references to practical situations creates unnecessary obstacles for understanding. Especially when proposed systems and methodological suggestions are intended for day-to-day use in legal work the demand for clearness becomes critical. *G. D. Wood*, directing our attention towards terminological discrepancies, is outspoken about how this aspect has been handled in the discipline of AI and law so far:

> This [communication problem] has had the unfortunate consequence of creating incommensurable vocabularies and misunderstanding, a 'tower of Babel' which has cut researchers off from each other and from the worlds of legal practice an legal scholarship. The failure to communicate has afforded some researchers the opportunity of shrouding their work in mystery and of avoiding criticism.[46]

44 Hamfelt, Wahlgren *supra* note 21 *and* Dahnell, O. *Ekonomiska aspekter på ett beslutstödsystem* (1990).

45 Some of these student projects are documented in Jansson, C-G., Wahlgren, P. *Expertsystem för juridik. Ett försök med avtalslagen* (1985).

46 Wood, G.D. *On the Classification and Evaluation of Knowledge-Based Systems in Law*, 9 (1990).

Being aware of these difficulties, one additional aim of this study is to discuss the issues that are approached in a language understandable both from a legal stand-point and from a technical perspective. This methodological consideration is reflected in this study by the fact that definitions and terminological issues are given a relatively high priority – technical definitions and special expressions are explained as they appear. In addition, some commonly abbreviated words and phrases are explained in the list of abbreviations. The ambition to clarify the underlying principles of AI and law is also reflected in the background descriptions of related work, which are intended to include also matters of basic nature.

1.4.2 Method vs Objectives

The method of decomposing the reasoning process in order to discuss potentialities for computer-based support follows the same approach as the one employed in the first elaborated article on the topic.[47] The need for a better understanding of legal reasoning processes has been thereafter identified and commented on by several researchers,[48] e.g. by Susskind who suggests that

> [J]urisprudence can and ought to supply the models of law and legal reasoning that are required for computerized implementation in the process of building expert systems in law. . . .

[47] Buchanan, Headrick *supra* note 4, at 53-60 *and* at 45: "Understanding and codifying the decisionmaking process of lawyers presents one of the greatest challenges of the proposed research."

[48] *Cf.* Chandler, J.P. *Computers and Case Law*, 217 (1974) "More must be known about the mental operations a lawyer performs when engaging in case law research before the computer can be programmed to aid him to the full extent of its capacity.", Berman, Hafner *supra* note 37, at 2 "A computer program for legal reasoning cannot be created without first characterising the task to be performed and the means by which the reasoning agent performs it." *and* Bing, J. *Legal Decisions and Computerized Systems*, 250 (1990) "Problems basic to our understanding of traditional legal decisions are also obstacles for the successful modelling of such processes". *But see,* Koers, A.W., Kracht, D., Smith, M., Smits, J.M. Weusten, M.C.M. *Criteria for the Classification of Legal Knowledge Systems. Advisory Systems on Legal Questions*, 26-30 (1990), who stress the importance of encompassing the structure of legal knowledge and the fact that knowledge should be derived from legal sources, but, on the other hand, consider differences between legal reasoning of a KBS and of a lawyer irrelevant as long as "the system comes up with the right answers."

> . . . Perhaps the reason that there is, as yet, no overwhelmingly successful system is that the vast corpus of apposite jurisprudential material has not yet been tapped in the construction process.[49]

Considering the wide-spread acknowledgement of the necessity of an in-depth understanding of legal reasoning, the strategy of relating technical contributions to various phases in the legal reasoning process is not far-fetched. It is also noticeable that a study in which the focus is set on the legal reasoning process meets the objectives that are mentioned above.

An obvious advantage is thereby that an investigation originating from the legal reasoning process is independent of initial technical considerations and limitations. This stands in contrast to many previous projects which were initiated with a more or less fixed formalization methodology (i.e. a certain programming language, an expert system shell, or a pre-defined notion of logic) and in which jurisprudential considerations have been given a rather restricted influence. Thus, an investigation originating from the reasoning process may provide a basis for more balanced discussions.[50] Such an investigation may also help to clarify the issue of how AI-applications and AI-methods may best support legal reasoning in a way that is understandable from the lawyer's point of view.

Simultaneously, as regards to the question of whether jurisprudence may be of value to AI, a description of the legal reasoning process (if it turns out well) may provide a modularized blueprint of how jurisprudentially sound legal AI-tools may be designed.

49 Susskind *supra* note 9, at 20.

50 *Cf.* de Vey Mestdagh, C.N.J. *How Artificial Should Artificial Intelligence be?*, 103 (1990) "Our general conclusion is that research in the field of artificial intelligence should start from models of human knowledge and human knowledge processing, not from the knowledge representation and processing formalisms that are available." *But see*, for a suggestion that classifications of support systems originating from activities are less appropriate, Sergot, M. *The Representation of Law in Computer Programs*, 9-10 (1991). The reason for the latter stand-point, it is argued, is that most systems are not designed to support one particular activity, and that common types of systems may be used in order to support several activities. The activities that are mentioned in order to illustrate these arguments are however all synonyms for legal decision making on a general level (design and drafting of legislation, drafting of documents, litigation, general advice giving) and not very detailed activities within legal reasoning (*Cf.* section 5.1 *infra*). It may also be argued that the fact that few systems actually support one particular activity is of little significance in a study starting out from jurisprudential presuppositions.

In connection with this it should be mentioned that increased understanding of the legal reasoning process is not only an aim of studies in the combined field of AI and law. In Sweden legal reasoning has also been recently identified as a primary jurisprudential research objective.[51] In consequence, a study originating from the legal reasoning process may be of interest also from a purely jurisprudential perspective.[52]

Finally, remembering that jurisprudence offers one of the most elaborate descriptions of reasoning that exist, an investigation of legal reasoning may reveal features that may lend themselves to be generalized from. Thus a study like this may contribute to a more general understanding of human reasoning – also of value to the AI-research in general.

1.5 Structure and Overview

This book is divided into three parts. The first part, chapters 1 – 4, in addition to this introduction, provides background descriptions. In chapter 2 some basic jurisprudential notions are outlined. The overview starts with a short description of some common assumptions of the nature of law, which are necessary for the understanding of the various contributions to legal reasoning that have been submitted. Thereafter, an overview of some methodological traditions is presented. In chapter 3 the history of computer science and AI is outlined in a perspective reflecting mechanical devices and theoretical development. Chapter 4 describes the integration of law, computer science and AI. Methodological experiments and the formation of the academic discipline of AI and law are given special attention.

The second part of the study, chapter 5, embraces a description of the legal reasoning process. In the first section of chapter 5 the model of the process forming the basis for this study is outlined. Thereafter each part

[51] Strömholm *supra* note 29, at 301. "Scientific, if possible empirically founded in-depth analyses of the structure of legal decision making are presently some of the most urgent research tasks within [the discipline] general theory of law." (original text in Swedish).

[52] *Cf.* Bing *supra* note 48, at 250, "We realize that in working with the problems of designing legal expert systems we have returned to basics: We are working with problems formerly seen as belonging to the philosophy of law or the theory of norms. But these problems have now ceased to be academic, they have become vital to the design of computerized decision and expert systems, which we except will be the tools of the legal trade in the years to come.

of the model (based on different phases of the reasoning process) is described in detail in the succeeding sections.

In the third part of the study the primary undertaking is to investigate methods and techniques for the automation of legal reasoning. The discussion in chapter 6 starts with an analysis of some non-technical aspects of relevance for all projects concerning automation. Thereafter various computational models and knowledge representation techniques are investigated and related to the jurisprudential model of legal reasoning outlined in chapter 5. In this context also composed solutions and integrated systems are discussed.

Chapter 7 contains a discussion of potentialities of further automation of legal reasoning. The analysis leads up to the formulation of a more general design strategy for legal AI-systems. In Chapter 8 a summary of chapters 1-7 is provided. In addition the conclusions of the study are articulated. Finally, some remarks on apparent future research objectives are submitted.

2 Jurisprudence and Legal Reasoning

2.1 Introduction

In jurisprudence methodological shifts of practical significance have seldom or never happened overnight. The discussion concerning legal methods and legal reasoning has been a challenge primarily for legal philosophers and many legal movements basically mirror a theoretical development.

Nor is it always an easy task to elucidate methodological aspects related to legal reasoning in works of jurisprudence. Contributions to the study of legal reasoning are often part of more general discussions on the nature of law. It is also noticeable that in comparison to studies devoted to the nature of law and related issues, studies focusing on legal reasoning are scarce.[1]

The relatively low interest in legal reasoning processes may perhaps be explained by the fact that this has been a less problematic aspect of legal theory. In a historical perspective it is plausible that the problem of, for example, justification of legal decisions and discussions about codifications have appeared as much more compelling issues. The fact that relatively few philosophers have devoted their efforts to legal reasoning processes is nevertheless surprising since all contributions to jurisprudence must include assumptions about legal reasoning.[2]

It should be however stressed that the scarcity of studies on legal reasoning is by no means all-embracing. Legal reasoning has been the object of numerous studies reflecting a variety of approaches. But although a number of important contributions have been submitted, it is not appropriate to claim that there exists a uniform theory of legal reasoning. The models of explanation that have been offered reveal far-reaching differences of how the process is understood. It is also apparent that detailed studies on physical operations, sequences, and sub-processes within legal reasoning are rare.

1 *See, e.g.*, Aarnio, A. *On Legal Reasoning*, 23 (1977) ''Philosophers of law have not aimed at creating a theory coverning [sic] prevailing legal thought. They have instead often stated the basic problem in the form: what is law? Thus they have tried to assign a precisely defined object to juridical research – and to legal thinking in general.''

2 *See, e.g.*, MacCormick, N. *Legal Reasoning and Legal Theory*, 229 (1978).

In the studies focusing on legal reasoning processes it is possible to perceive two major approaches. The most common approach is, perhaps, to analyze legal reasoning by means of decomposing the process into more or less detailed phases.[3] Many researchers have also described legal reasoning as a rule-guided activity. Various aspects of legal reasoning are then related to different kinds of methodological rules (often hierarchically ordered).[4] Several contributions reveal a combination of these two approaches.[5] It is also noticeable that some researchers have suggested that legal reasoning is an example-based or case-based activity.[6]

Studies on legal reasoning based on decomposition into phases, conceptions of rules, or examples are however not the only existing approaches. *Aulis Aarnio* has, for instance, submitted a hermeneutical approach,[7] and legal reasoning has been also discussed in sociological,[8] mathematical[9] as well as cognitive terms.[10] Moreover, it has been suggested that there exists a demarcation between legal reasoning in a narrow sense (denoting arguments justifying decisions) as compared to legal reasoning in a broad sense (referring to "psychological processes undergone by judges reaching decisions . . .").[11] Several researchers have also concentrated on logical aspects of legal reasoning[12] and some recent contributions have

3 *See, e.g.,* Wasserstrom, R.A. *The Judicial Decision,* 27 (1961), Strömholm, S. *Den juridiska argumentationens relevanskriterier,* 644 (1974), Buchanan, Headrick *supra* chapter 1 note 4, at 53 *and* Hansen, J. *Simulation and Automation of Legal Decisions* (1986).

4 *See, e.g.,* Dickinson, J. *Legal Rules: Their Function in the Process of Decision* (1931), Hart, H.L.A. *The Concept of Law,* 77-96 (1961), Alchourrón, C.E., Bulygin, E. *Normative Systems* (1971) *and* Hamfelt, A. *The Multilevel Structure of Legal Knowledge and its Representation* (1990).

5 *See, e.g.,* Gottlieb, G. *The Logic of Choice,* e.g. at 66-77 and 155 (1968) *and* Bing, J. *Fra problem til resultat: Model av den juridiske beslutningsprocess* (1975).

6 *See, e.g.,* Levi, E.H. *An Introduction to Legal Reasoning* (1949) *and* Rissland, E.L., Ashley, K.D. *A Case-Based System for Trade Secrets Law* (1987).

7 Aarnio *supra* note 1.

8 *See, e.g.,* Schubert, G. ed. *Judicial Behavior: A Reader in Theory and Research* (1964).

9 Goldberg, S.P. *On Legal and Mathematical Reasoning* (1981).

10 *See, e.g.,* O'Neil, D.P. *A Process Specification of Expert Lawyer Reasoning* (1987).

11 Golding, M.P., *Legal Reasoning,* 1 (1984).

12 *See, e.g.,* Tammelo, I. *Modern Logic in the Service of Law* (1978).

submitted models of explanation based on biological findings[13] as well as theories on neural networks.[14]

The variety of contributions is initially a bewildering feature. Legal reasoning is however a complex process and the fact that there exist different models of explanation does not necessarily imply that some contributions are less accurate than others. A number of things may explain the diversity. One obvious reason is that contrasting studies have often focused on various parts of the process. Some researchers have, for instance, concentrated their attention on justification, while others have devoted their interest to the role of logic during rule application, and so forth.

It is also apparent that studies of legal reasoning processes focusing on different areas of the law arrive at different conclusions about appropriate procedures. Likewise, the roles of legal decision makers may be of a very different nature.[15] That is to say that a judge who has to decide about sentencing in criminal court proceedings is in a different situation than a litigating lawyer who tries to predict the outcome of a trial concerning an infringement of patents.

Further complications originate from the fact that differences between prescriptive and descriptive arguments that appear in various discussions on legal reasoning have not always been made clear. In addition, an in-depth investigation of previous studies reveals that a number of things that initially stand out as dissimilarities may be explained by the lack of consistency in the use of terminology.

Reviewing various contributions to the theory of legal reasoning it is also apparent that diverse assumptions about the nature of law are reflected. It is therefore obvious that knowledge of different legal theories facilitates the understanding of methodological proposals. For this reason the following sections provide a short overview of some common theories on the nature of law.

13 Walter, C., Parks, M. *Natural Models of Intelligence* (1985).

14 Warner, D.R. *The Role of Neural Networks in the Law Machine Development* (1990).

15 *See, e.g.*, Patterson, E.W. *Logic in the Law*, 883 (1942).

2.2 *The Nature of Law*

Presently, legal theory accommodates two main models of explanation concerning the nature of law.[16] The first one is usually known as *positivism* or *normativism* and is founded on the assumption that law consists primarily of rules. The second model is known as *realism* and is based on the presumption that law is primarily behaviour.[17]

Legal realism and legal positivism may, in a historical perspective, be seen as two major approaches that have evolved in order to meet criticism concerning metaphysical foundations, as well as demands for more rigid and scientifically appropriate methods. In this respect both models emerged originally as a reaction to *Natural law*.

In theories based on Natural law the issue about the origin of law was explained with references to fundamental and eternal natural principles valid for all people and at all times; e.g. human instincts, common sense, or the will of God.[18]

Models of explanation based on Natural law can be traced back to the dawn of jurisprudence and can be found already in ancient Greek and Roman literature.[19] Criticism against the theories of natural origin was however raised at an early point and several captious arguments have been submitted, most intensely during the last two centuries. The existence of universal factors has, for instance, been argued to be false since it is difficult to find regularities in different legal systems. Natural law has also been criticized since it does not provide any means of finding out about the content of the law. In addition, it has been pointed out that there

[16] *See, e.g.*, MacCormick, Weinberger *supra* chapter 1 note 41, at 1-3 *and* Klami, H.T. *Föreläsningar över juridikens metodlära*, 13 (1989).

[17] Naturally a categorisation of jurisprudence into two basic models is a simplification. Alternative models have been submitted also during the latest decades and simultaneously a number of additional models coexist. A related distinction is for instance a division between models stressing *is* and *ought* aspects of the legal system. *Cf. also* Olivecrona who has suggested a demarcation between *voluntaristic theories* (a label for theories based on the notion that the law is the expression of the will of a supreme authority) and *non-voluntaristic theories* (denoting a number of theories embracing more realistic explanations concerning the nature of law). Olivecrona, K. *Law as Fact*, 79-85 (1971). To independent theories it is also common to refer the *Marxist doctrine*.

[18] *See, e.g.*, d'Entrèves, A.P. *Natural Law* (1971) *and* Strömberg, T. *Rättsfilosofins historia i huvuddrag*, 21-38 (1985).

[19] Strömberg *Id.* at 9-12.

have been continuous disagreements over basic legal principles among the advocates of various natural theories. This criticism has been persistent and victorious. In consequence, from the middle of the nineteenth century theories based solely on Natural law have rarely been submitted in the Occident, although in other cultural spheres vivid exceptions do exist, e.g. the religious fundamentalism movement in the Arab countries.

Legal positivism appears in various forms. Theories of legal positivism are sometimes said to stress the outer appearances of the law, its existence and content.[20] Within positivism there is also an on-going search for definitions of the validity of legal systems based on rationality and logic. The word positivism is however ambiguous. Many legal philosophers of various inclinations have been labelled positivists. In addition to that, positivism has a general meaning outside the field of jurisprudence. A summary is given by *Stig Strömholm*:

> The word 'positivism' is used in a confusing way. Within *jurisprudence* as a rule . . . in the way that entails that one only considers the 'issued' (e.g. enacted) or by authorities actually practiced law (apart from e.g. natural law, non legal customs and so forth). Additional variations appear . . . In the field of *general philosophy* the term is used *partly* – and originally – in order to denote the anti-metaphysical, simultaneously rationalistic and empirical program for studies in social science, introduced by the French philosopher Auguste Comte in the middle of the 19th century, *partly* in a weaker meaning in order to denote schools which are of the opinion that science only should consider visible, tangible conditions.[21]

The ideas of *Auguste Comte* (1798 – 1857) had a strong influence on the scientific community. Comte argued that each science (and all thinking activities) passes three phases: a theological, a metaphysical, and a positive phase. Comte had the ambition to advance the social sciences to the positive stage, and to end the metaphysical speculations. The social sciences,

20 *Cf.* MacCormick, Weinberger *supra* chapter 1 note 41, at 1 who refers to "what is practicioners of what is sometimes called 'black letter law'."

21 Strömholm *supra* chapter 1 note 29, at 89 note 1, (original text in Swedish).

formerly founded on metaphysics and assumptions about natural origin, should be transformed into empirical sciences.[22]

For jurisprudence the emerging perspective of positivism meant that investigations of social matters outside the legal system became legitimate. Hence, within the framework of legal positivism several rational explanations concerning the foundation of legal systems, more or less empirically rooted, have been suggested.[23]

Important movements which had a widespread impact on the development of positivism theories in continental Europe evolved in Germany during the later part of the nineteenth century. In these theories legal rules were conceived of as "governmental orders" or as an expression of "the will of the state." In such models of explanation the existence of an effective state organization, consisting of e.g. a police-force, courts, and other authorities, was also justified. Positivism in this form has been given the name *ideological legal positivism*.[24]

The general development towards positivism is also commonly related to *Jeremy Bentham* (1748 – 1832) and the theory of *utilitarism* – the notion that the utility of humans is the purpose of the legal order – and *John Austin* (1790 – 1859) and the so called *analytical school*, stressing that the law is an empirical fact, and that it should be considered to be founded on commands from a superior sovereign. Theories underlining the view that the law is an empirical fact and that empirical investigations are necessary in order to understand the true content of the law are sometimes referred to as *sociological legal positivism*.[25]

At the beginning of the twentieth century ideological positivism and *state-will-theories* met with a competition from other philosophical ideas known as *logical empirism*, or *logical positivism*. The logical empirism has its origins in philosophy and in general theory of science and was developed under the influence of the works of e.g. *Bertrand Russell* (1872 –

22 Comte, A. *Discours préliminaire sur lésprit positif*, (1844). *See also* Strömberg *supra* note 18, at 53-54.

23 *See, e.g.*, for more elaborated descriptions of legal positivism, Lee, K. *The Positivist Science of Law* (1989), Olivecrona *supra* note 17, at 7-64 *and* Hall, J. *Foundations of Jurisprudence*, 21-47 (1973).

24 Strömberg *supra* note 18, at 52.

25 *Id.* at 52-54.

1970), *Ludwig Wittgenstein* (1889 – 1951), and the so called *Vienna* and *Cambridge schools*.[26]

Through logical positivism, from ideals originating in mathematics and natural science, demands for a distinct terminology and strictly defined concepts were raised also in legal science. It was argued that if those methodological and rational demands were not met, the prospects for jurisprudence would be discouraging. Without the adoption of more rigid methods traditional jurisprudence could not be considered as a science and, in consequence, jurisprudence would have to be dismissed from the scientific community.

The ideas of logical positivism had a strong influence on jurisprudence and during the twentieth century the debate as to whether jurisprudence should or should not be acknowledged as a scientific discipline has been intense. Especially three aspects of jurisprudence have been attacked. In the first place, jurisprudence has been said to be based on ethically justified, but unprovable and unscientific foundations. In the second place it has been argued that the law operates with artificial concepts (rights, obligations, duties, etc.) which, since they cannot be related to reality, are proofs of unscientific methods. It has also been stressed that legal reasoning must include assessment of values. And since any assessment of that kind is often subjective, the use of such methods, it has been alleged, excludes jurisprudence from the scientific sphere.[27]

Legal positivism in contemporary jurisprudence has come to mean a perspective in which the legal rule system is taken more or less for granted. The emphasis in works based on positivism is often directed towards the elaboration of methods for manipulating, transforming and applying legal rules. Within the positivism paradigm, *legal dogmatics* (i.e. works aiming to clarify the content of the law in specific fields by means of systematization and interpretation of legal materials[28]) has emerged as

[26] The description of logical empirism and its influence on legal positivism and jurisprudence is based on the résumé in Strömholm *supra* chapter 1 note 29, at 87-90.

[27] *Id.* at 88. *See also*, about arguments raised in the Scandinavian realism movement, section 2.9 *infra*.

[28] *See, e.g.*, Aarnio, A, Alexy, R, Peczenik, A. *The Foundation of Legal Reasoning*, 423 (1981) "The task of legal dogmatics has generally been defined as (i) *the investigation of the content of the legal order*, and (ii) the *systematization* of legal concepts and norms". (Footnote omitted).

a major research approach. It should finally be stressed that various positivist movements, though they may share some methodological approaches embrace largely divergent opinions about the content and the origin of the law.

Legal realism, on the other hand, in contemporary jurisprudence usually stands as a label for various attempts to elaborate a more authentic theory of law. Within the framework of legal realism studies of relations between law, legal decision making, and factors outside the law have been undertaken. In this respect a number of methodological approaches are related to the realistic paradigm; e.g. *Sociology and the law*, *Psychological jurisprudence*, and *Jurimetrics*.[29]

Legal realism is not only an approach in which outside factors have been related to jurisprudence. It is also a theory in which the practicability of rules has been criticised. Legal realism can be therefore perceived as a reaction against all too formalized decision making based on rigid legislation. In consequence, in theories related to legal realism it is not rare that legal rules are accorded a more or less limited importance.

During the last century legal realism has grown to become a dominating paradigm in North-American jurisprudence. Legal realism is also a phrase connected with Scandinavian jurisprudence, especially with its distinctive profile it has achieved during the twentieth century. Scandinavian legal realism is however a notion that has evolved with little or no connection to the way in which legal realism has developed in the U.S.A. From the methodological perspective adopted in this study it is also difficult to maintain that any important similarities exist between the two.[30] Scandinavian legal realism is therefore discussed separately in this chapter and not in connection with the overview of the American development that is related in the following section.

It should be noted that legal realism and legal positivism are not theories that have been developed in isolation from each other. The notions have been synthesized in some approaches, whereas in other cases the advocates of various opinions have been in conflict with each-other. In

29 *See, e.g.*, for more elaborated descriptions of legal realism, Hall *supra* note 23, at 55-62 *and* Llewellyn, K.N. *The Common Law Tradition*, 508-20 (1960).

30 *Cf.* Lee *supra* note 23, at 29.

this study which focuses on legal reasoning the two approaches are perhaps best illustrated in a comparison between the so called mechanical jurisprudence (based on legal positivism) and rule scepticism (based on the conception of legal realism[31]).

2.3 Mechanical Jurisprudence and Rule Scepticism

The term mechanical jurisprudence sometimes appearing in jurisprudential literature naturally attracts a lot of interest from those who are interested in the potential of AI in law. The evolution of AI and computer science has, however, nothing to do with the origin of the expression mechanical jurisprudence. The name was coined as early as in 1908.[32] It was introduced in order to signify that legal reasoning may be looked upon as a process of deduction.

When legal practice is looked upon as a process of deduction the concepts used in legal rule descriptions are perceived as axioms. Legal reasoning is then seen as a formalized process of deduction in which concrete cases may be included under legal rule descriptions mechanically. Such a view on legal decision making is founded on several basic assumptions. Most importantly, the theory presupposes that it is possible to develop stable and unambiguous legal concepts. It also assumes, of course, that legal rules are conditional statements consisting of *if – then* elements.

In addition, a mechanistic view on legal practice presupposes a valid and well-defined rule system. The approach is therefore often said to lean on a positivist foundation. It should be underlined, however, that it is sometimes also possible to describe legal systems based on Natural law as closed axiomatic systems. Hence, as regards the possibilities to perceive legal reasoning as a process of deduction, there need not be any distinct

[31] Legal realism is hereinafter a phrase used in order to denote American legal realism.

[32] Pound, R. *Mechanical Jurisprudence* (1908). *See also*, for a similar illustration from this time, Flavius, G.J. (pseudonym for Kantorowicz, H.U.) *Der Kampf um die Rechtswissenschaft*, 7 (1906) "Die herrschende Idealvorstellung vom Juristen ist die: Ein höherer Staatsbeamter mit akademischer Ausbildung, sitzt er, bewaffnet bloß mit einer Denkmaschine, freilich einer von der feinsten Art, in seiner Zelle. Ihr einziges Mobilar ein grüner Tisch, auf dem das staatliche Gesetzbuch vor ihm liegt. Man reicht ihm einen beliebigen Fall, einen wirklichen oder nur erdachten, und entsprechend seiner Pflicht, ist er imstande, mit Hülfe rein logischer Operationen und einer nur ihm verständlichen Geheimtechnik, die vom Gesetzgeber vorherbestimmte Entscheidung im Gesetzbuch mit absoluter Exaktheit nachzuweisen."

differences between a legal system based on Natural law and a legal system founded on positivism.

The view of law as a more or less stable system of premises from which logical deductions may be drawn automatically is rather old and goes back at least to the Age of Enlightenment during which it played an important role in the endeavours for legal codification and perfect laws.[33] There is also a close methodological relationship between the notion of mechanical jurisprudence and the so called *conceptualism* (*Begriffsjurisprudenz*) which had a strong influence on the continental development, especially in Germany, during the nineteenth century.[34] During the nineteenth century conceptualism was also known as *Pandektwissenschaft* and as such included theories of formal logic as well as notions of ''a legal order without gaps, possible to achieve through explicitness and clearness in the conceptual system raised by jurisprudence.''[35]

Despite the fact that deductive elements are present in many legal theories it is not appropriate to talk about a mechanical legal tradition, or to claim that mechanical jurisprudence exists as a coherent school of thinking. The notion that legal reasoning is a process of deduction appears under a variety of labels. For instance, at the beginning of the 1960s the English legal philosopher, *H. L. A. Hart*, referring to *formalism* described the ultimate state as when

> . . . a general term is given the same meaning not only in every application of a single rule, but whenever it appears in any rule in the legal system. No effort is then ever required or made to interpret the term in the light of the different issues at stake in various recurrence.[36]

[33] Naturally, undertakings in order to codify laws are much older and in this respect, since it is not far fetched to assume that the reasons for codifications may have been similar during various ages, it may be appropriate to admit a methodological inheritance which is several thousand years old.

[34] Begriffsjurisprudenz has been used also as a label for an exaggerated form of conceptualism in which the concepts are the masters of the lawyers. Anners, E. *Europas rättshistoria*, 52 (1972).

[35] *Id.* at 51. *Pandectae* is a Greek name for a collection of ancient Roman legal texts (*Digesta*) within *Corpus Juris Civilis*, from which is was assumed that it was possible to form a more or less complete legal system through constructive conceptual analysis.

[36] Hart *supra* note 4, at 127 (1961).

A few years later *Julius Stone* described a hypothetical legal system under the headline *Juristic Axiomatics*:

> If a legal order were designed to contain within itself a sufficiently comprehensive set of legal propositions precise and stable enough in meaning so that only one answer could be deducted from them for every problem presented for legal solution, those who operated with it would need to use only formal logic.[37]

However, proposals for a legal method based on deduction have seldom been submitted without reservation.[38] Most authors acknowledge the limitations restricting the formation of a more or less complete legal system. The notion that legal reasoning is a deductive process has been also criticized by many. Criticism was raised already in the middle of the nineteenth century by German legal philosophers of a school known as *Historical jurisprudence. Friedrich Carl von Savigny* (1779 – 1861) then claimed that all codifications are harmful and unnecessary. Instead, the law should, as it has been interpreted, provide a manifestation of the "historically founded tradition of legal ideas as it was interpreted and expressed by historically trained legal philosophers."[39] von Savigny also stressed the dynamic aspect of legal systems:

> "For law, as for language, there is no moment of absolute cessation; it is subject to the same movement and development as every other popular tendency; and this very development remains under the same law of inward necessity, as in its earliest stages."[40]

Another German philosopher, *Rudolf von Jhering* (1818 – 1892), underlined the fact that in addition to formalized law, purpose is a necessary element of legal reasoning:

37 Stone, J. *Legal System and Lawyers' Reasonings*, 330 (1964).

38 *Cf.* Dworkin, R. *Taking Rights Seriously*, 15-16 (1977) *and* Simmonds, N.E. *The Decline of Juridical Reason*, 99 (1984).

39 Anners *supra* note 34, at 50.

40 von Savigny, F.C. *Vom Beruf unserer Zeit für Gesetzgebung und Rechtswissenschaft*, 27 (1815), (original text in German).

> The standard of law is not the absolute one of truth, but the relative one of purpose. Hence it follows that the content of law not only *may* but *must* be infinitely various. As the physician does not prescribe the same medicine to all sick people, but fits his prescription to the condition of the patient, so the law cannot always make the same regulations, it must likewise adapt them to the conditions of the people, to their degree of civilization, to the needs of the time.[41]

The advocates of Historical jurisprudence did not, however, oppose the idea of a valid legal system. In practice Historical jurisprudence, by stressing the value of the existing law as a result of past experiences in practice – and perhaps as a paradox – became an important factor in the development of positivism and conceptualism.[42]

Arguments against a narrow-minded focus on the importance of legal codification were also raised during the nineteenth century in Europe by an number of writers who later came to be referred to as the *Free law movement (die Freirechtsbewegung)* a school of thought which also absorbed and revived some ideas based on natural law.[43]

The critics of the deductive theory in the Anglo-American sphere soon found out that they could draw their arguments from the writings of *Oliver Wendell Holmes* (1841 – 1935). Holmes attacked the notion that the law could be based on formalizations and logic, and among other things proclaimed that ‘‘general propositions do not decide concrete cases’’, and that ‘‘the life of the law has not been logic: it has been experience.’’[44]

Holmes is also the father of the so called *prognosis theory* which has been interpreted from the frequently quoted statement that ‘‘The prophecies of what the courts will do in fact, and nothing more pretentious, are what I mean by the law.’’[45]

41 von Jhering, R. *Der Zweck im Recht*, 189 (1877), (original text in German).

42 *See, e.g.,* Anners *supra* note 34, at 53.

43 Olivecrona *supra* note 17, at 45. Sundberg, J.W.F. *fr. Eddan t. Ekelöf,* 159-60 (1978) as important forerunners explicitly mentions *F. Gény* and *H. Kantorowicz.*

44 Holmes, O.W. *The Common Law*, 5 (1881).

45 Holmes, O.W. *The Path of the Law*, 461 (1897).

Holmes is usually looked upon as one of the founders of the *American legal realism movement.*[46] During the beginning of the twentieth century the ideas of Holmes were elaborated by several writers[47] and the American legal realist movement in this way developed a perspective on law and legal reasoning usually known as *rule scepticism* – a deviation which still has its advocates in the American legal sphere.[48]

Thus, from arguments raised in the school of Historical jurisprudence, in the Free law movement, in American legal realism, as well as in other schools of thought the criticism of the deductive theory was submitted at an early stage in both the continental sphere and in Anglo-American jurisprudence. During the twentieth century several arguments of various weight and substance have been articulated in a more or less continuous discussion.

The debate whether or not legal decision making ought to be understood as a rule-based process of deduction is still going on. The criticism has been enduring and perhaps most outspoken in the legal realist movement.[49] In view of the lawyers leaning towards rule scepticism a number of reasons indicate that legal reasoning ought not to be described as a rule-based activity. The discussions include both descriptive and prescriptive arguments. Likewise, numerous discussions of the advantages and disadvantages – allegedly following from various deductive and rule sceptic positions – have been submitted. The positions in the debate have often been polarized. A frequently cited example is taken from *Karl Llewellyn*:

46 *See also*, on the influence from the teaching of *Cristopher Columbus Langdell* (1826-1896) at *Harvard Law School* during the late nineteenth century, Farnsworth, E.A. *An Introduction to the Legal System of the United States*, 16-19 (1983) *and*, generally on the development in the U.S., Stevens, R. *Two Cheers for 1870: The American Law School* (1971).

47 Peczenik, A. *Juridikens metodproblem*, 15 (1980) explicitly mentions *Jerome N. Frank* (1889-1957) and *Karl L. Llewellyn* (1893 - 1962).

48 *See, e.g.*, Smith, J.C., Deedman, C. *The Application of Expert Systems Technology to Case-Based Law*, 86 (1987) "While there is a variety of forms and degrees of rule skepticism the majority of the legal profession would probably consider themselves to be rule skeptics of one sort or another."

49 The idea of the legal decision process as a logical process of deduction has been given less flattering names during such attacks. *See, e.g.*, Wasserstrom *supra* note 3, at 14 who among other things mentions "slot-machine jurisprudence", "legal fundamentalism" and "the phonographic theory of law."

> "*rules* . . . are important to you so far as they help you see or predict what judges will do or so far as they help you get judges to do something. That is their importance. That is all their importance, except as pretty playthings."[50]

In the early 1960s the American theorist *Richard A. Wasserstrom* summarized the criticism and found that the deductive theory was criticized as

> . . . necessarily an incorrect account of the decision process of a nonstatutory legal system because it fails: (a) to take account of the fact that no two cases can ever be identical; (b) to realize that the operation of characterization [i.e. identification of concepts and situations] is a crucial but nondeductive procedure; and (c) to recognize that there cannot be *antecedent* legal rules binding on the judge.[51]

An overview of the American history of jurisprudence indicates that many of the arguments used in the debate between the advocates of the various forms of deductionism and rule scepticism are, typically, descriptive. Prescriptive arguments about legal reasoning and legal work have been much fewer. This has been commented on by Wasserstrom who concludes that "[T]here is a serious lack of clarity not only in the basis of the attack upon a logical decision process, but also in the proposal to substitute a realistic or sociological method for deciding cases."[52]

However, legal realism does not only represent critical or faultfinding approaches. In a comprehensive analysis of the criticism against the deductive theory Wasserstrom recognized that three alternative descriptions of the decision process had been submitted within the framework of legal realism. The first stresses the importance of the intuition of the judge; the second implies that the personality of the decision maker is an influential factor for the outcome of a case; and the third is based on the assumption that legal decision making is a reflection of the emotions or preferences of the judges.[53]

[50] Llewellyn, K.N. *The Bramble Bush*, 14 (1960).

[51] Wasserstrom *supra* note 3, at 21-22.

[52] *Id.* at 4. *Cf. also* Gardner *supra* chapter 1 note 5, at 22 "The effect of the legal realist movement, in short, was to destroy the old conceptualist paradigm and to put nothing in its place."

[53] Wasserstrom *supra* note 3, at 22.

Wasserstrom thereby pointed out that American legal realism embraces not only a rule sceptic notion; a more constructive but less often emphasised objective of American legal realism has been to throw light on the irregularities of and to identify inappropriate factors in legal decision making. The proposed approaches have often drawn attention to in-depth studies of the judicial process, and have also been oriented towards investigations of factors outside the rule system.

It can be noted then that the American realist school placed emphasis on the argument that legal reasoning and the law are not isolated phenomena and that also a perspective including a description of social factors may be useful. For this reason, in its attempt to explain and develop the legal system the American legal realist school became related to *The sociology of law*. This connection has been described in the following way:

> As lawyers, the American legal realists were as familiar with the normativity of legal rules as anyone. But they wished to construct a science of law, . . . They, therefore, used 'law' as a factual term of their sociology of law to signify factual patterns, *e.g.* of 'official behaviour'... Their important studies... were anything but applications of a behavioral theory of judicial decision.[54]

In relation to the description of American legal realism, it is therefore appropriate to mention something about The sociology of law.[55]

[54] Hall *supra* note 23, at 56.

[55] As indicated in section 2.2 it should be noted that a number of additional jurisprudential movements may be related to the strive to broaden the perspective and to develop scientific methods for law, e.g. *Psychological Jurisprudence, Law and Economics, The Critical Legal Studies Movement, Experimental Jurisprudence,* and so forth. Thus, the description of the sociology of law in the following section merely provides an illustration, important as it may be. *See also* section 4.2 on *Jurimetrics infra*.

2.4 *The Sociology of Law*

The study of the sociology of law is often said to have started with *Eugen Ehrlich* (1862 – 1922).[56] It should be mentioned, however, that several pioneers in the more general field of sociology also did relate social factors to the legal system.[57] An example is *Emile Durkheim* (1858 –1917) who tried to relate social changes to development of the legal system.[58] Nevertheless, sociology of law has developed into a separate discipline only during the twentieth century.[59]

Researchers devoted to the Sociology of Law are concerned chiefly with the general aspects of the legal system and its relationship with society at an aggregated level. The law is observed from the outside and the discipline imposes a division between law and society. The objectives of the research are to understand and explain in what way the phenomena on both sides are connected to each-other.[60]

The discipline has been characterized as one that is descriptive, generalizing and empirical.[61] That is, law is viewed here as a normative structure and a variable basically divided from, but at the same time inter-dependent on society. Furthermore, it is assumed that it is possible to empirically establish hypotheses about the relations between law and society.[62] Studies of sociological interrelations between the law and the factors outside the legal system may be performed at different levels, (micro, macro, individual, group, organization, society) and may embrace legal systems, legal norms, legal reasoning, and outside factors

56 Ehrlich, E. *Grundlegung der Soziologie des Rechts* (1913).

57 Forslund, A-L. *Vad är rättssociologi?* 59-66 (1978).

58 Lukes, S., Scull, A. *Durkheim and the Law* (1983).

59 In Sweden this topic was proposed as an element in the study of general theory of law in a official report in 1953. University courses started in the early 1960s and the first professor was appointed in 1972. Descriptions of the assimilation of the discipline in legal education in Sweden is given by Bolding, P.O. *Rättssociologin i den nya juristutbildningen* (1978) and in *Tidskrift för rättssociologi*, 2-6 (1983/84).

60 Mathiesen, T. *Rett og Samfunn*, 9 (1977).

61 Peczenik *supra* note 47, at 20.

62 Luhmann, N. *Rechtssoziologie*, 11 (1972).

of different size and numbers. In a simplified picture research hypotheses may regard law as either a determining factor in social development processes (law as an instrument) or as a product of social factors (law as a generated object).[63]

There is no general consensus as to how divisions and sub-topics in the sociology of the law ought to be organized and labelled.[64] Research activities have been divided into studies of the sociology of law in a narrow sense (activities closely connected to the general discipline of sociology, and conducted basically from the perspective of social science), and the sociology of law in a broad sense (more closely connected to legal research with the purpose of investigating how the rules of the law function in reality).[65] A proposal similar to the latter is described by *Roscoe Pound* (1870 – 1964) who named his approach *Sociological jurisprudence*; an applied science in which law was regarded as a social institution, embracing functions, social purposes and legal institutions.[66]

The methods employed in the sociology of law are basically the same as the ones used in the more general discipline of sociology,[67] e.g. interviews, observations, surveys based on questionnaires, statistical investigations, content analysis of texts, case studies, and sociometrical analyses.

2.5 *The Pure Theory of Law*

Rule scepticism, studies focusing on behaviour, and the sociology of law are three approaches aiming to put law in a broader perspective and integrate it with various factors outside the legal order. Hence, they are reflections of legal realism.

However, the ambition to develop more rigid scientific methods has also prompted investigations in other directions. Several philosophers

63 *Cf.* Forslund *supra* note 57, at 59.

64 *See, e.g.,* Stjernquist, P. *En aspekt på rättssociologisk forskning*, 15-16 (1983/84) *and* Cotterrell, R. *The Sociology of Law*, 8 (1984).

65 Hellner, J. *Rättssociologisk undersökning av skadeståndsrätten*, 20 (1969).

66 Pound, R. *Jurisprudence Vol. 1*, 291-358 (1959). *Cf. also* Beutel, F.K. *Some Potentialities of Experimental Jurisprudence as a New Branch of Social Science* (1957).

67 Forslund *supra* note 57, at 13. *See also*, for a general introduction to sociological methods, Rosengren, K.E. *Sociologisk metodik* (1975).

have pursued in-depth studies in the legal order and also put forward proposals concerning various means of approaching the law in a more scientific way, without necessarily confronting it with elements outside the legal order.

A legal philosopher who provided an important foundation for such a way of approaches was *Hans Kelsen* (1881 – 1973). Kelsen developed a theory in which the legal order was described as a more or less closed system and called it *Pure theory of law.* According to Kelsen, jurisprudence could be perceived as a science focusing on the relations between various kinds of rules. The theory is founded on a conception of the existence of a basic norm.

> [I]f we ask why a particular act of compulsion – the fact, for instance, that one man has deprived another of his freedom by imprisoning him – is an act of law and belongs to a particular legal order, the answer is, that this act was prescribed by a certain individual norm, a judicial decision. If we ask, further, why this individual norm is valid, the answer is, that it was constituted according to the penal state book. If we inquire as to the validity of the penal state book we are confronted by the State's constitution, which has prescribed rules and procedure for the creation of the penal statute book by a competent authority. If, further, we ask as to the validity of the constitution, on which repose all the laws and the acts which they have sanctioned, we come probably to a still older constitution and finally to a historically originally one, set up by some single usurper or by some kind of corporate body. ... This is the schematic formulation of the basic norm of a legal order. . . . The pure theory of law operates with this basic norm as with an hypothesis. Presupposed that it is valid, then the legal order which rests on it is valid also.[68]

Kelsen worked on his theory for a long period of time (it was originally outlined in 1911)[69] and later incorporated into it also a dynamic aspect concerning the creation of new norms. The basic norm was then described as a norm of competence.

68 Kelsen, H. *The Pure Theory of Law*, 518 (1935).

69 Knight, M. *Translators preface*, at v (1970).

> The norm system that presents itself as a legal order has essentially a dynamic character. A legal norm is not valid because it has a certain content, that is, because its content is logically deductible from a presupposed basic legal norm, but because it is created in a certain way – ultimately in a way determined by a presupposed basic norm.[70]

Kelsen's presentation made a distinction between two worlds: the world of reality, and the world of rules. The reality was referred to as the existing world, the "is" world, while the rule system was perceived as something that "ought" to be. According to the pure theory of law, jurisprudence should only be concerned with the rules, the "ought to" world. Kelsen, however, admitted that several relations between the two conceptions were necessary, e.g. that the rules may work as schemes of interpretation and that a legal system, in order to be valid, must be effective.[71]

The major contribution of Kelsen's theory is that seen in this perspective it provides a means of discussing legal norms and legal orders without necessarily obscuring the discussion with repeated speculations about the nature of law.[72] The notion of the legal order as a more or less closed world is thereby important as a framework for methodological discussions about legal reasoning. Such a model of explanation does not only provide a possibility of making the methodological discussions more lucid but also, when elaborated, provides an opportunity to systemize the – admittedly necessary – relations between the law and factors outside the legal order.

In addition, the concept of a closed legal system is an important basis for the development of legal positivism. This is, however, not the only function of this model. The notion of a legal system as a more or less closed world serves also as theoretical foundation for methodological approaches which may be collectively named as studies on *logic in law.*

70 Kelsen, H. *Reine Rechtslehre*, 198, (1970), (original text in German).

71 *Id.* at 3-4, 211-12.

72 *Cf.* Peczenik, A. *Rätten och förnuftet*, 186 (1988) *and* Strömholm *supra* chapter 1 note 29, at 114.

2.6 Logic in Law

Logic is a science which, at least in theory, can be employed in all domains. In modern logic it is thereby common to utilize symbolic representation, i.e. the subject-matter under investigation must be initially translated into a formal language. Several formal notations have been introduced,[73] some of them have been developed for the purpose of facilitating classification, while others have been elaborated in order to increase the understanding of inferences.

A number of studies in which logic has been employed in order to investigate various aspects of law and legal reasoning have been submitted.[74] One basic reason for the employment of logic in law is that it makes it possible to determine criteria for the validity of arguments by means of investigating the form of these arguments. Discussions concerning logical relations in law were submitted already by Bentham and Austin, although symbolic notations were not elaborated at that time. Further approaches were made by *Wesley Newcomb Hohfeld* (1890 – 1917) in the early twentieth century. Hohfeld developed a scheme consisting of eight basic elements – *right*, *duty*, *privilege*, *no-right*, *power*, *liability*, *immunity* and *disability* – trying at the same time to identify the logical connections between these elements.[75]

A contribution that made a significant impact was submitted in 1950 by the Finnish philosopher *Georg Henry von Wright.* von Wright using the label *Deontic logic*,[76] discussed the question of how concepts such as *the obligatory*, *the permitted*, and *the forbidden* could be treated in a logical argument. Deontic logic has been accepted since then as a label for numerous projects based on symbolic representation of law. During the succeeding forty years the development of symbolic logic especially designed for law has been a major objective of a number of philosophers. The elaborated form has come to include theories embracing not only the

73 *See, e.g.*, for an introduction to symbolic logic, Suppes, P. *Introduction to Logic* (1957) *and*, for an overview of various notations, Lübcke, P. ed. *Filosofilexikonet*, 335-43 (1988).

74 *See, e.g.*, on the foundations and prospects for logic in law, and for further references, Tammelo *supra* note 12 *and* Soeteman, A. *Logic in Law* (1989).

75 Hohfeld, W.N. *Fundamental Legal Conceptions* (1923).

76 von Wright, G.H. *Deontic Logic* (1951).

original concepts indicated by von Wright, but also basic types of legal positions, relations between positions, and relations between various legal aspects.[77]

Submissions employing more or less elaborated symbolic notations have been suggested.[78] Contributions have, for instance, consisted of cautious formalizations combined with elaborated discussions of the advantages and the disadvantages of a more formal language for specific purposes. This kind of approach was suggested by *Layman Allen* in the mid 1950s:

> ''This approach is a compromise between expressions in ordinary prose and expressions in the mathematical notation of symbolic logic – enough like ordinary prose to be understood easily by any careful reader, enough like symbolic logic to achieve some of its important advantages.''[79]

Allen proposed a process of ''pulverization'' and rearrangement of text elements in order to facilitate the discovery of schematic forms in ordinary legal text statements. In that process the text expressions were transformed into *if – then* statements, and then represented schematically in an abbreviated form. The notation included horizontal lines representing implications and it also supported the use of elementary connectives (*conjunctions, disjunctives, negations*). The method, Allen argued, could be of assistance in systematic interpretation and in drafting of legal documents.

Allen's contribution illustrates a careful step-wise integration of symbolic logic and legal material. Studies based on the use of symbolic logic in law may be however also of a different nature and comprise the use of one or several logical notations, with a few references to the pros and cons of symbolic representation in natural language.[80]

77 *See, e.g.,* Kanger, S. *New Foundations for Ethical Theory* (1957) *and* Lindahl, L. *Position and Change: A Study in Law and Logic* (1977).

78 *See, e.g.,* for a discussion of various approaches of logic in law in general, Lacock, D.D. *The Relevance of Logic to Law*, 13-23 (1964) *and*, especially on Deontic logic, Hilpinen, R. *Deontic Logic: Introductory and Systematic Readings*, (1981).

79 Allen, L.E. *Symbolic Logic: A Razor-Edged Tool for Drafting and Interpreting Legal Documents* (1957).

80 *See, e.g.,* for a more elaborated approach, Åqvist, L. *Kausalitet och Culpaansvar inom en*

The use of symbolic logic in the legal sphere has been criticized from various stand-points. Perhaps the most debated issue is the fundamental question of whether symbolic logic can be used in law at all.[81] Much of the criticism has thereby concentrated on the fact that symbolic logic is a method for making statements based on truth values. As is known, a presupposition in the employment of classical logic is that the propositions to be integrated into formal statements are either true or false (indicative statements). In law, it has been argued, statements are neither true nor false. Legal statements are the statements of an ''ought to'' world, (imperative statements) and therefore symbolic logic is not applicable to them.

Although the debate in this respect still continues, it has nevertheless been made clear that in many cases logic can be a useful instrument in jurisprudence. A variety of solutions have been proposed for the explanation of the paradox concerning truth values, e.g. that truth values are exchangeable with validity and invalidity values.[82] It has also been pointed out that in a practical situation rules are viewed in a different perspective and that those who employ rules during legal reasoning perceive them in a way which does not differ from the way indicative statements are conceived.[83]

Deontic logic may be criticized since the propositions – rights, duties, permissions, obligations, etc., may be claimed to be without practical value in legal reasoning. Since legal concepts of this kind may be acknowledged in actual legal work only as communication tools (i.e. high

logiskt rekonstruerad skadeståndsrätt (1973) *and*, especially on the use of analogies in law, Frändberg, Å. *Om analog användning av rättsnormer* (1973).

81 *See, e.g.*, Heather, M.A. *A Demand-Driven Model for the Design of a Half-Intelligent Common Law Information Retrieval System*, 78 (1985) ''The methodology for ascertaining the Law cannot be based on a legal calculus for (at present) none exist.''

82 *See*, about this so called Jørgensens dilemma, Jørgensen, J. *Imperatives and Logic*, 288-96 (1937/38), Kelsen, H. *Essays in Legal and Moral Philosophy* chapter 10-11 (1973), Alchourrón, C.E., Martino, A.A. *A Sketch of Logic Without Truth* (1989), Soeteman *supra* note 74, at 51-53 *and* Herrestad, H.B. *Norms and Formalization*, 29-36 (1990).

83 *See, e.g.*, Hamfelt *supra* note 4, at 19 ''A lawyer carrying out this function does not comprehend norms as commands, only as descriptions to be applied to fact situations.... If a description applies it is true relative to the fact situation, otherwise false.'' *and* Herrestad *Id.* at 36 (1990) ''I . . . find it natural to use true and false as semantic values as we are talking about an evaluation of information transmitted in a communicative act.''

level concepts representing sets of rules) without any corresponding subject matters in reality, the practical value of developing a formal logic based on such propositions has been challenged.[84] Also a number of technical limitations have been suggested and discussed, which issue will be addressed further in part three of this investigation.

Although the contributions based on symbolic logic have been many, outside the fields of *Computers and law* and *AI and law* it is difficult to see any practical influence of works based on the employment of logic in law. Legal logic has been a relatively isolated philosophical movement. An obvious reason for this is that symbolic representation confronts the lawyers without special training with vast problems as regards transparency; i.e. without a skill in reading and understanding the symbolic notation it is difficult to evaluate the usefulness of formal representations. Many submissions demand therefore strong analytic power from the readers. On some occasions these problems are quite persistent because various philosophers working with symbolic logic choose to use different symbolic notations. In addition, the closed world approach which usually makes up the greater part of the contributions based on symbolic notation may, for practically inclined readers, seem all too theoretical.

Nevertheless, various forms of logic are, naturally, highly relevant for a study in law and AI which is why various methodological approaches based on symbolic logic will be further discussed in part three of this work.

2.7 *Separation and Integration*

The debate between legal philosophers concerning different forms of legal positivism versus various offshoots of legal realism has sometimes been quite intense. The polarization of views on legal positivism was noticed and criticized at an early stage by several researchers, such as e.g.

84 *Cf., e.g.*, Gottlieb *supra* note 5, at 169 "... Deontic Logic which is the logic founded upon the premise that rules can logically contradict one another independently of their application. Such a premise necessarily entails the formulation of another premise about the unity and coherence of a will from which rules originate. We do not share these premises." *and* Sergot, M. *Representing Legislation as Logic Programs*, 13 (1985) "For many practical purposes, however, it will be unnecessary to import the whole of this [deontic] general mechanism into every given application. ... in practice, we can treat the conditions ... as a definition ... we shall rarely want to proceed beyond that ..." *See also*, for further comments on deontic logic, *infra* section 6.4.5.4.

John Dickinson who in his comment on the debate on deductive reasoning (although he used the label *legal determinism*) pointed out that

> The fact that legal rules do not always dictate the decisions of cases does not, however, mean that they may not have influence, and sometimes a controlling one, in the process of decision. Sceptics who minimize the influence of such rules often seem only disappointed absolutists, who expected the traditional theory of legal determinism to work out to the bitter limit of its clockwork logic, and on finding it play them false, react into an opposite extreme of naive unwillingness to recognize the less absolute, but none the less relatively effective, way in which legal rules do their work, holding an impossible exalted way of certainty, they insist on all or none.[85]

Dickinson was, of course, right. If legal reasoning can in no respect be related to a deductive process, it would then be arbitrary, and the arguments could be chosen at random. Such a state of the matter would naturally raise well motivated criticism. In the same way, it would be ridiculous to purport that law and legal reasoning is nothing more than mechanical rule-application.

Wasserstrom, in his analysis of the criticism directed against the deductive theory submitted the concept of *irrationalist fallacy*. He thereby made clear that deduction alone cannot explain how legal decision making is conducted, but similarly to Dickinson, argued that this fact does not justify a complete exclusion of deduction from legal reasoning. Irrationalist fallacy was described in the following way:

> The mistake . . . consists in this: The question of whether an argument is formally valid is confused with the question of whether there can be good reasons for believing a proposition to be true or false. It is recognized quite correctly that the canons of formal logic have a decidedly limited applicability. It is inferred quite incorrectly from this that all the questions which cannot be settled by appealing to formal logic cannot be settled in any manner which could be called 'reasonable' or 'logical'.[86]

85 Dickinson *supra* note 4 at 835-36.

86 Wasserstrom *supra* note 3, at 23-24.

The conclusion was summarized by stating that

> [I]t may not make much sense to describe the judicial process as a completely deductive one. But it makes even less sense to insist that for this reason courts could not (and should not) employ a procedure or set of procedures that permits of some kind of reasoned justification of the judicial decisions reached by those courts.[87]

The conclusion was clear and sound, but not very innovative. Reasonable well-balanced discussions leaving room for both deductive reasoning and discretion were wide-spread among legal philosophers already in the school of historical jurisprudence.[88]

Wasserstrom deserves, however, to be recognized for having provided a major theoretical breakthrough by introducing a model of legal reasoning based on a dichotomy. In the model, two phases in the legal decision making were recognized: a *process of discovery* and a *process of justification*, leaving room for both activities connected to rule application (in the process of justification) and for considerations of evaluation and individual factors in each case (in the process of discovery).[89] Wasserstrom provided in this way a theoretical foundation where arguments of deductive and non-deductive reasoning did not need be in conflict with each-other. In consequence, it may be alleged that the debate on whether or not legal reasoning is rule-guided has lost much of its importance.

The conflicting perspectives of the lawyers leaning towards positivism or realism have not however appeared only in discussions about whether or not legal reasoning is a deductive process. Various assumptions about the utility of a realistic approach have been also noticeable in the debate about the utility of the sociology of law. From a positivist perspective it has been argued that the results achieved by the sociology of law are of limited value. In the positivist view, a sociological approach may

87 *Id.* at 24.

88 *See, e.g.,* von Savigny *supra* note 40 *and* von Jhering *supra* note 41.

89 Wasserstrom *supra* note 3, at 25 "I will refer to the procedure by which a conclusion is reached as the *process of discovery* and to the procedure by which a conclusion is justified as the *process of justification.*" In this context it may be relevant to mention the apparent relationship with the contribution to general philosophy of science made by *John Herschels* in 1830, based on a distinction between "context of discovery" and "context of justification." *See, e.g.,* Losee, J. *A Historical Introduction to the Philosophy of Science,* 114-20 (1972).

admittedly provide a broad overview of the legal system and pin-point the irrelevant factors playing more or less appropriate roles in the legal work and in legal decision making. Such knowledge is, however, relevant only on a general level since a judge, according to the doctrine of positivism, must search for answers in the rule system. In line with this it has been underlined that "In principle and by its aim, the answer of the sociologist is of no direct concern for a judge in his work."[90]

Henceforth, the adherents of legal positivism emphasize that realistic approaches in the form of sociological findings and methods must be admitted solely on the grounds that they may deepen the understanding of how the law ought to be adjusted *de lege ferenda*.[91] In other words, sociological methods have – with a few exceptions – no place in actual legal decision making. Only in the relatively few cases when the rules directly indicate that the judge ought to investigate matters outside the legal system sociological methods are said to be appropriate, e.g. when the law refers to customs, or in sentencing, when personal factors such as social living conditions, etc. are to be taken into consideration when making a decision.[92]

This positivist position has been criticized, on the other hand, as narrow and conservative, and it has been argued that the positivist attitude makes it difficult to develop the law and the legal system in a more functional way – a development that for various reasons could be desirable.[93] The realist thereby argues that legal decision making ought to include considerations of social factors, scientifically investigated.

One can argue, of course, that such a polarization of various attitudes is unnecessary also in this case. The positivist claim that a decision maker should turn to the legal rules for answers in the first place, may be explained by means of articulating the underlying legal principle, viz. that in their reasoning judges must be guided by legal norms and legal

90 Strömholm *supra* chapter 1 note 29, at 50, (original text in Swedish).

91 *De lege ferenda*: "About the law that ought to be made" Statements de lege ferenda are statements about the law as one like to see it developed in the future.

92 *See, e.g.*, for an articulation of this perspective, Strömholm, S. *Något om sociologiens betydelse för juridiken* (1970).

93 *See, e.g.*, Rylander, S. *Strömholm och rättssociologin* (1970).

methods. In the decision making process a judge must not be affected by poorly defined, ad hoc determined factors outside the legal system. He may, of course, use all his wit in order to fully investigate the situation that is to be decided upon, but he cannot employ sociological methods in order to determine how the law should be applied in an individual case. Nor can he freely attach special importance to attributes that have not been previously described in the rule system. The reason for this is that such a method of decision-making could easily give rise to legal decisions that would be in conflict with the principle of predictability.

Predictability is in turn an important aspect of the so called *formal principles of justice*[94] and hence also one cornerstone of legal theory. The importance and the meaning of predictability have been described in the following way:

> "[It means] that court decisions must be predictable. Predictability is one of the basic foundations for human activities. If court decisions become different in similar or in analogical cases it is impossible for the citizens to make prognoses for their own future acting."[95]

It must however be stressed that the principle of predictability is by no means an obstacle to the use of sociological methods in general investigations of how the law is applied, in investigations of effects, and in investigations of how decision making is conducted.[96] Enhanced knowledge of social factors and the effects of the legal system and legal decision making is doubtless useful, for instance in order to achieve more efficient legislation, or more uniform sentencing. In those respects sociological methods may be of considerable importance, e.g. in the formulation of legal arguments *de lege ferenda* and *de sententia ferenda*.[97]

94 *Cf. e.g.*, about formal principles of justice and *the doctrine of precedent*, Coval, Smith *supra* chapter 1 note 29, at 36 - 37 (1986).

95 Aarnio, A. *Introduktion*, 17 (1988) in a discussion about *Rechtssicherheit* in relation to rules for judges formulated by *Olaus Petri* in 1540, (original text in Swedish).

96 The difference in views has been commented on by Roos, C.M. *Mot en verklighetsorienterad juridik*, 19 (1978), who makes a division between abstract legal analysis (focusing on logical consistence and semantic content of legal norms) and concrete legal analysis (including the relation between the norms and reality).

97 *De sententia ferenda.* About the court decision that ought to be made; statements de lege ferenda are statements about the law as one wishes to see it developed in court practice in the future.

2.8 Analytical Jurisprudence and System Theory

Jurisprudence has been discussed not only in terms of positivism and realism. In contemporary legal theory the phrase *analytical jurisprudence* appears also to refer to studies encompassing methodological discussions.

> [A]nalytical jurisprudence, which is that part of legal theory that seeks to promote a systematic, theoretical and general understanding of issues such as the structure of legal rules and legal systems, the nature of legal reasoning, the role of logic in law, and the interpretation of legislation and case law.[98]

The notion of analytical jurisprudence comprises primarily theoretical studies based on the concept of positivism.[99] It does not however include only works based on logic in law or static positivist perspectives. In analytical jurisprudence it is also possible to detect influence from legal realism. Moreover, a number of studies based on *system theory* are also commonly associated with it.[100]

System theory is originally not a jurisprudential invention. The general outline of system theory was given in the 1920s by the biologist *Ludwig von Bertalanffy* (1901– 1972).[101] In 1956, together with representatives from the fields of economy, physiology, and mathematics, von Bertalanffy formed *The Society for General Systems Research*. The general idea behind system theory is to identify elements that may be related to each other in order to facilitate descriptions of a scientific or explanatory nature. Issues and entities may be selected in an unlimited way in order to suit the research aim in the most effective manner.[102] Although definitions of the term *system* sometimes differ in their details, the word

98 Susskind, R.E. *Pragmatism and Purism in Artificial Intelligence and Legal Reasoning*, 7 (1989).

99 Ross, A. *Om ret og retfærdighed* 10-11 (1953).

100 Raz, J. *The Concept of a Legal System: An Introduction to the Theory of Legal System*, 1 (1970), Eckhoff, T., Sundby, N.K. *Rettssystemer. Systemteoretisk innføring i rettsfilosofien*, 1-2 (1976).

101 Eckhoff, Sundby *Id.* at 42.

102 *See, e.g.*, for a overview, von Bertalanffy, L. *General Systems Theory* (1968) *and* Weinberg, G.M. *An Introduction to General Systems Thinking*, 63 (1975).

usually denotes something like " . . . a set of objects together with relationships between the objects and between their attributes."[103]

Within this broad framework many system theories have appeared in almost every discipline. *Economic system theory*, for instance, has been developed in order to increase the understanding of economic relations at different levels, whereas *information system theory* has been developed to facilitate technical and administrative development.

It is not possible to make a complete list of all the approaches that have in some way contributed to system theory. Theories may originate from either objects or abstraction and systems may be perceived as open, closed, static, dynamic, complete, incomplete, natural, artificial, stable, unstable, etc. The particular relations selected in various works based on system theory may also emphasise many different aspects, e.g. functions, time aspects, hierarchic orders, statistical relations, etc.[104]

It is also necessary to underline that sometimes studies that may strike one as being elaborated contributions to system theory may actually evolve in a more or less unintentional manner. Within jurisprudence, for instance, only few contributions have been originally presented as examples of system theory – much of them are as much the result of various historical processes and practical necessities.

Despite a rather limited employment of system theory it is nevertheless important to recognize that analyses of this kind are important methodological means, and that it is possible to describe many works and many aspects of jurisprudence in terms of system theory.[105] In this respect it is also obvious that system theory is an important means of classification and description of various research approaches.

In a study focusing on the valid law in a certain jurisdiction it may, for example, be natural to describe the law as an intricate system of sub-topics and rules. Basic entities may thereby be formed from demarcations between different fields of law – criminal law, civil law, family law, etc.

103 Hall, A.D., Fagen, R.E. *Definition of System*, 81 (1968).

104 *See, e.g.*, about different kinds of systems, Eckhoff, Sundby *supra* note 100, 16-48 *and* Seipel, P. *Computing Law*, 197-211 (1977).

105 *See, e.g.*, Raz *supra* note 100, who especially discusses the theories of Hans Kelsen and John Austin.

In legal work such classifications are vital, e.g. for the systematization of legal material, and for efficient legal rule search.

It is also a well-known fact that studying legal rules apart from each other is insufficient, which is also why a large number of models have been submitted, in which rules of various kinds have been studied in relation to each other. Perhaps the most elaborate model of general system theory in law has been contributed by Kelsen,[106] but several other theories exist as well. A well-known distinction between two different kinds of rules has been introduced, for instance, by Hart who has presented a model based on the idea that rules exist on two different levels – the first level containing *primary rules* and the second – *secondary rules*.[107]

Legal sub-topics and legal rule systems are however not the only examples of the possible origin of system perspectives in law. Classifications of various kinds intended to facilitate methodological developments appear in many shapes and the later part of this century can be also characterized by systematic attempts to introduce new kinds of system perspectives in law. A first step in this direction was taken by *Joseph Raz* who related the works of several legal philosophers to a system perspective.[108] Another contribution in this respect is a Norwegian study by *Torstein Eckhoff* and *Nils Kristian Sundby*, published in 1976.[109] The authors presented a theory in which law was perceived as a open and dynamic system in which the main elements were argued to be rules and activities. Recently also a comprehensive analysis of the Swedish law on property has been presented by *Jan Hellner*, who investigates among other things systematical and structural aspects of different laws and relates them to various techniques and theories for legislation.[110]

It is also significant that the legal order has been described as a system consisting not only of rules but also of institutions, e.g. legislative author-

106 Kelsen *supra* notes 68 and 70.

107 Hart *supra* note 4. (These aspects of law will be elaborated on in chapter 5 and 6.)

108 Raz *supra* note 100.

109 Eckhoff, Sundby *supra* note 100.

110 Hellner, J. *Lagstiftning inom förmögenhetsrätten* (1990).

ities, courts, etc.[111] Of relevance to this study is, for instance, a number of contributions by which the process of legal reasoning has been divided and studied in more detailed ways.

In addition, an array of legal system theories based on information theory has been submitted during the last decades and several of the models presented in them have served as important theoretical foundations for the development of the fields of computers and law, and AI and law. In consequence, several works that are referred to in the following chapters may be without any doubt considered as contributions based on system theory perspectives and analytical jurisprudence.

2.9 The Scandinavian Development

In Sweden an independent theory was developed in the early twentieth century. The movement, known as the *Uppsala school of legal thinking*, has had a considerable influence on Scandinavian jurisprudence in the twentieth century. Three Swedes; *Axel Hägerström* (1868 – 1939), professor of practical philosophy, *Vilhelm Lundstedt* (1882 – 1955) and *Karl Olivecrona* (1897 – 1980) – the last two both professors of law – are considered to be the most prominent spokesmen.

Outside the country of origin the theories worked out by the Uppsala school of legal thinking appears sometimes under the name of *Scandinavian Realism*, and as such a number of legal philosophers from Norway, and from Denmark are usually also included.[112]

Hägerström, the founder of the Uppsala movement, initially attacked the traditional jurisprudential concepts like right, duty, etc., as being metaphysical and without theoretical value.[113] Also the wide-spread notion of the existence of a state-will was criticized as being un-scientific. Hägerström's theses were developed by Lundstedt who found that legal practice and questions concerning interpretation of the law should be guided by what is "good for society", which among other things included

111 *See, e.g.*, Flodin, M. *On Valid Law and Valid Moral Norms*, 51 (1986) *and*, for further reflections on system approaches in law, Seipel *supra* note 104, at 195-220.

112 Schmidt, F, *The Uppsala School of Legal Thinking*, 151 (1978) explicitly mentions *Torstein Eckhoff* and *Alf Ross* (1899 - 1979).

113 Hägerström, A. *Inquiries into the Nature of Law and Morals*, 8 and *passim* (1953).

a plea for general prevention in criminal law, and by Olivecrona who perceived legal rules as independent imperatives (orders without commanders) and described the legal order as a socio-psychological continuity of meaning.[114]

In this tradition the Dane *Alf Ross* (1899 – 1979) argued metaphorically that an outside viewer of a game cannot fully understand the game solely by observation. In a game of chess, for example, the players are affected by the theory and purpose of the game and in order to be able to play chess they must consider tacit presuppositions which provide a schemata of interpretation necessary for the full understanding of the game. Ross's illustration has been interpreted as an argument against theories depending solely on behavioural studies,[115] but the chess-example has been also used as an illustration of arguments directed against positivist perspectives leaning solely on the outer appearances of the law.[116]

Ross also opposed the notion of legal reasoning being perceived as a process of deduction and argued that explicit reasons given in legal decision making, although they may give the impression of deduction, often function merely as a façade for the justification of the decisions.[117]

Another issue taken up by the Scandinavian realist movement was the question of the utility of legal concepts such as "rights". This issue was addressed, among others, by *Per Olof Ekelöf* (1905 – 1990) who arrived at the conclusion that many legal concepts may be useful tools "vehicles of inferences" for legal language, especially if they are to signify a collection of prerequisites and/or a collection of legal consequences.[118]

Ekelöf also contributed to the theory of interpretation and legal reasoning by means of elaborating the notion that legal decisions should be guided by the legislator's intentions. The concept which is known as

114 *See, e.g.*, for overviews of the impact of the Uppsala school of legal thinking and for interpretations of their theses, Pattaro, E. *Il realismo giuridico scandinavo* (1974), Bjarup, J. *Skandinavischer Realismus* (1978), Schmidt *supra* note 112, *and* Strömberg *supra* note 18, at 58 - 69.

115 Strömholm *supra* chapter 1 note 29, at 92.

116 Aarnio *supra* note 1, at 3-10, among other things refers to the necessity to include also tactics and stategies.

117 Ross *supra* note 99, at 179.

118 *Id.* at 206-08. *See also* Ekelöf, P.O. *Är termen rättighet ett syntaktiskt hjälpmedel utan mening?* (1952) *and* section 5.3.3.4 *infra*.

teleology, has been discussed and included in a number of works on Scandinavian legal theory.[119]

Contributions to Scandinavian legal theory have also been submitted by the Norwegian theorists Eckhoff and Sundby who depict law as an open, dynamic system which encounters various forms of feedback from the outside world.[120] Recent submissions in contemporary Scandinavian legal philosophy include those of *Jacob Sundberg* who has elaborated the issue concerning the necessity to understand the nature of law and the doctrine of legal sources in a historical perspective[121] and of *Alexander Peczenik* who has named his theory *neorealism.* Peczenik in his discussions about the validity of legal systems, has underlined the importance of rationality in legal reasoning.[122]

In terms of realism versus positivism the Scandinavian development may be described as a synthesized theory, based on a positivist foundation and accepting legal norms as crucial elements of legal reasoning, but nevertheless admitting ''realistic'' relations with the outside world through explicit discussions about teleological reasoning and through elaborated theories of interpretation. Realistic elements are also present in the attempts to explain and justify the legal order in historical as well as in rational terms.

This basic perspective, with its rather well-balanced relation to the legal order, accepting the importance of rules and admitting realistic relations with the outside world, has provided the necessary foundation for the growth and development of research in the branch of jurisprudence known as legal dogmatics, i.e. for investigations aiming to meet the demands of the legal community for rational analyses and the systematization of legal material in various fields.

One can also notice a general tendency in contemporary Scandinavian jurisprudence towards elaborations of prescriptive arguments for legal reasoning. Several contributions of this sort, providing detailed descrip-

119 See, e.g. , Ekelöf, P.O. *Teleological Construction of Statutes*, 75-117 (1958).

120 Eckhoff, T. *Feedback in Legal Reasoning and Rule Systems*, 51 (1978).

121 Sundberg *supra* note 43.

122 *See, e.g.*, Peczenik *supra* note 72.

tions of legal reasoning intended to be used in tutorials have been submitted in recent years.[123]

However, the harmony seemingly prevailing in Scandinavian jurisprudence must not be over-estimated. A number of theoretical contributions show more than clearly that Scandinavian jurisprudence can be characterized in many cases by vastly divergent opinions. The following two quotations provide an excellent illustration of this state of affairs: the first quotation is from *Tore Strömberg*, who claims that "[t]he Swedish law, in our conception, appears as a *closed unified system. ...*"[124] The second quotation is from a recent book by *Hannu Tapani Klami* who suggests that "[t]he truth about the law must be therefore *system-related*, ... [the law is] an *open, social system*"[125]

2.10 Summary and Conclusions

As illustrated, a large number of different assumptions about the nature of law exist. Likewise it is clear that a number of different opinions – tacit or explicit – about the objectives of jurisprudence are present. It is also noticeable that a variety of methods have come into practice, and that sometimes the advocates of different approaches oppose each-others proposals. The discussion about the deductive theory provides also a good example of the lack of established terminology. In addition, it must be remembered that the various jurisprudential movements included in this overview, although revealing a number of different approaches, represent only a small sample of the on-going activities. A great number of other movements and divergent schools of thought exist.

In general, the development of legal theory may be seen as a reaction against metaphysical speculations and notions about natural law. It is, however, important to observe that different schools of jurisprudence have met the challenge coming from the empirical and positivist movements in different ways. This leads to the development of two basic

123 *See, e.g.*, Strömholm, S. *Allmän rättslära* (1973), Hellner, J. *Rättsteori*, 21 (1988) *and* Klami *supra* note 16.

124 Strömberg, T. *Rättsordningens byggstenar. Om normtyperna i lag och sedvanerätt*, 7 (1988), (original text in Swedish).

125 Klami *supra* note 16, at 21, (original text in Swedish).

perspectives: legal realism (focusing on behaviour), and legal positivism (focusing on the rule system and its appearance). Methodological approaches based on the assumptions that law may be primarily explained in terms of behaviour have initiated empirical studies focusing on a variety of factors outside the legal system. On the other hand, movements leaning towards positivism have focused on various technical and philosophical aspects of the legal system, and entailed that within the framework of positivism jurisprudence has in much concentrated on the development of consistency within legal rule systems. Realism and positivism, respectively, have grown to be at times the sole theoretical basis for undertakings in jurisprudence. In other approaches, the perspectives have became integrated in various degrees. In still other contributions the demarcation is just not relevant.

Different assumptions about the nature of law, and various methodological inclinations do not, however, tell the whole story behind the prismatic image of contemporary jurisprudence. Much of the diversity may be also explained by stressing the fact that works in jurisprudence may focus on many different things and that in many works the lines of demarcation between the approached elements have not been drawn very explicitly. At least six main objects of interest can be identified: legal concepts, legal rules, legal reasoning, legal systems, interactions between legal systems and the outside world, and foundations of law. Each of these topics can be in turn related to each other in various combinations and investigated with various means. In addition, many of the issues addressed in this context concern difficult philosophical questions, and in many cases further sub-division into even more detailed fields of knowledge seems necessary. The main elements of interest in jurisprudence may, nevertheless, be depicted as in figure 2.1.

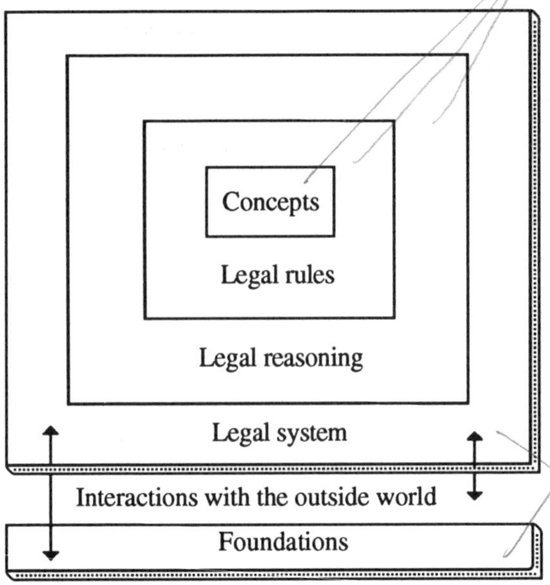

Figure 2.1 Studies in jurisprudence may focus on many different things and sometimes several aspects are approached simultaneously.

The existence of several major objects of interest is an important factor when it comes to explaining the relatively large number of movements that are apparent in jurisprudence. Different schools have emphasized various aspects of law, but this fact has not always been made clear. The existence of a variety of objectives in turn may be explained by the fact that different topics have appeared at various times and in different perspective as more or less compelling issues of concern. The existence of several objects of study explains, nevertheless, the sometimes confused debate on basic legal matters, in which various stand-points may at first glance seem totally inconsistent. A general observation would therefore be that many approaches within jurisprudence would presumably gain a lot from more distinct demarcation between the various objects of study.

One other observation following from this survey is that although there exist many schools of thought as regards the nature of law and the suggestions concerning the primary objects of study, the actual methodological approaches are relatively few. Basically three kinds of methodological approaches can be perceived: the use of sociological methods, manipulations with symbolic logic, and development of models of explanation by means of system theory.

It can also be seen that each methodological aspect foremost is used in order to study various objects. This is not to say that some methods are excluded from the study of certain topics in jurisprudence, it is merely to point out a general tendency. In a simplified picture, it may thereby be claimed that sociological methods are employed foremost in studies focusing on the interactions between legal systems and the outside world. Contributions based on sociological methods have been also to some extent orientated towards the foundations of legal systems and legal reasoning.[126] Symbolic logic, on the other hand, has been primarily used in studies aiming to develop the ability to manipulate and increase the understanding of the elements within the legal system, such as legal concepts, the relations between legal rules, and legal reasoning.[127] Although general studies encompassing all the elements are rare, more general undertakings are, as a rule, more or less explicitly based on system theory. Contributions of the latter kind appear sometimes under the label analytical jurisprudence. One illustration of this phenomena is given in figure 2.2.

126 *See, e.g.*, Schubert *supra* note 8.

127 Although exceptions exist. *See, e.g.*, Frändberg, Å. *Om rättsordningars giltighet* (1986).

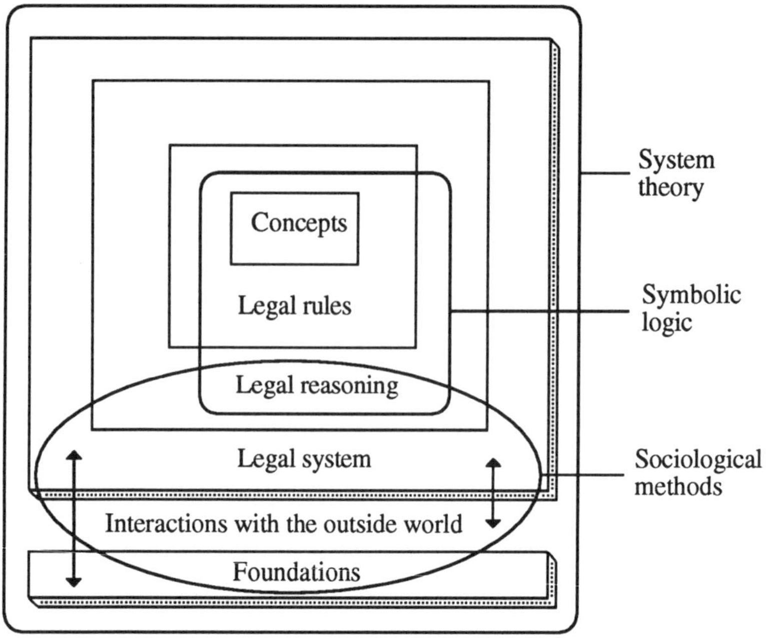

Figure 2.2 Several methodological approaches exist. Although a number of jurisprudential movements lay emphasis on different aspects of the law, basic legal elements are normally investigated with similar methods.

This study focuses on legal reasoning. From figure 2.2 follows that anyone undertaking such a project must be prepared to admit the relevance of several different methods.

3 Artificial Intelligence

3.1 Introduction

Compared with jurisprudence AI as a field of study has been in existence for a much shorter period of time. The term AI was coined as late as in the mid 1950s, whereas the forerunners of the first binary electronic computers appeared just before and during World War II. Mechanical calculators have been around however for several hundred years, and the notion of intelligent devices and thinking artefacts is much older than that.

As pointed out by *Hubert Dreyfus* – who in the writings of *Plato* finds certain epistemological demands similar to the desires of present day AI researchers[1] – and by *Pamela McCorduck* – who recalls *The Iliad* and *Talos* "a man of bronze whose duty is to patrol the beaches of Crete"[2] – it is possible to see a relationship between AI and various notions and concepts described already in the ancient Greek culture.

The ancient Greek mythology is not unique in this respect. During the recorded history of mankind notions about thinking Gods and stories about artefacts with human abilities appear in many cultures. The tradition doubtless reflects mostly human fantasy, although some mechanical devices imitating logical capacities and indicating knowledge may have been constructed, perhaps in the form of nodding statues, animated figures of saints and idols, etc. For natural reasons we know very little about these earliest attempts to mimic human intelligence.[3] Later expressions of this creative tradition may be however observed in the chess-playing Turk of baron *Wolfgang von Kempelen*,[4] in *Mary Shelley's*

[1] Dreyfus, H.L. *What Computers Can't Do*, xv (1972).

[2] McCorduck, P. *Machines who Think*, 4-5 (1979).

[3] *See*, for a survey and for further references to early projects and ancient devices, McCorduck *Id.* *and* Bowden, B.V. *Faster Than Thought*, 317 (1953).

[4] The chess playing Turk was presented as a robot and designed as a "life-sized wooden figure, turbaned and robed, seated in front of a wooden chest . . ." The Turk was however a fake and in the construction a man was hidden. The Turk was constructed in 1770 and toured Europe for some 40 years, without being revealed. *See, e.g.* Harmon, M. *Stretching Man's Mind*, 43-45 (1975).

Frankenstein,[5] in the science fiction literature of recent days, in modern toy stores, and in innumerable films.[6]

3.2 Philosophical Notions

Although AI is in its practical aspects intimately associated with the development of mechanical devices and the digital technique, the story of AI is not only the story of computers. AI touches upon the issues concerning the nature of knowledge, the process of learning, the meaning of language, the way our minds are related to the physical world, and other similar issues. In other words, studies in AI often stumble upon epistemological questions that have interested philosophers in all times. A background description must therefore include some references to various philosophical notions about the human mind.

To formulate a universally accepted explanation of natural intelligence is not an easy task. The definition of the word intelligence is constantly discussed and it tends to take on new meanings as time goes by. Various suggestions and interpretations have been submitted. One textbook overview purports that: "common definitions of intelligence include the ability to learn, to adopt to new situations, to represent and to manipulate symbols, and to solve problems."[7] A somewhat more detailed description also lists such abilities as:

> to respond to situations very flexibly; to take advantages of fortuitous circumstances; to make sense out of ambiguous or contradictory messages; to recognize the relative importance of different elements of a situation; to find similarities between situations despite differences which may separate them; to draw distinctions between situations despite similarities which may link

[5] Shelley, M.C. *Frankenstein: The modern Prometheus* (1817).

[6] *See also,* for a late contribution, Newsweek, *C-3POs for the display floor* (1990), about *Mannetron Productions, Glendale,* CA., U.S.A., a company selling "a line of androids designed to demonstrate products and give information in retail outlets around the country. For $26,000 a shop gets a pair of talking clerks made out of rubber, fiber glass and electronics – complete with swiveling heads and moveable limbs."

[7] Mayer, R.E. *Thinking, Problem Solving, Cognition,* 301 (1983).

> them; to synthesize new concepts by taking old concepts and putting them together in new ways; to come up with ideas which are novel.[8]

Attempts to formulate an all-encompassing definition of human intelligence reflect only one, even though rather important, aspect of studies concerning the processes of thinking. Since the time of *Aristotle* people have been trying to explain the reasoning process in terms of logic. In addition, several sciences have been founded on the study of various aspects of thinking. Mental abilities are approached, for instance, by psychologists, whereas theories concerning the nature and function of human language are tackled by linguists and so forth.

Perhaps the most well known attempt to define natural intelligence is the *psychometric approach,* focusing on mental faculties and assuming that each ability can be measured by means of testing. A systematic study of mental abilities was presented in the later half of the nineteenth century, and was later elaborated at the beginning of this century by the Frenchman *Alfred Binet* (1857–1911). The work initiated by Binet lead to the extensive use of *IQ-tests*.[9]

In addition to the uniform models of explanation and – perhaps as a reaction to the large number of diverse approaches in existence – a collective label for various methodological approaches has come into use, viz. *Cognitive science*. "[A] merger of philosophy, linguistics, and psychology with a strong influence from computer science."[10] Cognitive science is also a concept that has been related to AI:

> "In the last decade the awareness of these common issues has grown, leading to the emergence of a new interdisciplinary research domain, known as cognitive science. Being a cognitive scientist means that you are interested in a certain class of problems relating to natural and artificial intelligence."[11]

[8] Hofstadter, D.R. *Gödel, Escher, Bach,* 26 (1979).

[9] Mayer *supra* note 7, at 302-07. *See also,* for descriptions of psychological theories such as *Gestalt psychology, Associationism, Behaviorism* and *Cognitive psychology,* Johnson-Laird, P.N., Wason, P.C. eds. *Thinking* (1977), Sowa, J.F. *Conceptual Structures,* (1984) Turkle, S. *Artificial Intelligence and Psychoanalysis,* 242-43 (1988) *and* the appendix of this book.

[10] Sowa *Id.* at vii.

[11] Slack, J.M. *Cognitive Science Research,* 155 (1984).

In cognitive psychology, partly due to an intensive interaction with computer scientists, *information* has come to be an an important element in theory construction. In its most explicit forms this has lead to the formation of an *information processing model*, originally outlined in 1943 by *Kenneth Craik*,[12] where reasoning was perceived as processing of symbols. The information processing theory was elaborated in the 1950s by *Allen Newell* and *Herbert Simon* who assumed that there was a similarity between computers and brains in their capacities for executing and organizing elementary information processes. Newell and Simon made their information processing perspective explicit by suggesting that:

> "... the thinking human being is also an information processor, it should be possible to study the processes and their organization independently of the details of the biological mechanisms – the 'hardware'– that implements them."[13]

Newell and Simon also submitted their assumption in the form of a hypotheses known as the *Physical Symbol System Hypothesis* stating that "a physical symbol system has the necessary and sufficient means for general intelligent action."[14] The concept of the brain as an information processing unit has been discussed, transformed and elaborated by several researchers and the perspective has been recently summarized in the following way:

> These cognitive processes include: sensation and perception (reception and recognition of input stimuli), learning (encoding of input information), memory (retrieval of input information), and thinking (manipulation of perceived, learned and remembered information). These topics form the core of what has been called *cognitive psychology*, and to the extent that each involves active manipulation of information, each involves thinking.[15]

[12] Craik, K.J.W. *The Nature of Explanation*, 50-61 (1943).

[13] Simon, H.A., Newell, A. *Information-Processing in Computer and Man*, 256 (1964).

[14] Newell, A., Simon, H.A. *Computer Science as Empirical Inquiry*, 41 (1976).

[15] Mayer *supra* note 7, at 8.

Many approaches concerning natural intelligence and human thinking have focused on natural faculties, and in doing so they have paid lesser attention to how these abilities originate in nature. Approaches aiming to study intelligence by means of actually modelling the physical aspects of the human brain have been more rare. One such line of development is however the construction of so called *neural-networks* – an approach also known as *Connectionism*.[16] The basis for such an approach is that intelligence may be explained in terms of neuro-biological processes. The model was inspired by *Warren McCulloch* and *Walter Pitts* who in 1943 published a paper on the possibilities to simulate propositional logic in a network of neurons.[17] The notion behind this approach came to be later referred to as *Information theory*,[18] to which independent contributions were made by the American *Claude E Shannon*,[19] and by the father of cybernetics, *Norbert Wiener*.[20]

> The cybernetics theory of thought, with feedback as a central notion, seemed to promise the possibilities of imitating human cognition by modeling systems of neurons. This modeling was not based on detailed biological knowledge of the natural cell. . . . Instead, it seemed certain that the correspondence between the on-off behaviour of the neuron and the on-off behaviour of the electronic switch would be sufficient to allow significant modeling of neural systems, and then intelligent behaviour.[21]

The neural network approach has been criticised, among other things for being misleading and essentially statistical.[22]

16 *See, e.g.*, Schwartz, J.T. *The New Connectionism* (1988).

17 McCulloch, W.S., Pitts, W. *A Logical Calculus of the Ideas Immanent in Nervous Activity* (1943).

18 McCorduck *supra* note 2, at 46.

19 Shannon, C.E. *A Mathematical Theory of Communication* (1948). *See also*, Fleck, G. *A Computer Perspective*, 144 (1973).

20 Wiener, N. *Cybernetics* (1948).

21 McCorduck *supra* note 2, at 46. The theory on neural networks has been elaborated by a number of other researchers. *See, e.g.*, for a historical overview and for further references, Cowan, J.D., Sharp, D.H. *Neural Nets and Artificial Intelligence* (1988).

22 Reeke, G.N., Edelman, G.M. *Real Brains and Artificial Intelligence*, 144 (1988).

The debate concerning the two paradigms that are outlined above – symbol processing and connectionism – has been a main controversy in the history of modern AI. Symbol processing approaches have been so far dominant but in recent years connectionism has regained interest.[23] It is worthwhile to mention, however, that attempts have been made to design theories suggesting a natural symbiosis between the theories stressing physical aspects and the symbol processing approaches.[24]

Besides the various models of explanation concerning the functioning of the human mind, much of the philosophical discussion has concentrated on the relations between artificial and human intelligence. A basis for argumentation was thereby provided by the Englishman *Alan Turing* (1912–1954) who in 1950 submitted what has later come to be known as the *Turing test*.[25] In his contribution Turing reformulated the question "Can machines think", which he found difficult to address due to the vaguely defined words "machine" and "think".

Turing's proposed set up consisted of a person operating as an interrogator, alone in one room, communicating with two other persons, A and B, outside the room through a Teletype writing machine. The Turing test, as it normally is understood, is conducted by means of replacing A or B with a computer imitating human answers. If the interrogator is unable to determine whether A or B has been replaced, then the computer would have passed the test.[26] Thus the critical question is no longer is whether machines can think, but whether or not an interrogator, in a clinical test, can detect the difference between a human being and a computer.[27]

23 *See, e.g.*, Graubard, S.R. *The Artificial Intelligence Debate* (1988).

24 *See, e.g.*, Hillis, W.D. *Intelligence as an Emergent Behaviour* (1988).

25 Turing, A.M. *Computing Machinery and Intelligence* (1950).

26 The Turing test, which has been discussed in numerous versions, is an example of an approach which focuses on ability. The distinction between the nature of intelligence and faculties is however not always acknowledged to be relevant. *See, e.g.*, Searl, J.R. *Is the Brain's Mind a Computer Program?* 20 (1990), who points out that some AI-workers claim that a computer program that passes the Turing test would be a mind, in the same sense that the human mind is. Searl labels this approach *Strong AI*, and puts it in opposition to *Weak AI*, which is based on the "more cautious approach ... to think of computer models as being useful in studying the mind in the same way that they are useful in studying the weather, economics or molecular biology."

27 *See also*, for recent contributions to the discussion about natural and artificial intelligence with references to the Turing test, Sokolowski, R. *Natural and Artificial Intelligence* (1988), Waltz,

Various other submissions concerning the concept of intelligence have been also related to experiments with computer applications. An important insight has been made explicit, for instance, by *Douglas Hofstadter* who points out that the brain and the concept of intelligence – like computer systems – may be understood at several different levels, and that various levels need not necessarily exclude each other.[28] The relation between AI, the philosophy of mind and mental faculties has also been commented on by the American *John McCarthy*:

> AI is concerned with methods of achieving goals in situations in which the information available has a certain complex character. The methods that have to be used are related to the problem presented by the situation and are similar whether the problem solver is human, a Martian, or a computer program. . . .
>
> Much controversy surrounds AI's implications for philosophy, a subject about which there are strong views. AI tends to support rationalist and realist views of philosophical problems rather than empiricist, phenomenological, or idealist views. It encourages a piecemeal approach to the philosophy of mind, in which mental qualities are considered separately rather than as part of a grand package. This is because some systems have important, but rather limited, mental qualities.[29]

In addition, a dynamic aspect concerning the concept of intelligence has been underlined. The phenomenon is well-known to most researchers in the field of AI. It has been called the *Tesler's Theorem* and concerns progress in AI:

> [O]nce some mental function is programmed, people soon cease to consider it as an essential ingredient of 'real thinking'. The ineluctable core of intelligence is always in that next thing which hasn't yet been programmed. This 'Theorem' was first proposed to me by Larry Tesler, so I call it *Tesler's Theorem*: 'AI is whatever hasn't been done yet.'[30]

D.L. *The Prospects for Building Truly Intelligent Machines* (1988) *and* Penrose, R. *The Emperor's New Mind* (1989).

28 Hofstadter *supra* note 8, at 559 and *passim*.

29 McCarthy, J. *Mathematical Logic in Artificial Intelligence*, 308-09 (1988).

30 Hofstadter *supra* note 8, at 621.

That the concept of intelligence keeps changing its meaning is also apparent in the suggestion of Marvin Minsky, which focuses on problem solving:

> *Our minds contain processes that enable us to solve problems we consider difficult. 'Intelligence' is our name for whichever of those processes we don't yet understand.*
>
> Some people dislike this 'definition' because its meaning is doomed to keep changing as we learn more about psychology. But in my view that's exactly how it ought to be, because the very concept of intelligence is like a stage magician's trick. Like the concept of '*the unexplored regions of Africa*,' it disappears as we discover it.[31]

In other words, Minsky is content with an infinite definition. However, the changing nature of the concept of intelligence may also be related to the *superhuman human fallacy* – a phrase invented by *Seymour Papert*, expressing the fact that there exists "a very common modern view that machines can't be said to 'think' unless they show superhuman skills."[32] From this point of view the dynamic aspect of intelligence is often discouraging for AI-system designers. It suggests that many potential users will, as soon as they understand the underlying principles of a system, instantly declare that its performance is rudimentary.

It is obvious that many of the undertakings in the study of the human mind have depended on the various preferences and the different backgrounds of the persons involved. Cognitive science is thus a multifaceted discipline. It is, however, important to recognize that a diversity of perspectives does not need to entail problems. On the contrary, the development of AI has been a process in which many disciplines have provided valuable sources of knowledge. The manifold background also supply the AI researchers with a comprehensible methodological tool-kit for further advancements. The overview of different approaches towards the concept of intelligence will however not be elaborated to any greater extent in this

[31] Minsky, M. *The Society of Mind*, 71 (1985).

[32] McCorduck *supra* note 2, at 11.

background description. Some terminological statements about the basic notions approached in this study are nevertheless in place.

Intelligence is here conceived of as a series of intellectual faculties attached to human beings. In consequence, the study of *artificial intelligence* is defined as a study of mechanical devices that may take over any tasks previously performable only by human minds. AI is thereby used as a general label encompassing not only elements of computer science and information technology, but also methodological findings from other sciences. By this, no terminological invention is intended – the terminology that is outlined here is meant to be in line with the common usage of the concept of AI.[33]

Implicit in the definition of intelligence as a series of faculties lies the acceptance of a broad spectrum of levels of performance. That is to say, that although it is possible to specify a number of basic abilities that we usually associate with intelligence, it is clear that most faculties may be developed in various degrees. Furthermore, it is possible to allow for one or even several abilities to be lacking, but nevertheless to define the remaining qualities as intelligence. For example, certain individuals may have a bad memory and possess a low ability to manipulate numerical symbols. The same individuals may, on the other hand, be more than proficient in literature, painting, verbal abilities, etc, and it would be unjust

33 *Cf.* Hofstadter *supra* note 8, at 601 "One could define AI as coming into existence at the moment when mechanical devices took over any tasks previously performable only by human minds." *and* Susskind *supra* chapter 1 note 9, at 7-8, "In the present context, the term 'artificial intelligence' can perhaps best be regarded . . . as a label used to refer to what it seems that certain computer systems possess to some degree. Such systems – having been so designed and constructed to perform those tasks and solve those problems that together if performed by human beings are taken by us to be indicative of intelligence – can be said to exhibit artificial intelligence." *See also* Schank, R.C. *What is AI, anyway?*, 4 (1990) "One way to attack this [definition] problem is to attempt to list some features that we would expect an intelligent entity to have. None of these features would define intelligence – indeed a being could lack any one of them and still be considered to be intelligent. Nevertheless each is an integral part of intelligence in its way. . . . [T]he features . . . are: communication, internal knowledge, world knowledge, goals and plans, and creativity." *and* Sowa *supra* note 9 at vii: "Cognitive science is a merger of philosophy, linguistics and psychology with a strong influence from computer science. Artificial intelligence is the engineering counterpart; it pays more attention to programming tools and techniques than to philosophical issues." *But see,* for what seems to be a somewhat more comprehensive and ambitious approach, Genesereth, M.R., Nilsson, N.J., *Logical Foundations of Artificial Intelligence*, 1 (1987): "AI is the study of intelligent behaviour. Its ultimate goal is a theory of intelligence that accounts for the behaviour of naturally occurring intelligent entities and that guides the creation of artificial entities capable of intelligent behaviour. Thus, AI is both a branch of science and a branch of engineering." *Compare also* Minsky *supra* note 31.

to proclaim that the lack of one or several abilities instantly entails lack of intelligence. Likewise it appears unethical and impossible to conceive of a definition founded on the concept of certain levels of performance in various fields.[34]

It is clear that a definition of intelligence in terms of mental faculties does not answer any ontological questions about the outmost nature of the concept. It has not been intended to either. The prime objective of this study is to complete a practically oriented investigation, and by making these initial demarcations to exclude the hardest philosophical issues from the discussion. On the other hand, it should be noticed that no final statements about the importance of in-depth philosophical studies have thereby been made.

Keeping in mind that the main object of this study is legal reasoning (and thus problem solving), it should be mentioned that a definition that starts out from an investigation of faculties need not necessarily be in opposition to a definition of intelligence based on general problem solving. Problem solving capacity may be also looked upon as a faculty. Problem solving is, however, a complex ability which can be decomposed into smaller parts, and in this respect the faculties that are investigated in this study are all related to problem solving processes. The more detailed level is preferred since it seems to provide greater opportunities for systematic analyses.

3.3 Calculating Machines

A description of the origin of AI cannot be limited to the study of attempts to produce *androids* or Divine idols.[35] Neither is it possible to limit a study of AI to autonomous full-fledged intelligent Automats – simply because no such devices exist. AI inventions are still designed for more or less specific tasks. Hence, a background description must include

[34] Hofstadter *supra* note 8, at 26 "[T]o suggest that a sharp borderline exist is probably silly." *See also* Bowden *supra* note 3, at 319 *and* Schank *Id.*

[35] McCorduck *supra* note 2, at 5 n. 2, points out that purists make distinctions between different sorts of AI machines. *Automata* is the general term denoting all "self-locomoting contrivances". Humanlike automats are called *androids*, e.g. the creation of Dr. Frankenstein, and *robot* is a name for mass-produced special kinds of androids.

more down-to-earth projects, aiming to produce tools for isolated intellectual tasks. The most elaborated projects have thereby concerned various types of calculators.

Calculating machines appear for the first time in the seventeenth century.[36] The earliest known example was presented by *William Schickardt* in 1623.[37] Mechanical calculators were also constructed during the seventeenth century by the Frenchman *Blaise Pascal* (1623–1662), by the Englishman Sir *Samuel Moreland* (1625–1695), by the German *Gottfried Wilhelm Leibniz* (1646–1716),[38] as well as by several others.[39] The efforts to produce improved calculating machines continued during the eighteenth and the nineteenth centuries.[40] Although most devices were designed in order to facilitate some predetermined tasks of calculation, nevertheless, through the Englishman *Charles Babbage* (1792–1871), there exists a direct link to more general devices.

Babbage's first major project concerning calculators was a *difference engine* for the generation and printing of faultless tables.[41] In the nineteenth century the production of tables was a cumbersome task, engaging brigades of calculating clerks. Babbage's invention was a manually operated machine with moveable parts carrying numbers related to each other in such a way that numerical differences could be generated automatically when the machine was operated. In order to eliminate the appearances of errors during the complicated and prolonged printing process – at that time a major difficulty – the machine also included a

36 Devices assisting calculating are however much older. The abacus, which is still a standard calculating tool in large parts of Asia, is several thousand years old. Naturally, also the use of strings bearing knots, marks in pieces of wood, and similar utensils belong to this tradition.

37 Harmon *supra* note 4, at 17-19, Lund, J. *Från kula till data*, 27 (1988). The conception of calculating machines are nevertheless older and already among the manuscripts of *Leonardo da Vinci* (1452-1519) there exist notes describing a mechanical calculator. Harmon *supra* note 4, at 12.

38 Lund *Id.* at 27-30.

39 *E.g.* by the German *Philipp Matthäus Hahn*, (1939–1790) and by *Grillet de Roven. Id. See also, e.g.*, Harmon *supra* note 4, at 17-43.

40 Improved models were presented e.g. in 1709 by *Giovanni Poleni* (1685–1761), in 1775, in 1777, and in 1790, by *Charles Stanhope* (1753–1816). Harmon *supra* note 4, at 40-41.

41 A problem previously given attention in 1784 by the German *J.H. Müller* (1746–1830). Lindgren, M. *Glory and Failure*, 64 (1987).

printing mechanism. A prototype of the difference engine was presented in 1822, but the work on the full-scale version of the machine could not be completed and Babbage was finally forced to abandon the project in 1833.[42]

Despite the fact that the difference engine did not become operative, Babbage elaborated his ideas and started working on a device which he named *The analytical engine*. The analytical engine was a sophisticated machine which could be programmed by means of instructions coded on punch cards – an invention that Babbage had picked up from *Joseph Marie Jacquard* (1752–1834), a Frenchman who introduced punch cards in order to operate looms.[43] The instructions could be altered by means of changing the *Operating cards* which were handled in *the Mill* of the machine. The numbers that were to be computed were represented on another set of punch cards called *Number Cards*, which were deposited in *the Store.* The Store incorporated also, among other things, a computing apparatus, printing facilities, and a card punching apparatus.[44]

The analytical engine thus comprised the embryos of the components that can be found in modern computers – the *program* of the latter corresponding to the operating cards, the *processor* resembling the mill, the *memory* corresponding to the store, the *input facilities* existing in the form of punch card readers and the *output devices* present in the form of printing equipment and card punchers.

Babbage did not succeed in producing fully operative prototypes of his inventions, and the ideas of Babbage concerning machines for more general purposes did not have any direct influence on the development. Various constructions that were presented during the nineteenth century in much still aimed to facilitate predetermined and isolated tasks.

A major advancement was made in 1890 when the American *Herman Hollerith* (1860–1929) patented a mechanized tabulating machine, originally designed for the *U.S. Census Bureau*. Hollerith used electricity to

[42] *Id.* at 63.

[43] Harmon *supra* note 4, at 102. Jacquard also had a number of less known predecessors. *See, e.g.*, Zemanek, H. *Central European Prehistory of Computing*, 589 (1980).

[44] *See*, for a description of the design and the functions of the analytical engine, Buxton, H.W. *Memoir of the Life and Labours of the late Charles Babbage ESQ. F.R.S.*, 173-216 (1988).

sensor the holes in the punch cards and the machine was used in the 1890-census which was completed in less than two months. In comparison, the 1880-census which was tabulated manually, took 7.5 years to complete.[45]

Numerous mechanical calculating devices were also patented during the first decades of the twentieth century, although most of them had been still developed for designated tasks, e.g. for statistics, tabulating, book keeping, measuring, etc.[46]

The majority of inventions that were presented during the nineteenth century depended on discrete representation, i.e. on a representation in distinct steps. One line of development that was pursued during the later part of the nineteenth century, and in the first half of this century, leaned however on analog technique, i.e. it was based on a continuously variable representation, e.g. physical or electrical magnitudes. The notion of building analog computers was initially submitted by the Englishman Sir *William Thomson* (Lord Kelvin) who in 1873 specified a harmonic analyser and a tide predictor, and later a more general differential analyser.[47] The first machine "that was general enough to solve a wide variety of problems", *The Bush Differential Analyser*, was designed by the American *Vannevar Bush* (1890–1974), around 1930,[48] The successful results obtained from the differential analyser lead to the development of a number of electronic analog computers in the 1930s. A few elaborated versions were also completed during World War II.[49] Computers based on analogue representation would, however, soon become obsolete. The reasons for this may be found in a series of theoretical insights, as well as in practical advancements with digital technique.

45 Harmon *supra* note 4, at 103.

46 *See, e.g.,* for general overviews Fleck *supra* note 19 *and* Lund *supra* note 37.

47 Fleck *supra* note 19, at 15.

48 *Id.* at 116.

49 *Id.* at 134.

3.4 Logical Foundations

The origin of AI and computer science is not only a history of practical inventions. The development is also based on the utilization of theoretical conceptions and on the integration of various notions. This is most noticeable in the development and utilization of formal logic. In this respect advancements of crucial importance were made in the middle of the nineteenth century by the Englishman *George Boole* (1815–1864), who elaborated the theory of mathematical symbols in logic.[50]

Boole demonstrated that all conceivable classes of objects may be related to each other and represented by symbols, and that an algebra restricted to the values of 0 and 1 is sufficient for such a representation. Boole also showed how ''laws of thoughts'' may be used in order to relate symbols and to draw logical conclusions from symbolic representations.[51]

Boole is often thought of as the father of modern logic although he did not invent symbolic logic. Even though the development of symbolic logic was rather slow for a long time, the origins of symbolic logic may be already found in the ancient times.[52] Noteworthy proposals were also made in the seventeenth century by Leibniz who submitted the concept of *calculus ratiocinator*, a method for scientific thinking in general, based on symbols representing concepts on which logical operations could be executed by means of using exactly defined rules.[53] Leibniz was in turn inspired by others[54] but the ideas did not generate any practical results.

All the rules of symbolic logic, the so called *Boolean algebra*, that are now in use were not, however, developed by Boole; Boolean algebra has

50 Boole, G. *The Mathematical Analysis of Logic* (1847) *and* Boole, G. *An Investigation of the Laws of Thought* (1854).

51 *See, e.g.*, for comments on the contributions of Boole and for an overview of the history of symbolic logic , Lewis, C.I., Langford, C.H. *Symbolic Logic*, 3-25 (1932).

52 *Cf. Id.* at 3.

53 Leibniz also conceived a universal scientific language, *characteristica universalis*, common to all scientists and constructed in order to make the communication of scientific ideas more efficient, and to facilitate logical analyses by means of replacing ordinary language. The idea of *characteristica universalis* did not produce immediate results but the works of Leibniz are hold to have been of great importance as a source of inspiration to other logicians. *Id.* at 5-7.

54 E.g. by *Raymund Lullus. Id.* at 5.

been developed and refined by several succeeding logicians. One important line of development that was eventually integrated with the Boolean conception was also pursued by Russell and *Alfred North Whitehead* who in their well-known work *Principia Mathematica* (1910) tried to prove that all pure mathematics is part of formal logic.[55]

The operators ("and", "or", "not") which are the basic elements of Boolean algebra may be described by the use of so called Venn diagrams:

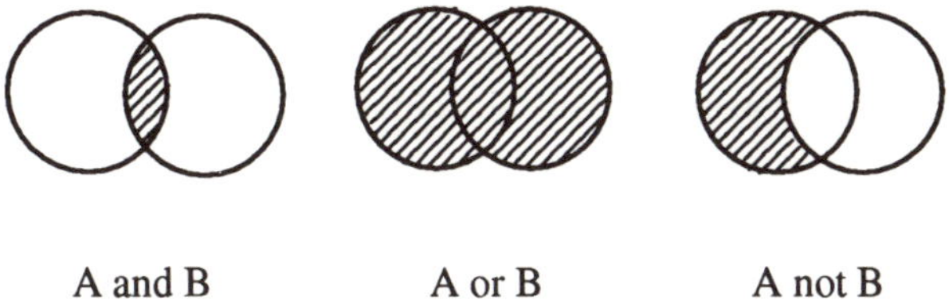

Figure 3.1 Graphic representation of the Boolean operators *and, or, not.*

In Boolean algebra. the variables may be added, multiplied and negated. Furthermore various combinations may be summarized in so called *truth tables*[56] where the possible combinations of variables which may carry either the value of 0 or 1 may be expressed.

The operators "and", "or", "not", in combination with the conditional expression "if . . . then . . ." are also the essential components of a formal system called the *Propositional Calculus*, although they then are represented by symbols like those presented below (figure 3.2) and labelled sentential connectives:[57]

55 Nagel, E., Newman, J.R. *Goedel's Proof*, 1679 (1956), von Mises, R. *Mathematical Postulates and Human Understanding*, 1741 (1956).

56 So named because 0 and 1 are sometimes referred to as false and true. *See, e.g.*, on truth tables, Dewdney, A.K. *The Turing Omnibus*, 75-83 (1989).

57 Suppes *supra* chapter 2 note 73, at 3, Tarski, A. *Symbolic Logic*, 1910 (1956).

& representing *and*, (conjunction)

V representing *or*, (disjunction)

~ representing *not*, (negation)

—> representing *if – then*, (implication)

<—> representing *if and only if*, (equivalence)

Figure 3.2 Symbolic representation of sentential connectives of propositional calculus.

Propositional calculus may be used in order to derive truth values through laws of relations. By means of using brackets and so called *atom symbols*, e.g. P, Q, and R, any well formed sentence[58] may be included in a formal system. In an additional step, different relations may be combined into complex expressions in certain well-defined ways by the use of predefined rules. Reasoning that depends only on the correct usage of these relations is named *propositional reasoning*. By applying syntactic rules of logic it is then possible to make statements about truth. The law of hypothetical syllogism gives for instance:

((P—> Q) & (Q —> R)) —> (P —> R)

The propositional calculus has been elaborated by several researchers, especially by the German *David Hilbert* (1861–1947) who assumed the existence a finite formal representation in which also the means of deducting formulas were mechanized. In the system conceived by Hilbert some classes of symbols were adapted to be axioms from which it was suggested additional classes of symbols could be deduced in a mechanized way in accordance with predetermined rules.[59] Such a system, if it existed, would be sufficient to prove or disprove all conceivable theorems.

[58] *Cf., e.g.,* Suppes *Id.* at 12.

[59] von Mises *supra* note 55, at 1751.

During the 1930s several innovations and additional theoretical breakthroughs appear. One important contribution to modern computing was made by Turing in 1936. Turing showed that a machine, by means of moving a tape filled with digital information back and forth and by printing and erasing the symbols, is capable of executing any kind of program expressed in the binary code of zeros and ones. "If we can express precisely the steps needed to accomplish a task, the task itself can be programmed and carried out by the machine."[60] Turing restricted himself to theoretical models, proving his theses without any practical construction work. The suggested concept is nevertheless known as the *Turing machine* and the ideas described by Turing are incorporated in all general computers. In the same paper, in opposition to the axiomatic notion proposed by Hilbert, Turing also proved that certain classes of mathematical problems cannot be solved by any fixed and definite process. This conclusion was also arrived at and proved by the Austrian mathematician *Kurt Gödel* (1906 –1978) in 1931.[61]

The binary code, which is an essential element in the works of Boole and Turing, is a representation based on a numerical system with the base 2. Such a system was first studied by Napier[62] and then by Leibniz.[63] Binary representation, Boolean operators, formal logic, and a number of mathematical findings form a theoretical basis for the present day computers and computer programs. There is also, however, a practical side to the development of electronic computers.

3.5 Electronic Computers

On the practical side the use of electronic computers is connected with the understanding and the manipulation of electronic components. Practical

60 Turing, A.M. *On Computable Numbers with an Application to the Entscheidungsproblem* (1936).

61 Weyl, H. *The Mathematical Way of Thinking*, 1849 (1956). *See also* Hofstadter, D.R. *Metamagical Themas*, 485-86 (1985).

62 Turnbull, H.W. *The Great Mathematicians*, 122 (1956).

63 Lund *supra* note 37, at 76.

construction work combining electronic equipment with Boolean algebra and binary representation started during the 1930s when, independently of each other, several prototypes of electronic computers were developed.[64]

Presumably the first project including computers in this sense was initiated in Germany by *Conrad Zuse* in 1934. Practical construction work of several prototypes, named *Z1, Z2,* etc, was commenced during 1936. Zuse did not publish his results until after the war, but in a review some forty years later he mentions that several technologies were then tested and used.[65] The computers in question were meant to be of a general nature and the program as well as the numbers to be calculated were transmitted to the machine through punched tape, initially old movie filmstrip. Zuse also integrated formal logic into the use of hardware (the physical equipment of the machine) and for this purpose employed the operators, ''and'', ''or'', and ''not''. The integration seems however to have been initiated rather because of practical requirements than due to any theoretical analyses:

> But I missed there the consequent confrontation with the calculus of propositions. For us the terms ''and'', ''or'', and ''not'' belonged to our daily language. We really worked with them and made the step to apply the mathematical logic to the computer design. I translated the logical rules systematically into switching algebra[66]

Because of the war, Zuse's work was interrupted several times and it finally came to a halt during 1945. One of the prototypes, the model *Z4*, was rescued but practical work could not be continued before 1948. In the

64 Although mechanical devices developed in order to solve logical problems appears earlier. In 1870 *J.W. Jevons* (1835–1882) demonstrated a logical machine consisting of a logical abacus with a number of separate wooden tables and a keyboard, Bowden *supra* note 3, at 183. In the 1880s the American *Allan Marquand* (1853–1924) completed a machine that could perform logical operations. Marquand later also conceived the possibilities to employ electricity for his machine. In 1903 the Italian *Annibale Pastore* (1868–1936) presented a mechanical device with moveable devices that that could be altered in order ''to represent any of 256 syllogistic structures.'' Fleck *supra* note 19, at 32-33. Noticeable is also a chess playing machine, that could play with a rook and king against the king of the human opponent, built in 1912, by the Spanish inventor *Leonardo Torres y Quevedo* (1852–1936), Zemanek *supra* note 43, at 598-99.

65 Zuse, K. *Some Remarks on the History of Computing in Germany* (1980).

66 *Id.* at 615.

meanwhile, Zuse turned to theoretical work and developed the first elaborated computer programming language, which he called the the *Plan–kalkül* (program calculus).

> The result was an amazingly comprehensive language . . . an extension of Hilber's *Aussagenkalkül* (propositional calculus) and *Prädikatenkalkül* (predicate calculus). Before laying his project aside, Zuse had completed an extensive manuscript containing programs far more complex than anything written before. Among other things, there were algorithms for sorting; for testing the connectivity of a graph represented as a list of edges; for integer arithmetic, (including square roots) in binary notation; and for floating-point arithmetic. He even developed algorithms to test whether or not a given logical formula is syntactically well formed, and whether or not such a formula contains redundant parentheses – assuming six levels of precedence between the operators. To top things off, he also included 49 pages of algorithms for playing chess.[67]

Although various earlier attempts to program calculating machines had been made by Charles Babbage and *Ada Lovelace* in the 1830s and 1840s,[68] by *Leonardo Torres y Quevedo* in 1914, by Alan Turing in 1936, as well as by the German *Helmut Schreyer* who assisted Zuse in 1939, Zuse was the first to extend and to adapt the propositional calculus for electronic computers. The Plankalkül was in this respect in much the first modern computer language.[69]

Several computers developed during the 1930s and 1940s were electromechanical devices operated partly by electricity and partly mechanically. The computers designed by Zuse, for instance, used electromagnetic telephone relays. A working electromechanical computer was also constructed in the U.S.A., at Bell labs., by *Georg Stiblitz*, who in 1938 built a

67 Knuth, D.E., Trabb Pardo, L. *The Early Development of Programming Languages*, 203 (1980).

68 Lovelace, A. *Translators Notes to Menebrea, L.F. Sketch of the Analytical Engine Invented by Charles Babbage, Esq.* (1842).

69 The manuscript of Zuse, basically comprised in 1945, with the exception of a few excerpts, lay unpublished until 1972. *Id.*

"complex number calculator, *Model I*, which consisted largely of relays and crossbar switches" and was based on a "mixed binary, decimal notation."[70] Electromechanical computers were also designed by *Howard Aiken* who in 1944, in a joint project between *IBM* and *Harvard University*, completed the first general-purpose digital calculator, *Mark I*.[71]

The first project based primarily on electronic components was organized in the U.S.A. by the American *John V. Atanasoff* who designed and built two electronic computers,[72] a prototype and a second version which was named *ABC*, an acronym for *The Atanasoff-Berry Computer*.[73] The ABC, like the computers of Zuse, operated on a binary basis, manipulating the numbers by means of employing the rules of logic, rather than by direct counting. Atanasoff introduced however also vacuum tubes in order to carry out the control and the arithmetic functions of the machine. He also decided to store the binary digits in capacitors. In addition, the ABC project differed from other projects at the time by means of separating the computer's memory unit from the processing unit. The ABC was constructed between 1937 – 1942. The project was then interrupted by World War II, and after that time the ABC was not developed any further. The principles of the ABC were however taken up by *John W. Mauchly* who was one of the men behind another, more famous computer project which resulted in *Electronic Numerical Integrator And Computer* (ENIAC). Despite this, it took a long time before Atanasoff got the full credit for his contribution.[74]

70 Fleck *supra* note 19, at 121.

71 *Id.* at 123, Harmon *supra* note 4, at 117-19.

72 *See*, for descriptions of the development of the project of Atanasoff, and the ABC computer, Burks, A.R., Burks, A.W. *The First Electronic Computer* (1988), Mollenhoff, C.R. *Atanasoff: Forgotten Father of the Computer* (1988) *and* Mackintosh, A.R. *Dr. Atanasoff's Computer*, 72-78 (1988).

73 Atanasoff in the work was assisted by *Clifford E. Berry. Id.*

74 The ENIAC patent ("the original electronic computer patent") was, according to section 3 of *Judge Earl R. Larson's* opinion in *Honeywell Inc.* v. *Sperry Rand Corp., et al.* October 19, 1973 at the U.S. District Court in Minneapolis, concluded to be invalid due to the fact that the men behind the ENIAC "Eckert and Mauchly did not themselves first invent the automatic electronic digital computer, but instead derived that subject matter from one Dr. John Vincent Atanasoff." (Quoted by Mollenhoff *supra* note 72, at 265).

The technique of combining logic with electronic circuits was first described in 1937 by Shannon.[75] Shannon illustrated how Boolean operators could be used for the description of the behaviour of electrical relays and switching circuits. Shannon also realized that a restricted two-valued algebra and Boolean operators could perfectly describe the behaviour of electrical relays, where any of them could be set on or off. In its ''on'' state a relay may thus correspond to the value of 1, and in its ''off'' state correspond to the value of 0. Thus, by means of combining several circuits and groups of circuits to each other, and by utilizing the technique of storing binary digits in electronic devices, the things that are to be represented are only limited by the number of circuits and switches.

The production of functional computers became one of the most crucial tasks during World War II, and the first electronic computers that actually came into daily use originate from this period. Two major projects whose researchers had little or no knowledge of the other project, were initiated during the war. The most famous project is the work that resulted in the ENIAC. The ENIAC project was initiated at the *Moore School of Electronics* at the *University of Pennsylvania*. The preparatory work started in 1943, but the machine was not completed until 1946, after the war had ended. Although the machine turned out to be for general use it was initially designed to calculate ballistic tables. The design work on ENIAC was lead by Mauchly and *J. Presper Eckert, Jr.* The project was sponsored by the *U.S. Army*. ENIAC was a gigantic machine.

> It had 30 separate units (plus power supply and forced-air cooling), occupied a space 30 by 50 feet, and weighed over 30 tons. It had some 18,000 vacuum tubes, 70,000 resistors, 10,000 capacitors, and 6,000 switches. It was a synchronous machine with a clock rate of 100,000 pulses per second. The ENIAC had 20 accumulators (for addition and subtraction), a multiplier, and a combination divider and square rooter. Input and output were by punch cards.[76]

[75] Fleck *supra* note 19, at 121.

[76] Harmon *supra* note 4, at 124.

Computers based on electronic techniques were also developed during World War II in England. The project was initiated by *The British Foreign Ministry*. The initial objective of the project was to break the German codes and the first machine that was constructed was a cryptanalytic device called the *BOMBE*. The machine could successfully break the code of a cryptographic machine employed by the Germans, called *ENIGMA*, and thus played an important role during the war.[77] A couple of years later, among other devices, an electronic computer named *COLOSSUS* was constructed. The machine was put into operation in December 1943.[78]

The early computers, although they often had a powerful calculating capacity, had to be programmed (or re-programmed) manually before any processing could be conducted. This was often a time-consuming and cumbersome task. Important improvements for electronic computers were however described in 1945 by an Hungarian-born American, *John von Neumann* (1903–1957), who submitted the conception of stored programs.[79] Stored programs made it possible to predetermine subroutines in the machine and to give instructions to the computer in the same form as the data to be calculated. Thus, time-consuming re-programming, which previously had to be done manually, could be eliminated which drastically increased the generality of computers. ''For the first time the, then, logical choices of program sequences could be made *inside* the machine, and the instructions could be modified by the computer as it went along.''[80]

77 Hodges, A. *Alan Turing, The Enigma* (1983).

78 Randell, B. *The COLOSSUS*, 88 (1980).

79 von Neumann, J. *First Draft of a Report on the EDVAC* (1945). There exist however different opinions about the origin of several early inventions connected to electronic computers. Mauchly, for instance, still after the 1973 court decision denied that Atanasoff played any important role in his and Eckert's conception of ENIAC. Mauchly, J.W. *The ENIAC*, 548-49 (1980). Eckert on the other hand claims that several ideas related to stored programs were conceived by him and Mauchly and that von Neumann got the idea from working with them. Eckert, J.P. *The ENIAC*, 532-36 (1980).

80 Fleck *supra* note 19, at 137.

The first computers with stored programs and binary arithmetic were constructed in England a few years later. (*The Manchester University Computer Mark I*, [81] and at *Cambridge University EDSAC*.[82])

In the U.S.A. the ENIAC project was followed by a number of development projects. Eckert and Mauchly founded a private company and designed the first American binary computer with stored program, *BINAC*. Eckert and Mauchly also designed *UNIVAC* – the first electronic computer that came into serial production (1951).

The development of electronic computers also triggered off a number of other activities connected with computer programming. In the U.S.A. von Neumann, in cooperation with *Herman V. Goldstein*, *Adele Goldstein* and *Arthur W. Burks*, developed during 1946–1947 a pictorial representation involving boxes containing mathematical notations joined by arrows, which they called *flow diagrams*.[83] Around 1950 contributions based on mathematical and algebraic notation were suggested by numerous researchers. In the beginning the work was very time-consuming and often related to specific tasks and special computers, but soon more appropriate methods based on the use of predefined subroutines, the development of compilers for generation of binary code, and similar advancements opened the way for a growing multitude of languages of a general nature. The first textbook on programming appeared in 1951, the first high-level language, *FORTRAN*, was presented in 1957, and the second one, *Algol*, was introduced in 1958, etc.[84]

During the last 35 years innumerable versions of improved electronic computers have been constructed. A number of factors have made such development possible. Succeeding generations of electronic components have not only improved access-time and reliability, but also made

[81] A prototype was designed and tested in 1948 and an operating machine was presented in 1950, Lund *supra* note 37, at 79-81.

[82] In 1949 Fleck *supra* note 19, at 155.

[83] Knuth, Trabb Pardo *supra* note 67, at 208.

[84] Dorn, P.H. *Commercial Data Processing: A Brief History*, 20-25 (n.d.). *See also,* on the early development of computer programs, Sammet, J.E. *Programming Languages* (1969) *and* Knuth, Trabb Pardo *supra* note 67.

significant miniaturization possible. The vacuum tube technology, which was the basis for the first generation of electronic computers, has been replaced by transistors.[85] Transistors, in turn, have been replaced by semiconductors and integrated chips.[86] Simultaneously a large number of inventions – e.g. improved memory technology and time sharing – as well as increased understanding of how to construct effective processors and improved, high-level computer programming languages, have made it possible to achieve high speed in data processing and to increase the amount of data which may be processed. Punch cards have been replaced as input/output vehicles by keyboards, optical character readers, computer screens, laser printers, and by a large diversity of peripheral equipment. Furthermore, the integration of computers and telecommunications has made it possible to access and retrieve data of almost infinite magnitude. In addition, mass-production and improved efficiency have made drastic cost reductions possible.[87]

3.6 Towards a Uniform Discipline of AI

Computer science has gone through dramatic changes since the middle of the 1950s. It has also been a manifold enterprise in which a large number of research groups and organizations with different interests have been established. Equally important, a number of commercial and political interests have been attracted. In consequence, the notion of AI has not been the only one competing for acknowledgment, and the relations between computer science and AI have sometimes been debated. From one perspective AI has been suggested to be a sub-field of computer science.[88] Others have argued that the notion of AI is the fundamental one, and that

[85] The transistor was invented in 1948, Gratte, I., Månsson, E. *Datorer?*, 14 (1985), and the first all-transistor logic computer was presented in 1958. Dorn *Id.* at 16.

[86] The integrated chip was invented in 1959, and it has been commercially available from the early 1970s. *See, e.g.*, Reid, T.R. *The Chip* (1984) *and* Dorn *supra* note 84.

[87] *See, e.g.*, for an overview over the recent years history of electronic computers, Dorn *supra* note 84 *and*, for the evolution of high level languages and so called expert system building languages, Hayes-Roth *supra* chapter 1, note 2, at 8.

[88] Weizenbaum, J. *Computer Power and Human Reason*, 8 (1976).

computers and information technology are merely devices for the realization of the former.[89]

Reviewing the early contributions, it is however obvious that many of the pioneers of computer science were, in various ways, aware of the similarities between electronic computers and the human intellect. Zuse, for instance, explains that "[b]ehind the Plankalkül there is a special philosophy based on my early conviction, that there is a steady way from simple numerical calculation to high-level thinking processes."[90] In 1950 Turing addressed the question of whether a computer can think[91] and in the same year Shannon published a paper in which he discussed the possibilities to teach a computer to play chess.[92] In 1953 *B. V. Bowden*, in an overview of the technique and its possible applications, discussed such questions as "can these new machines think, and if not, will it ever be possible to build machines which do?" Bowden also mentions that the issue was "widely discussed in the press – for example, in the correspondence columns of *The Times* last year." (i.e. 1952).[93]

The parallels between computers and human intelligence have however not been, however, always stressed – on the contrary – McCorduck retells the history of computer marketing around 1960 in the following way:

> [S]ales executives at IBM began to grow nervous lest the very machines they were trying to sell prove so psychologically threatening that customers would refuse to buy them. Thus they made a deliberate decision to defuse the potency of such programs . . . by conducting a hard-sale campaign picturing the computer as nothing more than a quick moron. Countess Lovelace's dictum, that the machine can do nothing more than we tell it to do . . . was raised to a universal truth, and parroted by every sales and service person connected with the company. It came to be a popular idea, a sort of slogan of the back-

89 McCorduck *supra* note 2, at 345 "[T]he impulse to make artificial intelligence has always been central to our project as a species."

90 Zuse *supra* note 65, at 625.

91 Turing *supra* note 25.

92 Shannon, C. *A Chess-Playing Machine* (1950).

93 Bowden *supra* note 3, at 316-17.

> lash, and is offered to this day by people who feel threatened by the idea of machine intelligence.[94]

If not sooner, the concept of a uniform discipline devoted to the study of thinking artefacts and its potentialities, becomes explicit a few years later when a seminar takes place in *Dartmouth*, U.S.A., and one of the organizers, McCarthy, coins the label AI (1956).

Since the 1950s AI has continuously achieved greater admission as a worthwhile area of research. The development has been related in several ways. The history of AI has been, for instance, described as consisting of three distinct periods. A *classical period*, with the emphasis on the problems related to game playing and theorem proving, stretching from 1950 to the publication of *Computers and Thought* – a collection of early papers on topics in AI published in 1963.[95] A *romantic period*, from the mid 1960s to the mid 1970s, with a focus on computer understanding, succeeded by a *modern period* "characterized by an increasing self-consciousness and self-criticism, together with an orientation towards techniques and applications."[96]

In a somewhat more detailed description six distinct periods have been listed: A pre-World War II "root-period" distinguished by the development of formal logic and cognitive psychology; a pre-AI period stretching from 1945 to 1954, in which computers are developed and in which a number of trend-setting papers appear; an initiating period, 1955–1960, during which AI-research is prompted, among other things, by the growing availability of computers, the Dartmouth conference, and by the development of information processing psychology; 1961–1970 a period devoted to the search for general problem solvers – and also a period of general development and redirecting; the succeeding decade, 1971–1980, described as the years of specialization and success, in which a number of advanced computer programs appear, but which is also remembered for the discovery of knowledge-based systems and knowledge engineering;

[94] McCorduck *supra* note 2, at 159-60.

[95] Feigenbaum, E.A., Feldman, J. *Computers and Thought* (1963).

[96] Jackson, P. *Introduction to Expert Systems*, 8 (1986). *Cf. also* McCorduck *supra* note 2, at 335.

finally, from 1981 onwards, a period marked by a rush for applications, international competition and commercial ventures.[97]

Of course, also potentialities and desirable solutions have been a subject of debate. Such issues were addressed already by Turing in his 1950 paper and by Bowden who in his early contribution assumes that "[o]ne can imagine that in a few years' time a single machine might replace hundreds of the clerks in an insurance office, but under no circumstances could it ever replace the board of directors."[98] The attitude towards AI has been, however, often ambiguous. Bowden, for instance, in a succeeding discussion acknowledges that the issue whether or not a machine may be able to think depends in much on how one prefers to define thinking. He also concludes that "[i]t is hard to deny that many of the activities of a digital computer are such as would normally be regarded as evidence of conscious thought were they to be undertaken by a human being."[99]

Early ambitions were set high, but many of the problems that were addressed then soon proved to be more difficult than it was initially anticipated. As a consequence, a number of project failures and drawbacks have occurred, which in turn have been the basis for criticism.[100] Although the development of AI has been sometimes uncertain, it is now an accepted field of research. Recent undertakings represent a variety of approaches in which a number of questions, concerning both detailed sub-problems as well as general theories, are being addressed. In addition, fresh perspectives often appear and inspiration is thereby obtained from many sources.[101]

97 Harmon, P., King, D. *Expert Systems: Artificial Intelligence in Business*, 4 (1985).

98 Bowden *supra* note 3, at 257.

99 *Id.* at 336.

100 One well-known controversy originated from chess playing programs. Simon and Newell predicted in 1957 that within ten years a computer would be the world's chess champion. (Simon, H., Newell, A. *Heuristic Problem Solving: The Next Advance in Operations Research*, 7 (1958)) When the prediction failed the American, Hubert Dreyfus, used this as a starting-point for a broad attack on AI, whose contributions were referred to in terms of intellectual smog and similar phrases. (Dreyfus *supra* note 1, at xxix - xxx.).

101 In a recent Swedish study AI has been for instance related to occupational skills and to art experiences. Göranzon, B. *Det praktiska intellektet* (1990).

A number of sub-topics are being approached and from the multitude of existing approaches it follows that the efforts to establish distinct schools of thoughts are frequently challenged. A survey of recent textbooks reveals the following, more or less distinct fields of interest: logic programming, automatic programming, natural language processing, speech recognition, robots, machine learning, cognitive science, problem solving, planning and operations research, text processing, computer vision and perception, game playing, computer aided instruction, intelligent knowledge based systems, and expert systems.[102] Moreover, AI-applications are being developed in many disciplines; e.g. in medicine, engineering, control and surveillance, economy, etc., and in such enterprises a number of additional aspects are being stressed.

Financial support has been supplied by the computer industry, various research and development foundations and, in considerable portions, by defence departments and the defence industry.[103]

From the large number of diverse approaches it appears that AI is not a uniform discipline and this multiplicity is illustrated by the fact that contributors often argue about appropriate lines of development. The discussions concern fundamental assumptions as well as more specific issues, e.g. questions related to the problems of formalisation. It is also possible to perceive a constantly on-going debate among purists – oriented towards basic research – and pragmatists, aiming for usable devices. In addition, the relative importance of various components; e.g. programming theory, logic, hardware development, studies in cognitive science, etc., is under debate.[104] Furthermore, various opinions exist about terminology and about how demarcations in the field ought to be carried out.

102 *See, e.g.*, for further examples and additional references, Webber, B.L., Nilsson, N.J. eds. *Readings in Artificial Intelligence* (1981), Susskind *supra* chapter 1 note 9, at 8 *and* Hofstadter *supra* note 8, at 601-02. *See also*, Reeke, Edelman *supra* note 22, at 146.

103 *See, e.g.*, especially on the support from the *Defence Advanced Research Projects Agency*, DARPA, in the U.S., Rothfeder, J. *Minds Over Matter*, 182-218 (1985).

104 During the short history of AI is has for instance been a debate between so called *Scruffies* (practically oriented researchers) and *Neats* (theoretically oriented researchers emphasising the role of logic). A persistent discussion has also concerned what has been known as the *procedural – declarative controversy*, i.e. the question whether it is best to represent knowledge on *knowing how*, or on *knowing that*. Sowa *supra* note 9, at 22-25. *See also*, about *formalists* and *experimentalists*, Genesereth, Nilsson *supra* note 33, at vii - viii *and*, about traditional (rule based) and connectionism approaches, Graubard *supra* note 23.

3.7 Decision Support Systems

The main object of this study is legal reasoning. This in much limits the investigation of AI applications to the functions which are possible to relate to the elements of reasoning, to decision support systems (DSS), and to the technique behind such systems.

From a practical point of view the emphasis on DSSs is not a limitation. DSSs are among the relatively few AI-applications that have reached the market in large numbers. Many DSSs have also been evaluated and discussed in terms of quality, user friendliness, etc. In addition, there exists a considerable bulk of recorded experiences about system developing methods.

DSSs begin to appear during the 1970s. Experiments with reasoning computer programs were, however, conducted earlier than that. The first example, "The Logic Theory Machine" – a program capable of proving theorems in elementary symbolic logic[105] – was designed by Newell and Simon and presented at the Dartmouth seminar in 1956. The development of DSS with elaborated, domain-specific knowledge begins some ten years later when work on *DENDRAL* – a system capable of helping chemists discover the structure of an unknown compound – is initiated.[106] Another early project commenced in the 1960s is *SAINT* – a line of work which in the 1970s resulted in a system capable of handling symbolic mathematics (*MACSYMA*).[107]

During the 1970s several well-known systems emerge: e.g. *MYCIN*, a system for "assisting and educating physicians who need advice about appropriate antimicrobial therapy" for infectious diseases;[108] *PROSPECTOR*, a system containing knowledge on mineral deposits relationships;[109]

105 Newell, A., Shaw, J.C., Simon, H.A. *Empirical Explorations with the Logic Theory Machine* (1957).

106 Buchanan, B.G., Sutherland, G., Feigenbaum, E.A. *Heuristic Dendral: A Program for Generating Explanatory Hypothesis in Organic Chemistry* (1969).

107 *See also*, about early system developments, Hayes-Roth *supra* chapter 1 note 2, at 6-11.

108 Shortliffe, E. *Computer-Based Medical Consultations: MYCIN* , 233 (1976).

109 Duda, R., Gaschnig, J., Hart, P.E. *Model Design in the PROSPECTOR Consultant System for Mineral Exploration* (1979).

and *R1*, an application for the configuration of computer systems.[110] Although a lot of activities are initiated during this period, few systems are brought into daily use. The 1970s may therefore be characterized as a decade oriented basically towards research and development.

In the 1980s, as the market and the technique mature, DSSs start to reach larger groups of users and appear in a greater number of domains. The development during the past decade was ever accelerating and presently numerous systems are employed in many areas of application. Likewise the number of commercially available products is considerable.[111] It must however be noticed that in comparison to many other kinds of computer programs, DSSs are seldom used on an every-day basis. It is, nevertheless, possible to perceive a trend not only towards a broad acceptance but also towards a general agreement about the feasibility of the technique.

The terminology concerning DSSs is varying. For a long time "expert systems" was the most frequently used label for computer programs aiming for decision support. In recent years the phrase has been gradually replaced by "intelligent knowledge based systems", (IKBS), or, shorter, "knowledge-based systems", (KBS)[112] – the latter phrase favoured also in this study.

There are several reasons for this shift in the DSS terminology. Perhaps most noticeably the phrase "expert system" is a misleading name. The use of the term "expert" originated presumably from the necessity to cooperate with experts, i.e. persons highly specialized in the domain selected for system application, during system construction.[113] The term "expert" has been, however, often wrongfully interpreted to be an attribute tied to the

110 Bachant, J., McDermott, J. *R1 Revisited* (1984).

111 Diaper *supra* chapter 1 note 32, at 11 "Expert systems and Knowledge-Based Systems now form a market worth annually billions of dollars, yen and ECUs". *See also*, Morris, A., Reed, A. *Directory of Expert System Tools* (1989).

112 Also the label KS, for knowledge systems, appear in many contributions. *See, e.g.*, Harmon, King *supra* note 97, at 5: "Early systems were usually called 'expert systems', but most knowledge engineers (persons trained in AI techniques) now refer to their systems as 'knowledge systems'."

113 *Id.* "The first systems were built by interviewing a recognized human expert and attempting to capture that expert's knowledge, hence the term 'expert systems'."

systems that have been produced. Moreover, the term "expert systems" may be even perceived as a provoking label, for instance in cases when computers are introduced to employees with long experience in the field in question.[114]

A terminological change has been also motivated by the fact that the phrase "expert systems" seems to be insufficient. AI-technique may be employed not only in order to design systems aiming to provide expertise knowledge. Various applications may also reflect different levels of ambition and the technology may be used in order to develop functions of many different kinds.[115] So far, e.g. interactive check-lists, search tools, planning programs, associating storing archives, decision support systems, experimental research prototypes, and a variety of combinations of the above have been presented.

Not all researchers have accepted the replacement of the name expert system with the phrase KBS. All kinds of differences between KBS and expert systems have been suggested. The terminological aspect, for instance, has been addressed by Susskind:

> (IKBS) [Intelligent Knowledge-Based Systems] . . . are systems that contain representation of knowledge which can be deployed in the solving of given problems. Expert systems (despite the fact that this term is often considered to be synonymous with IKBS), are, more precisely, a type of IKBS. Expert systems are computer programs that have been constructed (with the assistance of human experts) in such a way that they are capable of functioning at the standard of (and sometimes even at a higher standard than) human experts in given fields. They are used as high-level intellectual aids to their users, which explains much of their alternative epithets: intelligent assistants. They differ from IKBS in that the latter may recognize speech, perceive images, or indeed solve problems in a fashion that undoubtedly is dependent on knowl-

114 *See, e.g.*, Simon, Gaes *supra* chapter 1, note 24, at 198, who describes a strategic change of name of a system called 'expert', in order "to reinforce the position that the program was not a substitute for knowledge . . . but an aid in the process."

115 Harmon, King *supra* note 97, at 5, "Recently, however, several systems have been built that contain knowledge of a difficult decision-making situation that is quit useful, but hardly the equivalent of a human expert. To avoid suggesting that all systems built by means of knowledge engineering techniques capture the knowledge of a human expert, 'knowledge systems' is rapidly becoming the preferred name."

> edge yet that requires no particular human expertise. Only those IKBS that embody a depth and richness of knowledge that permit them to perform at the level of an expert in a particular (and normally highly specialized) domain, therefore, ought then to be designated expert systems.[116]

One way of describing KBS is to compare them to conventional computer systems:

> In contrast with [conventional computer] programs like this (which will be called *algorithm-based*) are the more recent *knowledge-based* systems. Here the whole focus is on knowledge in the ordinary meaning of the term, i.e. facts about the task domain, and heuristics or rules of thumb that guide the use of knowledge to solve problems in the domain. Most current knowledge-based systems are divided, not into code or data, but into a corpus of knowledge and a comparatively simple mechanism for applying the knowledge in an opportunistic way to solve problems. The power of the system does not come principally from the knowledge application mechanism (*the inference engine*) but from the richness, pertinence and redundancy of the knowledge itself.[117]

The focus on knowledge may be explained by the comparison of the theoretical foundations of KBS and those of conventional computer systems. During the development of the latter, *data* is a basic element. According to the standard terminology in computer science data is "a representation of facts, concepts or instructions in a formalized manner suitable for communication, interpretation or processing by humans or by automatic means."[118] Data is normally perceived as a static representation and usually numbers, e.g. binary code, characters, and similar symbols are looked upon as data. In order to achieve meaning, data must be interpreted by human beings, and in that process *information* emerges. Due to

116 Susskind *supra* chapter 1 note 9, at 9. *See also* Harmon, King, *supra* note 96, at 5 "Throughout this book we use 'expert systems' and 'knowledge systems' as synonyms, but we generally refer to large systems as 'expert systems' and smaller systems as 'knowledge systems'."

117 Quinlan, J.R. *Fundamentals of the Knowledge Engineering Problem*, 34 (1982).

118 SIS, *Dataordboken*, 61 (1989).

the fact that various persons interpret data differently, information includes a considerable amount of elements of subjective nature.

Data is an important element also in the construction of KBS, but in the development of KBS *knowledge* which is a broader concept is used as a complement. "Knowledge is more than a static encoding of facts; it also includes the ability to use those facts in interacting with the world. A basic premise of AI is that knowledge of something is the ability to form a mental model that accurately represents the thing as well as the actions that can be performed by it and on it."[119] In other words, a representation of knowledge includes predefined structures determining how data may be used and interpreted in various situations. The relations between data and knowledge have been addressed by *Dan Diaper* who submits that

> The most plausible understanding of the term 'knowledge' is in its contrast with the use, in computer science terms, of either data or information . . . data consists of things that are potentially available to a computer system, as records for example, and information can be characterised, at least here, as data that is accessed by a human user. Within this framework, it is the user who supplies the intelligence to the human–computer system such that it is the human–machine composite that could be called knowledgeable. It appears that the term knowledge has been coined to denote the importing of the intelligent manipulation of data into computers, not necessarily with any claim being made to psychological validity, so that they may be called knowledge based, rather than data based systems.[120]

Susskind, discussing legal expert systems describes the distinction between data and knowledge in the following way :

> Expert systems will not be designed to provide the legal profession with raw *data* (the formal sources of law) of the legal reasoning and legal problem-solving processes, based upon search requests formulated in terms of key-words in combination, as existing database systems in law do; but rather,

119 Sowa *supra* note 9, at 2.

120 Diaper *supra* chapter 1 note 32, at 23.

> they will serve as the embodiment of a corpus of *knowledge* – the result of interpretation of the raw data – to which users may gain access.[121]

The attempts to define KBS and expert systems have been many and *Sture Hägglund*, after a review of various definitions of expert systems, concludes that:

> These definitions, although relatively uniform, in practice provide large room for different interpretations concerning the type of programs that may be considered to be expert systems. Today there is a clear tendency to use the comprehensive term *knowledge-systems* . . . . There are strong reasons for the use of this term, which emphasizes the central role of knowledge in a deeper meaning compared to the manipulation of data in accordance to well specified algorithms within traditional data processing.[122]

The differences in construction approaches have entailed that KBS basically aim to assist other kinds of functions than conventional computer systems. The latter are best suited for the development of functions for tasks which may be described in detail in a more or less predefined way, e.g. word-processing, book-keeping, counting, etc.

The way a KBS operates is – within certain limits – determined by the type of data it encounters. In comparison to conventional computer programs a KBS is in most cases able to handle data that are less specified. To be able to do that the systems must employ procedures in order to translate the given data into appropriate (in relation to the given task) levels.[123] For this reason, a KBS must have a *knowledge base* which contains not only a representation of the facts about a certain domain, but also the structures and rules related to those facts.

In order to provide decision support, a KBS must embody procedures for problem solving. For this purpose an *inference engine* is used. An inference engine includes inference methods, and a number of high level

[121] Susskind, *supra* chapter 1 note 9, at 13.

[122] Hägglund, S. *Datorstödda kunskapssystem i framtidens kontor*, 21 (1986), (original text in Swedish).

[123] *Cf.* Hayes-Roth *supra* chapter 1 note 2, at 170, "to convert a problem description in lay term into an internal representation convenient for processing with its expert rules".

rules regarding e.g. information retrieval strategies and dialogue controlling modules. Among the general inference methods that may be formalized are *forward chaining* – a procedure in which the inference pattern is determined according to input data, and *backward chaining* – a procedure in which the system tries to verify or falsify a hypotheses by means of a systematic investigation of its sub-elements. The inference engine also includes control procedures for the coordinating of the various parts of the system.

Most KBSs are capable of obtaining data from the users by means of conducting a two way dialogue, and, in addition, a KBS may have to exchange data with other computer systems. Hence a KBS must possess an *interface*, handling the communication with users and other computer systems, a *register of questions*, functioning as a knowledge acquisition module, and a *working memory*, containing a representation of the facts that are encountered during the session. A KBS must also, in order to be accepted as a decision support aid, be able to explain and justify its recommendations and therefore possess a *register of explanations* supporting the user interface. Although the components of various designs may vary, the basic entities of a KBS may be depicted as in fig 3.3:[124]

124 *See generally,* about basic entities of KBS, e.g. Harmon, King *supra* note 96, at 34, who makes a division between knowledge base, working memory, inference engine, knowledge acquisition subsystem, explanation subsystem and user interface. *See also* for a similar design the VF system in Hamfelt, Wahlgren *supra* chapter 1 note 21, at 41. *Compare* Statskontoret. *Social Assistance and Knowledge-Based Systems: PLUTO - A Support System*, 5 (1988) who in the description of the KS *PLUTO* makes an initial division between the knowledge base and the inference mechanism, which in turn is divided into a information gathering module, a calculation module, a search module and a report module *and* for a different terminology Hayes-Roth *supra* chapter 1 note 2, at 17, who in addition to a knowledge base employ a justifier, a language processor, a blackboard, an interpreter, a scheduler and a consistency enforcer. *See also* Karpf, J. *Modularization of Legal Expert Systems* (1989) who defines five main modules: user module, query module, facts module, law module, and control module.

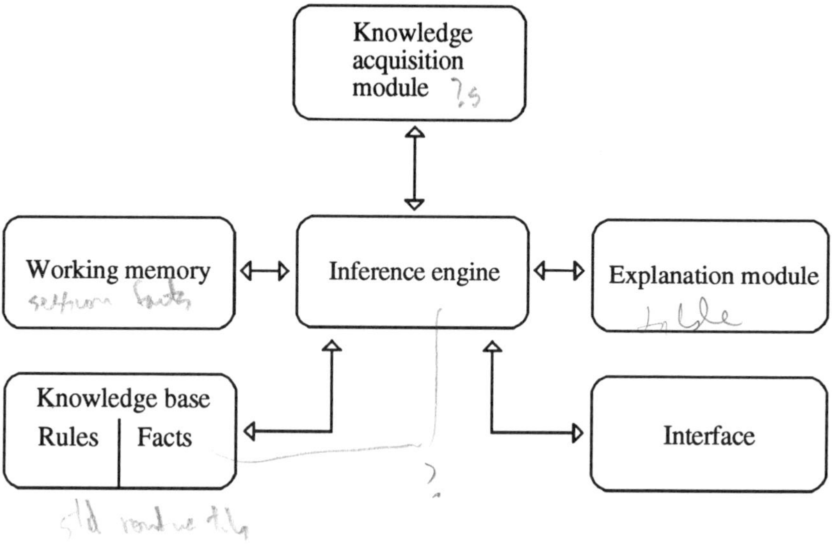

Figure 3.3 Schematic overview of basic components of a KBS.

3.8 System Development Methods

The aim in KBS development is to create a representation of knowledge in such a form that it may be stored in and manipulated by a computer. The representation must also be, however, authentic and understandable to human users. That is to say the representation must be able to respond to two different requirements, and that it must be able to combine two different semantics and two kinds of syntax.[125]

A large number of methods have been developed in order to facilitate the construction of KBS. The focus on knowledge has entailed that the methods that are employed have became known as *knowledge methods*. For the same reason persons trained in the use of these methods have been called *knowledge engineers*.

125 This has been referred to as the *knowledge representation hypothesis*: "Any mechanically embodied intelligent process will be comprised of structural ingredients that a) we as external observers naturally take to represent a propositional account of the knowledge that the overall process exhibits, and b) independent of such external semantic attribution, play a formal but causal and essential role in engendering the behaviour that manifests that knowledge." Smith, B.C. *Prologue to "Reflection and Semantics in a Procedural Language"*, 33 (1982).

The KBS development strategy is often described as consisting of phases: *Frederick Hayes-Roth* , *Donald A Waterman*, and *Douglas B. Lenat*, for instance, recognize five different stages: identification, conceptualization, formalization, implementation, and testing.[126]

Paul Harmon and *David King*, likewise, see system development as a process consisting of stages and state that the first concern is to define the problem. The definition should be followed by a generation of a search space and of an examination as to whether conventional computer technology may be amenable. If the KBS technique turns out to be appropriate, the examination should be succeeded by knowledge identification – a development of a knowledge framework consisting of ''a mix of inference and representation.'' The construction process is completed by the implementation, test and revision phase.[127]

In a similar but a rather more detailed step-by-step approach Diaper lists eleven ''necessary stages'' for KBS design:[128]

'' 0. Pre-project feasibility study

1. Organisational modelling

2. Personnel identification

3. Knowledge elicitation } Knowledge acquisition

4. Knowledge representation } Knowledge acquisition

5. Knowledge encoding } Knowledge acquisition

6. User interface design

7. Prototype testing

8. Delivery system implementation

9. Delivery system installation

10. Delivery system evaluation''

126 Hayes-Roth *supra* chapter 1 note 2, at 24.

127 Harmon, King *supra* note 96, at 6.

128 Diaper *supra* chapter 1 note 32, at 29.

KBS development is a complicated and cumbersome task. Various approaches exist and most authors underline that the phases overlap and that the various activities connected with system developing interact with each other. In this study no attempt is made to refer to system developing methods in a more or less handbook-like approach.

A close study of the knowledge-based methods is nevertheless important for the understanding of the potentialities of a joint effort of AI and law. A more thorough investigation is however best done in connection with the discussion about the potentialities of automation that is undertaken in part three of this study.

4 Integration

4.1 Predictions

As described in chapter 2 the perspective in which legal reasoning is perceived as a more or less mechanical process is an old and frequently criticised approach. Much of the discussion, as for instance the arguments raised among American legal realists at the beginning of this century, has not, however, been supported by empirical experiments. With a few exceptions it has been a theoretical discussion founded on various assumptions about the nature of law, and reflecting different opinions about the objectives of the legal system.

The actual importation of new technology into legal work is limited to the last 40 years, but, compared to many other disciplines, surprisingly many aspects of legal work are still unaffected by computer technology and other forms of automation. Experiments and prophesies, originating from computer science as well as from legal research, have nevertheless been numerous.

The first explicit references to law and computer technology are the contributions discussing potential applications. The connections between computer technology and law may however be more or less direct. *Jon Bing*, for instance, recalls that Boole in his 1854 paper used a problem from Jewish dietary law as an illustration, and that Hollerith's tabulating machine from 1890 was initiated by the need to count people in advance to presidential elections, originating from legislation.[1]

It may be noted that during the twentieth century digital computers are not the only implements included in the discussions about the automation of legal work. Various other devices have been suggested at different times. In an early background description *Louis Kelso* mentions among other things Dictaphones and electrical typewriters,[2] and Bush, in 1945, in connection with a description of a retrieval tool for microfilm (MEMEX)

[1] Bing, J. *Handbook of Legal Information Retrieval*, 253 (1984). *See also,* Tapper, C. *Computers and the Law*, 93 (1973) who mentions an experiment in the late 1930s with drafting of insurance documents by application of symbolic logic.

[2] Kelso, L.O. *Does the Law Need a Technological Revolution?*, 380 (1946).

suggests that "[w]holly new forms of encyclopedias will appear, ready made with a mesh of associative trails running through them, ready to be dropped into the MEMEX and there amplified. The lawyer has at his touch the associated opinions and decisions of his whole experience and of the experience of friends and authorities."[3]

Another early contribution was submitted in 1946 when Kelso, partly inspired by the article of Bush, conceived the LAWDEX and suggested that new technology should be employed for legal research, thus focusing on information retrieval functions.[4] In a more general perspective Wiener, in 1950, in a book about cybernetics and society, devoted a chapter to law and communication in which he discussed, among other things, a technique by which the "concepts of justice can be made effective."[5] Simultaneously *Jerome Frank*, previously one of the hardest critics of the so called mechanical jurisprudence, presented a balanced discussion about the prospects and the advantages of logical machines and a science of legal predictions.[6]

For obvious reasons, the possibilities to utilize digital computers soon became, nevertheless, the dominant issue of concern and a few years later, in 1953, Bowden, in one of the first books about the impact of digital computers, conceived the idea of an advanced decision support tool and declared that

> [I]t is interesting to speculate on the possibility of using such a machine to help a lawyer in his judgement of a case which was presented to him in such a way as to allow him to decide it entirely by a logical interpretation of statutes and by reference to a well-indexed library of leading cases.[7]

Several early suggestions concerning law and automation were submitted by persons who were not lawyers. In consequence, it is sometimes possible

3 Bush, V. *As we May Think*, 57 (1945).

4 Kelso *supra* note 2.

5 Wiener, N. *The Human Use of Human Beings*, 105 (1954).

6 Frank, J. *Courts on Trial*, 206-08 (1950).

7 Bowden *supra* chapter 3 note 3, at 336.

to detect a scarcity of jurisprudential insight. Bowden, although he underpins his proposal with references to various legal statements, gives an example of this when he suggests that "if the findings of the machine seemed to lack something of the spontaneity and variety of current legal verdicts, the careful and judicious use of the random number generator might help to mitigate the harshness of pure logic."[8]

4.2 Jurimetrics

An attempt to systematise various methodological approaches that had a relatively widespread effect was presented in 1949 under the name of *Jurimetrics* – a term intended to signify scientific investigations of legal problems. During the late 1950s and the 1960s Jurimetrics was applied as a name for several attempts to develop jurisprudence. Some activities that have been undertaken in the name of jurimetrics are of high relevance to the works done in the field of AI and law. The notion will therefore be presented in some detail:

The article in which the term appeared for the first time – "Jurimetrics – the next step forward" by *Lee Loevinger* – was a frontal attack on traditional jurisprudence. Loevinger began his paper with an outspoken critic of the legal system. The law was described as a "recondite mystery that is . . . incomprehensible to the public and scarcely intelligible to its own votaries"[9] and in several other similar phrases. Loevinger recognized a number of proposed remedies – more policemen, moral renaissance, better education, new laws, better public relations between lawyers and the public – but in the usual suggestions for changes he saw only attempts to put the present law into practice. The trouble, however, was that the law itself needed change and progress. According to Loevinger, further attempts to force the law onto society with inadequate means would only increase the bewilderment, and the lack of respect for the law would remain.

The hypothesis was supported by a historical description of the development of legal thinking. Starting with references to the *Code of Hammurabi*

[8] *Id.*

[9] Loevinger, L. *Jurimetrics*, 3 (1949).

and the old Greek philosophers, discussing *St. Thomas Aquinas*, and referring to the ideas of various legal writers and philosophers, Loevinger found arguments for that the law may be described as

> "[T]he dictate of God, of Nature, of Reason; that it is Justice, Equality, Liberty, custom, command, rules, decisions; that it is found in the will of a personal sovereign, of the people, of the legislature, in the decisions of the courts and in the words of the judges."[10]

It was then argued that jurisprudence had been basically concerned with meaningless speculations.

> [T]he fact remains that we are no nearer agreement on answers to the fundamental questions of law than we were two thousand years ago. It seems about time for some one to begin to suspect that we are either asking the wrong questions, or looking for answers in the wrong way, or doing both.[11]

The question about the nature of law was from Loevinger's point of view without practical value and he therefore claimed that law was an abstraction, an invention of the human mind, that it could not be called right or wrong, and that it could not be proved or disproved. Furthermore, it was argued that the persistent but meaningless speculation about the nature of law had diverted the attention from a more scientific and practically oriented research. Loevinger also alleged that the result of the total agreement as to the basis of law, the end and purpose of law, definitions of justice etc., would be worth nothing at all.[12]

In an overview of the general theory of science, Loevinger compared the progress made in other sciences with the persistent confusion within jurisprudence. A variety of examples were given in order to pin-point the need for fresh perspectives and the new questions in legal research. The conclusion was that the next step after jurisprudence must be "to jurimetrics – . . . the scientific investigation of legal problems." A more scientific

[10] *Id.* at 5.

[11] *Id.* at 15.

[12] *Id.* at 32.

approach was supposed to generate a new research program for legal science. Loevinger elaborated his ideas of these new perspectives and proposed nine areas of study: (a) The behaviour of witnesses, (b) the behaviour of judges, (c) the behaviour of legislators, (d) legal language and communication, (e) legal procedure and recordation, (f) non-aberrant personal maladjustments, (g) aberrations of behaviour, (h) unintentional personal injury, (i) macrolegal techniques of investigation.[13]

Loevinger did not concentrate his discussion on computers, but made references to Wiener, declaring that:

> Machines are now in existence which have so far imitated 'thought processes' that they can solve differential equations and other 'logical' operations of equal or greater complexity. The machines can be constructed to solve equations with virtually any number of variables, and with large numbers of variables the operation is much faster than when performed by the human mind. Why should not a machine be constructed to decide lawsuits? The complexity of the problems presented, measured by the number of variables involved, is well within the limits of existing machines.[14]

The assumptions about the immediate feasibility of computers were perhaps over-optimistic, but Loevinger correctly foresaw the problem of legal knowledge representation "The difficulty is that we have no terms to put into the machines, as the scientists have numbers and symbols. Legal terms are almost all vague verbalisations . . ."[15]

Various activities have been recognized under the name of jurimetrics. Jurimetrics has been also used as a collective name for periodical publications, books, conferences and educational programmes, especially in the U.S.A.

[13] *Id.* at 32-36.

[14] *Id.* at 19.

[15] *Id.*

4.3 Information Retrieval

The first computer applications that came into practice in the legal field were the so called information retrieval (IR) systems. Work with such systems was initiated in the late 1950s and, beside word processing and other forms of non domain specific support systems, legal IR-systems are still most dominant among computer applications that have been integrated into legal practice. Although the input-output devices and the storage techniques have changed, the underlying principles of most IR-systems are basically the same today as they were thirty years ago. The IR-technique has been also successful in many fields outside the legal domain.

In a computer-based IR-system data are stored electronically in one or several data bases. Legal data bases usually handle texts, and texts are divided into documents. Documents may be long, e.g. provide the full text of cases, but they may also be short, e.g. be limited to bibliographic references.[16] For each data base in a IR-system an index file is created. In the index files all the words[17] in all the documents are stored alphabetically. To each word pointers to the documents in which the word appear are attached.

The user of the system may retrieve the documents by means of submitting search requests to the system.[18] Search requests are formed from words by means of using a search language. The system compares the words in the search request with the index file. The number of documents in which the word (or words) occur is then indicated. The indicated documents may be retrieved and presented through one or several output devices.

Documents in a data base may be indexed, and index codes or other kinds of added terms, such as e.g. key words, numbers, etc., may be used as elements in search requests. In some systems it is also possible to

[16] Bing *supra* note 1, at 70, 74-84, relates legal documents to legal sources and recognizes three typical forms of documents: "indexes", "abstracts", and "authentic texts".

[17] Since not only words but also index codes, dates, numbers etc. may be used as index terms it would be more adequate to use the phrase "string of characters". "Word" is used here, however, for the sake of simplicity, as a synonym of the more technical phrase. It should also be noted that in most systems very common words (e.g. articles, conjunctions, prepositions) are excluded from index files.

[18] *See*, for a more detailed description of various functions in IR programs, Bing *supra* note 1.

designate the search to certain fields of the documents; e.g. to titles, abstracts, etc.

In order to create elaborated search queries it is usually possible to combine several words with Boolean operators ("and", "or", "not"), and through truncation and mask functions retrieve words with unspecified units. Normally, the so called right hand truncation is used as a means to create search queries consisting of word stems, including all possible endings. In addition, many systems handle left hand truncation and in most modern systems it is also possible to search within a document, i.e. to find out where in a certain document a specific word, or a combination of words, appear.

As alternatives to full text presentation, the retrieved documents may be presented in many different ways, and in many modern legal IR-systems it is possible to shift between various forms of presentation, e.g. focusing on headlines, tables of contents, etc. In early experiments sometimes *KWOC presentations* were used as an alternative to *KWIC presentations*. A KWOC (Key Word Out of Context) presentation may simply list the word's occurrences, indicating the documents in which the words appear by means of presenting pointers. A KWIC (Key Word In Context) presentation may include one or several lines of text surrounding the requested word.

The presumably first project on a legal IR-system was initiated at *The Health Law Center* at *The University of Pittsburgh* in a work administered by *John F. Horty.*[19] The project started out in 1956 as a study aiming to improve the health statutes of Pennsylvania. The work originated as a project employing conventional technique. Horty and his collaborators began the writing of a manual for health law. After some time they encountered problems with the unification of indexes from various states, which gave the impulse to contact the Computing Center of the university. The complete text was then registered on punch cards and thus a machine-readable copy of the text was created. It then became possible to retrieve

19 *Cf.* Biunno, V.P. *History of Electronic Methods for Legal Research,* 100 (1960) who also mentions earlier experiments in the 1950s with manually punched and sorted punched cards, and a project in the U.S. Patent Office for retrieval of patent documents and literature.

all the occurrences of a certain word, word combinations, or all variations of a word.[20]

Within a few years after Horty's experiments a large number of projects were initiated.[21] One well-documented work was commenced in 1962 by the *U.S. Air Force*. The *LITE-system*, an acronym for *Legal Information Through Electronics*, was a full text information retrieval system intended for the fiscal legal field. In 1965 the system contained "the full text of all Titles of the United States Code, all published decisions of the Comptroller General of the United States and the Armed Services Procedurement Regulations."[22] It was further reported that by the end of June 1966 the data base would include some forty million words "each and every word of the text data bases . . . stored on magnetic tape and available for machine processing and retrieval."[23]

The first commercially available legal IR system originated in a project initiated by the American lawyer *Ellias Hoppenfeld*. The company that Hoppenfeld founded, *Law Research Service Incorporated* (LRS), was established in 1963. The LRS-system was an index system oriented towards case law, and it became operative in February 1964. To each case in the system descriptors were added and initially the users had to present their request to an editor.

> The user filled in a form specifying the nature of his problem in his own words with some indication of any background material and a designation of the area concerned. This form was then sent to the computer centre where it was passed on to a search editor for that area of law. The editor then framed a computer question in in terms of the descriptors which he knew were used in the system. . . . The computer produced a list of case names and references which was then scanned by a human editor to select the four which seemed to

20 Bing *supra* note 1, at 257-258. Tapper, C. *Lawyers and Machines*, 133 (1963).

21 Tapper *Id.* at 132, reports "twenty-eight separate projects in the field of law in the United Stated alone". Duggan, M. *Legal Research Projects*, 83-86 (1965) lists 55 projects relating to computers, logic, decision theory and law. The majority of them conducted in the U.S. One year later an additional 25 project is listed. Duggan, M. *Legal Research Projects, supplement*, 97-99 (1966).

22 Davis, R.P. *LITE: Legal Information Through Electronics*, 138 (1965).

23 *Id.*

> him most relevant to the original question. The full text of these decisions was then micro-filmed and posted off to the inquirer together with a full list of the citations produced by the computer from which the four had been selected.[24]

In 1966 it was reported that LRS had enroled "over five thousand attorneys, comprising a majority of the largest law firms in New York State."[25]

LRS soon encountered financial and technical difficulties however. The company was sued for giving misleading information at the time public shares were issued in 1965. In addition, *West Publishing Company* brought a suit against LRS, claiming that part of the West Key Number digest indexes had been copied in the computerized system, thereby infringing West's copyrights.[26]

In a historical overview of early legal IR-systems Bing also mentions RIRA (*Reports and Information Retrieval Activity*) – a project initiated by the *U.S. Internal Revenue Service* (IRS) in 1962. RIRA was intended as a tool to solve coordinating problems between different offices and lawyers within the IRS. The ambition was that RIRA would facilitate the realization of a uniform praxis and the control of the status of pending cases. The cases that were handled in RIRA had been coded in accordance with an indexing system and the computer-based retrieval system had been integrated with microfilm devices for output facilities.[27]

Also Horty's system became a part of a commercial venture. The material Horty had used was in 1968 integrated with the products that were offered on the market by *Aspen Systems Corporation.* Aspen also engaged Horty and soon presented a variety of computer-based services, among other things "a bill-drafting service (QUIK-DRAFT), bound KWIC-indexes, production of compilations of statutes in force in a printed form, etc."[28]

24 Tapper *supra note* 1, at 184-185.

25 Hoppenfeld, E.C. *Law Research Service/Inc.*, 50 (1966).

26 Bing *supra* note 1, at 266-67.

27 *Id.* at 268-271, Tapper *supra* note 1, at 200-203.

28 Bing *supra* note 1, at 260-61.

Experiments with IR-systems soon took off also in Europe. Perhaps the most well known pioneer project is the one known as the Oxford Experiments, initiated by the Englishman *Colin Tapper.* Unlike Horty, Tapper based his experiments on case law. Tapper was also the first researcher to systematically compare the computer-based information retrieval technique with manual search techniques.[29]

Around 1970 experiments of various scope were initiated in many countries; beside in the U.S and in the U.K. projects were launched in *Belgium*, *Canada*, *France*, *Germany*, *The Netherlands*, *Norway* and *Sweden.*[30] In addition, some international organizations initiated similar kinds of activities and in 1967 the *European Communities* set out to develop an automatic document retrieval service, CELEX, focusing on Community legal documentation.[31]

During the 1980s the IR technique became expanded and commercialized. In many countries the IR systems have established themselves as important tools of legal research, serving a great number of lawyers on a daily basis. In an overview over current systems from 1984 Bing devotes some 230 pages to a presentation covering legal IR-systems in some 25 countries. Some systems have become very large and comprise several millions of documents.[32]

4.4 A Discipline of Computers and Law

Legal IR-systems are not the only subject matter that has been studied in the emerging field of computers and law. In the early 1960s a number of additional areas of interest were outlined, e.g. behaviour analyses of learning, problem solving and decision making, the use of symbolic logic,

[29] Tapper *supra* note 20, at 132, Tapper, C. *British Experience in Legal Information Retrieval* (1964). *See also,* for a description of the early development of legal IR, Bing, J. *Legal Information Services* (1984).

[30] Bing *supra* note 1, at 722-23. *See also,* for references to the literature on the early development of IR-systems, Seipel, P. *Om användning av automatisk databehandlingsteknik inom juridiken,* 722, n. 2 (1970).

[31] Bauer-Bernet, H. *Computerised Legal Documentation System of the European Communities.* 2-3 (1976).

[32] Bing *supra* note 1, at 272-504.

statistics, and probability theory, the investigations of structural linguistics, the quantitative analysis of judicial behaviour and social processes, the application of communication and information theory to legal expression, and the use of mathematical logic in law.[33] Despite the large number of topics addressed it is, nevertheless, difficult to find practical applications from this period, except in the area of legal IR systems.

Methodological undertakings related to mechanization have been initiated under various names. As already mentioned, several contributions have been submitted under the name jurimetrics. As the development proceeds, however, the term jurimetrics is more and more often replaced with the phrase *Computers and law*. The shift in terminology is natural enough, considering the growing impact of computer technology. Computers and law is, nevertheless, not an uncontested label. The study of law, computers, and information science is sometimes referred to in Europe as the study of *Law and informatics*, whereas in the Scandinavian countries *rättsinformatik* (Sweden), *rettsinformatikk* (Norway), *retsinformatik* (Denmark), and *oikeusinformatiikka* (Finland) are used as collective labels for studies related to the methodological issues and the regulative aspects of computers and law. The corresponding German name is *Rechtsinformatik*, and in Italy the discipline is known as *Informatica giuridica*. In France the phrase *Droit et informatique* is predominant. Contributions of relevance to the field of computers and law also appear under other labels.[34]

The emerging field of computers and law achieved an important forum in 1959 when *Layman Allen* started the edition of a periodical newsletter with the name of *Modern Uses of Logic in Law* (M.U.L.L.). Besides legal logic, many articles in the early volumes were devoted to legal information retrieval, statistical methods, technical aspects of law, and application studies.[35] M.U.L.L. was sponsored by the *American Bar Association*,

33 *See, e.g.*, Baade, H.W. ed. *Jurimetrics*, 1 (1963), Loevinger, L *Jurimetrics: The Methodology of Legal Inquiry*, 8 (1963) *and* Allen, L.E., Caldwell, M.E. eds. *Communication Sciences and Law*, xvii-xx (1965).

34 *E.g.* "Computer Jurisprudence", "Computer Science and Law", "Law and Computer Technology", "Law and Information Technology", "Law and Communication Science".

35 M.U.L.L. *Cumulative index* (December 1963).

(ABA) through an almost simultaneously launched special committee on electronic data retrieval.[36]

During the 1960s the Committee provided demonstrations of research by computers, arranged meetings within the area, and in 1966 published an *Introductory Handbook on Computers & the Law*.[37] In 1968 the committee, together with a similar group working on communications, formed the ABA's *Standing Committee on Law and Technology*. The new committee continued the work of its predecessor and in 1969 published a second edition of the Handbook on Computers & the Law. Jurimetrics was then used as a headline for articles on symbolic logic, analyses of prediction of judicial decisions and legal education.[38] The support to M.U.L.L., which in 1966 changed its name to *Jurimetrics Journal*, continued under the new committee.

The committee was reorganized in 1974 and became the *Section of Science and Technology*. A third edition of the handbook was issued in 1981.[39] In the third edition articles on symbolic logic, judicial decisions and legal education are found under the headline *The Computer in Law Practice*. The support to the Jurimetrics Journal continues and the publication is now (1992) in its thirty-second volume.

The Bar Association was not the only organization that was apt to give attention to judicial implications of computers. In 1960-61, *The Association of American Law Schools* formed a *Jurimetrics Committee* with the objective to observe the developments in science and technology and its relations to law.

During the 1960s several conferences and symposiums were arranged, e.g. in 1960 and in 1962, *National Conferences on Law and Electronics* at UCLA, in 1963 *The Jurimetrics Conference of the Associations of American Law Schools*, and in 1965 *The Rockefeller Institute Conference on Law and Science*.[40]

36 M.U.L.L., 1 (September 1959).

37 Bigelow, R. ed. *Computers & the Law* (1966).

38 Bigelow R. ed. *Computers & the Law* (2:nd ed. 1969).

39 Bigelow, R. ed. *Computers & the Law* (3:rd ed. 1981).

40 Jones, E.A. *Foreword*, x-xi (1965).

In the 1970s it is possible to perceive a widening of the perspective, when also regulative issues are included. Although the focus on the IR-systems remains central, several articles addressing legal problems concerning computers, computer programs, and telecommunications appear. Examples of this may be found in various numbers of Jurimetrics Journal, in the 1970 launched *Rutgers Journal of Computers and the Law*,[41] and in the forerunner of the British newsletter *Computers and Law*, initiated in 1974. An important contribution in this respect is also the monograph *Computers and the Law* by Tapper, published in 1973.[42]

In the late 1960s and during the 1970s, in addition to legal IR-systems, more complex computer applications appear. An early example, which is still operational, is *The Swedish Judiciary Information System* (JI), initiated in 1966,[43] combining several functions, such as information retrieval, word processing, production of statistics, report generation, etc.[44] The technical progress, as well as the theoretical build-up has thereafter been swift and multifaceted.

This development has been reflected by several researchers. For instance *Peter Seipel*, focusing not only on technical devices, but also in more general terms has described the early development of the emerging field of computers and law as consisting of three major phases:

"– the period of forerunners: until about 1960
– a period of growth: the 1960s
– a period of maturing: begins around 1970"[45]

41 A publication issued by *Rutgers Law School*, New Jersey, U.S.A.. The editorial board in the first volume of the journal declared that beside legal research and other methodological aspects "Substantial emphasis will be placed on the substantive law implications of computer usage. . ." Volume 1970, spring no 1, at v.

42 Tapper *supra* note 1.

43 *See, e.g.*, Alpsten, B. *ADB-planeringen inom rättsväsendet*, 44 (1988).

44 *See also*, for a description of a system initiated by the Federal Judicial Center in the U.S. in order to "support services for court management and for study and evaluation of court procedures and processes", Ebersole, J.L., Hall, J.A. *COURTRAN: A Modular Management Information and Research System for the Judicial Process* (1973).

45 Seipel *supra* chapter 2 note 104, at 112.

The evolving discipline computers and law has recently been analysed also by *Giancarlo Taddei Elmi* who, besides giving references to the historical development, provides an overview of theoretical and systematical approaches that have been submitted in the field.[46]

In the decade around 1970 it is possible to see the commencement of systematic studies of computers and law on a general and broad basis. Reviewing theoretical contributions from this period and onwards, it can be also seen that the demarcation between various objects of study within the discipline of computers and law is a question that is often addressed. It has been discussed now and again, for instance, whether or not the methodological aspects and the regulative issues ought to be handled as one complex topic, or as two separate disciplines.[47]

The accelerating development and the formation of the discipline of computers and law are reflected in the organization of a number of research institutes in the field. A few examples may illustrate this.

In Sweden a *Working Party for EDP and Law* was established in 1968 at the faculty of law at *Stockholm University*. In an initial document a number of activities encompassing both legal and methodological issues were outlined. Especially, legal problems concerning patents, computer contracts, and liability were mentioned.[48] The group soon started to conduct systematic research on legal IR and in 1981 it was reorganized and became the *Swedish Law and Informatics Research Institute* (IRI). The work of IRI is documented in the series *IRI-reports*, where up till 1990 some 90 research reports in various topics related to computers and law were published.[49]

In Norway a research group was organized in 1970. Initially as a section of the department for Private law at *Oslo University*. It was later

46 Taddei Elmi, G. *Origine, sviluppo, attualita' e prospettive dell' informatica giuridica* (1989).

47 *See, e.g.*, for further references and arguments in both directions, Seipel *supra* chapter 2 note 104, Blume, P. *Jurauddannelsen og retsinformatikken – nu og i fremtiden* (1988), Fiedler, H. *Rechtsinformatik* (1988) *and* Taddei Elmi *Id.*

48 Hellner, J. *Arbetsgruppen för ADB och juridik (The Working Party for EDP and Law)* Cir. no. 1, 15 October 1968.

49 The series *IRI-reports* was preceded by the series *ADBJ-reports*. *See also*, for a more comprehensive background description of the Swedish IRI, Seipel, P. ed. *From Data Protection to Knowledge Machines* (1990).

reorganized into the *Norwegian Research Center for Computers and Law* (NRCCL). The orientation of NRCCL is similar to that of IRI, i.e. the center devotes its interest to both regulative issues and to methodological development. The center publishes the *CompLex* series and up till 1990 some 140 volumes were issued.[50]

Several research institutes have been also organized in Italy. The most outstanding one, *Istituto per la documentazione giuridica* of the *Italian National Research Council* (IDG), was established in 1968. IDG devotes its interest to law and informatics in a broad sense and research activities are oriented among other things towards legal decision making, theoretical and practical development of legal informatics, documentation technology, and lexiographic research.[51] IDG publishes *Informatica e diritto*[52] – a journal on computers and law consisting of two parts: one bibliographical part (*The International Bibliography on Computers and Law*, BID) and one part devoted to research papers. The journal is now (1991) in its seventeenth volume.

In France, a working group, later named the *Centre de recherche et developpement en informatique juridique*, was established in 1967. Other research centers appeared also in Germany around 1970, e.g. the *Institut für Datenverarbeitung im Rechtswesen* (IDR),[53] and a couple of years later in Canada when the *Canadian Law Information Council* (CLIC) was set up.[54] During the late 1970s and the 1980s numerous groups emerged, often within the organizational frameworks of universities. At this time also a large number of journals and newsletters appeared.

In addition to research centers, computer, EDP, and law societies have been formed. In the U.K., for instance, in 1973 the *Society for Computers and Law limited* was founded. The Society was preceded by a *Scottish*

[50] *Complex* was preceded by the publication series *Skriftserien JUS og EDB*.

[51] *See*, for further details, Hiselius, P. *The Institute for Legal Documentation (IDG)*, 12 (1991).

[52] Informatica e diritto was preceded by *Bollettino bibliografico d'informatica generale e applicata al diritto* (1972-73). Bing *supra* note 1, at 408.

[53] *See*, for further details of the formation of research organizations in the field of computers and law, Bing *supra* note 1, at 272-504.

[54] Bennion, F.A.R. *Computers and Law in Canada*, 8-10 (1976).

Legal Computer Research Trust, established in 1970.[55] In 1974 the Society started a newsletter which was later transformed into the journal *Computers and Law.* In February 1990, when 62 issues of the journal had been published, a new series was commenced with the same name.

In Sweden and Norway societies for EDP and law were established around 1980, and since 1984 the organizations have been jointly publishing a *Nordic year-book of law and informatics.* Since 1989 also representatives from Finland and Denmark have been cooperating in the editorial work of the Year-book. The organizations in the Scandinavian countries also participate in the arrangement of joint conferences on law and informatics – events that have been arranged on a yearly basis since 1983.

During the 1980s similar groups were founded in a number of countries and in 1988 *The International Federation of Computer Law Associations* (IFCLA) was launched. In 1990 the federation listed thirteen member organizations and has so far (1992) arranged three international conferences.

In 1990 a plan for the setting up of yet another international organization, the *International Law & Information Technology Association* (ILITA) was outlined. At the initial gathering in Malta 49 organizations were invited to participate.

The frequently close connections between research groups and universities have entailed that educational activities in the area of computers and law commenced at an early stage. Educational initiatives have, naturally, also emerged in order to meet practical demands, e.g. concerning the operation of legal IR-systems. Presumably the first organization with this objective was the previously mentioned Jurimetrics Committee of the Association of American Law Schools (set up in 1960-61).[56] After that, during the 1960s and 1970s educational activities have been initiated in a number of countries.[57] The development in the U.S. has been, perhaps, the

55 *See, e.g.*, for a collection of cited articles on the establishment of the organization, *The Society for Computers and Law Limited Newsletter* no 1, summer 1974.

56 Allen, Caldwell *supra* note 33, at xiv.

57 *See*, for a summary of early experiences in Sweden, Seipel, P. *Introducing Law Students to Computers: Swedish Experience* (1970) *and*, for a discussion about educational consequences from a general point of view, Seipel *supra* chapter 2 note 104, *passim.*

most extensive and in 1974 some twenty universities reports on-going activities related to computers and law.[58]

On an international basis, the *Council of Europe* recommended in 1980 that each member country should in several ways encourage and initiate research and training in the field of computers and law.[59] Also, in 1985 the Council arranged an international conference on educational aspects, and presently (1992) a second updated version of the recommendations is being considered.[60]

Educational projects in the area of computers and law have been increasing steadily and organizational frameworks are still being established and/or adjusted in order to meet the technical development. One example is the *Law Technology Center for U.K. Law Schools* which commenced its activities in 1987. The center also acts as a secretariat for the *British and Irish Legal Technology Association* (BILETA) which was formed in 1986.[61]

Presently it is possible to see a trend where law schools are gathering resources in order to set up advanced computer laboratories.[62] The purpose of such initiatives is not only to teach law students to manage commercially available systems, but also to take advantage of the computer technique in the process of teaching law, and to train the students so that they are able to utilize computer technology in active and creative ways.

4.5 A Discipline of AI and Law

The development of AI and law is intimately interrelated with the growth of the broader field of computers and law. Sometimes the connections are

58 Jurimetrics Journal, *Education in Jurimetrics*, 69-107 (1972) *and* Jurimetrics Journal, *Education in Jurimetrics, supplement*, 166-171 (1974).

59 Council of Europe, *Recommendation No. R (80) 3* (1980).

60 Seipel, P. *Rättsutbildning och informationsteknologi i ett internationellt perspektiv* (1991), (The revised text of the draft is appended).

61 The Law Technology Center and BILETA jointly publish the *LTC and BILETA Newsletter* (The first issue was published in 1987).

62 Projects of this kind has been initiated e.g. in the U.S.A. and in Sweden. *See*, for overviews, Trautman, D.T. *The Computer in American Legal Education* (1990) *and* Seipel, P. *LEXLAB: A Computer Laboratory for Legal Teaching and Training* (1991).

fundamental and, looking back at the development from a methodological perspective, the concept of AI and law appears more to reflect a terminological evolution than a technical revolution. This is perhaps best illustrated by the fact that predictions about the use of computers in the analysis of legal decisions appear already in the 1950s and in the 1960s. An early categorisation of computer-based tools indicated for legal work was, for instance, provided by *Lucien Mehl* in 1958:

> One may imagine two basic types of law machine: (1) the documentary or information machine, or – in more familiar terms – the machine for finding the precedent (or relevant text), (2) the consultation machine; less properly, the 'Judgment machine'. There is no fundamental difference between these two types of machine; the degree difference is one of degree rather than of essence.[63]

A few years later *Reed C. Lawlor* predicted that "In a few years lawyers will rely more and more on computers to perform many tasks for them. They will not rely on computers simply to do their bookkeeping, filing or other clerical tasks. They will also use them in their research and in the analysis and prediction of judicial decisions."[64]

The evolutionary nature of the development of AI and law is also reflected in the technical development as it has been addressed by researchers in the field. One example is provided by *Roland Tranmüller* who recognizes five generations of information processing devices and correlates each of them to different types of applications in law: the first generation emerging around 1943 with the basic ability to provide numerical computation and accompanied by statistical applications; the second generation yielding legal IR-applications around 1958; the third generation around 1968, introducing data processing in law and administration; the fourth generation of personal computers and networks, generating the first decision support systems around 1975; the fifth generation based on advanced integration and related to KBS and logic programming around

63 Mehl, L. *Automation in the Legal World*, 759 (1958).

64 Lawlor, R. *What Computers Can Do*, 344 (1963).

1985, introducing expert systems and more advanced decision support systems in law.[65]

An additional observation is that there exist no sharp borderline between the applications presented as ordinary computer-based systems and the systems originating from research in the field of AI. This is among other things illustrated by categorisations of technical solutions originating from various periods, which have in much remained remarkably stable over the years.

In 1970 Seipel mentions, for instance, a variety of computer-based functions aiming for legal decision support and analysis, legal IR, mathematical-statistical calculation, legal problem simulation, legal education, and legal administration.[66] Some ten years later, in 1981, *Constantino Ciampi*, in a retrospective analysis recognizes three lines of research: the first line devoted to "automatic retrieval of legislative, jurisprudential, doctrinal data and other data of legal interest in the general sense"; the second line focusing on "automatic drafting of legal documents"; and the third line concentrating on "the representation of the content of the laws in a formal language for automatic application of the laws themselves or, more modestly, to help the jurist in his work of interpretation and application of rules in actual cases."[67]

A subsequent categorisation of knowledge-based legal applications is provided by *Graham Greenleaf*, *Andrew Mowbray* and *Alan Tyree*, who, besides advising systems, recognizes systems for document generation, tuition, enhancements of IR, and case management and support. The group

65 Traunmüller, R. *The Entrance of Informatics into the Domain of Law*, 145 (1988). Bing, in a similar review, although with a somewhat more limited perspective focusing on computerized systems for public administration, perceives three generations: "The first generation emphasized use of data bases and computers for calculation, as well as 'computer oriented legislation.' The second generation lifted the forms, which structure the case work, onto the computer screens. And the third generation is being born from the current efforts to design integrated work-stations, using knowledge based methods." Bing, J. *Three Generations of Computerized Systems for Public Administration and Some Implications for Legal Decision Making*, 219 (1990).

66 Seipel *supra* note 30, at 263-65 and *passim*.

67 Ciampi, C. *Artificial Intelligence and Legal Information Systems*, 160-61 (1982).

also specifies some sub-divisions and stresses the fact that several functions may be apparent in the same applications.[68]

Similar categorisations have been also recently submitted by *The Expertise Centre for Juridical Software* in the Netherlands, where in 1990 a distinction was made between programs for the analysis of juridical data, IR-systems, systems for administrative functions, decision support systems, communication software in a broad sense, and software for computer assisted instructions.[69]

The formation of the field of AI and law is however not only reflected in more or less interrelated technical solutions. There also exist a number of theoretical contributions of significant importance. The first explicit discussion about a combination of AI and law was made in 1970 in an article by *Bruce G. Buchanan* and *Thomas E. Headrick*.[70] Initially the authors discussed the reasons why IR-systems are limited and argued that there was a need for more sophisticated programs. The article also suggested that the time had come for serious interdisciplinary work between lawyers and computer scientists to investigate the potentialities of computers in law. It was argued that such interdisciplinary work could lead to a deeper understanding of the legal reasoning process, and also facilitate the design of machine methods for performing parts of it.

In order to strengthen this point a couple of models for legal reasoning were outlined. Different legal problem solving processes were then related to the performing capabilities of an AI-program (the *Heuristic DENDRAL* program).[71] Finally, the authors concluded that AI "may have something to contribute to law . . ." and that "the only way of finding out whether the relationship will be fruitful is to explore it seriously."[72] They also pointed out certain potentialities, e.g. that a

68 Greenleaf, G., Mowbray, A., Tyree, A. *Legal Expert Systems: Words, Words, Words. . .?* 119-20 (1987).

69 Franken, H. *The Expertise Centre for Juridical Software*, 6 (1990).

70 Buchanan, Headrick *supra* chapter 1 note 4.

71 Feigenbaum, E.A., Buchanan, B.G., Lederberg, J. *On Generality and Problem Solving* (1971).

72 Buchanan, Headrick *supra* chapter 1 note 4, at 60.

"computer system might make good service available to a larger segment of society", but at the same time mentioned risks, e.g. that lawyers may lean too heavily on poorly developed systems. Also several difficulties in the process of developing legal AI systems (psychological, financial, and technological obstacles) were recognized .[73]

In the early 1970s from the number of contributions it is possible to see a growing interest in the mechanization of legal reasoning. This is for instance illustrated by *Jeffery Meldman* and *Anatol Holt* who presented in 1971 an article on legal knowledge representation based on theoretical proposals related to computer science. The authors argued that such a theory would "enable better analysis and understanding of complex systems, legal systems included. It would aid in the detection and clarification of ambiguities and inconsistencies in the natural-language descriptions of systems, and it would also permit straightforward computer simulation."[74] In 1973 in a review of a Canadian report *Philip Slayton* emphasised the need for more advanced programs in addition to conventional IR-systems and, among other things, argued that such programs should be developed after "research into the nature of legal thought processes" and "development of the experimentation with advanced 'artificial intelligence' systems . . ."[75] During the 1970s several experiments with advanced computer systems and knowledge representation techniques for law were started. A number of frequently mentioned projects from this period are the automated logical analyses of legal rule systems initiated by *Peter B. Maggs and Cary G. deBessonet,*[76] the legal consultant program *Judith* by *Walter G. Popp* and *Bernhard Schlink,*[77] the *TAXMAN-project* on the representation of the structure of legal concepts by *L. Thorne McCarty*,[78] the *LEGOL-project*

73 *Id.* at 61.

74 Meldman, J.A., Holt, A.W. *Petri Nets and Legal Systems*, 65 (1971).

75 Slayton, P. *Electronic Legal Retrieval – The Impact of Electronic Computers on a Profession*, 39 (1973).

76 Maggs, P., deBessonet, C.G. *Automated Logical Analysis of Systems of Legal Rules* (1972).

77 Popp, W., Schlink, B. *Judith: A Computer Program to Advice Lawyers in Reasoning a Case.* (1975).

78 McCarty, L.T. *Reflections on TAXMAN* (1977).

aiming for a representation language for legal rules and regulations developed by *Ronald Stamper*,[79] the elaborated theoretical work on legal knowledge representation by Meldman,[80] the work on conceptual legal IR by *Carole Hafner*,[81] and the project with a rule-based DSS for the analysis of liability claims documented by *Donald Waterman* and *Mark A. Peterson.*[82]

It is, however, noticeable that very few of the systems that are presented are put into use outside the development laboratories. The emphasis is in much laid on technical aspects and especially problems related to legal knowledge representation stand out as a central issues of concern.

In the 1980s another large number of systems were presented. Simultaneously, a number of elaborated theoretical contributions, several of them being academic dissertations,[83] made it possible to establish the identity of the discipline of AI and law. In the later half of the 1980s also some commercially available DSS, as well as systems developed for legal administration, were presented. Examples of these may be found in the U.S.A., where a system aiding criminal sentencing has been introduced,[84] in the U.K., where systems concentrating on dismissal law[85] and on latent damages[86] have been made commercially available, in Belgium where systems on social security are offered to social field workers,[87] in the Netherlands where systems on inheritance law, dismissal law, sentencing and custody

[79] Stamper, R.K., Jones, S., Mason , P.J., Mudarth, P.E. *The LEGOL Project* (1976).

[80] Meldman, J. *A Structural Model for Computer-Aided Legal Analysis* (1977).

[81] Hafner, C.D. *An Information Retrieval System Based on a Computer Model of Legal Knowledge* (1978).

[82] Waterman, D.A., Peterson, M.A. *Rule-Based Models of Legal Expertise* (1980). *See also*, for references to additional projects from this period, Susskind *supra* chapter 1 note 9, at 258-61.

[83] *See, e.g.*, Michaelsen, R.H. *An Expert System for Federal Tax Planning* (1984), Susskind *supra* chapter 1 note 9 *and* Gardner *supra* chapter 1 note 5.

[84] Simon, Gaes, *supra* chapter 1 note 24.

[85] Expertech, *supra* chapter 1 note 21.

[86] Capper, Susskind, *supra* chapter 1 note 14.

[87] Robben, F., Herbosch, E., van Buggenhout, B., van Bulck, K. *The Computer Supported Development of Juridicial Advice Systems Based on the Decision Table Technique*, 50 (1990).

have been marketed,[88] in Finland where a support system for the determination of house allowances has been brought into action,[89] in Denmark, where a large number of systems have been introduced by both private organizations and public authorities,[90] and in Sweden where decision support for administrative officers has been implemented and tested in the social sector.[91]

Experimental prototypes still dominate, however. Theoretical contributions categorize them into rule-based systems, example-based systems and more general programs.[92] In the classification of systems the focus is also set on the applied domain and the type of legal material (cases or statutes), the type of program (AI shell or expert system), and on whether or not the systems are commercial.[93]

In the 1980s the development was stimulated by a number of international conferences. An important meeting in this respect was sponsored by the *Science Research Council of the United Kingdom* and held at the *University College of Swansea* in 1979.[94] One other conference (*Artificial Intelligence and Linguistic Problems in Legal Data Processing Systems*) was arranged by the *Council of Europe* in Thessaloniki in 1981.[95] The same year IDG in Florence arranged the first international conference on

88 van Noortwijk, C. *Criteria in the Juricas Project*, 36 (1990).

89 Hynynen, R., Salokivi, J. *Datorprogrammet Aatu hjälper* (1988).

90 Karpf, J. *Danish Expert Systems in Law* (1991).

91 Statskontoret, *supra* chapter 3 note 124.

92 Gardner *supra* chapter 1 note 5, at 70-81. *See also*, for a categorisation originating from various forms of reasoning (rule based, operating with open-textured concepts, precedent based, etc.), Rissland, E.L. *Artificial Intelligence and Law: Stepping Stones to a Model of Legal Reasoning* (1990).

93 Susskind *supra* chapter 1 note 9, at 258-61, who also, in tabulated form, takes notice of the existence of heuristics, data base, transparency, and flexibility. *See also*, for a a recent overview of current activities in Europe, Council of Europe, *Systems Based on Artificial Intelligence in the Legal Field* (1991) *and*, for a historical analysis, Susskind, R.E. *General Survey of the Situation in Europe Concerning Artificial Intelligence Systems in the Legal Field* (1991).

94 Niblett, B. *Computer Science and Law* (1980).

95 Council of Europe. *Artificial Intelligence and Linguistic Problems in Legal Data Processing Systems* (1982).

Logica, Informatica, Diritto.[96] One year later a *Colloquium on Data Processing and the Law* was held in Leicester, England.[97] A second international conference on Logica, Informatica, Diritto was arranged by IDG in 1985[98] and in the U.S.A. two conferences were organized in Huston, in 1984[99] and in 1985.[100] An additional event – *the First International Conference on Artificial Intelligence and Law*, initiated and sponsored by *the Center for Law and Computer Science* at *Northeastern University* in cooperation with *Association for Computing Machinery Inc., Special Interest Group on Artificial Intelligence* (ACM SIGART) – was arranged in Boston in 1987.[101] The same year a workshop dedicated to legal expert systems was held in Tübingen.[102] A second International Conference on Artificial Intelligence and Law was held in Vancouver in 1989.[103] The same year also two international conferences were organized in Italy: in Bologna, where the *Center for Law and Computer Science* at the *University of Bologna*, arranged an *International Conference on Expert Systems in Law*,[104] and in Florence where IDG arranged the third International Conference on Logical, Informatica, Diritto.[105] In 1991 the third International Conference on Artificial Intelligence and Law was gathered in Oxford.[106] At that occasion also an International Association for AI and Law was formed.

96 Ciampi, C. ed. *Artificial Intelligence and Legal Information Systems* (1982), Martino, A.A. ed. *Deontic Logic, Computational Linguistics and Legal Information Systems* (1982).

97 Campbell, C. ed. *Data Processing and The Law* (1984).

98 Martino, A.A., Socci Natali, F. eds. *Automated Analysis of Legal Texts* (1986).

99 Walter, C. ed. *Computing Power and Legal Reasoning* (1985).

100 Walter, C. ed. *Computer Power and Legal Language* (1988).

101 *Proceedings ICLAI-87* (1987).

102 Fiedler, H., Haft, F., Traunmüller, R. eds. *Expert Systems in Law* (1988).

103 ICAIL-89 *supra* chapter 1 note 13.

104 Partly documented in *Ratio Juris* vol. 3 no. 2 (1990).

105 Martino, A.A. ed. *Pre-proceedings ICLID-89*, Vol. I, II, and appendix (1989).

106 *Proceedings ICAIL-91* (1991).

In the same year a *First International Workshop on Deontic Logic in Computer Science* was held and noticeable is also that two international journals on Artificial Intelligence and law has been advertised for 1992.[107]

The short time-span during which the notion of AI and law has been made explicit makes it difficult to perceive general trends. Reviewing theoretical and practical contributions, as well as the the documentation from the conferences during the 1980s, it is, however, possible to make some general observations.

Most apparent in the field of AI and law is perhaps that the submitted contributions – with a few important exceptions – are remarkably technically oriented. The studies on various detailed aspects of legal knowledge representation and the elaborations of various logical systems have often been made major objects of concern.

At the same time comparatively little attention is given to studies on the jurisprudential aspects and the practical consequences of automation. Assumptions about the nature of legal reasoning are in many cases implied or completely tacit. Conflicting perspectives concerning the nature of law, reflecting both the realist and the positivist perspectives, can be, nevertheless, detected through contributions focusing either on case-based or rule-based reasoning. This development will be, however, addressed in more detail in chapter 6.

107 Kluwer Academic Publishers *Artificial Intelligence and Law. An International Journal* (1990) *and* Triangle Books Ltd. *Law, Computers and Artificial Intelligence* (1991).

Part 2

The Legal Reasoning Process

5 Legal Reasoning

5.1 Introduction

The analysis undertaken in this chapter starts from a decomposition of the legal reasoning process into six different sub-processes. Each process is addressed separately (sections 5.2 – 5.7). Thereafter some remarks about the learning process which is necessarily related to legal reasoning are submitted (section 5.8). The important characteristics as well as the modus operandi of the sub-processes and their relations to each other are described. The description of the sub-processes is essentially rule-based, i.e. it is assumed that many mechanisms that are incorporated in legal reasoning may be described in terms of methodological rules.[1] In the concluding section (5.9) the various kinds of methodological rules as well as other kinds of influential factors that have been discussed are summarized.

To start with, it should be pointed out that a rule-based *description* of legal reasoning does not say anything about the outmost nature of the process. In other words, the analysis of legal reasoning that is outlined here is not intended to address the question as to whether or not the process will eventually and in its ultimate meaning turn out to *be* rule-based. The objective of this exploration is to develop a jurisprudentically sound model of legal reasoning that may facilitate investigations concerning automation. The reason why a rule-based approach is preferred is thereby merely the fact that rules provide a feasible (easily understandable and traditionally well established) way to describe how lawyers (and people in common) appear to reason.

5.1.1 Definitions and Terminological Remarks

The word *lawyer* is used in this part of the study as a collective description of many different legal professions (e.g. judges, advocates, law-teachers, prosecutors, company lawyers, and administrators in the public

[1] Methodological rules are of a different nature as compared to *rules of substantive law* or *primary rules* (focusing on original legal problems) in the sense that methodological rules do not deal with issues of substantive nature, but instead govern the legal decision making process and also determine how rules of substantive law may be applied, interpreted and changed. The phrases *secondary rules* and *meta-norms* are sometimes used as synonyms of methodological rules. *See, e.g.*, Hart *supra* chapter 2 note 4, at 77-96 *and* Bing, J., Harvold, T. *Legal Decisions and Information Systems*, 19 (1977).

sector). The criterion of qualification is that the decisions made by the persons involved, in their normal work situation, must concern legal rules.

Legal rules appear both as rules of substantive nature and as methodological rules. Legal rules are the rules that lawyers have to consider in their work due to the doctrine of legal sources (a collection of theories about origin, validity and application of legal rules) or because of other legally authoritative reasons. Usually this includes rules that are reflected in statutes, in legislative preparatory material (*travaux préparatoires*), in precedents, in work of jurisprudence, or, as a last resource, in regularities that may be perceived as customs.

Within jurisprudence there is an on-going discussion concerning the relevance and the hierarchical order of legal sources and rules of different status. As indicated in chapter 2, there also exist several theories concerning the justification of legal systems, the authorization, and the principles of legality. Although some aspects of these issues remain unsettled, this study adopts initially a perspective in which the validity of legal rules is taken for granted. In this respect this study rests on a positivist tradition. In the Scandinavian legal environment this is not an extreme position since there is a consensus on the relevance of the majority of legal sources. Nevertheless, in the description of the legal reasoning process that is carried out below, there are reasons to return to classifications and different attributes of legal rules. It may be therefore worth remarking right at the start that one characteristic, frequently reappearing feature is the distinction between the representation of legal rules (the written law) and rules of a semantic nature (as they are perceived by lawyers during legal reasoning).

Legal reasoning is used as a collective label for a number of mental processes leading to a legal decision. Some of these mechanisms focus on the event that has initiated the current issue and concerns situation-identification, interpretation, and fact evaluation. Other aspects of legal reasoning include law-search and involve choices between available rules and arguments. The process also comprises a constant evaluation of possible decisions and formalization activities. Legal reasoning is a crucial task since reasons that are formulated and choices that are made during the process will be used as arguments in favour of a decision. Haphazardly conducted legal reasoning and superficial analysis lead to poor arguments and result in legal decisions of low quality.

A legal reasoning process may be also very comprehensive and drawn out. It may also engage several individuals. The latter is, for instance, the case in a legislative drafting process. Likewise, it must be mentioned that in practical situations (e.g. in the preparation of litigation) it is a standard legal procedure to analyse and prepare several lines of reasoning that in a later instance may be employed alternatively depending on the kind of opposing arguments that are encountered.

Legal decisions are the result of the legal reasoning processes, and they may be more or less explicit. Legal decisions may be, for instance, visible in the way that they have a direct effect due to formal reasons (e.g. the decision of a judge closing a court proceeding, or the decision of a solicitor performing a transaction on behalf of a client). On the other hand, legal decisions may be also indirect and their effects may be hidden due to the fact that they are elements of complex situations. This is what happens in the usual counsel situation, with or without trial or connection to a dispute, and also in the legal teaching situation. The advice, the argument, or the description of the law is founded on a previous decision of the lawyer concerning the ways in which to handle the issue of the situation at hand. If the client follows the advice, if the court is in favour of the proposal, or if the student accepts the guidance, the decision may have effect. Naturally, due to misinterpretation, negligence or poor quality, legal decisions may also lack any effect, and between these extremes, many possible consequences may be perceived.

It should be also stressed that in many situations (e.g. during negotiations or court-proceedings) legal decisions are tentatively suggested in an argumentative manner and often reformulated, e.g. when the opposing party produces obstacles in the form of new information and counter-arguments. In other words, there is a close relation between the legal decision and the legal reasoning process due to the fact that a legal decision may give rise to more or less foreseeable effects, of which some may challenge and provoke the decision in such a way that a transformation is motivated.

5.1.2 Legal Reasoning – Overview

A legal reasoning process starts when a lawyer is confronted with a legal issue. For example, a potential client may visit a lawyer in a legal office and describe a situation, or a district attorney may put forward an alleged crime before a judge in a court-proceeding, or a company lawyer may receive a telephone-call from his manager to be informed of a possible legal problem emerging in a contracting situation, or a civil servant may find in his morning mail an unusual request from a citizen, regarding partly classified documents with references to the freedom of information act.

Rarely does the initial confrontation with a problem give the lawyer enough information to let him arrive at a legal decision. On the contrary, the lawyer usually has to find additional information. Depending on how familiar he is with the situation, the effort that he will have to make may be more or less time-consuming and cumbersome. Two extreme cases are possible to visualize; (i) the case when the lawyer immediately recognizes the description and makes a decision instantly without any additional efforts whatsoever, (ii) the case when the lawyer does not recognize any piece of information at all – everything, the whole situation as well as its elements, is a total mystery. Between these extremes, a continuum of alternatives can be imagined, and in some cases, as for instance in the case of court-proceedings, the lawyer will be obliged to follow formal rules guarding his decision making.

As to (i) it is necessary to underline that it is often possible to arrive at rule applications quite easily. This is for instance the case in situations in which the nature of the upcoming issues can be easily determined in advance and in which the law is stable and clear. In many fields of the law this is not an unusual situation. Anyone who has spent some months, for example issuing creditor's bills at a district-court in Sweden would probably willingly testify that problems related to the identification of the relevant law are extremely rare. Likewise, the vast majority of such cases provide few opportunities for mistakes concerning the identification of relevant facts. The same applies to many other kinds of legal issues of frequent occurrence, like for example cases concerning inheritance, traffic incidents, various taxation issues, etc. This aspect of legal reasoning is often neglected in works of analytical jurisprudence, but is reflected in the writings of *Benjamin Cardozo*.

> "Of the cases that come before the court in which I sit, a majority, I think, could not, with semblance of reason, be decided in any way but one. The law and its application alike are plain. Such cases are predestined, so to speak, to affirmance without opinion."[2]

The fact that rule applications may be arrived at with little or no effort does not, of course, mean that the underlying principles of reasoning cannot be of a complicated nature. The fact that legal reasoning often appears unproblematic indicates, however, that it is possible to generalize the process so that it can be easily executed. This, naturally, is an encouraging and important observation to keep in mind in any discussion on automation.

In the second, more complicated case (ii), the lawyer must try to determine the relevancy of the encountered facts and identify the legally relevant elements, resolving any uncertainty surrounding them. In many situations a lawyer must also try to extract more information. Depending on the nature of the case (and on the quality of the description of the situation that is communicated to the lawyer) these tasks may be more or less cumbersome. The objective of these initial activities is nevertheless in each case to be able to compose a legally relevant description of the issue. This may be called the *identification process.*

Identification is a process that is activated together with a *law-searching process*. The lawyer must find a description in the legal system that will reflect the current situation. This is the result of the if-then-syntax of legal rules. Legal rules can be always described in the form of conditional statements that is to say, they consist of an *if*-side – the antecedent or a situational description – and a *then*-side – the consequent.[3] The description of the antecedent must cover the facts of the actual event if the rule is to be applicable. The consequent of the rule is then indicated as a logical

[2] Cardozo, B.N. *The Nature of the Judicial Process*, 164 (1921).

[3] Sundby, N.K. *Om normer,* 197 (1974). *See also*, for a general comparison between various theories in legal philosophy, stressing the consensus, and the terminological discrepancy, of so called conditional statements (if *p* then *q*) in legal rules, Susskind *supra* chapter 1 note 9, at 128-39.

effect of the similarity between the current facts and the rule-antecedent. This means that rule application must always start with a comparison between the actual event and the available legal knowledge. Any law-search is, of course, guided by the identification that is being performed; the facts relevant to the current situation lead the lawyer in his search for adequate legal propositions.

Due to the fact that legal descriptions are sometimes of a fragmented nature, any law-search may turn into a complicated and lengthy procedure. It is also clear that the result of a law-search may indicate that an additional shift back into the identification activities is necessary. This is the standard procedure in cases when the situational description retrieved from the rule system indicates that under the given circumstances additional facts ought to be investigated.

From a broader perspective the initial activities within legal reasoning may be seen as a search process following two lines. The lawyer must try to form a general description of the case which includes a search for relevant facts. At the same time he must search for a legal proposition that will enable him to form a legal rule that is applicable in a given case, i.e. a rule that contains a description of a similar situation. The objective of the process is to be able to subsume the specific situation under a general description of a situation in the legal-system.

Legal subsumption must not be, however, performed haphazardly. Rule application is normally guided by a number of elaborated methodological rules of a formal nature. Methodological rules determine and explain not only the presuppositions for rule applications, but they also determine how rule applications ought to be completed. In this context it is therefore proper to acknowledge a special *rule application process*.

By definition it is impossible to find a prefabricated description reflecting a new situation. The law cannot be constructed in such a way that would allow for direct mapping of new cases. Legal propositions are often designed so that they can be used as general descriptions, covering numerous individual cases. Alternatively, as in case decisions, the available legal material may reflect only separate events and have no reference to general principles. From this follows that descriptions in the legal system must be interpreted. Elements to scrutinize are thereby not only descriptions of complete situations, but more often detailed prerequisites, e.g. concepts, agents, time aspects, and relations. Some of the elements are thereby probably recognized by the lawyer without difficulties – others may be new to him and require the use of conceptualization and/or transformation activities. In this study such transformations of legal notions are viewed upon as components of an *interpretation process*.

Another important aspect of legal reasoning with strong implications for interpretation strategies is the potential effect of the intended rule application. Depending on how interpretation and identification guide the lawyer in his search for applicable rules, different consequences of legal rule applications are indicated. Some of these effects may be acceptable, others may seem less appropriate and indicate that another situational mapping ought to be tried. Such anticipation may lead the lawyer back to one additional round of identification, interpretation, law-search, etc., with a purpose of arriving at a rule application that will be different in some aspect from the previously intended one. In jurisprudence this method of adjusting legal reasoning to some perceived purpose is often referred to as a teleological method.[4] It may here be appropriate to call it the *evaluation process*.

Finally, after several rounds of identification, interpretation and evaluation, when the rule application has been completed, the lawyer must formulate the decision. Formulation activities, just like evaluation activities, may indicate that additional instances of identification, etc., are necessary. Depending on the situation, formulation may also be completed in many ways. In a legal counseling situation or in a hearing in front of a judge, the decision may be formulated in speech and submitted in an argumentative manner. On the other hand, in a contracting situation in which messages are exchanged by mail, or if a written statement is going to be submitted, the decision must be transformed into text. Disregarding the medium actually used, this may be called the *formulation process*. Formulation terminates the reasoning process by means of revealing a decision – which may, of course, immediately become an element in a new reasoning process.

In addition, legal decisions as well as reasoning processes that do not result in formulated decisions are likely to be remembered, which is why

4 Ekelöf *supra* chapter 2 note 119.

legal reasoning is also related to the learning ability. (Learning may be naturally also a consequence of a systematic investigation of legal material.)

The different aspects of the legal reasoning process and the main relations between them form a model of legal reasoning which may be depicted as in figure 5.1:

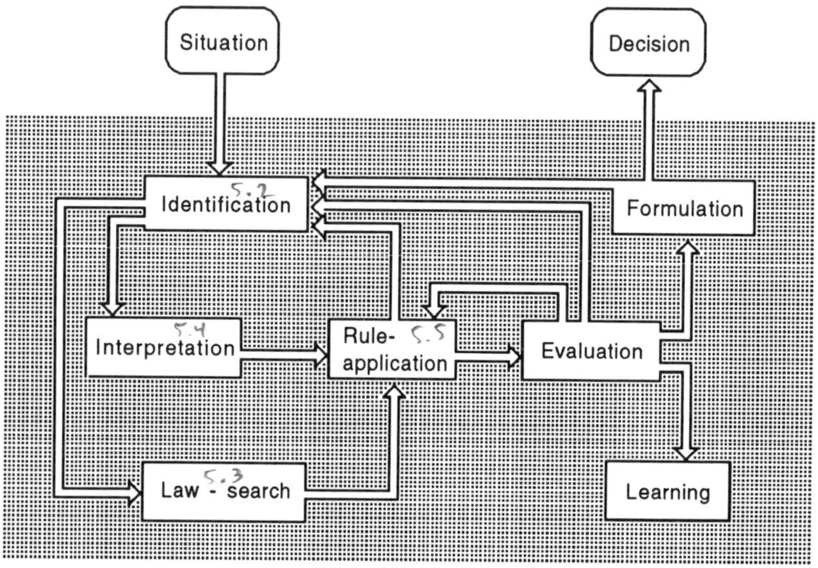

Figure 5.1 Overview – mechanisms involved in the legal reasoning process.

5.2 *Identification*

5.2.1 Introduction

The aim of identification is to be able to define a situation in a legally relevant way. Various factors influence the way in which relevancy is determined but in the legal identification process there is little doubt that the encountered facts must be related first and foremost to *the legal system.*[5] From this follows the fact that the process of identification interacts with the processes of search for legal descriptions, and with the lawyer's recollection of prerequisites used in legal descriptions. Interaction here means that the attention of the lawyer must oscillate between the actual situation and legal descriptions.

> [T]here is the process of fact recognition and characterization. The facts suggest some possibly applicable rules; these rules and the cases using them suggest the relevance and importance of certain facts. The rules that are being explored will influence the decision about which facts are relevant. Working with these interrelations is one aspect of recognizing relevant facts in legal problem solving.[6]

The fact that legal reasoning presupposes the establishment of a connection between upcoming situations and corresponding descriptions in the legal system is uncontroversial and probably quite well-known. Nevertheless, it leaves a number of questions concerning legal identification unanswered, providing rather superficial explanations as regards the legal identification process. Analysing legal identification more closely it is clear that various sub-processes may have to be completed during the process. At least three general procedures can be perceived here:

[5] *Cf.* Wilson, A. *The Nature of Legal Reasoning*, 278 (1982) "In this process the judge performs the mental operations of 'identification' and 'classification': identification of the empirical data – be it a present object or evidence of parts action – and its classification under a relevant legal figure . . ."

[6] Buchanan, Headrick *supra* chapter 1 note 4, at 51. *See also* Wilson *Id.* at 279 "The process of reasoning involved in the judge's interpretation of facts as legally relevant is made up of two heterogeneous, irreducible elements: his knowledge of the normative – legal system, whose rules, principles, categories and definitions provide the scheme of interpretation, and the evidence of the facts in the case at hand."

i) A description of a situation, as it is first encountered often contains redundant information, i.e. elements which from a legal perspective, are irrelevant. Sometimes the amount of unnecessary information is huge. Simultaneously, facts relevant to the case may be few. This may, for instance, be the case in an emotionally affected client report. A lawyer must then be able *to recognize the relevant facts and to omit the irrelevant elements.*[7]

ii) Encountered information may be incomplete. In such cases one or more additional facts have to be established before a legally relevant situation may be comprised.[8] This is a normal condition in all kinds of legal work. Hence, lawyers must be able *to find additional – supplementary – facts.*

iii) The components of a description may be disputed and sometimes mutually exclusive or inconsistent facts appear. This is, for example, an ordinary situation for a judge listening to opposing parties in trials. Likewise, the concepts used in situational descriptions may be vague.[9] Legal identification presupposes therefore an ability *to establish uncertain facts.*

5.2.2 To Recognize Relevant Facts

A crucial observation when it comes to determining relevancy is that a lawyer encountering the situation for the first time has no knowledge as to which elements he should scrutinize. In many cases this does not need to be a problem, though. For example, when a lawyer meets an upcoming issue in a field with which he is familiar, he may be able to instantly recognize the relevant facts. In other cases, however, he may encounter difficulties in the recognition of relevant items in an encountered description. In some cases there may be even some doubt as to the relevant legal area. To commence a process of identification from a vague description of a

[7] Bing, Harvold *supra* note 1, at 18 (1977) refers to this as "extracting the legal problems out of the totality".

[8] *Cf.* Alchourrón, Bulygin *supra* chapter 2 note 4, at 33 who refer to "gap of knowledge".

[9] *Cf.* Hart, H.L.A. *Positivism and the Separation of Law and Morals*, 607 (1958) who discusses "problems of the penumbra" *and* Alchourrón, Bulygin *supra* chapter 2 note 4, at 33 who refer to "gap of recognition".

situation is therefore not always a trivial and easy task. Bing expresses a truly valid observation when he writes that this "may easily be perceived as one version of the paradox on what came first, the egg or the hen: The relevant facts cannot be qualified without knowledge about the applicable rules – and, . . . the rules cannot be found without a basis in the relevant facts."[10]

Initially, it may however be assumed that the process of identification is triggered off by the encountered situation.[11] That is to say that a process of legal reasoning is normally initiated by external factors, not by a lawyer's salient contemplation of legal issues. The establishment of the relevant facts poses, nevertheless, apparent problems for several reasons. Difficulties with relevancy may appear, for instance, in extremely complex situations in which many elements of various kinds are integrated. Problems concerning relevancy may also appear when the encountered situation is vague and obscure. All this looks even worse when we realize that right from the start a lawyer does not have immediate access to any written representation concerning the relevancy of the encountered issue – except, perhaps, in highly formalized situations, i.e. in situations in which the nature of upcoming issues can be foreseen. The vastness of the accumulated legal material and the fact that different parts of the legal system may turn out to be relevant in different situations make such instant access impossible.

5.2.2.1 The Use of Background Knowledge

The lack of access to relevant legal sources in the initial stages of the legal identification process is not an insurmountable obstacle. Assuming that the lawyer has a typical professional background, as a rule he will be able to discover the necessary indicators on how to proceed, even when the description of the situation is vague. In such situations the *background knowledge* of the lawyer will function as a tool for classification. In other

[10] Bing *supra* chapter 1 note 48, at 228.

[11] *Cf.* Bing, Harvold *supra* note 1, at 20 "To us it is important to stress that our model takes the *facts* of the case, rather than the legal *norms*, as the point of departure".

words, one can say that lawyers are spontaneously aware of a number of general criteria that are embedded in the legal order.[12]

Relations between a current situation and a legal description may be confirmed at various levels of detail. The particularization that has to be completed is determined basically by the generality of the legal system. If a legal description is very detailed, the identification of a situation may have to include patient scrutiny of the corresponding facts. Other rules may, on the other hand, force lawyers to generalize from the encountered elements in order to find related legal concepts.

The existence of various levels of descriptions and the fact that, depending on their experience, different lawyers may have had the opportunity to memorize a greater or smaller number of illustrations and examples entail that in the initial stages the process of identification may be individualized to a large extent. An experienced lawyer may recall a large number of previously instanced facts without difficulty and be well aware of how different elements are interrelated with each other in the legal system. An inexperienced lawyer, on the other hand, may have to repeatedly initiate the search processes and consult "external" legal sources (written material, colleagues, etc.) in order to determine the relevancy and the relations between the encountered facts.

The nature of background knowledge and the general criteria within the law, however, are not very well defined phenomena. As pointed out in chapter 2 divergent opinions have been put forward, not only about the nature of law but also about appropriate classification of legal elements. And, as will be illustrated further on, different assumptions about the basic entities mentioned above are also present in discussions about legal identification and background knowledge. The claim that the number of opinions is at least as large as the number of legal philosophers would not be far from the truth[13] but at a more general level two basic theories may

[12] *See, e.g.*, Bing *supra* chapter 1 note 48, at 228 "The lawyer may lack a detailed understanding of the relevant legal rules, but he or she probably will have some *general* understanding of that area of law. And even if that is lacking, the lawyer has a general understanding of what types of facts or circumstances the law recognizes".

[13] Discussing the elements in background knowledge it may be appropriate to recall the words of Cardozo *supra* note 2, at 13 "In this mental background every problem finds its setting. We may try to see things as objectively as we please. None the less, we can never see them with any eyes except our own." *and*, on a general level, Wittgenstein, L. *Philosophical Investigations*, 115

be detected. These two models correspond in much to the previously described notions of legal positivism and legal realism.

5.2.2.1.1 The Positivist Approach

In legal systems leaning towards positivism much work focuses on legal dogmatics. In other words one central aim of jurisprudence is to systematize and clarify *legal concepts* and *legal rules*.

Legal rules are entities that may be studied at various levels. At the aggregated level the legal order is not seldom perceived as a *system of rules*,[14] which is why contributions to the legal theory are often based on subdivisions of that system, e.g. civil law, criminal law, etc. Within a legal sub-area it is in turn common to systemize the rules in various ways, e.g. around some legal issue or as decompositions of general and special parts. Various aspects, e.g. objects or functions, may then be used as a means of classification. For a long period the notion of *rights* has played an important role. Likewise, a lot of effort is spent on penetrating the content and meaning of legal concepts. And, just like legal rules, legal concepts are entities that may be studied at different levels.

Implicit in the positivist approach is also the pursuit of ways to reduce the existing gaps and inconsistencies. The analysis is basically held on a general level and in e.g. Scandinavian legal theory the task of providing theoretical knowledge of this kind is held to be central. Ross concluded in 1953 that "The task of jurisprudence is also to systemize the legal rules, i.e. to provide a representation of the law that is as simple and perceptible (overskuelig) as possible."[15]

The assumption that law may be described in terms of legal rules is intimately integrated with the legal curicula. At law school students learn to recognize legal rules and concepts in different areas of law. The courses focus on the study of the existing legal system, as it is codified in statutes

(1953) "The mental picture is the picture which is described when someone describes what he imagines."

[14] *See, e.g.,* Aarnio, Alexy, Peczenik *supra* chapter 2 note 28, at 423. "The legal order is the sum of legal norms which have been put together (systematized) on a certain basis."

[15] Ross *supra* chapter 2 note 99, at 207 (original text in Danish). *See also, e.g.,* Aarnio, Alexy, Peczenik *supra* chapter 2 note 28.

and other kinds of legal material, but they also include investigations of various issues and factors appearing in previously settled cases, as well as discussions about facts in hypothetical examples. In this way, in the process of education law students become accustomed to identifying and relating the upcoming situations to the relevant legal sub-areas, the corresponding legal rules and concepts. There is therefore no doubt that one basic function of legal education in the positivist paradigm is to communicate and develop a conceptual structure that is ready to function as an effective fact recognition and classification tool.[16] Likewise it is obvious that the basic components that are employed in this process are legal rules and concepts.

5.2.2.1.2 The Realist Approach

In the tradition of legal realism, i.e. in Anglo-American jurisprudence, it is usual to a adopt a critical position vis-a-vis the concept of legal rules. Instead, the importance of *cases* and *examples* is often underlined.

The emphasis on cases and examples is also reflected in North-American legal education[17] where the value of oral discussions has been given a more predominant place. As a reflection of this and following the old Greek tradition the process of legal education is often compared to the Socratic method of reasoning. *Michael Dyer* and *Margot Flowers* have summarized the perspective in the following way:

> [A]lthough numerous legal crib notes exist which attempt to explicitly formulate the rules of contracts, most lawyers look down on learning law in this

[16] *Cf.* Dickinson *supra* chapter 2 note 4, at 849 "The operation of rules is to make certain factors the primary elements before the judge's attention and to push other considerations into the background until he has reached conclusions on those which the rules single out as primary. It thus helps him to decide without making the ultimate decision for him; it supplies a structure for his thought to follow . . ." (footnote omitted), Kelsen *supra* chapter 2 note 70, at 4 "The judgement that an act of human behaviour, performed in time and space, is 'legal' (or 'illegal') is the result of a specific, namely normative, interpretation." and "The norm functions as a scheme of interpretation" (original text in German) *and* Gottlieb *supra* chapter 2 note 5, at 157 "The concept of rule developed in this book characterizes rules as devices for the guidance of *mental processes* of inference leading to choices, decisions, actions, attitudes, judgements, conclusions and the like."

[17] The notion that law can be learned from cases was introduced by the American Law professor C.C. Langdell in the 1870s and "[b]y the end of the first decade of this century these techniques had been generally accepted in law schools throughout the country." Farnsworth *supra* chapter 2 note 46, at 16-17.

> way. Instead law schools claim to teach by a socratic method of reasoning and debate which is extremely example-based. Law students examine famous and prototypic cases.[18]

The focus on cases and examples has also a definite influence on how legal identification is understood. Dyer and Flowers illustrate this by stating that "In our experience, when a lawyer is given a situation to analyse, he or she immediately recalls one or more prototypic cases which involve similar issues."[19] As regards the topic of background knowledge, the American researcher *Peter O'Neil* further elaborates this perspective by concluding that:

> The reasoning and problem solving behavior demonstrated by our expert involves the construction of rich semantic models developed on the basis of prototypical stories and expectations from previous case experiences across multiple contexts. These previous case experiences are used for gathering information to develop theories about the case, gauge what typically fits within expectations, notice anomalies, and generate mentally simulated predictions about how the new case may be concluded . . . . Mental models are summarized in the form of 'stories' and 'legal theories' by our expert and reflects particular characterizations and instantiations of the components models outlined.[20]

Thus, legal realism as compared to legal positivism reflects different assumptions about the nature of basic entities of legal background knowledge, and, with little doubt, these assumptions reflect different ways in which legal systems and their components are perceived. From the citations above one can nevertheless see that despite different legal traditions

[18] Dyer, M.G., Flowers, M. *Toward Automating Legal Expertise*, 57 (1985).

[19] *Id.*

[20] O'Neil *supra* chapter 2 note 10, at 57. The suggestion that lawyers store legal experiences in the form of prototypical stories and expectations from previous case experiences is similar to the concept submitted by Dyer, Flowers *supra* note 18, at 53, where, after analysing an actual instance of case identification, the authors conclude that a crucial aspect is the access to "a legal memory organized around abstract *conceptual issues*." Moreover, it is submitted that "[t]he indexing scheme for these issues had been built up in the lawyer's mind through the experience of attending law school."

the *functions* of the legal system are to a large extent similar. That is to say that, although on the surface exist huge differences in the way the legal order is perceived and described, an important function of the legal order in both positivism and realism is to provide effective fact recognition and fact classification assistance in legal reasoning. In addition, there is little doubt that initial legal identification is possible due to the fact that legal classification schemata of a general nature are reflected to a large extent in the background knowledge of lawyers.

In other words, legal identification is affected not only by the kinds of elements contained in the situation (the nature of the facts) and by the existing legal descriptions about similar things (available concepts, decided cases, and rules of a substantive nature), but it is also heavily influenced, especially in the initial stages, by the lawyer's immediate recollection of relevant legal categories (the nature and richness of general legal notions in the background knowledge).

It should be noticed furthermore that the relation between the elements of upcoming situations and the legally relevant concepts need not be direct. Through chains of inferences associating arrays of concepts of a non legal nature (sub-concepts, co-ordinated concepts, attributes, higher level classifications, etc.), elements of an encountered situation may also provide indirect relations to the law. In this respect it may be concluded that effective legal identification in many cases presupposes also elaborated domain knowledge of a non legal nature.

5.2.2.2 *Tentative Identification*

The existence of legal background knowledge is not the only factor involved in the commencement of the initial identification process. An analysis of legal identification must also consider the tentative and the interactive nature of the process.

This aspect is illustrated by the observation that even vague situational descriptions usually contain pointers to certain parts of the legal system. For example, in encountered situations reflections of rule-functions, requirements of actors, and various legal concepts may serve as triggers for the initial identification activities. These pointers may in turn, by means of extracting interconnected concepts in background knowledge, direct the mind of the lawyer to related sub-concepts, relations, and attributes, etc., which may be used as check-lists for additional eliciting activities. Of course, these initially perceived pointers may be inadequate, but even superficial scanning of different legal fields usually helps the lawyer to solve the dilemma of choosing the way to proceed.[21] A superficial investigation of rule-structures in family law, for instance, will indicate whether any of the issues raised in the current situation are anywhere near the situations regulated in that field. Presumably, in most cases the first round of such research is done causally and without any search-tools.

It should also be mentioned that many legal concepts may be used as *disqualifying facts* in order to pin-point a relevant legal field by means of trial and error. Some concepts that may be used in this way are very general. For instance, the most important parts of criminal law may be ruled out if the initial fact-eliciting regarding the actor shows a lack of intent. Family law will be ruled out if the persons involved are not related to each-other, etc.

The fact that situations as they are described in rules normally consist of several relevant prerequisites indicates that a strategy of finding one disqualifying fact that excludes whole situations, or eliminates a large number of possibilities, is probably the most effective method in initial identification phases. There are also reasons to believe that initial identification is sometimes conducted by means of a systematic and tentative investigation of disqualifying facts.[22] In other words, it may be assumed that experienced lawyers are normally well aware of concepts that may be employed as disqualifying facts, and can therefore easily identify and rule out the facts that are irrelevant to the upcoming issue.

21 Bing *supra* chapter 1 note 48, at 228 "[T]he initial extraction of relevant facts or circumstances is *tentative*. The lawyer has available, as a latent resource, the full bag of details comprising the problem as part of the world, with all its parties, witnesses and documents. At any time, the lawyer may refer back to this wealth of details, sift through them once more for extracting new facts to replace or supplement those made available in the first selection."

22 *Cf.* Dickinson *supra* chapter 2 note 4, at 849 "[I]t may thus be said that legal rules, even of a highly specific character, operate on the decision mainly by determining whether or not any issues, and if so which ones, remain to be decided . . ." *See also* Hamfelt, Wahlgren *supra* chapter 1 note 21, at 28 *and* Hayes-Roth *supra* chapter 1 note 2, at 44 "Expert behavior seems to demand that blind search through large numbers of hypotheses be avoided in favour of quick elimination of many possibilities in each inferential move."

5.2.3 To Find Supplementary Facts

As the identification during a legal reasoning process progresses, with or without the assistance of external legal material, and guided by continuously increasing perception of legal rule-descriptions, the facts that are to be investigated and identified in the current case become more and more clear. The question now is no longer what to look for, but how to find the missing elements in an effective way. At this stage the problem is not to establish the kind of legal situation, but to determine the existence of elements that are related to an already perceived description in the legal order.

Methods of eliciting additional facts vary with the situation at hand. If the lawyer knows what kind of information he is looking for, he will be able to choose the best way to find it. In a face-to-face confrontation he can ask questions using a more or less free interview-technique. Alternatively, he may request information by mail or telephone from different sources. Naturally, there are many more or less efficient ways of conducting this kind of fact collection, and, one important ability in this phase of legal reasoning is undoubtedly to be able to act as an apt fact-finder. In this respect it is, of course, also essential to be able to use communication facilities effectively.

In addition, psychological aspects, as well as the use of power and authority, must be taken into consideration. In some situations (e.g. in client consultations) it is important for a lawyer to be able to establish confidence. In other cases (as in court proceedings) it may be necessary to have access to means of pressure in order to extract relevant facts from individuals that for some reason are unwilling to impart their information.

The process of fact eliciting is not always an activity that can be conducted in a casual way. On the contrary, in some situations strictly formalized rules for fact collection must be followed. At least two different kinds of regulations that guard fact eliciting may be detected. One type of methodological rules focus on *sequences*, where rules determine in a step-by-step fashion the outer order of the fact collecting process. This is for instance the case in criminal proceedings where a well defined order determining how and when questions may be asked applies. Similar regulations may be found in procedural law and in regulations concerning activities of public authorities. Methodological rules of this kind may be, however, also of an informal nature and evolve more or less spontaneously for practical reasons.

Other kinds of standards applied in fact elicitation appear as *lists of prerequisites* that must be established in order to determine a certain situation. Registers of the latter kind may be more or less formalized. They may be composed of, for instance, prerequisites that can be found in statutes and/or precedents. On such occasions prerequisites from various legal sources may have to be juxtaposed in order to form complete check lists. The length of a check list used for fact elicitation depends, of course, on the complexity of the situation (i.e. on the number of prerequisites that have to be established).

It is difficult to determine a particular category of issues that might generate any fixed procedure in the legal identification process. Formalized sequences and check lists for legal identification are tools that may appear in different shapes in connection with any process that is frequent enough. In legal work informal routines develop sometimes into more or less firmly established check lists. At the same time the qualities of effectiveness, the achievement of equality, and the principle of predictability (to be explained) often impose strong limitations on any serious departure from the instituted orders of fact collection.

Regulations of legal fact elicitation may, in addition, be issued for situations that are for some reason considered to be especially important. The most obvious examples are court proceedings, but one can also observe established fact eliciting sequences integrated into work processes in various organizations, companies, etc. (An obvious and tangible example of this is the wide-spread use of printed forms.)

It should be also noticed that established regulations for fact eliciting may include preventive clauses in order to hinder the examination of some facts. There may be several reasons for such limitations. Within legal systems it is, for example, often explicitly stated that certain kinds of information (e.g. political or religious preferences of the persons involved) should be considered irrelevant for the judgement of cases. Other reasons imposing restrictions may be founded on considerations related to personal integrity, and in some cases the examination of certain facts may be in conflict with the purpose of the related rule (for instance, in order to secure the intentions behind a regulation concerning freedom of information it may be forbidden to investigate the identity of persons approaching public authorities with the objective to take part of public documents).

Although regulations in the legal order as well as elaborated check lists may be a good help in fact elicitation, it must be admitted that in many fields of law it is not possible to find formalized indications on how to proceed with the process of identification. Likewise, it is obvious that the existing check lists often account for only a small part of the knowledge that must be accessed if effective identification is to be accomplished.

In spite of this, in the process of collecting supplementary facts it must be assumed that access to useful sequences and to more or less elaborated check lists for the purpose of fact eliciting is an important condition for effective identification in the legal reasoning process. Moreover, since often only fractions of methodological knowledge of this kind can be to obtained from written sources, the nature and richness of the background knowledge of lawyers play undoubtedly a crucial role also in this aspect of legal identification.[23]

5.2.4 To Resolve Uncertainty

The third aspect of legal identification that is dealt with in this study concerns the ability to resolve uncertainty. In legal reasoning, problems concerning lack of certainty must be always solved in an explicit manner. This is one consequence of the *non liquet* prohibition. The principle of non liquet entails the fact that courts must not refuse to make a decision on the grounds that a situation is not covered by the law, or by claiming that the situation is vague or poorly defined. A judge who does that is guilty of *déni de justice,* which is considered to be a serious fault.[24] The doctrine of déni the justice is specifically defined for judges presiding in courts, but similar conventions apply even outside the courts. Practicing lawyers, e.g.

23 Hamfelt, Wahlgren *supra* chapter 1 note 21, at 45.

24 The doctrine of *déni de justice* was introduced in *Code Civile,* article 4, after the French revolution and gradually imported into the Scandinavian legal system during the 19th century. *See generally,* on *déni de justice,* Sundberg *supra* chapter 2 note 43, at 146-48 *and,* on *non liquet,* Stone *supra* chapter 2 note 37, at 186-92, 213-14 *and* Strömholm *supra* chapter 1 note 29, at 362-65.

during client consultations or negotiations, would accomplish little by suggesting that they do not know how to handle the issue, or by stating that they are unable to decide.

Several things may cause uncertainty, which in turn may concern the identity of isolated facts as well as the nature of complex situations. Perhaps the most common reason for the appearance of uncertainty is that the lawyer fails to recognize the elements that are communicated to him due to the fact that the reports he receives are imprecise or incomplete from a legal point of view, e.g. because of the witnesses' poor memory, or because written information concerning some details is missing. Uncertainty may be however also due to the fact that people make mistakes about what they have seen, or because some information about past events is no longer available. A similar common reason for prevailing uncertainty may be that conflicting reports of past time occurrences are presented, which may be due to the fact, for example, that opposing parties have different opinions about how to describe a situation in front of a lawyer, or simply because people consciously tell lies.

Problems concerning uncertainty in identification instances, do not, however, depend only on the quality of the evidence for a case. Also the nature of the situation that is to be investigated must be taken into account. That is simply to say that in some cases the encountered facts may be few and easily identified, whereas in other situations the facts to be established may be very intricate. The facts under scrutiny may be, for instance, the elements of various prerequisites that have been indicated by a party in order to prove a sequence in a story comprising numerous crucial facts. Simultaneously, an opposing party may give a different account of how the relevant chain of events ought to be understood. Some events may therefore stand out as main themes of proof, others as supporting, or opposing themes of proof, and so forth.[25] In such cases the process of the

[25] Within legal theory special terminology and a considerable literature has evolved around the *evaluation of evidence*. The proposition that is to be identified is often denoted as the *theme of proof* and may in a standard case be a fact corresponding to a prerequisite in a legal rule. The element that is invoked in order to establish the theme of proof is sometimes denoted as the *evidentiary fact*. An evidentiary fact is a circumstance from which it is possible, by means of employing *propositions of experiences*, to draw conclusions about the theme of proof. A theme of proof may in turn be a evidentiary fact for an other theme of proof in a *chain of evidence*. In such a chain "the farthest theme of proof, . . . is always a legal fact, i.e. a fact to which a legal consequence is connected according to a legal norm." A theme of proof may be supported by a number of facts of evidence which in turn may be of various strength; that is to say that the

examination of the existing evidentiary facts may be a cumbersome and prolonged procedure.

Recognizing the fact that the process of determining uncertainty is related to the nature of the upcoming situations it must be admitted at the same time that problems with uncertainty are intimately related to the nature of the existing legal descriptions of certain issues. This is a natural and necessary result of the fact that legal situations are ultimately defined by the legal system. It is furthermore rather obvious that the identification of situations reflected in many prerequisites of abstract nature will imply a higher degree of difficulty as compared to situations that may be described in a few prerequisites of a tangible nature. From this also follows that the recurrence of situations of uncertainty in a certain field of law may indicate that the quality of the underlying legislation and/or the consistency of the leading cases related to the issue is of a less satisfactory nature.

5.2.4.1 Formalized Support

More or less formalized methodological rules designed to facilitate the process of identification of disputed and/or vaguely defined facts have been in existence for a long time. Rules related to the resolution of uncertainty are linked by a common objective to find a balance between trustworthiness and the necessity to determine each issue that is being submitted. The methods that have been employed in order to reduce uncertainty have varied from time to time and, as in many other cases, the most elaborated regulations concern court proceedings. The possibilities to find effective solutions to these kinds of problems are for natural reasons limited and the attempts to establish a more formalized process have resulted sometimes in solutions that appear quite odd from the modern perspective.

A historical example can be found in the old Swedish procedural code in which a rule stipulating that unanimous statements made by two witnesses

proposition of experience may be more or less plausible and sometimes this relation is described in terms of *evidentiary values*. In a similar relation a fact of evidence may be affected by *auxiliary facts*, which in turn may be of a positive nature (i.e. strengthening the value of a evidentiary fact) or of a negative nature (i.e. weakening the value of the evidentiary fact). *See*, for further elaborations, Ekelöf, P.O. *My Thoughts on Evidentiary Value* (1983), quotation from page 11.

should be treated as undisputable evidence.[26] In France a similar rule was employed, but there, if the witnesses were female, three unanimous statements were necessary to establish sufficient evidence.[27]

In more poorly developed forms of legislative systems not only more or less tangible (race, social class, etc.) and formalized attributes (e.g. confessions, disregarding the fact that they may be the result of torture) but also various forms of purely metaphysical tokens have been – and sometimes still are – used in order to resolve issues of indeterminacy.

The possibilities to establish substantive truth values about the past events using formalized rules of evidence have turned out, however, to be limited. As a result of this one can perceive that many judicial systems are abandoning detailed regulations in favour of a more or less free process, accepting less restricted principles such as "the best evidence rule".[28]

Important indications of how evidence is to be evaluated still exist, nevertheless. Rules of this kind are the reflections of the accumulated experience, indicating that in some situations and for various reasons the collected information may be biased or inexact. A common example of this are rules limiting the weight of evidence coming in the form of testimonies received from witnesses with family relations to persons involved in the issue that is to be decided.

Other kinds of methodological rules stipulate the way in which facts are to be submitted, e.g. that certain kinds of evidence must appear in written form, and how judges are to act if those requirements are not met. If, for example, the standards concerning witnesses' signatures are violated a judge may be obliged to exclude such evidence for formal reasons.[29]

Still other rules prohibit the importation of certain kinds of evidence. An example of the latter is the hearsay rule in the legal system in the

26 The Swedish procedural act (RB 17:29) wording of 1918.

27 Ekelöf, P.O. *Rättegång: Fjärde häftet*, 16, note 24a (1977).

28 Lindell, B. *Sakfrågor och rättsfrågor*, 62-95 (1987).

29 Cf. Summers, R.S. *Form and Substance in Legal Reasoning*, 710 (1986), who illustrates this with the requirement of the signatures of two witnesses for a valid will. "The court requires the signatures of two witnesses regardless of the over-riding weight of contrary substantive reasons emergent in the circumstances (e.g., testimony of forty Bishops who did not sign, yet saw the testator make the will, combined with gross hardships to a deserving beneficiary if the will is held invalid and the property goes to undeserving parties)."

U.S.A., entailing that a witness in front of a court must be able to give a first-hand account of the topic he or she is questioned about.[30] A similar regulation is the principle of directness in the Swedish procedural law, limiting the matter to be decided upon to the elements that have been presented to the court during the trial.[31] Methodological rules with a similar function appoint the burden of proof in court proceedings; in civil procedures it is, for instance, normally up to the party that refers to a certain fact to prove the existence and the relevance of that fact.[32]

Other forms of support of how to handle uncertain facts appear in the form of indications on various degrees of *evidential strength (degrees of certainty, degrees of probability)* that must be present if a legal proposition is to be applied. Guide-lines of this kind are often integrated into the legislative system and appear in surprisingly many forms. Swedish legislation, for example, provides a rich selection of more or less well defined levels of confirmation. In certain statutes it is therefore stipulated that legal consequences may occur if a certain condition can be *assumed*. In accordance with other statutes, rules may apply with a growing degree of evidential strength depending on whether something *is reasonable*, *may be presumed*, *may be suspected*, *for good reasons may be suspected*, *for good reasons is beyond any reasonable doubt*, *is obvious*, and so forth.[33]

Although phrases of this kind indicating various degrees of evidential strength and looked upon as isolated expressions may seem imprecise, most of them have been discussed and debated upon within jurisprudence for a long time. Thus, indications of this kind enable practicing lawyers to

30 Rules of these kinds have several important exceptions. Without violating the hearsay rule it is, for instance, possible to refer to official written statements, e.g. police reports, and to declarations from dying persons, etc. Similar exceptions exist concerning demands for written evidence and for principles of directness. *See, e.g.*, Farnsworth *supra* chapter 2 note 46, at 103-05.

31 *See, e.g.*, on the principle of directness in Sweden, Ekelöf *supra* note 27, at 42-44.

32 *Cf.* Alchourrón, Bulygin *supra* chapter 2 note 4, at 32. "The central position is occupied by the general principle of the *onus probandi*, according to which all those who assert the existence of a fact must prove it, for if the alleged fact has not been duly proved, it is held to be non-existent."

33 In Swedish e.g. *troligt* (e.g. SFS 1976:727, section 10), *rimligt* (e.g. SFS 1977:1160, chapter 6, section 17), *kan förmodas* (e.g. SFS 1936:81, section 13) *kan antas* (e.g. SFS 1990:1342), *kan anses* (e.g. SFS 1921:351, section 9), *kan misstänkas* (e.g. SFS 1987:672, chapter 7, section 16), *skäligen kan misstänkas* (e.g. RB 23 chapter 23, section 3), *skäligen kan befaras* (e.g. RB chapter 15 , section 9), *sannolikt* (e.g. SFS 1990:932, section 21).

find pointers toward relatively well defined methodological sub-rules and/or illustrations describing the nature of evidence that is required. It is however noticeable that support of this kind is significantly of a domain dependent nature.

Discussing degrees of evidential strength it should be also mentioned that several attempts have been made to develop methods for the application of numerical values to various degrees of evidential strength.[34] Some researchers have also argued that in cases when many facts are involved, it may be feasible to employ mathematical formulas for the resolution of uncertainty.[35]

5.2.4.2 *Expert Behaviour*

Despite the existence of methodological rules concerning the evaluation of evidence it is clear that when indications on how to deal with uncertainty run out, lawyers are often left on their own. This does not necessarily mean that identification must be done at random. As their experience accumulate lawyers develop, no doubt, efficient means of how to handle uncertainty also in cases when formalized indications are lacking. At least three general approaches that may be employed in order to resolve instances of uncertainty can be distinguished.

One obvious way to clarify uncertainty is to undertake a *contextual investigation*. In such an investigation the lawyer must ask himself whether a given story or situation makes sense when taken as a whole if a disputed fact is instantiated. A discussion concerning this particular method to

[34] Each theme of evidence may be thereby given a numerical value, e.g. between 0 (the fact does not say anything about the theme) and 1 (the fact proves the theme). Two main approaches are possible to perceive, *the theme method* and *the evidential value method*. The theme method suggests that from the submitted evidence on a certain theme it is also possible to draw conclusions about the negation of the theme. According to the evidential value method nothing can be inferred about the negation of the theme. Recent Scandinavian jurisprudence shows that the discussion between proponents of the various theories is often of a theoretical nature. *See, e.g.*, for further elaborations, Lindell *supra* note 28, at 134-69 and *passim, and* articles in Klami, H.T. ed. *Rätt och sanning* (1990).

[35] One recent illustration is provided by Åqvist, L. *Towards a Logical Theory of Legal Evidence* (1989) who, inspired by the Swedish legal scientists *Bolding* and *Ekelöf*, has illustrated various categories of this kind. *See also*, for a number of various contributions to this discussion from the Anglo-American sphere, Cohen, L.J. *The Probable and Provable* (1977), Jurimetrics Journal Vol. 22 at 1-120 (1981) *and* Boston University Law Review. *Symposium: Probability and Inference in the Law of Evidence* 377-952 (1986).

establish uncertainty has been recently submitted by one of the most well-known Swedish theorists who also points out that the method employed for the coherence analysis of evidence can be detected in various case reports.[36] Noticeable is that a contextual investigation has been also suggested to be most effective when applied to problems with conflicting facts. It has been thereby argued that the best way of resolving uncertainty in such cases is to investigate which of the two conflicting stories that accounts for the largest number of elements in the disputed chain of events.[37] *Neil MacCormick* has illustrated this approach in the following way:

> I suggest that the only type of test which we have available to us for verifying contested assertations about the past is this test of 'coherence'; taking all that has been presented to us in the way of real or testimonial evidence we work out a story that hangs together, which makes sense as a coherent whole.[38]

The second method of resolving uncertainty that can be employed in legal reasoning may be labelled the *definitional approach*. The important observation underlying this approach is that normally it is not the tangible facts as such that are to be established, but more often the *evidence of facts*.

Reflections of this way of approaching the problem are sometimes exposed in the way that lawyers interrogate witnesses who are unwilling to expose their knowledge on some issue. The strategy used in these cases is to try to make the witness confirm some seemingly irrelevant evidential fact which, as an element of a sophisticated chain of evidence conceived by the lawyer in advance, may be employed later on in order to demonstrate that also the debated theme of proof can be established.

To some extent the definitional approach employs the tentative process that may be initiated during determination of relevancy. That is to say that it includes decompositions and/or generalizations of the encountered components in order to find some element at another level of abstraction that

[36] Ekelöf, P.O. *Om vărdering av strukturala bevis* (1990).

[37] Lindell *supra* note 28, at 255-56.

[38] MacCormick *supra* chapter 2 note 2, at 90.

may be a reflection of some concept in the legal system. It may be assumed, however, that this process may be also employed consciously and with the focus set on more detailed aspects of the encountered situation, which may be decomposed and investigated in a piecemeal manner.

If such an analysis indicates that some subject matter may be related to the legal system (if only through several succeeding steps) it may then be possible to initiate alternative fact eliciting sequences and the established facts contained in the elaborated chain of evidence may be eventually linked to explicit prerequisites in the legal system.

The third way of pursuing the process of legal identification through instances of uncertainty is *to shift into law-search*, i.e. to actively try to find some legal proposition that is better suited to define the encountered situation or the contested fact. This is simply to say that when efforts to find legal propositions corresponding to factual elements fail, an obvious way to proceed is to try to find an alternative legal proposition which would make it possible to approach the issue in a different way.

Thus, this avenue of thought may in turn lead to the conclusion that subject matters of different nature ought to be investigated. Alternatively, if the result of the excursion into law-search indicates that the problem has to be solved with the available legal descriptions, active interpretation may have to be initiated in order to transform the existing propositions.

5.3 Law-search

5.3.1 Introduction

If the available background knowledge does not provide sufficient material for rule application, lawyers must turn to law-search. Like many other mechanisms in legal reasoning law-search is a complex matter. It is also evident that the successful result of law-search is related to the effective management of several sub-processes.

All discussions about law-search must, for instance, consider the close relationship between form and substance in law, and the fact that text is the fundamental communication medium. In practice this means that law-search almost always depends on the effective retrieval of legal documents.

It is also noticeable that the notions conceived during the identification process must now be transformed into explicit terms in order to activate external information systems. (For instance, the employment of a subject index in a legal library requires the conscious use of one or several index terms.) A good sense of the language, an ability to transform the encountered fact descriptions into legally relevant language, as well as elaborated and rich background knowledge are, of course, of good help in this phase.

Moreover, in order to conceive relevant legal descriptions several retrieved concepts may have to be related to each other. Law-search is in this respect a process that may have to be activated repeatedly, and often with different objectives in mind. The complexity of the process and the frequently intricate nature of the material thus entail that law-search may sometimes be a very time-consuming activity. The task of finding the relevant point of law and the ability to decide when all the relevant items of legal knowledge have been established are of critical importance here, as any mistake during this phase may be fatal to the outcome of the decision. Most lawyers are well aware of this and recognize the fact that law-search is one of the most crucial aspects of legal reasoning.[39]

[39] An IRI-survey covering different categories of lawyers indicated that law-search was the most desirable activity to rationalize in legal work. Wahlgren, P. *ADB, telekommunikationer och juridiskt arbete*, 58 (1983).

5.3.2 The Doctrine of Legal Sources

Now and then it is possible to find explicit guide-lines on how to proceed in the process of law-search. Most noticeable is perhaps the existence of an established hierarchical order among different kinds of legal material. This so called *doctrine of legal sources*[40] provides sometimes rather firm indications on how law-search ought to be conducted.[41] For example, it says that elements of a lower dignity may have to be extracted only if higher level material fails to give sufficient information.[42] The relations between various kinds of legal knowledge may be thereby determined by the fact that the material originates from producers of different levels of dignity, or by "their long customary practice".[43]

The doctrine of legal sources is basically a theory about substantive law. In this respect the doctrine of legal sources may be looked upon as a collection of methodological rules or "managing rules"[44] and as such it is essential for the guidance of law-search in many ways. In continental jurisprudence, for example, the investigation of the prevailing legislation is almost always the most important. Thereafter, legislative preparatory materials may have to be inspected. In addition, case reports may supply examples on how a rule is to be applied in practice. And, if the official legal material and the previous cases fail to supply sufficient knowledge, equity and customs may provide guidance. Important legal knowledge may also be found in works of jurisprudence.[45]

40 *See, e.g.*, Raz, J. *The Authority of Law*, 53 (1979) "It is common ground to all legal positivists that the law has social sources, i.e. that the content and existence of the law can be determined by reference to social facts and without relying on moral considerations."

41 *See, e.g.*, Peczenik *supra* chapter 2 note 72, at 242-45 "rules for legal sources".

42 *Cf.* Hart *supra* chapter 2 note 4, at 92-93.

43 Hart *supra* chapter 2 note 4, at 92.

44 *Cf.* Hart *supra* chapter 2 note 4, at 92-93 (*rules of recognition*) *and* Strömholm *supra* chapter 1 note 29, at 297-98.

45 It should be noticed that although the doctrine of legal sources provides often a rather firm framework of how various items of law are to be related there is an on-going debate about the relative weight which ought to be ascribed to certain detailed legal materials in various fields of the law. The conditions in this respect also vary between different jurisdictions. *See, e.g.*, for a comparative analysis of statutes and legislative preparatory materials, MacCormick, N., Summers, R. eds. *Interpreting Statutes* (1991) *and*, for a discussion concerning the order between legal sources in the Scandinavian legal systems, Strömholm *supra* chapter 1 note 29 at 289-349 *and*

Various legal sources may in turn be composed of material of different kinds. Legislation, for instance, may include constitutional rules, federal rules, state laws, and regulations issued by public authorities, legislative preparatory materials embrace a number of materials of different origin and status, and case law may include decisions from courts of various dignity, etc. The existence of sub-divisions within legal sources sometimes implies that even more detailed regulations defining appropriate sequences for law-search are developed.[46]

The doctrine of legal sources undoubtedly facilitates the processes of law-search in many cases. In spite of this, it is not possible to work out some universal code comprising an elaborated search strategy for legal material based on the hierarchical order of legal sources. The most apparent obstacles to such an approach are the facts that law is an all too complex phenomenon, and that legal sources are ascribed various degrees of importance in different jurisdictions.[47] In addition, the conditions vary depending on the area of the law. For example, in a stable field of the law where precedents are rare, case decisions may be considered to be of a relatively high importance as compared to case decisions concerning rapidly changing areas of the law where litigation is frequent. In some jurisdictions, legislative preparatory material may have a high dignity. In still other fields of the law, due to the age of the material, changing presuppositions, new precedents, legislative amendments, etc, the legislative preparatory material may provide information of a less important nature. Likewise, works of jurisprudence may be more or less updated, produced by more or less acknowledged jurists, and so forth.[48]

It must be also remembered that there is an on-going discussion about *the nature of knowledge* that can be extracted from legal sources. The frequently debated issues here are whether or not it is possible to extract

Sundberg *supra* chapter 2 note 43, *passim. See also*, for a similar description of legal sources in the the English legal system, Capper, Susskind *supra* chapter 1 note 14, at 54 *and* for a description of rules of priority in the legal system of the U.S.A., Farnsworth *supra* chapter 2 note 46.

46 *Cf.* Farnsworth *supra* chapter 2 note 46, at 55-57 *and* Hellner *supra* chapter 2 note 123, at 66.

47 MacCormick, Summers *supra* note 45, *passim.*

48 *Cf.* Hellner *supra* chapter 2 note 123, at 55-57.

legal rules, and/or whether additional considerations must be included. Some legal philosophers have intensively emphasised the incorrectness of perceiving the legal system as a collection of predefined rules. It has been also stressed that in addition to knowledge that may be found in legal sources, lawyers must also consider knowledge of a subjective nature.[49] At least two additional aspects have been named as necessary elements in a more "realistic" doctrine of legal sources: *moral considerations*[50] and *practical considerations*.[51] Some researchers have also argued that the material that can be found in legal sources is to be understood primarily as the part forming (transformable) components to be considered during legal reasoning. In line with this the label *legal source factors* is a commonly utilized phrase.[52] An example of a researcher who has articulated the latter view is Eckhoff who claims that what may be found in legal sources is merely *raw-material*.[53]

The model of legal reasoning outlined in this study is based on the admission that the doctrine of legal sources does not constitute sufficient means to explain how relevant legal knowledge may be established. Likewise, it is acknowledged that elements of a subjective nature are essential for the outcome of legal reasoning. From the decomposition of the legal reasoning process suggested here follows, nevertheless, that it is improper to distort the discussion on law-search with concepts like legal source factors. The observation that legal sources cannot provide

49 *Cf.* Capper, Susskind *supra* chapter 1 note 14, at 54, "As well as the written sources of legal knowledge there are also human sources. We are referring in this respect to . . . 'private' knowledge. Some legal knowledge, no doubt, remains inarticulated and untapped in the heads of human beings." *and* Strömholm *supra* chapter 1 note 29, at 297-98.

50 *Cf.* Simmonds *supra* chapter 2 note 38, at 99-100.

51 Eckhoff, T. *Rettskildelære*, 20 (1971) (*reale hensyn*). *See also* Capper, Susskind *supra* chapter 1 note 14, at 55 "Clearly, human experts solving hard cases will bring to bear far more than a body of rules. Rather, on the basis of experience, no doubt, they will exercise judgement; and the expertise relied upon will be far less formal than that contained in a body of rules."

52 Strömholm *supra* chapter 1 note 29, at 296-98, Eckhoff *Id.* at 19-23.

53 Eckhoff *supra* note 51, at 19. *Cf. also*, on categorisation of legal knowledge, Susskind *supra* chapter 1 note 9, at 56-57, who suggests a demarcation between *academic legal knowledge* "law-formulations together with legal commentaries on these materials . . . 'the repositories of law'" and *experimential legal knowledge* "knowledge of the day-to-day practical administration of the law" and, on the relation between legal rules and legal sources, Bing *supra* chapter 1 note 48, at 230.

predefined solutions for each upcoming case is undoubtedly relevant. But the fact that the retrieved legal knowledge must be normally adjusted to a current case is looked upon in this study as an example of *interpretation*. In a similar fashion moral and practical considerations are perceived primarily as processes that are related to *evaluation*. These aspects of legal reasoning are therefore dealt with separately (sections 5.4 and 5.6).

5.3.3 Legal Knowledge Structures

In order to pursue the investigation of law-search further, it is nevertheless necessary to complement the doctrine of legal sources with some additional explanations. A detailed theory of law-search must also consider the nature of the material that is to be retrieved. The assumption behind this hypothesis is simple, viz. that all search activities must be adjusted to the ways in which the law is represented, organized, and stored. (Or – in somewhat more cautious words – that search activities ought to be best adjusted to how we *understand* the representation, organization, and storing of the law.)

Over the years, the issues related to the nature of law have been discussed extensively, and, as indicated in chapter 2, often with little consensus among the various contributors. The variations between the submitted theories suggest that one cannot reasonably expect to be able to find some objective and uncontroversial description of the law based on a single aspect like rules, cases, institutions, etc. The approach that is suggested here is therefore of a different kind and the description of legal knowledge that is submitted in this section is not based on one basic notion. Instead, the discussion is based on the analysis of *relations between different kinds of legal knowledge*. The law is thereby perceived as a network of component structures appearing on different levels of abstraction. The following sub-sections provide some illustrations of the above.

5.3.3.1 Document Level

The way legal knowledge may be approached depends intimately on how the law is represented. This entails that in practice law-search is closely related to document retrieval.

Search for legal documents is a normal, but often cumbersome task in legal reasoning, showing a number of well-known characteristics and distinguished by frequently reappearing problems. The most common difficulty is perhaps that the amount of material that is related to a certain issue may turn out to be immense. Legal documents may have been accumulated for long periods, and often large volumes of material may have to be investigated. This means that lawyers are very dependent on search aids, and that law-search is to some extent related to practical skills of various kinds concerning the physical operation of retrieval facilities, familiarity with library organisation, legal subject indexes, etc.

A related complication is that legal documents appear in many shapes, and that because of this various kinds of documents must be often investigated before a legal issue can be isolated,[54] e.g. case reports, law reviews, statutes, legislative preparatory materials, books of jurisprudence, court files, individualised agreements, etc. The identification of the relevant documents often imposes therefore a problem. In this respect, knowledge of legal publications series and other kinds of secondary structures, e.g. of document organisation in various kinds of in-house files and similar matters, are also important for effective law-search. Likewise, it may be a cumbersome task to extract large numbers of documents from various sources. Legal document search may therefore not only raise problems of an intellectual nature. Also physical arrangements, distance and other tangible aspects may be of relevance for the ability to complete the process in an efficient manner.

In spite of these complications, there is nevertheless, little doubt that the legal knowledge appears foremost in written form – and that lawyers in law-search must concentrate on the investigation of legal documents.

54 Several different categorisations of legal documents have been suggested. Bing *supra* chapter 4 note 1, at 74-84, for example, recognizes three basic types, *indexes*, *abstracts*, and *authentic texts*.

5.3.3.2 Text Level

Looking somewhat closer at legal knowledge representation it becomes obvious that the final aim of law-search can seldom be to read a document from the beginning to the end, or to find a document *per se*. For instance, in statutes it is usually one specific section that provides the relevant knowledge, in case material a lawyer may devote his initial interest towards final statements, in a legal handbook it may be sufficient to read a paragraph or a chapter, and so forth. Hence, in authentic search situations the objective of law-search is to identify various subdivisions of legal documents.

Effective text-browsing, in turn, presupposes familiarity with the ways in which the material is organised in various legal documents, e.g. the awareness that final statements in appealed court decisions are to be found after the description of the circumstances, that subject indexes in law reports may appear in the latest issue of each volume, etc. A professional search for text paragraphs is also related to the understanding of document organization at a general (i.e. non-legal) level. Knowledge of the latter kind is often used, no doubt, in an unconscious way. Nonetheless, general knowledge concerning document organization may be employed in a procedural manner and it is not far-fetched to assume that the inspection of e.g. titles, tables of contents, summaries, headlines, etc., in legal documents is often conducted in a similar way.

Also, at this level of organization, it is obvious that material from various legal sources must be combined. A certain issue may have been discussed and described in many different texts originating from various producers. In other words, lawyers must normally juxtapose and inspect several interrelated texts. From this follows in turn that lawyers must be able to utilize reference systems of various kinds (footnotes, literature- and name-indexes, and so forth).

5.3.3.3 *Concept Level*

An in-depth analysis of law-search must go beyond the text-representation level. An additional, crucial observation could therefore be that law-search in authentic situations is domain-related and that any subject matter that is perceived in a given situation may eventually provide the first association to a legally relevant concept. This implies (as has been already indicated in the discussion about identification) that an essential condition for the ability to initiate search processes effectively is to have immediate access to a rich spectrum of *legal concepts*. In a discussion of law-search it must be observed, however, that each instantiated legal concept may have a decisive influence also on the succeeding sequences of the search process. This follows from the basic function of legal concepts, which is to tie elements to each other in a legally relevant way.[55]

Sometimes this connecting function of a legal concept may be highly technical. This is, for instance, the case when a legal concept is to provide links to explicit legal definitions appearing in legal rules of substantive nature (e.g. *robbery* is a legal concept used in order to communicate information about certain related elements, such as physical or psychological threat, felonious removal of property, intent, and so forth). The concept is of a technical nature since in an instance of rule application each prerequisite has to be established in an indisputable way. If any component is lacking, then robbery is not an adequate term in that case.

Legal concepts may be however less technical. That is to say, legal concepts need not be of any immediate relevance to rule application. The main function of a concept may be to provide a convenient, general label in order to facilitate communication about a number of related legal concepts.[56] *Criminal law*, for instance, is a concept interrelating a great

55 This technical aspect of legal concepts has been extensively discussed by Lars Lindahl who submits that "The connecting function of a legal-technical concept is a special case of a general phenomenon . . . On the whole, it is even possible to claim that the connecting function is a presupposition for a *concept*." Lindahl, L. *Definitioner, begreppsanalys och mellanbegrepp i juridiken*, 43 (1985), (original text in Swedish).

56 *Cf.* Frändberg, Å. *Till frågan om de juridiska begreppens systematik*, 84 (1985), who makes a division between legal concepts with a function of systematization (*systematiserande R-begrepp*) and constituting rule elements (*regelkonstituenter*).

number of legal concepts dealing with different acts of crime. The basic function of a legal concept structure may be illustrated as in figure 5.2:

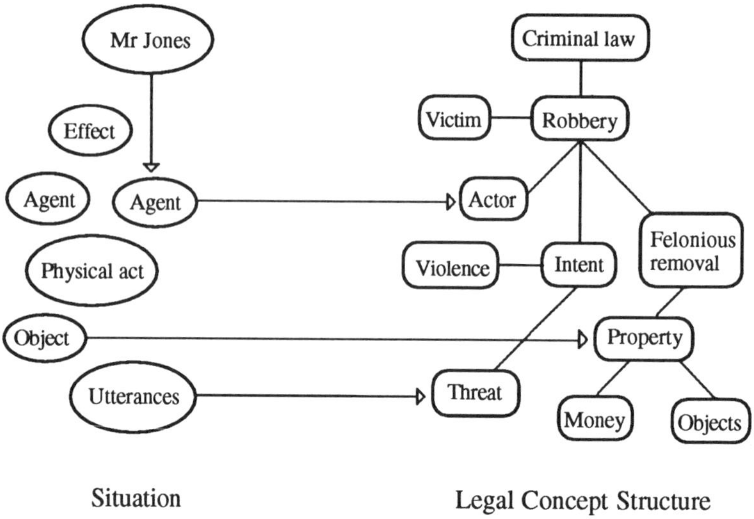

Figure 5.2 Law-search may be perceived as an activation of legal concept structures. Any activated concept may in turn provide associations to additional legal concepts.

The observation that concept structures play a crucial part in legal thought processes may seem trivial and obvious. It is however important to observe that conceptual structures constitute the fundamental corpus of legal knowledge, and that various kinds of legal concepts are basic building blocks in all fields of the law. Legal concepts appear in almost innumerable versions and, depending on the domain, together form more or less elaborated structures. The clarification of the meaning of legal concepts and their relations with each other are the major objectives of continental (dogmatic) jurisprudence. In consequence, in all detailed discussions on law-search it must be accepted that legal concept structures are vital for the understanding of how relevant legal knowledge may be retrieved.

5.3.3.4 Rule Level

As mentioned before, the primary objective of all processes of law-search is to find a legal description that matches the current case. Descriptions appear as antecedents or consequents and in their law-search lawyers may aim for either kind. To initially aim for descriptions in the form of antecedents is perhaps most common, but sometimes the primary objective is to scrutinize descriptions in consequents. The latter is for instance the case when hypothetical scenarios are to be evaluated during planning sessions.

It is important, however, to observe that it is often pointless to terminate the process of search when one, seemingly relevant description has been found. In order to get something out of a legal description the lawyer must be able to find the corresponding antecedent or consequent. In other words, the objective of a law-search is to find a *complete legal rule*, and not only an isolated description.

Additional complications may arise from the fact that a consequent description in one rule is also frequently an element of an antecedent description of another rule. Lawyers must therefore often sift through hierarchically ordered chains of rules

The relations between conditional elements in legal rules are sometimes easily spotted, e.g. when the complete rule is expressed in a single text section. The process of relating the elements of legal rules to each other may pose problems, however, for several reasons. One difficulty is that the interrelated conditional elements of a rule often appear in different parts of e.g. a statute.[57]

The difficulty may consist not only in being able to find the interrelated conditional elements of legal rules. It may be also cumbersome to comprise complete antecedent and consequent descriptions. That is to say, that in order to perceive a complete description of a legally relevant situation it may be necessary to investigate more supplementing material. A vague definition in a statute may, for instance, have to be combined with an illustration of a prerequisite in a case-report or in an amended regulation. In jurisprudence this is commonly referred to as *legal rule fragmenta-*

57 In theoretical contributions the phenomenon of dispersed rule elements is sometimes explained by means of indicating a demarcation between rules and rule expressions. *See, e.g.*, Peczenik, A. *Rättsnormer*, 9 (1987), (“norms” and “norm expressions”).

tion.[58] Thus, inter-related rule-fragments may be dispersed in a limited field of the law but from time to time it may be necessary to investigate seemingly remote areas for guidance on some aspect.

Illustrations of rule fragmentation have been provided by several legal philosophers, e.g. by Ross, who has demonstrated that the sole function of many legal concepts is to provide systematic connections between facts (f) and consequences (c) – to work as *vehicles of inference*.[59] Likewise, Eckhoff has underlined that the same phenomenon can be perceived at the rule level,[60] i.e. each (f) and each (c) related to a legal rule may be composed of rules on a lover level (f_1 in figure 5.3 below may include, for instance, rules concerning purchase, f_2 rules concerning inheritance, c_1 rules concerning the registration of rights in property, etc.).

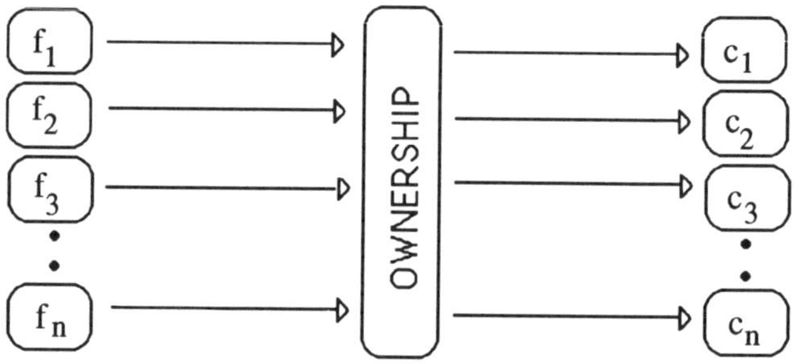

Figure 5.3 Rule fragmentation. Law-search may be perceived as an ability to identify and combine a number of interrelated legal rules.

58 *See*, generally on rule fragmentation, Sundby *supra* note 3, at 387. Eckhoff *supra* note 51, at 44-51.

59 Ross, A. *Tû – Tû* (1951). Ross thereby illustrated that legal concepts of rights were primarily technical tools for representation. *See also* Eckhoff, *supra* note 51, at 48-51 (1971) *and*, for a recent contribution on this subject, Lindahl *supra* note 55.

60 Eckhoff *supra* note 51, at 50.

5.3.3.5 *Rule System Level*

A further investigation of the law-search process shows that within substantive law, rule fragments are not the only structures that have to be extracted. Lawyers must also pay attention to other kinds of relations. One important legal structure that must be considered reflects legal rule systems. It means here that legal rules may be complete *per se* but in spite of this in practical work it may be necessary to handle them in combination with other kinds of legal rules.

Within analytical jurisprudence several suggestions concerning rule systems have been submitted. Perhaps the most well-known division between different kinds of rules has been introduced by Hart, who has presented a model based on the concept that rules exist on two different levels and are divided into *primary* and *secondary rules*.

> Thus they [secondary rules] may all be said to be on a different level from the primary rules, for they are all *about* such rules; in the sense that while primary rules are concerned with the actions that individuals must or must not do, these secondary rules are concerned with the primary rules themselves. They specify the ways in which the primary rules may be conclusively ascertained, introduced, eliminated, varied, and the fact of their violation conclusively determined.[61]

Hart divided the secondary rules further into: *rules of recognition* (similar to Kelsen's basic norm, deciding criteria for the validity of other kinds of legal rules), *rules of adjudication* (defining a procedure for identifying the individuals and the procedures to be followed when primary rules have been set aside), and *rules of change* (defining procedures for the change of primary rules).[62]

The notion of a secondary system has been also accepted by *Carlos E. Alchourrón* and *Eugenio Bulygin* who recognize two groups of rules within the secondary system:

61 Hart *supra* chapter 2 note 4, at 92.

62 *Id.* at 92-96.

> We have given the name of secondary system or judge system to the set of norms regulating the actions of judges as such. These norms may be divided into two groups: (i) those that determine in what conditions the judges may judge and what types of question they may resolve (norms of competence); and (ii) those that establish obligations and prohibitions for the judges.[63]

A related, but rather controversial sub-division of entities in law is the separation between rules and principles, suggested by *Ronald Dworkin*. Principles are proposed here to serve as a complement to rules denoting a set of ''standards that do not function as rules'' and are to be adhered to ''because it is a requirement of justice or fairness or some other dimension of morality.''[64]

Submissions stressing various kinds of rule systems have been also submitted by a number of Scandinavian legal philosophers, e.g. by Ross who recognizes three different rules of competence (regulating *personal competence, procedural competence, and substantial competence*);[65] by *Tore Strömberg* who makes a distinction between *rules of conduct* (describing patterns of activities), *rules of qualification* (defining legally relevant qualities), and *rules of competence* (defining legally relevant competences);[66] and by *Alexander Peczenik* who, among other things, separates between *constituting norms* and *regulating norms*.[67] Decompositions similar to Dworkin's sub-division into rules and principles have been proposed by Sundby, who proposes a division into *rules* and *guide-lines* (*retningslinjer*),[68] and by Eckhoff and Sundby.[69] A related demarcation is

63 Alchourrón, Bulygin *supra supra* chapter 2 note 4, at 151.

64 Dworkin *supra* chapter 2 note 38, at 22. The notion of legal principles is discussed in more detail in section 6.4.4.

65 Ross, A. *Directives and Norms*, 96 (1968).

66 Competence in Scandinavian jurisprudence has been extensively commented on by Strömberg *supra* chapter 2 note 124, *passim.*

67 Peczenik *supra* note 57, at 15-32.

68 Sundby *supra* note 3, at 190-306. (Among other things, Sundby also analyses norms of competence.)

69 Eckhoff, Sundby *supra* chapter 2 note 100, at 128.

suggested by *Nils Jareborg*, who makes a distinction between *dogmatic rules* and *rules of thumb*.[70] Sub-divisions based on a demarcation between rules and principles (and similar concepts) have been however criticized as being inappropriate and unnecessary.[71] In several studies of jurisprudence various relations between legal rules have been also depicted graphically.[72]

The operative function of various kinds of methodological rules may be illustrated by the fact that alleged criminal acts must be examined in accordance with the rules in the penal code. The examination, in turn, is guided by rules determining the ways in which evidence is to be evaluated. Simultaneously, rules on how sentencing ought to be performed must be taken into consideration. In addition, to be able to fully understand the penal code and the criminal procedure it may be also necessary to consider the rules of formality, governing the way in which the court proceeding ought to be managed. The latter type of rules is in turn closely related to rules on how judges are appointed, how jury members are selected, etc. In other words, the rules of substantive law (dealing with the original legal problems) must be related to various kinds of methodological rules, as well as to rules of formality (regulating the way in which rules of substantive law may be applied).

Categorisations of various kinds of legal rules are not elaborated on here. Further decompositions, as well as the operative function of various kinds of methodological rules and rules of formality are however discussed in sections 5.4 – 5.8, as well as in chapter 7. In this context it may be sufficient to conclude that in law-search lawyers must be able to perceive and extract rule-systems. Extending the meaning of the terminology concerning rule fragments, it may be therefore appropriate to say that lawyers must pay attention to various forms of *law fragmentation.*

70 Jareborg, N. *Värderingar,* 87-97 (1975).

71 *See, e.g.*, Frändberg, Å. *Rättsregel och rättsval,* 42 (1984) *and* Klami *supra* chapter 2 note 16, at 75. *See also* the objection in section 5.3.2 suggesting that elements related to interpretation and evaluation ought to be separated from discussions on the nature of law.

72 *See, e.g.,* Raz *supra* chapter 2 note 100, at 98-100 *and* Eckhoff *supra* note 51, at 25.

5.3.4 Concluding Remarks

A list of possible ways of describing the relevant legal elements can be easily extended and all aspects of the legal knowledge that have been mentioned here may be further analysed in a much more detailed way. Documents and text units, concepts, legal rules, and rule systems are only a few examples of the components of the complex network that constitute legal knowledge. Some levels of the network (e.g. document structures with explicit references between associated documents) are clearly visible, others (e.g. rule-structures) can be only perceived after a thorough investigation of legal texts. Yet others (e.g the insights of experts) may be individualized constituting a part of the background knowledge of lawyers.

It may be also noticed that some of the component-structures mentioned here necessarily generate secondary structures. Document categorisation, for instance, implies supplementary structures, reflecting authors, publication series, and so forth.

Although legal knowledge structures may be extremely complex and of a dynamic nature, it is clear that a structural description of legal knowledge, like the one outlined here, makes it possible to enhance the understanding of law-search. The most important observation refers therefore to the fact that legal knowledge is by necessity of a manifold nature (components of various kinds are necessary presuppositions for each other) and, in consequence, that law-search may be described as an activity with the aim to accomplish several different objectives.

To illustrate the latter point let us consider the following. In the initial phases of legal reasoning a lawyer will probably search for a legal description of a general nature, reflecting the current case as a whole. The objective would then be to determine the adequate field of law and to delimit the issue from the legal point of view. In the succeeding sequence, in order to obtain a more distinct picture of the situation, the attention may have to be shifted towards legal rules and definitions of interrelated concepts (prerequisites). Thereafter, some particular methodological rule may have to be investigated, e.g. a rule concerning the evidential value that may be ascribed to an identified fact. In the final stages of legal reasoning search activities may aim for explicit references (documents) of a formal nature, and so forth.

5.3.4.1 Individualized Structures – The True Nature of Law

Looking closer at authentic instances of law-search it becomes obvious that in addition to a more or less accepted doctrine of legal sources, individualized legal knowledge influences the process. Accepting the fact that lawyers' understanding of the law is of a subjective nature, it may be furthermore concluded that their individualized knowledge of the law contains components derived from many different levels of abstraction, e.g. knowledge about documents, rules, central concepts, etc.

Likewise, it may be hypothesized that individualized legal knowledge often contains meta-structures encompassing general and/or secondary knowledge about a number of interrelated structures. For example, lawyers working within in a certain field may have a more or less elaborated knowledge about where to find the relevant documents and the formal rules, whether or not there exist important cases of a principal nature that have to be investigated, whether there exists a detailed specification concerning the definition of a legal concept, etc. In this respect, individualized structures may, of course, also encompass case descriptions and a number of more or less causally remembered concepts – legal or not.

In other words, a further observation following from the above is that a structural perspective may shed some more light on the sometimes confused debate about the nature of law. That is to say that a description of the law encompassing component structures at different levels of abstraction allows for the fact that one's understanding of the law may be, at least to some extent, of a subjective nature. This, despite the fact that legal knowledge of high quality presupposes, naturally, also a good knowledge of basic legal structures. The relations between various forms of legal knowledge may be illustrated as in figure 5.4:

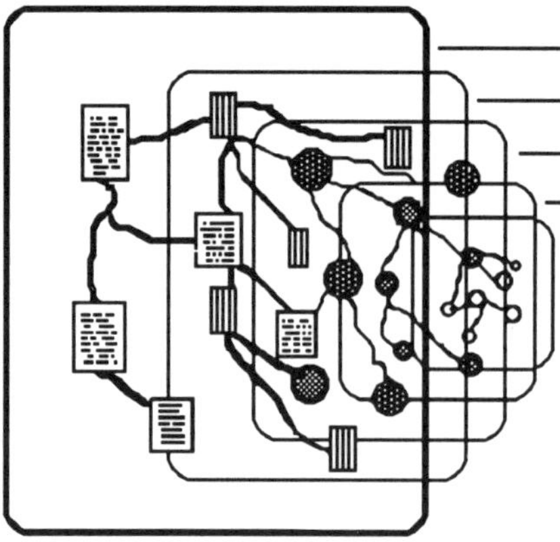

Figure 5.4 In law there is a close relationship between form and substance, which is why legal knowledge necessarily interweaves components derived from many different levels of abstraction, e.g. knowledge about documents, rules, central concepts, etc. Depending on the nature of the current issue and on how the legal reasoning process has been conducted, law-search entails the activation of legal structures of various kinds.

5.4 *Interpretation*

5.4.1 Introduction

In many cases it is obvious that it is not possible to arrive at an indisputable rule application instantly and that legal subsumption is not a straightforward process. Facts of the upcoming cases as well as fact descriptions in the legal system rarely appear in the same shape, where not only the use of the language, but also the levels of description may be different. The upcoming legal problems normally appear in the form of case descriptions without references to general principles. Modern law systems, on the other hand, rarely provide detailed case descriptions. Statutes or other forms of legal knowledge tend to provide general descriptions of abstract situations and if detailed case descriptions do appear – as e.g. in the case-based legal systems – there will always be some differences between the previously decided cases and the upcoming issues. On many occasions it is also evident that differences in the levels of description are sometimes the reason for approaching a lawyer. That is to say that if a case is initially described in a general and legally relevant way, the need for a lawyer will be much smaller in most cases.

As indicated in section 5.2 the differences between the upcoming cases and the legal propositions sometimes force the lawyer to utilize active transformations during identification. On such occasions the encountered facts may have to be looked upon from a different perspective, or handled as component elements at some other level of generalization. (In the discussion on legal identification this was looked upon as the establishment of relevance and the elimination of uncertainty through a tentative and/or definitional approach.)

The process of reaching the rule application stage involves, however, another activity, and to accomplish it, more or less far reaching transformations with respect to the existing legal knowledge may have to be performed. In other words, in legal reasoning not only the situations that are to be identified, but also the available legal propositions have to be adjusted. This latter aspect is defined in this study as interpretation.

Interpretation is, just like identification, an obligatory element of legal reasoning. That is to say that all the actual instances of legal reasoning *must* include the establishment of a connection between a legal proposition (appearing in a legal text or in the background knowledge) and a conceived rule.[73]

In many cases the establishment of this link between a legal proposition and a conceived legal rule may provide little or no problems. When difficulties do occur, however, they are normally related to various kinds of *vagueness* with respect to the legal material. A standard jurisprudential illustration of this problem is how to understand the legal proposition "No vehicles in the park."[74] How does the concept vehicle refer to various kinds of movable objects (skateboards, toy cars, electrically propelled wheelchairs, airplanes, World War II tanks for exhibition purposes, etc.)?

73 *Cf.* Gottlieb *supra* chapter 2 note 5, at 101 "The main problem of interpretation . . . [is n]ot what the meaning of words in the rule is, but whether the words authorized the inference made in reliance on them."

74 *Cf.* Hart *supra* chapter 2 note 4, at 123-26. Vagueness or indeterminacy of legal propositions is within jurisprudential literature often referred to as *open texture*.

Complications arising in connection with interpretation may also occur when several legal propositions seem to apply simultaneously or when legal propositions can be interpreted in different ways. On such occasions the law can be described as being ambiguous. As compared to the problems connected with vagueness, which appear most frequently on the concept level, these difficulties occur more often on the rule level and are then referred to as instances of *rule collision*[75] or *rule conflict.*[76]

In works of jurisprudence it is possible to distinguish several approaches aiming to reduce difficulties connected with vagueness and ambiguity. The most obvious and uncontroversial approach is here to clarify legal propositions by means of finding explicit indicators on how to handle a certain issue within the legal system. This is hereinafter referred to as *contextual interpretation.*[77] As a complement, when indicators from the legal system cannot be utilized for some reason, lawyers may have to transform legal propositions by means of applying various kinds of technical approaches (hereinafter *supplementing interpretation*).[78]

When rule collision occurs, lawyers may employ one or several methodological rules concerning the priority of legal propositions. This is referred to in this study as *interpretation of priority*.[79]

75 Peczenik *supra* chapter 2 note 72, at 305.

76 Strömholm *supra* chapter 1 note 29, at 388

77 *Cf.* Hellner *supra* chapter 2 note 123, at 65 *and*, for a somewhat different perspective, Jackson, K.T. *Definition in Legal Reasoning*, 379-84 (1985) on applying various types of legal definitions to facts.

78 Hellner *supra* chapter 2 note 123, at 69-73.

79 As compared to the model of legal reasoning that is outlined in this study numerous contributions to the theory of legal interpretation have been submitted from alternative standpoints (not all of them comparable to the decomposition of legal reasoning that is suggested in this study). This may be illustrated by the frequently mentioned *canones* of interpretation. The expression is derived from a categorisation outlined by von Savigny, F.C. *System des heutigen Römischen Rechts*, 206-330 (1840) who submitted four basic canones (guide-lines) of legal interpretation; (i) textual factors, (ii) logical, systematical factors, (iii) historical factors, and (iv) functional, teleological factors. Methods of interpretation have been thereafter addressed by many researchers and on a more detailed level 120 years later Llewellyn identified and analysed a large number of techniques ("canons on construction"), which common law lawyers had adopted in the process of handling law. Llewellyn *supra* chapter 2 note 29, *at* 77-120, 521-35. A common way of categorisation is also to distinguish between interpretation in accordance with the purpose of the legislation and interpretation done by means of composing various factors (Hellner *supra* chapter 2 note 123, at 62-63). *Cf. also*, for further examples, Gottlieb *supra* chapter 2 note 5, at 102 ("Interpretatio extensiva", "Interpretatio lata", "Interpretatio declarativa", "Interpretatio stricta" and "Interpretatio restrictiva"), Eckhoff *supra* note 51, at 117-45 ("innskrenkende", "utvidende",

5.4.2 Contextual Interpretation

In order to explain how contextual legal interpretation may reduce problems connected to vagueness it is necessary to go back to the nature of legal knowledge and, especially, to recall the distinction between legal knowledge representation and legal rules of a semantic nature. As indicated in the discussion on law-search, this distinction implies sometimes that legal propositions appear in a fragmented form. As a consequence, in order to conceive a legal concept or rule a lawyer may have to identify and juxtapose a large number of fragments from different sources.

The fragmented nature of legal knowledge is obviously the cause of many problems connected with interpretation. It must be noticed, however, that law fragments often provide a solution to many problems of this kind. That is to say, when vagueness is encountered it is often possible to clarify and adjust legal propositions by means of associating any number of interrelated law-fragments with each other.[80] The following subsections provide some illustrations of the above.

5.4.2.1 Definitional Support – Specializations and Generalizations

Perhaps the most common way of solving legal interpretation problems is to try using various levels of descriptions within legal propositions. This is in principle the same method that was indicated in the discussions on identification and law-search at the concept level. It may be noticed also that interpretation by means of generalization and specialization is a general phenomenon, not referring typically to legal reasoning. The most apparent difference when compared to many other fields of knowledge, is, perhaps, that various levels of generalization are often relatively well reflected in various kinds of sources. This correspondence is however not always present. On many occasions explicit definitions of general propositions may

"analogisk" and "antitetisk tolkning"), Strömholm, S. *Idéer och tillämpningar, passim* (1978), MacCormick, Summers *supra* note 45, at 531-32 on the *prima facie* ordering of linguistic arguments, systemic arguments, teleological-evaluative arguments, as well as arguments from intention and other transcategorical arguments in statutory interpretation *and* section 5.6 *infra*.

80 From a functional point of view it is thereby also clear that the fragmented nature of legal knowledge representation is a vital presupposition for a dynamic legal system. That is to say that the fact that law fragments may be combined in various ways implies that legal rules may be adjusted to the special features of numerous upcoming cases.

be found in legal sources of similar kind, and sometimes even in the same statutes.[81]

The fact that situations and objects may be described at various levels is easily illustrated by the fact that each description of a situation or of an object may be decomposed into *concepts*, *sub-concepts*, *attributes* and *relations*. The concept ''car'' may be divided, for instance, into sub-concepts, e.g. engine, wheels, chassis. Engine may be in turn subdivided into engine-block, cylinders, carburettor, cables, bolts etc. Examples of car attributes would be, for instance, registration number, colour and size; attributes of an engine smell, sound, colour, and so fourth. It is also possible to form higher levels of descriptions, or, as they are sometimes labelled, *classes*. ''Car'' may be for instance seen as a sub-concept of the class vehicle.[82]

To understand the legal interpretation process it is crucial to observe that descriptions contained in the legal rule system may be perceived in a similar way. A statute, for example, may contain descriptions of general concepts. Related sub-concepts and attributes may be defined and exemplified in court-decisions or in legislative preparatory material and jurisprudential literature, etc. To adopt a definitional approach during interpretation may therefore imply a search for a level of description that would be more in line with how the current case has been encountered and conceived.

The particular character of the available legal sources determines the way in which the process of interpretation may be developed. For example, in the Swedish jurisdiction the obvious way to proceed when a problem connected with the interpretation of the concept ''vehicle'' appears would be to turn to the statutes concerning classification of vehicles. These statutes provide a very large number of various kinds of detailed definitions, listing even rare types of vehicles. For example, one special statute concerns the classification of *stone removal vehicles*, another one classifies

81 One reason for this is then often to minimize the amount of text that is necessary to include in a certain statute. By means of collecting elements that are common to several propositions and/or paragraphs unnecessary recurrence may be avoided.

82 *Sub-concepts, classes,* and *attributes* are terms originating from the so called structured object languages. *See*, for an overview of different approaches in AI, Brachman, R.J., Levesque, H.J. eds. *Readings in Knowledge Representation* (1985).

fork-lift trucks, and so forth.[83] Thus, in a large majority of cases the lawyer will be doubtless able to find explicit definitions helping him to decide whether or not the current situation involves a vehicle in a legal sense.[84]

In a different type of jurisdiction – lacking special statutes on the classification of vehicles – the way to approach the lack of precision in a given case may be to try to analyse the previously decided cases and consult other kinds of legal sources that may specify the general concept in a way that is more in line with the encountered object. This may finally provide more explicit descriptions, even though the information gathered from e.g. the study of previous decisions, may have to be first put together. On an aggregated level it may thereby be noticed that an initially vague concept will be continuously related to an increasing number of illustrations as decisions are accumulated. Provided that the legal decision making is consistent and that the decisions are well documented, this will eventually diminish the problems connected with vagueness.[85]

Problems originating from the fact that legal descriptions reflect different levels of abstraction appear, however in many shapes. When the propositions appear as general concepts (e.g. as in the vehicle prohibition) it is obvious that the lawyer must first solve the problem concerning the lack of precision by means of specifying the concept crucial to the case (e.g. "vehicle") so that it gets a distinct meaning (interpretation by means of specification).

If, on the other hand, the legal system is based on case descriptions (or if the available legislation is of a casuistic nature) interpretation may have to include also generalizations. The latter is for instance the case when the financial losses issuing from the misbehaviour of the dog *Pluto* (e.g. an attack on the mail-man) are to be decided upon when the only available

83 *Vägtrafikkungörelse (SFS 1972:603)* sections 1-4, *Kungörelse (SFS 1954:617) ang. klassificeringen av så kallade stenröjningsvagnar, and Kungörelse (SFS 1952:45) ang. klassificeringen av vissa gaffeltruckar.*

84 In a jurisdiction encompassing a large corpus of knowledge about general concept of this kind it may even be presumed that the concept vehicle in the park regulation is chosen explicitly in order to *avoid* problems with interpretation.

85 *See, e.g.*, about this development of *opinio necessetatis* (necessary argument), Bing, J. *Om tolkning av enkeltord – særlig i lovtekst*, 141-42 (1986) *and* Aarnio *supra* chapter 2 note 1, at 21.

propositions on similar matters describe merely how e.g. financial losses issuing from the misbehaviour of the bull *Ferdinand* (e.g. an attack on the milkvan), and of the cat *Felix* (e.g. the theft of fish), as well as of an unidentified fox (e.g. the killing of eight hens) have been decided. To find an appropriate level of description in such cases it may be necessary to establish a number of associating links. In the first instance, legal propositions contained in the available cases may have to be generalized in order to find a level of abstraction that contains no contradictions (interpretation by means of generalization). In the succeeding phase these generalizations must be related to the current case (by means of specification).

In contrast, in the statute-based jurisdiction the misconduct of Pluto may be more easily interpreted as an instance of a general legal proposition, stating e.g. that "owners of domestic animals are liable for all kinds of damages made by such creatures." The rule may be arrived at in the latter case solely by the specification of the elements contained in the general rule.[86]

It may be noticed that interpretation by means of specification and generalization means that many different components may have to be adjusted to different levels of abstraction. This has been illustrated, for instance, by Stone discussing interpretation with illustrations from a well-known

86 On an aggregated level the development of legal propositions of general nature may thus be looked upon as a presupposition for an effective legal system. That is to say that without access to representation of hierarchically ordered general legal propositions lawyers must in each upcoming case try to generalize from more or less ad hoc related cases. This is not only a time-consuming enterprise, but also an undertaking that involves great risks with respect to the principles of predictability and equality (*Cf.* section 5.5. *infra*). The strive towards a well organized legal knowledge representation is also reflected in undertakings in many jurisdictions where efforts in this direction appear under many names, (legal dogmatics, restatements, reformulations, etc.). *See, e.g.*, for further illustrations of this stand-point, Susskind *supra* chapter 1 note 9, at 78 who among other tings submits that "[I]t is desirable for those whose concern is the administration of the law to recast these law-formulations as a body of structured, interconnected, coherent, simple (in so far as possible), and comprehensive law statements." Aarnio *supra* chapter 2 note 1 at 266-67, MacCormick, Summers *supra* note 45, at 18-23 and *passim, and* Berman, D.H., Hafner, C.D. *The Potential of Artificial Intelligence to Help Solve the Crisis in Our Legal System*, 928 (1989) "The American legal system is widely viewed as being in a state of crisis, plagued by excessive costs, long delays, and inconsistency leading to a growing lack of public confidence. One reason for this is the vast amount of information that must be collected and integrated in order for the legal system to function properly. In many traditional areas of law, evolving legal doctrines have led to uncertainty and increased litigation at a high cost to both individuals and society. And in discretionary areas such as sentencing, alimony awards, and welfare administration, evidence has shown a high degree of inconsistency in legal decision making, leading to public dissatisfaction and a growing demand for 'determinate' rules." (Footnote omitted).

English tort-case in which a plaintiff had found a dead snail in an opaque ginger beer bottle.[87]

> *Facts as to the Agent of Harm.* Dead snails *or* any snails, *or* any noxious physical foreign body, *or* any noxious foreign element, physical or not, *or* any noxious element . . . .
>
> *Facts as to Vehicle of Harm.* An opaque bottle of ginger beer, *or* an opaque bottle of beverage, *or* any bottle of beverage, *or* any container of commodities for human consumption, *or* any containers or any chattels for human use, *or* any chattel whatsoever, *or* any thing (including land or buildings).
>
> . . .
>
> *Facts as to injury of plaintiff.* Physical personal injury, *or* nervous or physical injury, *or* any injury . . .[88]

5.4.2.2 Intentional Support

Rule fragments appear in many different shapes and not only as elements that may be employed in inferences of a specifying or generalizing nature. In an analysis of contextual interpretation it is also necessary to note that a legal system can often provide also more general indications on how to proceed when legal propositions appear to be imprecise.

In other words, it is sometimes possible to find explicit statements concerning *intentions* behind legal propositions within the legal system. Intentional support may appear in the legal system in addition to definitional support, but it may also play a crucial role when one runs out of explicit definitions or when those are non-existent. The latter may, for instance, be the case when a general proposition is newly issued and when no examples and illustrations have yet been generated.

To illustrate this we may consider the problem concerning vehicle prohibition. In this case, if a lawyer is unable to obtain explicit definitions of the vague concept "vehicle", he may still be able to make an extensive

87 Donoghue v. Stevenson (1932) A.C. 562.

88 Stone *supra* chapter 2 note 37, at 269-70 (footnote omitted).

analysis of e.g. legislative preparatory material[89] and through it find out that the *purpose* of the legal proposition is to ensure silence in the park (e.g. because it is situated near a hospital). Such an *intentional law fragment* gives rather firm indications on how to interpret the concept "vehicle" in each and every case – namely that the quality of being noisy will be a crucial attribute when a lawyer has to decide whether or not a certain object is to be subsumed under a general concept. The construed rule may turn out to be on such occasions something like "no objects generating noise must be allowed in the park." This may in turn impose rules that e.g. electrically propelled tram-cars may be allowed in the park, provided they are quiet, and simultaneously rule out horses pulling carriages on stone pavements.

If, on the other hand, the lawyer is convinced for some reason, e.g. by the inspection of the underlying city plan regulation, that the intention with the vehicle prohibition is to ensure that no heavy objects appear in the park generating vibrations (e.g. because of unstable ground conditions of the buildings nearby) this will instantly impose a different interpretation of the concept "vehicle". On such an occasion electrically driven tram cars may have to be excluded because they are too heavy, while horse pulled carriages may present little or no difficulties.

5.4.2.3 Methodological Support

In addition to definitional and intentional support, in legal knowledge representation it is sometimes also possible to obtain *explicit methodological support*. The latter is the case when legal propositions of a substantive nature are interconnected with methodological rules. One example of such a rule of a very distinct nature appears in the Swedish legislation concerning vehicles, where the third section in the statute on road traffic (SFS 1972:603) stipulates that if a certain vehicle or type of vehicle cannot be

[89] It may be noticed that legislative preparatory work in various jurisdictions is admitted various degrees of importance. In some jurisdictions, as in e.g. the European community legislation, legislative preparatory work is more or less omitted from the decision making process. In Sweden, on the other hand, legislative preparatory work is often referred to, although the the discussion about its role in legal decision making for a long time has been intense. *See, e.g.,* for recent comparative study and for further references, MacCormick, Summers *supra* note 45 *passim and,* especially on the Swedish situation, Bratt, P., Tiberg, H. *Domare och lagmotiv* (1989).

classified in accordance with the lists of vehicles in the statute, the issue of classification should be submitted to the *Road Traffic Security Administration.*

The most common reason behind this kind of regulation is perhaps that many aspects of modern society are of a very complicated nature and that the legislator tries in this way to ensure that legal decision making preserves a high standard. Similar rules appear e.g. as regards issues related to the development of chemical compounds, construction techniques, etc. In addition, it may be noted that besides providing methodological support a regulation of this kind also ensures that the relevant authorities are notified when new, previously undefined phenomena appear. This in turn may facilitate the process of adjusting the rule system whenever the need arises.

An approach that is similar from the methodological point of view is when issues of interpretation are delegated to a jury during court proceedings.

Methodological rules may be however also less explicit and less decisive. An example of a methodological rule of a more general kind can be found in the previous wording of the Swedish penal code (in force during the NCA project) which stated merely that in each upcoming case and in their interpretation of the legislation concerning sentencing lawyers must consider factors concerning both the resocialization of the criminal as well as those concerning general prevention.[90] In this way, methodological support may be very similar to intentional support by means of merely pointing out the relevant factors that have to be considered.

As a final remark concerning contextual interpretation one should mention that various forms of contextual interpretation may be combined and interconnected. That is to say that efficient interpretation implies that a lawyer must be able to sift through large volumes of text encompassing not only a lot of legal matter of a substantial nature, but he must also consider legal propositions of intentional and methodological nature originating from different kinds of legal sources.

90 *Brottsbalken (SFS 1962:700),* (The Swedish Penal Code).

5.4.3 Supplementing Interpretation

5.4.3.1 Interpretation by Analogy

Even though sufficient support for interpretation cannot be obtained from the legal system, the lawyer must still decide whether or not the current case is to be subsumed under a legal proposition. *Åke Frändberg* describes this dilemma in the following way: "On the one hand, the judge is supposed to be loyal to the legislator and, on the other hand, he is bound by the *non liquet*-prohibition, i.e. he is not allowed to refuse deciding cases where the laws are obscure or missing."[91]

In cases when the legal system does not provide enough support for interpretation a lawyer may have to extend the investigation beyond the available legal propositions and include also knowledge about previously described legal *solutions*. That is to say, if a lawyer is able to find a solution that seems to be appropriate for the current case, he may try to apply the antecedent proposition that is related to this solution to the case he has to decide. This may be done only by means of *replacing* one or several concepts in the extracted legal proposition with concepts in the current case with *similar* attributes. Simultaneously, the lawyer must also try to consider any possible general aspects and intentions of the legal system. If those general aspects do not violate the intended replacement, the lawyer may be able to arrive at a rule application. The inference is based in such a case on *analogy* – a method of interpretation in which legal propositions are transformed in an active way.

Interpretation by analogy can be perceived on different levels of generalization. Depending on the nature of the available legal propositions it is for instance possible to conceive analogical inferences originating not only from legal concepts but also from legal propositions describing intentions.[92]

91 Frändberg *supra* chapter 2 note 80, at 176.

92 An additional categorisation related to this kind of interpretation is the division between statute-analogy (*analogia legis*) and law-analogy (*analogia iuris*). Statute-analogy is described as interpretation by analogy from the more or less well-defined propositions in the legislation. Law-analogy is described as interpretation by analogy from vaguely described general principles that are valid in the legal system. However, from the perspective that is adopted in this study – that expressions of substantive law in statutes and in general principles are basically of the same kind, although they may be represented in different kinds of materials – this kind of division seems less appropriate.

Interpretation by analogy is a rather well-established method of legal interpretation and for several reasons, especially when contextual interpretation is insufficient lawyers may prefer a process of analogical reasoning to e.g. an ad hoc solution. Most apparent is, perhaps, that interpretation by analogy minimizes the efforts related to evaluation. That is to say that since all the consequences of interpretation must be evaluated, a method making use of a previously established solution usually entails a lesser risk of unforeseeable consequences. Secondly, the employment of a method of interpretation based on analogy may facilitate the preservation of conformity in legal decisions (as well as in legal systems). Moreover, in actual instances of legal reasoning it may be important from a psychological point of view to be able to relate a conclusion to the existing legal propositions.[93]

5.4.3.2 Reasoning e contrario

Interpretation by analogy is in direct opposition to the so called *reasoning e contrario.*[94] Reasoning e contrario results in the fact that the analyzed situation is *not* comparable to a given legal proposition. There are basically two reasons for this kind of conclusion. The most obvious one is that a situation may not be comparable to a rule-description due to contextual discrepancy – considering the necessary functional and logical standards, the expressions that are used to describe the rule and the current case cannot be regarded as similar in any way. (Conclusions of this kind may be also due to the fact, for example, that there exist disqualifying facts, or other rules, explicitly indicating that the current situation is not comparable to the rule-description and hence that it must not be subsumed.)

A second factor that may indicate that reasoning e contrario is appropriate in a given case is the syntactical form of the rule-expression, i.e. when a rule-description lists prerequisites and concepts in such a way that it is possible to deduce that everything that has been left out is doubtless

93 *Cf.* Strömholm *supra* chapter 1 note 29, at 407.

94 Hellner *supra* chapter 2 note 123, at 71-72.

outside the criteria stated by the rule. The *silence of the law* guides the lawyer in the interpretation process.[95]

In this description of supplementary interpretation it should be finally underlined that interpretation by analogy is primarily a mode of reasoning in which certain legal presuppositions and encountered facts are to be looked upon as expressions of similar phenomena. Likewise, reasoning e contrario is a mode of reasoning implying that certain legal presuppositions and encountered facts should not be looked upon as expressions of similar phenomena.

The major characteristics of the inferences resulting from these modes of reasoning, as compared to ad-hoc solutions, are that they in each case are supposed to be explicitly related to some previously known legal proposition. In this respect, what has been said about the advantages of the possibilities to preserve conformity and the ability to relate legal decisions to the legal system for psychological reasons in connection to interpretation by analogy, is therefore also valid for reasoning e contrario.

5.4.3.3 Extensive and Restrictive Interpretation

Problems concerning vagueness are not something that is unique for law. Vagueness constitutes a general limitation for effective communication and language whose effects can be reduced but not eliminated by the introduction of technical terms and legal concepts.[96] Legal interpretation is therefore also related to general rules of a lexical nature operating on the concept level.

It is thereby obvious that the starting point for interpretation must normally be the understanding of the natural meaning of the concept (or the word in the text representation) and that the number of lexical and semantical rules that can be applied in a given case provide general limitations for how legal propositions may be transformed.[97]

95 Strömholm *supra* chapter 1 note 29, at 411.

96 *Cf.* Alchourrón, Bulygin *supra* chapter 2 note 4, at 32.

97 *Cf.* Evans, J. *Statutory Interpretation*, 2 (1988) *and*, on *logical-grammatical interpretation*, Strömholm *supra* chapter 1 note 29, at 397-401.

In this respect, a crucial observation concerning interpretation is that legal prerequisites as they appear in written form may be interpreted in both *extensive* and *restrictive* ways.[98] Extensive interpretation may then be used as a method of widening the obvious application area of a concept, while restrictive interpretation may be used as a method of limiting the application area, e.g. by the sole means of subsuming the situations of textual coherence or conceptual identity.

Discussing this aspect of interpretation it is also noticeable that the ways in which a concept may be interpreted vary with respect to the nature of the concept. The result of this is that different kinds of issues may cause bigger or smaller problems concerning interpretation and that it is possible to see a continuum from strictly defined to vaguely defined concepts. Examples of strictly defined concepts which provide little or no problems with interpretation are numbers, weights, measures. Concepts that may be vaguely defined are e.g. the previously mentioned vehicles and domestic animals. Noticeable is also that a large number of entities that are expressed in legal propositions reflect notorious and more or less genetic elements, e.g. man, woman, which leave little room for individualised interpretations.[99]

5.4.4 Interpretation of Priority

A special kind of interpretation may have to be employed in cases when more than one rule seems to be applicable. There are several reasons why such instances may occur. The most important reason is, no doubt, the fact that rule systems are often inconsistent, e.g. because they have been developed over a long period of time.

Problems of rule conflict may be solved by any of the techniques mentioned above, e.g. by means of interpretation by analogy and e contrario. In addition, however, a legal system may also include other more explicit rules in order to solve this kind of dilemma.[100]

98 *See*, on extensive and restrictive interpretation, Evans *Id.* at 174-232.

99 *Cf.* Bing *supra* note 85, at 136-39, who recognizes three main categories measurable *quantities*, *natural states* and *legal states*.

100 The comparative analysis in MacCormick, Summers *supra* note 45, at 527-30, indicates that various legal systems have generated different kinds of methodological rules concerning conflicts

Firstly, if the conflicting rules vary in status due to formal reasons, the principle of *lex superior legi inferiori derogat* may be employed. The lex superior principle gives precedence to the rules of a higher order over the rules of a lower order.[101] The order of dignity in the rule hierarchy is thereby an attribute that may be derived from the status of the issuing authority, or perhaps from a long time customary practice.[102] Secondly, if one of the conflicting rules is older than the other, the principle of *lex posterior legi priori derogat* may be used as a method of solving the problem, giving the more recent law precedence over the older law.[103] Thirdly, if one of the conflicting rules can be seen as a more specialized regulation of a certain issue, the principle of *lex specialis legi generali derogat* may come into use giving the more specialized law precedence over the more general one.[104]

5.4.5 The Limits of Interpretation

Analogical interpretation and reasoning e contrario as well as extensive and restrictive interpretation are methods that may generate conclusions of a contradictory nature. The same is true to some extent as regards the principles concerning interpretation of priority.

Sometimes the choice between the various methods of interpretation may provide little or no difficulty. This is for instance the case when intentional or methodological support can be obtained. If no such support is available, however, interpretation must be tied up with the process of evaluation and with the purpose of the legal system. That is to say that in order to make a choice between the various modes of interpretation a

of this kind, and that "no system has yet succeeded in establishing any clearly articulated picture of the law at this level . . ."

101 Sundberg *supra* chapter 2 note 43, at 200.

102 Hart *supra* chapter 2 note 4, at 92.

103 Strömholm *supra* chapter 1 note 29, at 451.

104 *Id.* at 414. *See also*, for a more comprehensive analysis of how to make choices between several possible rules, Frändberg *supra* note 71 *passim*.

lawyer must relate the existing alternatives to the resulting rule applications and the foreseeable effects of his final decisions.[105]

This necessary interdependence between interpretation and evaluation can be easily noticed in one special form of active interpretation, viz. *interpretation by means of reduction*.[106] In those cases the lawyer reduces the apparent application area of the rule in an effort to apply transformations that will achieve a more or less conscious goal and in which the evaluative aspects will actively influence the process.[107] One extreme form of this kind of interpretation is the *elimination of the rule*[108] e.g. because it is regarded as obsolete. (The relation between interpretation and evaluation, as well as additional reasons that may impose active transformations of legal propositions are addressed in more detail in section 5.6.)

5.5 *Rule-Application*

5.5.1 Introduction

The major objective of legal reasoning is to find a legal description that can be related to the current situation in order to accomplish an instance of rule application. Rule-application is performed when an individual case has been *subsumed* under a general description. Subsuming denotes thereby a process in which descriptions of factual elements and legal propositions are to serve as expressions of similar notions.

105 *Cf.* Sundby *supra* note 3, at 202 "[T]he issue should be resolved in accordance with the result of the evaluation.", Frändberg *supra* chapter 2 note 80, at 176 "The reason for analogical use of legal norms cannot be explained without examining the ideology of legal decision making, an ideology closely connected with political ideology." *and* Peczenik, A., Bergholz, G. *Statutory Interpretation in Sweden*, 318 (1991) "The fact that one must make a *choice* between the use of analogy and *agumentum e contrario* shows that these concepts do not indicate the content of interpretation but are mere argument forms, each supported by a set of reasons which a judge has to weight and balance."

106 Strömholm *supra* chapter 1 note 29, at 412.

107 Interpretations entailing that a rule is treated in a way that is different from the normal understanding of the law is sometimes motivated by the principle "*Cessante ratione cessat ipsa lex*" (the rule cannot be applied when there is no reason for the rule). *See also* Gottlieb *supra* chapter 2 note 5, at 113, who illustrates the role of purpose in the process of rule application with the obvious conclusion that a an ambulance ought to be allowed in the park in order to rescue an injured child. "The consequence of . . . [a prohibition] is clearly incompatible with the policy behind the whole body of law designed to promote the safety of individuals."

108 Peczenik *supra* chapter 2 note 72, at 286.

As described in the previous sections, rule application is preceded by the acts of identification, law-search and interpretation, on which processes it is highly dependent. These processes are, in other words, the necessary premises of the rule application process.

In an actual instance of legal reasoning, however, a decision cannot be the result of a rule application based on the factual elements of the case and the interpreted legal propositions only. The consequences of the intended decision must (or, at least, ought to wisely) be also taken into consideration. Thus, before the decisions are formulated, the possible consequences of the rule applications must be evaluated. In addition, since the foreseeable consequences of legal decisions may be more or less acceptable,[109] the intended rule applications may have to be adjusted, making that in the stages preceding formulation the character of legal reasoning must be of a *significantly tentative nature.*

A discussion about rule application should examine not only the iterating nature of the process. In order to accomplish rule application of any reasonable quality, at least two additional aspects should be considered. If they were not considered, each might put the decision in peril. The first of these two aspects concerns the formal validity of the intended decision and reflects the fact that there exists a large number of formal rules governing the process. Formal aspects do not only set out standards for decision makers. In many cases formal rules also explicitly point out and limit the rules of substantive nature that can be applied in a given situation.

The second complementing aspect of rule application discussed in this sub-section reflects some basic legal principles which in addition to formal rules are of relevance for the rule application process. Among other things such factors fulfil the function of ensuring that in each case the applied legal rule is the one that is best suited to the current situation. These aspects are referred to here as accuracy.

109 *Cf.* Gottlieb, *supra* chapter 2 note 5, at 74 "Every decision necessarily leads to some reasonably foreseeable consequences for the parties and for those closely associated with them. These may at times be diametrically opposed to the purposes of the rule which governs the decision, or conflict with the interests and policies normally upheld by the legal system. Harsh results may require modification of the rule applied."

5.5.2 A Recurrent Process

The dynamic and iterating nature of the legal reasoning process has been a major predicament of legal theory for a long time and, as indicated in chapter two of this study, the necessity to incorporate various realistic considerations (evaluations) into legal reasoning has been often seen as an obstacle to the possibilities of making use of logical deduction. The complications following from a demand for evaluation have been however understood and explained in many different ways. Some researchers have tried, for instance, to incorporate elements of evaluation into the logical reasoning process by means of adding further premisses to the perceptible process of deduction.[110] Others have elaborated those models of legal reasoning which have incorporated evaluative considerations by means of utilizing, often hypothetical or assumed intentions of the law-makers.

The ways in which processes of rule application may be initiated and developed depends, naturally, on the nature of the upcoming issue in each case. The intention of this section is, however, not to discuss the ways in which the substantive aspects of law are affected by the instances of evaluation. Those aspects, as well as the nature of the factors governing the outcome of the evaluation process, will be discussed in some depth in section 5.6. The intention of this sub-section is of a more limited scope, viz. to discuss some general observations following from the fact that the process of rule application is of a tentative nature and that it actually incorporates several interrelated sub-processes.

Thus *the focus is set here on sequences* and characteristics of the recurrent process that can be perceived in the light of the analysis that has been undertaken in the preceding sections.

The main assumption submitted here is thereby that, whenever it is possible, lawyers seek to start with the evaluation of a rule application on a rather high level of generalization. It is furthermore assumed that through repeated instances of adjustments, the process proceeds in the direction of evaluation of increasingly better specified rule applications.

110 *Cf.* Peczenik *supra* chapter 2 note 72, at 32-33 and *passim*. *See also*, for a critical view on approaches based on logic and for further references to Scandinavian literature, Strömberg *supra* chapter 2 note 124, at 165, especially note 1.

Perhaps the most important reason for these assumptions is the existence of a general current in human reasoning to eliminate as many steps as possible from each mental operation.[111] In legal reasoning this is reflected in the obvious fact that there is little meaning in spending a lot of time on a detailed analysis of numerous elements if the intended rule application should turn out to be inconceivable when looked at from a broader perspective. The conclusion that rule application often starts with a few general concepts in mind is also strengthened by the fact that in initial stages of legal reasoning lawyers must often depend on background knowledge[112] – and by the fact that it is difficult to remember many sub-elements and attributes in a limited time-sequence.

The assumption that the activation of various concepts on a rather general level makes it possible to arrive at a tentative rule application implies that this step must then be evaluated. The evaluation may give either positive or negative indications. If the indications are positive, i.e. if the tentative rule application seems reasonable, the process enters the next more detailed phase of analysis, where the selected facts are scrutinized and divided into sub-concepts, which are then related to accompanying items of legal knowledge. A well-trained lawyer, even a very experienced one, will then often make use of external knowledge representation, e.g. by reading the description of the available representation of the rule in a statute or a case, and mapping all the relevant prerequisites one by one onto the elements of the current situation. If everything fits, the lawyer will be ready to formulate a decision.

If, on the other hand, the consequences of the intended rule application do not seem to be acceptable, this usually means that some other facts ought to be held as relevant, that some other legal concepts should be extracted, or that some alternative means of interpretation should be employed.[113] From this it can be seen that evaluation may indicate not only that legal concepts have been instantiated at some less appropriate level of

[111] *Cf.* references in note 23 *supra*.

[112] *Cf. supra* section 5.2.2.

[113] Gottlieb *supra* chapter 2 note 5, at 109, "Purpose can thus be used to *preclude* the application of a rule in situations which seem to fall squarely within its language when such application would lead to results entirely alien to its purpose."

generalization. A tentative evaluation may also indicate that the rule application was substantively inadequate, and that the process should rather go along different lines of reasoning.

In such a case, additional rounds of identification, interpretation and law-search may have to be initiated. The objective of such repeated analysis is to arrive at a rule application that is different in some respect.[114] Here again the adjusted rule application is tested in an instance of evaluation, and is eventually subjected to yet another round of identification, law-search and interpretation. This process, depending on the complexity of the issue and the experience of the lawyer,[115] may have to be repeated many times.

Rule application can thus be described as a recurring process in which a lawyer is able to specify more and more adequate rule-applications through the succeeding and recurring instances of identification, law-search, interpretation, and evaluation. Rule-application described in this way stresses the fact that many phases of the legal reasoning process depend on each other and are conducted in a more or less parallel way.

114 Strömholm *supra* chapter 1 note 29, at 297.

115 *Cf.* Bing *supra* chapter 1 note 48, at 232-33 "As the understanding of the problem changes, the basis for the first search request also changes, and it may be appropriate to formulate a new (primary) search request. This may, of course, once more teach the lawyer additional features of the legal domain he or she has entered, making a new search for facts or circumstances necessary, and so on. Indeed, this observation emphasizes that the retrieval process also is a *learning process*, in which the background knowledge of the lawyers become an in-depth understanding, which may have a lasting effect on the background knowledge itself."

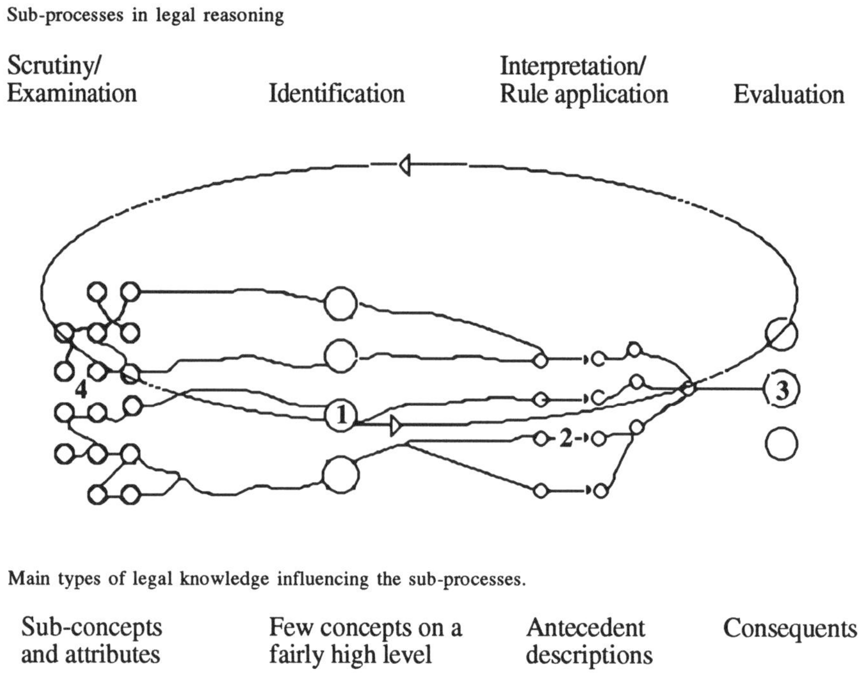

Figure 5.5 Sequences applied in legal reasoning: the process commences from a description consisting of a limited number of concepts at a fairly high level (1). The identified situation indicates a certain rule application (2) which is evaluated (3) and scrutinized (4), often in a repeated process.

5.5.3 Formal Aspects

The process of rule application is affected not only by the nature of the upcoming issue and by the rules of substantive law that match that issue. Nor is it a process which is based solely on these factors in connection with the evaluation of intended decisions. In particular instances of rule application it is also necessary to consider *formal rules.*

Following Hart's terminology,[116] formal rules are secondary rules, which is to say that when compared with rules of substantive law they function on a different level. In this respect formal rules are similar to the

116 Hart *supra* chapter 2 note 4, at 92.

previously discussed methodological rules governing the process of interpretation. There is also little doubt that the functions of formal rules are similar to those of methodological rules. That is to say, there are good grounds for assuming that the majority of formal rules have been developed with a more or less conscious intention to provide stability to the decision making process and to make possible the accomplishment of rule applications of high quality.

5.5.3.1 When, Where and by Whom?

Although functional similarities exist between formal and methodological rules it should be noted that formal rules also differ in several respects from methodological rules. The most important difference lies in the fact that methodological rules regulate different things than formal rules. While methodological rules give instructions on how rules of a substantive nature may be extracted and transformed, formal rules *define when and where rules of substantive law may be applied*.

The aspects of time and place are, however, not the only segments of the legal reasoning process that are administered by formal rules. Formal rules *define also the appropriate legal forum for and the necessary competence of legal decision makers*, i.e. they decide where, by whom and by which authority a given set of substantive rules may be applied. As a consequence three major kinds of formal rules can be distinguished: *promulgation rules*, *rules concerning jurisdiction* and *rules concerning competence*.

Promulgation rules focus on time aspects and appear in different shapes. Some simply state that a certain statute is valid from a certain date. Others, in addition to the information supplied above explicitly invalidate previous statutes and also regulate the way in which issues combining events that occurred during a period of time in which different laws were valid are to be handled.

Also rules concerning jurisdiction can be divided into different groups. Some jurisdiction rules simply indicate that cases occurring within a certain territory fall within a given court's jurisdiction (*territorial jurisdiction*). Jurisdiction can also follow from the fact that a person is physically present, or has some relations to a certain territory (e.g. by means of citizenship, marriage to someone that lives there, etc.). This is often referred to as *personal jurisdiction.*[117] Rules concerning jurisdiction are, however, related not only to territory. At times formal rules also define the *subject matter jurisdiction* by means of explicitly describing the particular categories of cases that a certain court or a certain authority has the power to determine.[118]

Rules defining subject matter jurisdiction are similar to the third main category of formal rules – rules of competence which define the necessary qualities of legal decision makers and give individuals (or more precisely individuals occupying certain positions) the competence to act as legal decision makers.[119] In other words rules of competence give individual decision makers certain powers. These special powers are often defined in a related category of formal rules, viz. legal *rules of qualification.* Rules of qualification give the person concerned, and/or the acts of that person, a certain legal quality, from which follows, in turn, different legal abilities and consequences. A legal decision maker in, for instance, a criminal-court proceeding must be able to support his act on a rule of competence if his decision is to have any effect whatsoever. The rule of competence says here that he should be an appointed judge. Rules of qualification tie different qualities to the concept ''judge'', such as among other things, the authority to lead criminal court-proceedings, to send persons to prison, to dismiss charges, etc.

It should be noticed also that in most legal systems certain factors may have the effect that a decision maker will not be able to exercise the powers following from the rules of competence. The most important of those factors are perhaps the existing personal relations between the decision maker and the issues concerned. Rules concerning such relations appear in most procedural law-systems and the facts that they refer to may

117 *See, e.g.,* on territorial and personal jurisdiction Eek, H. *Folkrätten,* 405-06 (1980) *and,* on the relations between various principles of jurisdictional competence, Brownlie, I. *Principles of Public International Law,* 298-320 (1979).

118 *See, e.g.,* for an illustration of various kinds of subject matter jurisdiction in the International Court of Justice, Shabtai, R. *The World Court,* 81-111 (1989). Principles of subject matter jurisdiction also determine the competence of various kinds of courts (e.g. criminal courts and administrative courts) that may be found within a certain country or a certain territory.

119 Strömberg *supra* chapter 2 note 124, at 42-62.

be of either substantial or formal nature (i.e. the decision maker may have an interest in a certain issue due to his direct personal involvement or merely because he is related to someone who is involved in the case).

5.5.3.2 Authority

Formal rules do not only differ from methodological rules by the fact that they focus on different aspects of the reasoning process. Formal rules also appear on a higher level in the hierarchy of rules, that is to say that *formal rules are authoritative rules.* This means not only that lawyers are obliged to follow them, but also that a violation of a formal rule is likely to invalidate the whole decision.[120]

In comparison, the results of the violation of a methodological rule, e.g. a failure to make an adequate interpretation, may lead to a decision of low quality that can be easily criticised. A mistake of this kind may also indicate that there are good grounds for an appeal. It is, however, extremely rare that mistakes concerning the employment of methodological rules as such will actually make the decision invalid – anyone who wants to criticise that decision on the grounds that some methodological rules has been violated must be prepared to incorporate into his argumentation references to issues of substantive nature in order to support his point.

It must be mentioned that formal rules do not only have the authority to exclude the use of certain rules of substantive nature but that they may also explicitly indicate the collection of rules that is relevant to a certain issue. In this respect, the fact that formal rules operate at a different level of the rule hierarchy may sometimes entail that the employment of rules that have been indicated by the rules of formality may seem totally inconsistent from a substantive point of view. On other occasions, the intended rule-application may be completely in agreement with the rules of substantive law, but still impossible to be performed due to formal

120 *Cf.* Summers *supra* note 29, at 703 "Once the legal rule of ineffectiveness for lack of a writing or the like is clearly established, the application of that rule usually shuts out from consideration particular substantive arguments in favour of validity or enforcement, however weighty."

reasons, e.g. because of the lack of rules of competence and/or qualification.[121]

Returning for a moment to the discussion about sequences, the conclusive nature of formal rules clearly indicates that in authentic instances of legal reasoning a close inspection of these high-level rules may save a lot of time. That is to say that in many cases it would seem wise to investigate formal rules before any, more detailed aspects of substantive law are inspected and before methodological rules are employed. In other words, it is possible here to look upon formal rules as rules possessing the capacity to disqualify (disqualifying facts),[122] or else to perceive them as indicators of authority since their function is sometimes to actively determine the adequate set of substantive rules.

In practice, however, it is seldom possible to start the examination of a legal issue by going over sets of formal rules. The obvious reason for this is that many kinds of formal rules are highly domain-dependent and that it is impossible to identify the relevant formal rules without first building some opinion about the issue from the point of view of substantive law.

The fact that formal rules are highly domain-dependent entails in turn the fact that in various fields of the law in actual instances of legal argumentation it is more or less feasible to consider arguments based on those. In other words, in areas with well established statutes that are in daily use it is often pointless to submit arguments claiming that a given law is invalid for some reason. In many cases it may thereby also be assumed that the scrutinizing of formal rules has a rather low priority and on some occasions it may be even assumed that formal rules are inspected only as a last resort when substantive law has failed to provide material for conclusive arguments.

Simultaneously, in other fields of the law arguments based on formal rules may be a crucial part of everyday legal reasoning. This is the case, for instance, in the rapidly changing fields of law or in areas where rules concerning jurisdiction are often in conflict with each other, as is the case

121 *Cf. Id.* at 705 "[S]tatutes of limitation, jurisdictional rules and so on, often require decisions to be made without examination of substantive reasons which would favour a different decision."

122 *Cf. supra* section 5.2.2.2. It should be noticed that not all kinds of formal rules are of an absolute nature in the sense that a violation always rules out the decision. A violation may be without effect, e.g. because nobody challenge the decision.

e.g. in international law, where it is not always clear which country's laws should apply.

As a final remark concerning formal rules it should be stressed that all that has been said about rule and law fragmentation in section 5.3 is also valid as regards formal rules. In practice lawyers must therefore remember that formal rules appear in many different legal sources. Some rules of formal nature may appear, for instance, in a country's constitution, while others are found in statutes or in authoritative court decisions.[123] In this context it is therefore also worthwhile noting that the occasionally fragmented nature of formal rules makes it sometimes difficult to detect and adjust to this kind of rules. This is also, no doubt, the reason why legal decisions in some fields are frequently attacked on formal grounds.

On the other hand, from the fact that formal rules are often valid for a number of rules of substantive nature at times follows that they are expressed in special statutes or that they appear in certain, easily identifiable parts of the law. Such is the case in the Swedish legislation in which rules concerning jurisdiction are often to be found in a certain chapter or a text paragraph and where promulgation rules normally appear at the end of statutes.

5.5.4 Accuracy

The third aspect which is relevant for the discussion of legal rule-application concerns accuracy, i.e. the necessity to be exact and correct.

The obligation to be accurate is, of course, present in most work situations and is not something that applies to legal work only. It may be, however, argued that accuracy is of special importance in legal reasoning. One reason for this is that the results of the reasoning process will be often closely examined by the opposing party with the object to find errors and level criticism at any badly conducted rule application procedure. An inability to use legal concepts and legal rules in a way that is acceptable with respect to the standards previously set out by the legal community may cause that a decision may be easily overruled.

123 It is also noticeable that formal rules may be derived from matters of status, e.g. martial or citizenship status.

In legal decision making the necessity of accuracy follows also from a couple of fundamental principles which by no doubt function as meta-rules governing legal rule application – *the principle of legality*[124] (also known as the *the doctrine of the precedent*[125]) and *the principle of equality before the law.*[126] These principles seriously delimit the free choice of lawyers and also entail that rule application must be preceded by close investigations of both legal presuppositions and current situations.

The principle of legality is a reflection of one of the most important aspects of a legal system – the previously mentioned social demand for predictability. The principle of legality has been perhaps most explicitly discussed within criminal law,[127] where the famous sentence *nulla poena sine lege, nulla poena sine crimine, nullum crimen sine poena legali* (no punishment without law, no punishment without crime, no crimes without criminal law) was formulated by *Paul Johann Anselm von Feuerbach* at the beginning of the nineteenth century.[128] Striving for predictability in the legal system entails also, however, that the principle of legality is important in all fields of the law.[129]

Also the principle of equality before the law (imposing that cases which are similar from the legal point of view should be decided alike) is of fundamental importance, not only for the legal reasoning process but also for the legitimacy of the legal system.[130] Anyone who comes in contact with

124 *See, e.g.*, Alchourrón, Bulygin *supra* chapter 2 note 4, at 176.

125 Coval, Smith *supra* chapter 1 note 29, at 36-37.

126 *Id. and* Strömholm *supra* chapter 1 note 29, at 276.

127 The principle of legality in criminal law is explicitly mentioned in the Swedish constitution (RF chapter 2, section 10).

128 *See, e.g.*, on the principle of legality in criminal law, Jareborg, N. *Kriminalisering*, 38-41 (1980) and Frankel, M.E. *Criminal Sentences: Law Without Order*, 3-5 and *passim* (1973).

129 *See, e.g.*, RF chapter 8, section 3, Strömberg, H. *Allmän förvaltningsrätt*, at 73-74 (1984) *and* Coval, Smith *supra* chapter 1 note 29, at 37 "[The doctrine of the precedent] follows from the principle of reason that unless we employ predicates and other terms in a consistent manner we have neither consistency in, nor predictability from, our arguments."

130 *See also*, on the importance of the principle of equality, Schmidt, F. *Domaren som lagtolkare*, 296 (1955) ". . . perhaps the proposition of value that is most deeply rooted in our western social order." (original text in Swedish).

the legal system (e.g. when facing a trial or simply submitting an application to a legal authority) has the right to equal treatment, disregarding when and where within a certain jurisdiction the issue is to be decided. A legal order that does not meet these requirements would soon loose its authority and trustworthiness. This in turn entails the fact that legal decision making must not be affected by the individual preferences of the lawyer and that legal decision makers must be able to adjust the process to legal and historical traditions.[131]

It may be noted that the principle of justice is especially important to uphold in certain kinds of legal decisions. Foremost, in decisions in which the outcome can be described in exact measures and in which irregularities are easily perceived and of great importance to the persons involved. This is for instance the case in criminal law and the law of damages, where sentencing and damages are to be decided in terms of time and money. In some judicial systems this aspect of legal reasoning is reflected in the development of very detailed rules, for example, in the so called sentencing guide-lines in the U.S.A.[132]

In practice, the principles of legality and equality (as well as the doctrine of precedent) imply that sanctions or other restrictions imposed by legal decisions must be done in accordance with the law. From the principle of legality it thereby follows that lawyers must never go beyond the legal propositions that are explicitly stated in the law.[133] It must be noticed, however, that acting in accordance with the law in this respect does not only mean that every prerequisite in the rule-antecedent must have a corresponding fact in the current situation. The principles related to accuracy in legal decision making also entail that a situation that is subsumed under a legal rule must not include any additional facts that

131 The necessity to adjust legal decisions to historical factors has been addressed by many authors. *See, e.g.* Cardozo *supra* note 2, at 104-05, Sundberg *supra* chapter 2 note 43, *passim and* MacCormick, Summers *supra* note 45, at 44, 221, 469, 514, and *passim.*

132 *See, e.g.* Jareborg, N., von Hirsch, A., Hanrahan, K.J. *Påföljdsbestämning i U.S.A.* (1984).

133 Alchourrón, Bulygin *supra* chapter 2 note 4, at 176 "Judicial decisions must be grounded on legal norms. . . . it is held that every decision requires not merely grounds, but grounds of a special kind: they must be legal. The judge must not go beyond the sphere of law, by appealing to non-legal (e.g. moral) norms, except in cases where the law itself authorizes him to do so. And even in these cases the ultimate ground for the decision will be a legal norm."

make the situation different from the previous situations that have been subsumed under a certain rule. Thus the principles of legality and equality not only compel lawyers to carefully examine all the prerequisites and the factual elements that are involved in a certain rule application, but also make that in instances of rule application lawyers must be certain that no disqualifying element is contained in the current situation, or in another rule-fragment.[134] In this way the legal system is insured against a development into which unprecedented and perhaps irrelevant circumstances are incorporated.

The general demand for predictability also means that interpretation by analogy and other forms of supplementary interpretation cannot be employed in all situations. For example, interpretation by analogy must not be used in order to extend criminal prohibitions, explicit statutory exceptions or tax regulations.[135] Works of jurisprudence also stress that reasoning e contrario must not be used as a general method, and that it is normally excluded from interpretations of case decisions.[136]

In individualized instances of the legal reasoning process the necessity to be careful in this respect means that lawyers must be exhaustive in their activities concerning the processes of law-search and identification and that it is not wise to terminate these activities if any other, seemingly relevant element has been found. A thorough investigation of the legal material and/or of the current situation may indicate in many cases that some additional prerequisite or circumstances must be considered as it may be of great relevance for the outcome of the decision.

134 Disqualifying factors may appear in many different shapes. Factors indicating that some other rule application may be appropriate may be found for instance in the form of explicit exemptions on every detailed level in the legal system (e.g. as a last remark in a promulgation rule). Legal rules that make an intended rule application inappropriate may also appear in different places in the legal system, e.g. on a higher level of generalization. This is for instance the case where the social security officer suddenly finds out that the widow Smith is not entitled to a widow's pension in spite of the fact that she fulfils all the requirements in the social security act (her husband is dead, no formal rules concerning jurisdiction are violated, she is unsupported and needing, and so forth). The reason for the exception may then be that the officer finds out that the widow has actually murdered her husband and that there exists a general rule imposing that no one should benefit from his or her own wrongdoing.

135 MacCormick, Summers *supra* note 45, at 472.

136 Hellner *supra* chapter 2 note 123, at 71-72, 82.

5.6 *Evaluation*

5.6.1 Introduction

Every rule application indicates certain possible effects. Some of these effects may be desirable and easily recognized, whereas others may not be so obvious. Certain effects may be also for some reason dubious or inappropriate. This is for instance the case when a legal decision is in conflict with the obvious purpose of the legal system. A conceived legal decision may be also unacceptable with respect to the political and moral standards prevailing in the society. On such occasions the intended legal decision may have to be abandoned and a different avenue of thought approached. To be able to make such decisions a lawyer must always evaluate the intended rule application.[137]

As mentioned before, evaluation is a process that is interconnected with interpretation, so much so that in some cases it may be even difficult to distinguish between the two. Some distinctions can be nevertheless perceived. The most obvious difference is perhaps the fact that the processes of interpretation and evaluation operate on different kinds of material. During interpretation the objective is to relate a *legal proposition* to a legal rule. During evaluation, on the other hand, it is the (intended) *legal decision* itself that is investigated. From this in turn follows that there exist a sequential order between interpretation and evaluation – a contemplated decision can be only evaluated when the legal proposition has been interpreted and the intended rule application conceived.[138]

The fact that evaluation affects the legal reasoning process in this sequence, i.e. that it is applied after interpretation, means that from the functional point of view it may be appropriate to look upon the principles of evaluation as *methodological meta-rules*. In line with this, the process

137 *Cf. supra* section 5.4.5. *and e.g.* Cardozo *supra* note 2, at 102, "[T]he goal, is the main thing. There can be no wisdom in the choice of a path unless we know where it will lead. The teleological conception of his function must be ever in the judge's mind." *and* Jackson *supra* note 77, at 386 "Even transparently simple applications of settled law to facts entail teleological (means-end) reasoning."

138 *Cf.* on sequences in legal reasoning, Strömholm *supra* chapter 1 note 29, at 426. and MacCormick, Summers *supra* note 45, at 531.

of evaluation may be also perceived as the process of interpretation of hypothetical rule application.[139]

A close investigation of the reasoning process indicates thus that interpretation and evaluation are guided by two different kinds of methodological rules. The methodological rules concerning interpretation focus on the ways in which legal propositions may be established and transformed. The rules concerning evaluation, on the other hand, indicate and describe the factors that may be used in the assessment of decisions. In practice this entails that evaluation is very much a process during which legal decisions are related to the *goal and purpose* of the legal system.

5.6.2 The Relative Importance of Evaluation

5.6.2.1 Goal Rationality and Rule Rationality

There is a great variety of opinions concerning the degree to which the process of evaluation may actually affect the outcome of legal reasoning. It is sometimes suggested that evaluation is the most influential part of the process and that the active use of legal rules merely fulfils the function of providing a façade legitimation of the decision that has been arrived at with the help of an informal use of juridical discretion of a subjective nature.[140]

Others have argued that legal reasoning is a process guided by *goal-rationality* which means that the final goal is perceived as a decisive factor indicating the ways in which the legal reasoning process will develop. From the perspective founded on goal rationality it is assumed that the methodological rules that come into use are the ones that will let the lawyer arrive at the goal in the most effective way.

[139] *Cf.* Gottlieb *supra* chapter 2 note 5, at 76 "The contemplated applications of the rule advocated play a considerable role in shaping it."

[140] In this discussion it is easy to see the reflections of the previously mentioned debate between legal positivists and legal realists. *See e.g.* Ross *supra* chapter 2 note 99, at 179, Frank, J. *Law and the Modern Mind,* 148-59 (1930) "[M]uch effort is devoted 'keeping the record straight'; that is, to making it appear that decisions and opinions have more of the logical and less of the psychological than is possible" (citation from p 156). *Compare* MacCormick, Summers *supra* note 45, at 16-18.

The critics of this approach, on the other hand, argue that the goal-oriented process of legal reasoning would run the a risk of being determined by subjective considerations or political assumptions and would thus be of a very unpredictable nature. In line with this it has been suggested that law's purpose should be allowed to influence only the final phase of legal reasoning and, furthermore, that the goal oriented approach may be employed only as a method for evaluating rule applications which are indicated by supplementary interpretation (e.g. analogical interpretation or interpretation by means of reduction). The latter form of reasoning is sometimes referred to as legal reasoning guided by *rule-rationality*.[141]

5.6.2.2 Teleology – Subjective and Objective Evaluation

The process of determining the purpose of the law is discussed not only in terms of goal and rule rationality. A somewhat more moderate approach that may help to explain in what way evaluation may affect the reasoning process is often referred to as the teleological method.[142] The approach has been extensively discussed in legal theory. Two major forms of teleological method may be perceived: the *objective teleological method* and *the subjective teleological method*.[143]

The objective teleological interpretation may be roughly described as a process in which the lawyer has to determine the objective purpose of the law. Objectivity means here that the inquiry does not need to be restricted to the discovery of the intention of the lawmaker. Besides that it is possible to adjust the hypothesized original purpose to the succeeding social changes, etc.[144] This approach gives the lawyer a considerable

141 *See, e.g.*, on goal and rule oriented legal reasoning, Bruun, N., Wilhelmsson, T. *Rätten, moralen och det juridiska paradigmet*, 708 (1983).

142 *See, e.g.*, Strömholm *supra* chapter 1 note 29, at 321-22, 344-45, 404, 428-37 *and* MacCormick, Summers *supra* note 45, at 26, 43, 44, 514, 518-21. 523-24.

143 *Cf., e.g.*, Strömholm *supra* chapter 1 note 29, at 403-05, MacCormick, Summers *supra* note 45, at 93, 316, 518-21. A variant of teleological interpretation similar to legal reasoning guided by goal rationality that sometimes appears in works of jurisprudence is *the radical teleological method*, stating that the purpose of the law should guide the lawyer during the whole process of legal reasoning, and not only in the final evaluation phase. *See e.g.* MacCormick, Summers *supra* note 45, at 317.

144 *Cf.* Strömholm *supra* chapter 1 note 29, at 403.

freedom to form legal decisions in line with his personal views, but it does not give the decision maker unrestricted liberty since it is assumed that inferences must be drawn from the propositions contained in substantive law and that accepted methodological rules as well as rules of formality will be considered.

The subjective teleological interpretation means, in contrast, that the lawyer must try to find out about (and rely on) the intentions of the law-maker such as they were when the law was formulated. The advocates of the latter doctrine also indicate several, more or less controversial ways of establishing the true intentions of the legislator.[145] In this respect the subjective teleological method is similar to intentional interpretation. That is to say that in order to reveal the true meaning of the law a lawyer may have to turn to legislative preparatory material of various kinds.

In jurisprudence, a vivid debate goes on among the supporters of different approaches to the teleological method. The objective teleological interpretation is not, for instance, an undisputed method for the adjustment of rule applications. A variety of approaches ranging from ideological conceptions to sociological and statistical evaluations of rules in action have been suggested as a means of determining the goals of the legislator in a more or less objective way in cases when formal reasons and other legal indications are difficult to find. It is also clear that various solutions to legal issues are often suggested by lawyers with different preferences. Likewise, different lawyers become spokesmen for various ideas. In consequence, critics argue sometimes that objective teleological interpretation puts the principles of legality and equality in peril.

The subjective teleological method is not, however, completely uncontroversial either. To arrive at a clear and indisputable solution of a legal issue by means of determining the intended purpose of the legislator may be quite a difficult task for several reasons. An obvious complication here is that occasionally more than one purpose is embedded in a statute, e.g. that a given rule should give a solution to a certain issue but also that the consequences of that rule application should be in harmony with the rule-system as a whole. On many occasions it may be also very difficult to establish the true purpose of the legislator because of the length of time

145 *Id.*

that passed since the law was issued. Additional problems, concerning e.g. vagueness may appear in the process of interpreting the intentions that may have to be identified.[146]

In this context it is worth noticing that texts containing final statutes often reflect the fact of political compromise and that a certain amount of vagueness remaining in legal propositions may have been intended by the lawmaker, e.g. for political reasons. Similar instances of vagueness may be reflected in legislative preparatory material as well as in legal decisions. The reasons behind this may be in the latter case not only that the decisions are based on compromise, but also that in some cases it is very difficult to establish the underlying reasons for a certain decision in an explicit and uncontroversial manner.

In practice, the conflict between the two kinds of teleological interpretation is sometimes apparent. That is to say that a given view on how to evaluate a certain issue may be crucial to the outcome of a decision in a difficult case, e.g. a complicated issue in a field of law where there are few statutes and precedents. Simultaneously, however, in areas with well established rules, as for instance in fields where a large number of consistent decisions can be found and where common problems are well identified and easily predictable, the possibilities of choosing between the various teleological methods may be very restricted.[147]

5.6.3 General Standards for Evaluation

5.6.3.1 Canons of Interpretation

Despite the existence of various assumptions about the role of evaluation in legal reasoning some rather obvious factors can be found that may facilitate the evaluation process and indicate whether a legal decision is of acceptable quality.

[146] Noticeable is thereby also that in some jurisdictions the utilization of legislative preparatory material may be restricted due to formal reasons or the doctrine of legal sources. *Cf. e.g.*, on "the U.K. prohibitions against the use of committee reports and records of parliamentary debates.", MacCormick, Summers *supra* note 45, at 472.

[147] *Cf.* Gottlieb *supra* chapter 2 note 5, at 114. *See also*, for further elaborations on the role of evaluation in legal reasoning, e.g. MacCormick 100-29, (second order justification) *and* Wasserstrom *supra* chapter 2 note 3, at 138-71 (two-level procedure of justification).

Several attempts have been made to describe such factors and their influence on the legal reasoning process. Moreover, many considerations of evaluative nature have been submitted in a rule-like form. These are often referred to as *canons of interpretation* or *canons of construction.* One rather elaborate example was provided by Llewellyn in 1960 who listed a large number of maxims in a tabulated form such as: "To effect its purpose a statute may be implemented beyond its text."[148] and "[I]f extreme hardship will result from a literal application of the words, this may be taken as evidence that the legislature did not use them literally."[149]

On many occasions guide-lines of this kind will no doubt give explicit answers to difficult questions. The principles of evaluation are, nevertheless, seldom unbiased and uncontroversial. An important observation that may be made here is therefore that the existence of a large number of legal evaluation principles does not necessarily facilitate the process. After analysing the contributions from several legal philosophers *Gidon Gottlieb* observes that "there is scarcely a rule of statute interpretation, however orthodox, which is not qualified by large exceptions 'some of which so nearly approach flat contradiction that the rule itself seems to totter on its base'."[150] Gottlieb also reminds us about the comments provided by Llewellyn who concludes that "there are two opposing canons on almost every point."[151]

It is therefore obvious that although the canons of interpretation, may have a decisive influence on the choice between various methods of interpretation in some cases, they cannot be a sufficient means of describing the way in which the evaluation of legal decisions must be completed. The existence of contradictory principles as regards interpretation indicates that the rational principles of evaluation must be sought after at an even higher level of abstraction. In this way, canons of interpretation constitute

148 Llewellyn *supra* chapter 2 note 29, *at* 522.

149 *Id.* at 529 (citing Ballon v. Kemp, 92 F.2d 556, 558 (D.C. Cir. 1937).

150 Gottlieb *supra* chapter 2 note 5, at 102, with reference to Wurzel, *Methods of Juridical Thinking,* 311 (1917).

151 Llewellyn, K.N. *Remarks on the Theory of Appellate Decision and on the Rules or Canons About how Statues are to be Construed,* 401 (1950).

a middle level in the hierarchy of methodological rules related to interpretation and evaluation.

The following subsections discusses various factors that may facilitate the evaluation process. To some extent, factors and/or general principles that may be of relevance for the evaluation of legal decisions are reflected in the legal system as well as in works of jurisprudence. This is, however, not always the case. It is obvious that legal decisions must be also related to the elements of a general, i.e. non-legal nature.[152] In consequence, two general approaches can be perceived in the process of evaluation: the utilization of a) factors and indicators that (in addition to canons of interpretation) may be found within the legal system (*legal evaluation*), and b) general standards for decision making (*supplementary evaluation*).

5.6.3.2 Legal Evaluation

As a starting point for a discussion of the general principles of evaluation it is important to point out that evaluations of actual cases include a study of the consequences following from *individual* legal decisions. Since it is obvious that legal decisions will produce different kinds of consequences in different fields of the law it should be kept in mind that *evaluation is a highly domain-dependent process* and that legal principles employed for evaluation purposes that would be of a truly general and substantive nature are rather difficult to find.

Some guide-lines that may help to evaluate legal decisions are reflected, nevertheless, in legislation and other kinds of legal sources. One example is provided by the Swedish constitution which sets forth general rules for the evaluation of intended legislation. The rules are thereby restricted to a very special kind of legal decision making. As suggested in the introductory section of this chapter, however, from the functional point of view there would be little reason to make a distinction between the process of legislation and the process of legal reasoning – the process of legislation necessarily involves the activation of all the mechanisms that

152 *Cf. e.g.* Gottlieb *supra* chapter 2 note 5, at 120 on "legal rules as a sub-species of rules" *and* Summers *supra* note 29, at 713.

appear in individual legal decisions, and the existing similarities between the two processes become most apparent in the evaluation phase.[153]

The rules that appear in the Swedish constitution are addressed to *The legislation council* – a board of senior judges whose function it is to comment on proposed legislation from the legal point of view. According to this regulation the council is obliged to investigate a proposed statute with respect to

> "1. how the bill is related to the constitution and to the rest of the legal order,
> 2. how the rules within the bill are related to each other,
> 3. how the bill is related to the demands concerning the rule of law (*rechtssicherheit*),
> 4. whether the bill is designed so that the intentions may be accomplished."

The council must also

> "5. make an inventory of the problems that may appear in the employment [of the intended legislation]."[154]

The use of a legislation council is an example of a method by which evaluation issues can be submitted to a special group of persons. In this respect there are similarities to the previously discussed process of submitting issues of interpretation to public authorities and/or juries.

It should be mentioned that a procedure by which a certain issue is delegated to a special group of persons (or to a certain authority) does not necessarily change the nature of the factors that may be important for the outcome of the evaluation process. On the other hand, delegation may be a way to ensure that the existing expert knowledge is actually being used. To submit issues of evaluation to a council of senior judges is thus a way to ensure that legal aspects are considered in a professional manner. Likewise, submitting a certain issue to a jury will ensure that common moral and ethical standards will become incorporated into legal reasoning.

153 *See*, for similar standpoints, Cardozo *supra* note 2, at 103 "the final principle of selection for judges, as for legislators, is one of fitness to an end." *and* Hellner *supra* chapter 2 note 110, at 19-20, 158.

154 RF chapter 8, section 18, paragraph 3, (original text in Swedish).

5.6.3.2.1 Consistency

The analysis of the substance of the above mentioned rules concerning the evaluation of the intended legislation shows that the aspects of consistency play an important role in any particular instance of evaluation.

The desire for consistency is well recognized in the legal domain and it is also something that often appears in discussions concerning legal reasoning.[155] Issues related to consistency has been previously discussed in this study also in section 5.2. concerning the utilization of background knowledge in the identification phase and in section 5.5.4. in relation to accuracy in rule applications.

The only noticeable difference when comparing the considerations of consistency during the processes of identification and rule application with similar considerations in the evaluation of legal decisions is that in the latter, evaluation may have to examine a composed decision or a set of rules on an aggregated level. Many of the underlying guide-lines that are discussed in the above mentioned sections (e.g. predictability, equality, etc.) are therefore of direct relevance to evaluation as well. In the process of evaluation consistency means that legal decisions (bills) must be in line with previous decisions (statutes), not contradicting them. In practice, this means that if there is a statute or a legal precedent concerning similar matters, it must be possible to relate the intended decision to the previous proposition. Alternatively, it must be shown in a convincing way that the current situation differs from the matters in question in some vital part.

5.6.3.2.2 Generality

Evaluation is guided not only by the aspects of consistency. When previous decisions or authoritative rules cannot be extracted, other factors must be considered. This means, of course, that when rules of a substantive nature cannot be used lawyers will feel in most cases obliged to search for solutions that can be described in general terms, the ultimate objective being to be able to refer to a rule. If this is not possible, however, it may be assumed that lawyers will more or less consciously try

155 *See, e.g. The Statute of the International Court of Justice,* Article 38, Alchourrón, Bulygin *supra* chapter 2 note 4, at 172, Peczenik, A. *The Basis of Legal Justification,* 91 (1983) *and* MacCormick, Summers *supra* note 45, *passim.*

to arrive at a decision that will be valid for a group of (eventually hypothesized) decisions. In practice it means that legal decision making should try avoiding too detailed specifications of legal concepts.[156]

This makes it easy to see that the general desire for consistency in legal reasoning is closely related to the basic need of procuring solutions of, at least to some extent, general nature.

This general wish for generality in legal decision making is well documented in works of jurisprudence[157] and it is doubtless a reflection of the awareness of the fact that ad hoc solutions may be often easily ruled out. Decisions based on generalizations force the lawyer to contemplate the implications and the consequences of his conclusions in a more extensive manner. A desire to attain general solutions may thus also help a lawyer to arrive at legal decisions that are more sound.

5.6.3.2.3 Relevance

In the process of assessing the intended legal decisions it must be also noticed that there exists an upper limit as to the extent to which a legal decision may be generalized. That is to say that a decision or an argument must not be so general that it may be used to motivate any conclusions whatsoever. In other words, a legal decision must stand out as relevant and be related in some way to the elements that appear in the situation.

Relevancy may in turn concern several different things. A legal decision may not only appear to be irrelevant due to the fact that the conclusions have been based on too high levels of generalization. A legal decision may also be irrelevant due to the fact that the relations between the facts and the implied consequences are to some extent inappropriate. In other words, the relations between the purported concepts and the alleged consequences must not be too far fetched or illogical.[158]

156 *Cf.* on the advantages and disadvantages of various degrees of *schematising* in legislation, Hellner *supra* chapter 2 note 110, at 207.

157 *See, e.g.* Cardozo *supra* note 2, at 102-03 ,"The rule that functions well produces a title deed to recognition. Only in determining how it functions we must not view it to narrowly. We must not sacrifice the general to the particular."

158 *See, e.g.*, Peczenik *supra* chapter 2 note 72, at 120-29, Hellner, *supra* chapter 2 note 123, at 39-49, who makes a difference between logical rationality, reasonable rationality and intellectual rationality (intellectual honesty) *and* Strömholm *supra* chapter 1 note 29, at 423-24.

In actual instances of legal reasoning this latter aspect may create many difficulties as, e.g., in deciding the extent to which various chains of events may be considered as relevant from the legal point of view. As a result, a vast jurisprudential literature has accumulated on such matters as *adequate causality* and examples of what a (hypothesized) *bonus pater familias* (reasonable man of ordinary prudence) ought to have done or foreseen in various situations.[159]

5.6.3.2.4 Explicitness

When discussing evaluation one must not forget that a legal decision must be acceptable not only from the formal and the legal points of view, but also that it must be comprehensible to the persons involved. In other words, a legal decision must not only be in accordance with the professional standards as regards the use of technical legal concepts but it must also conform to the common understanding of the words and concepts that are employed.[160] Legal decisions are quite often addressed to persons without legal training and from this follows that lawyers must always remember that in legal reasoning it is not possible to use words or concepts in an unlimited way. In other words, expressions that have a distinct meaning in ordinary language cannot be transformed so that they contradict that meaning.

The fact that decisions must be understandable from the layman's perspective also sets up standards concerning the necessity to motivate decisions in a comprehensible and logical way. Explicitness is therefore an aspect that to a large extent depends on the nature of the concepts and notions involved. That is to say that a decision based on highly technical legal concepts makes relatively higher demands on the standards of the explicitness of the accompanying explanations.

159 The concepts of adequate causality and bonus pater familias are examples from the field of the law of damages. *See, e.g.*, for the elaboration of corresponding notions (remoteness of damage and standard of care) in Anglo-American law, Fleming, J.G. *The Law of Torts*, 102-08, 170-227 (1983).

160 *Cf.* Strömholm *supra* chapter 1 note 29, at 441-42.

5.6.3.3 Supplementing Evaluation – The Limits of Law

Despite many attempts to formalize evaluation, i.e. to formulate general principles governing it, it is clear that discussions about the objectives of any legal system at a certain level of abstraction will encounter problems and show differences of opinions. It is, for example, easy to see that certain aspects of legal consistency and those of explicitness may occasionally clash. This can be noticed, e.g. in the use of technical legal concepts as opposed to ordinary, everyday language understandable to people that are not trained in law. The reason for this is simply that people possess different kinds of background knowledge and understand legal propositions in different ways.

A similar conflict can be perceived between the evaluative aspects based on the principles of generality and the demand for relevance.[161] An attempt to provide general solutions may easily conflict with the need to adjust the decisions to some specific factors of the current case. (Is the ultimate objective of the legal system to solve actual cases so that balance between the interests of the parties involved is preserved, or is it to furnish a structure that will provide predictability and stability on a general level?) An example from Wasserstrom may illustrate this dilemma:

> Imagine the plight of Widow Jones, who lives with her six children on an old and heavily mortgaged farm. It is winter and perhaps a light snow has begun to fall. The date upon which the mortgage payment was due has come and gone. Bachelor Smith, already the richest man in town, holds the mortgage on the land. He goes into court seeking an order which would foreclose the mortgage and evict the widow. What decision would a court be justified in giving?[162]

After a discussion of various solutions Wasserstrom remarks that a decision in favour of Smith "considering merely the respective positions of

161 *Cf.* Peczenik *supra* note 155, at 90.

162 Wasserstrom *supra* chapter 2 note 3, at 141. A distinction between different kinds of goals in legal reasoning appears in works of jurisprudence under various names. *See e.g.* Hellner *supra* chapter 2 note 110, at 178 (primary goals and end goals).

the parties before the court . . . would be heartless and inhuman . . ." He concludes nevertheless that

> The practice of adjudicating mortgage cases on this basis might have the effect . . . of destroying the utility of those security devices upon which mortgage transactions depend. Potential creditors might quite understandably be reluctant to lend money to those persons who probably would be hurt most by forfeiture of the mortgaged property in case of default. Thus, those who were most in need of some device by which they could borrow money would probably be unable to find willing lenders.[163]

From this example it is clear that the underlying reasons for the standards giving preference to solutions that impose consistency are quite strong. In some situations, however, the facts that they appear in the current case may be of such a special nature that they outweigh the arguments that can be derived from consistency aspects. Such a stand-point has, for example, been expressed by *Robert S. Summers*:

> It is important to be clear that formal reasoning is nearly always subject to limitations. At some point in the application of even the most formal reason, it may become appropriate to examine substantive reasons and even to allow substantive reasons to outweigh formal reasoning.
>
> . . . if the statute seems to lead to absurd or outrageous results, substantive reasons may outweigh the formal reasoning involved in literal application.[164]

In situations of the above kind, implied by Summers it is clear that when the legal system cannot provide sufficient support other forms of arguments will have to take over. It may be therefore concluded that in addition to easy access to a more or less comprehensible corpus of legal knowledge, a good understanding of what may be acceptable in the social environment of the intended legal decision as well as experience and knowledge of previous completed rule applications including their effects are doubtless other important aspects of legal expertise in this phase. The

163 *Id.* at 142.

164 Summers *supra* note 29, at 705.

distinctive and domain-bound nature of legal reasoning makes it in turn possible to assume that lawyers have to a large extent rely on their own practical experiences derived from legal decision making. This may be tentatively expressed as the knowledge of consequence structures. In this respect we are back at the point where it is possible to claim that law is experience and a legal system cannot provide much assistance.[165]

As this investigation of legal reasoning has shown, however, there is little need to resort to this kind of rule scepticism. The decomposition of the legal reasoning process shows that in the course of the process the law provides the decision maker with a rather elaborated methodological support, minimizing the influence of irrationality and chance. Thus, although it must be admitted that under certain conditions legal rules will lose their effectiveness and other kinds of considerations will take over, it must be emphasised that factors of a non-legal nature have normally a rather restricted influence. This is at least the case in well-developed legal systems.

It is beyond the scope of this study to incorporate any extensive discussion concerning factors of a non legal nature and their ultimate effects on the process of evaluation. As a final observation to keep in mind it may be, however, remembered that the types of arguments that may be employed for the justification of a legal decision are domain-bound and that the factors which are relevant in this aspect of legal reasoning are to a large extent the reflections of the moral and the ethical standards of the social environment surrounding the legal system.[166] In addition it would be reasonable to assume that e.g. economic factors and efficiency aspects might also influence the process.[167] Likewise, it has been convincingly

165 *See, e.g.*, Cardozo *supra* note 2, at 102 "This means, of course, that the juristic philosophy of the common law is at bottom the philosophy of pragmatism." *and* Wasserstrom *supra* chapter 2 note 3, at 138 "[The] procedure has as its rule of decision the rule which prescribes that a decision is justifiable if and only if is deductible from the legal rule whose introduction and employment can be shown to be *more desirable* than any other possible rule." (Italics added.)

166 Gottlieb *supra* chapter 2 note 5, at 61 "facts and cows have this in common: they may be sacred in India but not in the U.S. The importance of cows and the relevance of what happens to them depends on their place and function in the community".

167 MacCormick, Summers *supra* note 45, at 469.

demonstrated that in many cases also irrational aspects (e.g. the personality of the judge) may affect the outcome of a legal decision.[168]

5.7 *Formulation*

The process of legal reasoning terminates with the formulation of the decision. Formulation may be performed in speech or in writing, or even by means of combining the two. Like many other sub-processes of legal reasoning the formulation activities are also governed by formal rules setting up explicit standards. That is to say that in some cases formal rules along with established traditions provide rather firm frameworks as regards the form and the content of legal decisions. This is perhaps most apparent in the case of written decisions.

Methodological rules concerning formulation are often of an authoritative nature which means that a violation of a rule, concerning e.g. the requirement to present a given decision in the written form may easily obliterate the effects of the reasoning process.[169] It is also noticeable that in many cases rules concerning formulation require that not only the final decision but also the reasons behind a certain conclusion must be made explicit.[170] On some occasions several rules governing formulation are interconnected, which makes that a rather formalized procedure is required for the formulation of a legal decision. This is for instance the case when the rules stipulate that certain documents must be a) in a written form, b) signed by the persons involved in the act, c) signed by witnesses and d) marked with a stamp or similar token indicating that e.g. a given act has been registered by a public authority, and e) accompanied by instructions concerning the submission of appeals.

It is also necessary to note that a large number of facts of a non-substantive nature may sometimes have to be included in (or added to) a legal decision. Examples of such facts are the names and addresses of the parties

[168] *See, e.g.*, Schubert *supra* chapter 2 note 8, *passim* and SARI. *Straffmätning*, 13 (1980).

[169] *Compare* Summers *supra* note 29.

[170] This is for instance the case in Sweden where courts and authorities are obliged to explicitly state the reasons for their decisions. *See* RB chapter 17 (concerning decisions based on civil law), section 7, chapter 30, section 5 (criminal law) *and* (SFS 1971:291) section 30 (administrative law).

involved, the identification code of a decision, the name of the presiding judge, the name of the deciding court, instructions for appeals, and so forth.[171] In this respect it should be remembered that the process of formulation is not only extremely domain-bound, but that it also depends on the kind of decision which is to be formulated. For example, a decision that is communicated in an in-house memorandum may be in most cases formulated in a different manner than a court decision.

Authoritative rules concerning the formulation of legal decisions do not, however, determine only the outer form of the final statement. In addition, formal rules may limit the possibilities of an individual formulation of the reasons for a given decision. In some cases a lawyer may be forced to use predefined forms, and, as in Swedish courts, he may have to adhere to administrative rules as regards the systematic aspects of decisions.[172]

In practice it can be also noticed that standard-texts often guide the formulation of legal decisions. This is especially common in situations where a lawyer has to handle mass-cases or make legal decisions under time constraints, as is often the case in courts and in public service. Under such conditions a lawyer often works with forms or with previously defined decision-alternatives. Former decisions may also direct influence the outcome of a given decision in extreme cases – the task of formulating a more precise and comprehensive decision may be so exhausting that it may be wise to employ a formulation that has been elaborated and refined in a previous decision. Naturally, such a method of formulation may endanger the quality of the decision, since a more subtle formulation would express certain aspects in a more precise manner perhaps. Nevertheless, lawyers may use this kind of formulation-technique in a conscious way, especially in work-situations where they are pressed for time. In a similar way, quotations and legally adopted phrases serve the same purpose, although in various degrees, e.g. when frequently appearing forms of evidence are to be discussed or when standard motivations are to be used.

In complicated cases the situation is different. Here the skilful use of written language is an obvious and necessary aid to legal expertise. Thus,

[171] *See, e.g.*, for further examples the *Rules of the International Court of Justice*, Article 95.

[172] *See e.g.* Domstolsverket, *Bestämmelser om avfattning av dom och slutligt beslut i brottmål m.m.* (1986).

the demand for expert performance usually increases with the complexity of the case and with the ambiguity of the legal propositions that are to be applied. It may nevertheless be presumed that an even more important aspect concerning the need for expert skill in formulation is probably the frequency at which a legal issue appears. This is simply to say that also issues of a difficult and complicated nature may have been decided on previous occasions. Provided that the relevant features of the decisions in questions are similar and that the previous decisions are of high quality it may be possible (and time saving) to consult the files in order to extract the previously elaborated formulations. In many kinds of legal work this is probably a very common way of solving difficult issues related to formulation.[173]

Generally speaking, formulation becomes a more complicated task when decisions are based on analogical inferences or other forms of supplementing interpretation. That is to say that interpretation by analogy and similar approaches may have to include an extension of legal propositions and may therefore also require more cautious formulation activities incorporating, perhaps, extensive motivations and discussions of pros and cons of various solutions.

The fact that legal decisions often become a part of a larger corpus of legal knowledge means that also an extensive and skilful use of various kinds of reference techniques is an important element of legal writing.[174] By referring to the previously published and well-established legal material (e.g. statutes, precedents, etc.), lengthy motivations and repetitions may be avoided.

It is also noticeable that the writing process may be rather time-consuming. This, in addition to the fact that writing forces the lawyer to formulate his decision in an, at least seemingly, logical, and convincing manner, makes it possible to infer that the analysis conducted during the writing process is often one of the most significant phases in legal reasoning. In cases where the formal rules concerning formulation stipulate that also the

173 We are here basically relying on observations and personal experiences from Swedish district courts. This aspect of formulation is however also reflected in ''semi-authoritative'' publications on legal writing which include also lists of common legal phrases as well as recommendations concerning the use of such phrases. *See e.g.* Svea hovrätt. *Språket i domar och beslut* (1987).

174 Hellner *supra* chapter 2 note 110, at 244-48.

reasons behind a certain decision must be submitted in a written form, it may be even assumed that the process of formulating a legal decision will have a strong influence on the outcome of the decision. The process of writing makes it easier not only to systematize one's arguments and reasons but it also enables one to detect any logical lapses. Formulation activities may therefore often indicate that another round of legal reasoning is necessary.

In addition, several technical aspects which are related to writing skills may be mentioned. These include the ability to systemize (a large-scale organization of issues and arguments as well as a small-scale organization of paragraphs and sentences), a cautious use of undefined concepts (i.e. a frequent use of explicit explanations), the ability to sustain logical rigidity, and so forth.[175]

It should be also kept in mind at all times that legal decisions are intended not only for the use of individuals trained in law. A legal decision must be therefore formulated and phrased in such a way that it is understandable to all the parties involved in the issue – also the laymen. The formulation of legal decisions in writing requires therefore not only skilful handling of the technical and semantical aspects of conformity with respect to the legal material, but also a pedagogic skill concerning the ability to describe these concepts and notions in a non-technical way, ''digestible'' and comprehensible to the average reader without legal training.[176]

When it comes to the formulation of legal decisions in spoken language, other kinds of abilities come into focus. In addition to a talent for expressing arguments and descriptions of various kinds verbally, rhetorical and psychological elements play an important role. It is, for instance, obvious that arguments may be submitted in a more or less persuasive way and that the ability to express one's authority, inspire confidence, as well as overall

175 *See e.g.* for general standards for legal writing and for further references, *Id.* at 217-251, Svea hovrätt *supra* note 173 *and* Squires, L.B., Rombauer, M.D. *Legal Writing* (1982).

176 *Cf.*, on the rational evaluation of legal decisions, *supra* section 5.6.3 *and see,* on the formulation of court decisions in Sweden, e.g. Heuman, L. *Rättspraxis*, 122-126 (1988) who discusses two major alternatives in the formulation of legal principles – casuistic and general formulation. Heuman also recognizes that the courts often prefer precise expressions of a legal nature as compared to formulations understandable to laymen.

personal appearances of the presenter can greatly influence the way in which an orally submitted decision will be received.

Finally, it should be mentioned that the effects of legal reasoning naturally are also closely related to the kinds of distribution and communication facilities that are available.[177]

5.8 *Learning*

Any realistic model of legal reasoning must consider that fact that since law has dynamic nature, profound, high quality legal knowledge cannot be static either. In consequence, legal reasoning must be also related to the learning ability – all lawyers must be able to cope with changes and to incorporate new elements into the ever-growing corpus of legal knowledge.

Changes, in turn, may be of very different kinds. They may not only concern details (a new case, for example, may provide a new interpretation on some particular concept) but may also affect basic rule-structures (as in the case of the launching of a new statute or a group of statutes, e.g. a new tax-system).

As to the nature of legal systems taken as a whole, it may be postulated that in the majority of cases the occurring changes concern details. This is a reflection of the ordinary activities in the legal domain. In other words, amendments, refinements and minor elaborations normally appear as consequences of day-to-day legal work, as it is conducted in courts, by public authorities, etc. Changes of a fundamental nature, on the other hand, are preceded by the introduction of legislative acts, lengthy processes of preparatory work, etc. and occur more seldom.

The changing nature of the legal system may give rise to complications affecting legal reasoning. The fragmented nature of legal knowledge and the fact that changes often concern details cause that it may be difficult to know when the law has been modified in some aspect. From this in turn follows that effective legal reasoning is to some extent related to the existence of a control system that may help the lawyer to detect and draw consequences from changes in a large number of legal sources. In practice this means that lawyers are dependent on communication facilities and

177 These aspects are not addressed in this study. *See,* for a comprehensive analysis and for further references, Bing, J. *Rettslige kommunikasjonsprosesser* (1982).

legal information systems of various kinds (e.g. libraries, periodical publications, etc.)

When discussing the learning process one must also keep in mind the fact that legal knowledge appears in many shapes and that learning cannot only concern the external changes occurring in the legal system on an aggregated level. As indicated in the previous subsections of this chapter, legal knowledge is based to a large extent on the lawyer's personal experience and his background knowledge. From the fact that one's own experience plays an important role in the learning process follows also that the elements and facts memorised by a lawyer will be of a highly individual nature (e.g. the recollection of clients, situations in court, etc.). As a consequence, legal knowledge structures of a secondary nature may play a vital role in the learning process, by providing a structure for the organisation of legal knowledge.[178]

The fact that background structures are rather significant components affecting the way in which the learning process will develop emphasises again the characteristic and subjective nature of legal reasoning. It is also clear that the occurring changes affect not only legal knowledge of a substantive nature. Modifications may also be related to various forms of methodological and/or formal rules. In this way one can easily see that learning is a continuous, subjective process advancing on many levels and developing together with the growing experience of the lawyer.

5.9 Summary and Conclusions

The decomposition of legal reasoning into phases makes it possible to identify and categorize the factors influencing the ways in which each phase is operated. Or – in a less pretentious perspective – to identify the factors that – according to the legal theory – ought to determine how each phase should be operated.

Hence, an obvious conclusion that can be drawn from the survey conducted in this chapter is that a considerable number of factors governing the legal reasoning process can be found within the legal system. Legal propositions that have a decisive influence on the process appear both in

178 Bing *supra* chapter 1 note 48, at 233.

the form of substantive law and as various kinds of secondary knowledge structures.

In terms of generality, extensiveness, etc. the nature of the relevant legal propositions varies, not only as regards the different fields of law, but also by the nature of the issues that are approached. Another conclusion that may be drawn here is therefore that legal reasoning is to a large extent a domain-dependent activity. That is to say that the legal reasoning process and its components are directed by the structure of the relevant substantive law and by the methodological rules applying to the particular issue. In consequence, it may be claimed that there are no indications concerning the existence of any general legal problem solving mechanism.

It must be also acknowledged that legal factors and their role in legal reasoning are limited and that sometimes factors of a non-legal nature may have to be taken into consideration. This is especially obvious when it comes to the evaluation of decisions.

With these background considerations in mind, the investigation of the legal reasoning process and the analysis of various kinds of sub-processes, significant factors, and methodological rules may be summarized in the following way:

Identification is a process that may be decomposed into three sub-processes, the *establishment of relevancy*, the *identification of supplementing facts*, and the *resolution of uncertainty*. It may be furthermore assumed that these sub-processes are activated one after the other and that they are of a *recurrent* nature. The success of the identification process – and especially the establishment of relevancy – depends on the lawyer's access to a legal scheme of interpretation, i.e. a *background knowledge reflecting basic legal concepts and notions* of a substantive nature. In the process of identification of supplementary facts, the lawyer relies also on his ability to utilize *legal conceptual structures* in a more or less check-list fashion.

The process of the resolution of uncertainty is facilitated by – in addition to the access to legal background knowledge – the access to *elaborated domain knowledge* of a non legal nature. It may be furthermore assumed that the efficiency of identification is inseparably related to the extensiveness and the quality of the available background knowledge.

Law search is a process interacting with identification and it is also therefore a process of a recurrent nature. The process is activated by the factors that have been instantiated during the successive phases of the identification process and depends on the activation of different kinds of *legal structures*, i.e. relations between legal components at various levels of abstraction. Legal structures are thereby activated by association, the objective being to find legal propositions that will be similar to the current fact or situation. Usable structures to activate may be either of an external nature (e.g. consisting of documents and texts in legal publications) or of an internal and/or individual nature (e.g. consisting of legal concepts, rules and issues reflected in the background knowledge of lawyers). Many legal structures are necessarily interrelated with each other and may come to use in the successive phases of the process. In relation to the external structures of legal knowledge, various *search tools* have been developed (e.g. legal IR-systems, indexes, library classification systems, etc.) The activation of such external tools presupposes often in turn the ability to transform the conceived legal concepts into explicit terms.

In most legal systems it is also possible to gain support from a *doctrine of legal sources,* which guides the establishment of the *hierarchical order* of various forms of legal knowledge. The existence of a hierarchical order between various forms of legal knowledge may require that material on a lower level is extracted only if a higher level fails to provide sufficient knowledge. The hierarchical order reflects in turn the origins and/or the established customary use of different kinds of legal material. Rules governing the sequencing of the search process may be frequently immanent in the latter case in the physical organization of the process of legal work.

During *interpretation* a legal proposition of a substantive nature must be related to a legal rule. Two general kinds of problems may arise – problems concerning *vagueness* and problems concerning *rule conflicts*.

From the legal system it is possible to obtain at least three types of support when problems with vagueness appear: *definitional support* (explicit representations of legal conceptual structures), *intentional support* (descriptions of goals and purposes of legal concepts and legal rules), and *methodological support* (descriptions of appropriate facts and procedures that are to be considered in the process).

Interpretation may have to be complemented with *supplementary approaches* where legal propositions are construed in an active way. The most common of those is the use of *analogy* – a process in which some element of an available antecedent rule-description is replaced by a fact in the current case so that the lawyer may arrive at the desirable, previously described solution. In another approach – *reasoning e contrario* – logical inferences are established on the basis of differences between the current situation and some legal proposition.

Interpretation may be also approached from the *lexical and the grammatical* point of view. In this mode of reasoning, the meaning of legal propositions may be *extended* or *restricted* by means of transforming or elaborating the meaning of the words in the legal knowledge representation. Supplementary interpretation as well as various forms of lexical and grammatical interpretation are reasoning methods of a general nature. They stand in contrast with contextual interpretation which is domain-bound.

As to the problems concerning rule conflict, in many legal systems one can find a number of relatively well-established rules of priority (originating e.g. from the date of origin, the hierarchical order, or levels of specification).

Legal propositions that have been interpreted are then applied in a tentative and recurrent manner in the process of *rule application*. In this phase the process must be adjusted to a number of *formal rules of competence* which determine when, where, and by whom legal decisions may be made. During rule application a lawyer must also consider the *formal principles of legality and equality* which impose certain standards as regards accuracy.

In order to know whether or not the identified facts and legal propositions are relevant, and to understand in which situations different methods of interpretation are suitable, legal decisions must be *evaluated*. For evaluation certain maxims – canons of interpretation have been developed. These may be described as *methodological meta-rules*. Canons of interpretation are however often of a conflicting nature and evaluation implies also that the intended legal decision must be related to the *purpose and the objectives of the legal system.* When the objective has been established, it is possible to adjust the various sub-processes to that objective. Opinions about the relative importance of evaluation vary, but there is a general consensus in jurisprudence as regards the necessity to adjust legal decisions to the principles of *consistency, generality, relevance, and explicitness*.

This may be described as the process of handling the *rules of evaluation.* In individual instances of evaluation it must be admitted, nevertheless, that even *political and moral aspects*, as well as other forms of personal, subjective judgements, may have to be included.

Depending on the domain and the kind of decision that is to be made, in the *formulation* of his decision the lawyer must be also prepared to adjust to *formal rules*. Formal rules concerning formulation may determine not only the *form and content* of the final decision but they may also become a framework for the motivation of the decision. In many instances of legal reasoning it may be assumed that formulation is a very significant process.

The law changes and develops all the time, making that legal reasoning of high quality is always related to the continuous process of learning. In this respect, the lawyer must be prepared not only to accept changes concerning legal phenomena of substantive nature, but he must also be able to change and adjust his understanding of the methodological and the formal aspects of legal knowledge.

Part 3

Potentialities of Automation

6 Automation of Legal Reasoning

6.1 Introduction

The jurisprudential model of legal reasoning (JLR) elaborated in chapter 5 points out the various kinds of legal knowledge that influence legal reasoning. Furthermore the model helps to identify the major kinds of inferences that may have to be activated. The aim of this part of the study is to investigate the ways in which various solutions from the field of AI relate to these premisses.

From the basic assumption that any device intended to assist (or mimic) legal reasoning must have access to a comprehensive representation of legal knowledge follows that an initial undertaking in any analysis of the potentialities of automation must be to explore whether knowledge acquisition is a feasible process in the field of law. Thereafter, the related question concerning the extent to which it is possible to represent legal knowledge so that it may be employed in a legal AI-system must be investigated. These issues no doubt are among the most central ones in all investigations of AI in law. In consequence, they are given comparatively much attention.

Before knowledge acquisition and knowledge representation are scrutinized, however, it is important to recognize the relevance of a large number of non-technical factors determining the presuppositions for all projects in the field of AI and law. This is an obvious and well-known fact and various criteria for a successful AI-system implementation have been discussed during a relatively long time now. Discussions about the suitability of the technique for the performance of various tasks in different domains appear in pure AI literature[1] as well as in the documentation concerning various projects in the field of law.[2]

Hence, section 6.2 provides an overview of some non-technical premisses of a general nature, which are related to the crucial issue concerning the levels of ambition in all AI and law projects. Thereafter, in section

[1] *See, e.g.*, Hayes, Roth *supra* chapter 1 note 2, Harmon, King *supra* chapter 3, note 97 *and* De Salvo, D.A., Liebowitz, J. eds. *Managing Artificial Intelligence & Expert Systems* (1990).

[2] *See, e.g.*, Oskamp, A. *Het ontwikkelen van juridische expertsystemen* (1990), Susskind *supra* chapter 1 note 9, Karpf, J. *A Contribution to a Classification of Legal Models*, 8 (1989), *and* Kracht, de Vey Mestdagh, Svensson *supra* chapter 1 note 33.

6.3, various methods and experiences from legal knowledge acquisition are described. Finally, section 6.4 addresses the important problem of legal knowledge representation. In this way, section 6.2 provides a framework for the analysis undertaken in sections 6.3 - 6.4 which are of a more detailed and technical nature.

6.2 *Preliminary Considerations*

6.2.1 Economic Aspects

Many considerations related to the development of AI-system are well known from the introduction of computer systems of more traditional kinds. In this section, therefore, foremost factors of relevance for legal KBS-development, as they have been identified in the system development projects undertaken in this work will be mentioned.

A basic factor that must be given attention to in all system development activities is for instance the economics of the project. Important to observe right from the start is thereby that economic resources do not only determine the choice between large-scale projects and small-scale systems, but they also affect the possibilities to choose between standard ("off the shelf") systems and customized solutions.

Economic considerations must naturally include estimation of costs as well as possible savings related to the intended system development projects. It is, however, clear that depending on the nature of the domain and the task that is approached, cost/benefit factors may appear in many different shapes. In the commercial sector, for instance, economic advantages may appear in the form of gain of time, less constrained personnel resources, enhanced productivity, etc. Simultaneously, costs may originate from investments in software and hardware, licensing fees, knowledge engineering, maintenance, etc.[3] It is also noticeable that system development necessarily presupposes participation of domain experts and that AI-projects may put a strain on the existing resources in many different ways.[4]

[3] *See*, for further decompositions of cost and benefit aspects, Thompson, D.M., Feinstein, J.L. *Cost Justifying Expert Systems*, 110-11 (1990).

[4] Harmon, King *supra* chapter 3, note 97, at 200.

The fact that AI is a new phenomenon means that in certain domains the economic consequences may be difficult to predict. It is important to note also that costs and benefits related to AI system development may adopt indirect forms. For example, it may be possible to describe certain benefits only in terms of intangible quality aspects.[5] Likewise, the decisions concerning the physical environment, reflected, for example, in previous choices concerning computer system investments, may give rise to the fact that an import of new technology may be exceptionally costly and that AI-technology cannot be integrated without difficulties.

Economic consequences may be also detected and identified when subject matters in a certain domain are scrutinized.

In the legal sector, for instance, it may be argued that a number of principles and procedures (e.g. the right to oral proceedings, the right for the public to attend court proceedings, the principle of directness, etc.) must be vindicated and retained even if a support system should be introduced and despite the fact that these principles and procedures may have initially appeared as economically inefficient from the point of view of a computer consultant.[6]

At the same time more or less stable organizational preconditions may be too expensive to be changed, which will seriously delimit the possibilities of introducing AI-systems in an effective way.[7] Of relevance to system implementation are also the economic consequences connected with the education of the work force, the need to reorganize the organizational structures, to replace people, and similar aspects.[8] It should be also noted that in some cases it may be necessary to compare the prospective benefits following from the system development project with other kinds of options. For example, the operations of a commercial organization (e.g. a law firm) may become constrained due to a demand

[5] *See*, for a number of examples, Thompson, Feinstein *supra* note 3, at 106-09.

[6] From this does not follow, of course, that in the legal sector a reduction in the number of appeals, a higher percentage of successful cases and similar indications cannot be simultaneously a reflection of enhanced quality. On the other hand, pure economic gains, originating e.g. from reduction in time spent on court proceedings, may appear as unmotivated if arguments showing that quality aspects can be vindicated or improved cannot be presented.

[7] Thompson, Feinstein *supra* note 3, at 102-04.

[8] *Id.* at 109-11. *See also*, on the estimation of cost benefit aspects in relation to KBSs in law, Dahnell *supra* chapter 1 note 44.

for a fast return of the investments. System development projects may therefore have to compete with other kinds of urgent and potentially profitable undertakings.

In addition, in the evaluation of cost and benefit aspects it must be remembered that it may be difficult for a single organization to change some of the preconditions. This happens, for instance, when competitive reasons make it impossible not to adjust to some technical standard. In some cases for similar reasons it may be impossible to introduce the AI-systems into an organization, i.e. because the cooperation with other organizations demands the use of computer standards of different kinds.

Finally, it should be mentioned that difficulties related to the calculation of costs and benefits in purely economic terms are especially apparent in the scientific domain. When it comes to research and development projects, short-time economic considerations are obviously less relevant. As a result, in the estimation of the consequences originating from research projects, the calculated benefits may have to be discussed in terms of potential, but rather uncertain long-time advancements of a theoretical and/or methodological nature.

6.2.2 Objectives and Goal Conflicts

In chapter one several motives for undertakings in the field of AI and law were mentioned. The overview indicated that a number of objectives can be present, which is an important factor to consider when the potentialities of automation of legal reasoning are scrutinized.

Sometimes the contrasting interests are the reflections of the various backgrounds of the people involved, which is why they appear in so many different shapes. Occasionally, the lack of a common background results in goal conflicts of an explicit nature. This is the case, for example, when the people involved in a system development project disagree about the purpose of the system or when the submitted research approaches are criticised. In other cases, the lack of a common background is of a less explicit nature and is merely reflected in misinterpretations of various contributions as well as in mistakes occurring during system development.

For natural reasons it is not possible to make a complete inventory of how various motives may affect system development. As a general observation it may be noticed, nevertheless, that different attitudes towards the question what is to be considered as relevant objectives of the undertakings related to automation of legal reasoning are often present among lawyers and technically oriented researchers.[9] In this respect lawyers are more often inclined to perceive tangible systems intended to support practical problems in day-to-day legal work as major objects of concern. Researchers with a technical background, on the other hand, often seem to consider the question as to whether the addressed issue poses a practical problem to be comparatively less important. From the latter point of view a primary objective may be to tackle intricate formalization difficulties, e.g. problems concerning the representation of some aspect of legal knowledge in computer programs. For researchers with technical background it may be also more than sufficient to illustrate the advantages of their contributions by supplying a small-scale prototype, which is comprehensible only to those who master the programming language of the computer in use.[10]

The differences of opinions between technicians and lawyers which concern the objectives of the AI-systems development are not the only factors to be considered in the projects related to the automation of legal reasoning. Conflicting perspectives on what is to be considered to be the major aim may also evolve within organizations, e.g. between various hierarchical levels of an authority. A lawyer working in a public authority may prefer, for example, a support system which will enable him to adjust his reasoning process in an unrestricted way so that he can

[9] It is also obvious that there is a difference in opinion as to whether AI or law should be considered the principal object of concern, and which of the two has the most to gain from an interchange of ideas. In an article from 1981 *Brian Niblett* predicts "that the value of an expert system will recede not in its conformity to some jurisprudential theory, but on the quality of advice it provides. . . . a successful expert system is likely to contribute more to jurisprudence than the other way around". Niblett *supra* chapter 1 note 7, at 3. Susskind *supra* chapter 1 note 9, at 20, opposes the conclusion purported by Niblett and suggests that "[J]urisprudence can and ought to supply the models of law and legal reasoning that are required for computerized implementation in the process of building all expert systems in law." Gardner *supra* chapter 1 note 5, at 189-93, in a concluding discussion explicitly mentions some ways in which law may gain from AI. Prospects for AI are not made as clear, but in the last sentence of the book it is admitted that the disciplines may learn from each other.

[10] The existence of various inclinations among the contributors in the field of AI and law has been commented on by Susskind who recognizes two basic types of contributors; "pragmatists" and "purists". The main aim of the pragmatist is suggested to be "to develop and implement working computer systems that can actually assist in solving legal problems", whereas the "major goals for the purist are to clarify the nature of legal reasoning, of human and artificial intelligence, and of computational models of law". Two types of purists – AI purists and jurisprudential purists – are identified. Although the author admits that many researchers combine both the pragmatic and the purist attitude he claims nevertheless that most of the researchers in the field lean towards one side rather than the other. Susskind *supra* chapter 2 note 98, at 2-3.

individualize his decisions in such a way that previously unidentified factors will be continuously reflected. The head of that same institution may prefer, on the other hand, solutions which will limit the possibilities for the lawyer-employees to individualize the outcome of their decisions, e.g. in order to minimize the number of appealed cases and to achieve the highest possible efficiency within the organization as a whole. In the long-time perspective the introduction of DSSs in the field of law may also mean that an increasing number of tasks will be transferred from lawyers to paralegals or administrative staff,[11] a development which seems hardly desirable from the point of view of legal professionals.

Examples of various goal conflicts can be also perceived within various groups working on different tasks on the same organizational level. Some lawyers, handling, for example, administrative tasks may find that case management systems are the primary matters of interest. Others, active, for example, in litigation, may arrive at the conclusion that efficient document retrieval in combination with advanced word processing facilities should be the major functions to be developed, and so forth.[12]

Different preferences appear also among technically oriented researchers. Some contributors would lay emphasis on advanced methods reflecting a high level of technical sophistication and would devote less energy to document retrieval systems and word processing facilities,[13] whereas others would, without hesitation, incorporate the functions originating from conventional computer technology into advanced AI-techniques.[14] Additional differences of attitude exhibited by this group may be found when we look at the preferences shown in the selection of computer programming languages, the employment of expert system shells, and similar matters.

11 *See, e.g.*, Wahlgren *supra* chapter 1 note 42, at 103-04. *Cf. also* Magnusson, C. *New Roles in the Shaping of the Law* (1990).

12 *See, e.g.*, Wahlgren *supra* chapter 5 note 39, at 46-59 *and* Wahlgren *supra* chapter 1 note 42, at 128-55.

13 *See, e.g.*, Sergot *supra* chapter 1 note 50, at 3 "Most applications of computers to law fall outside the scope of this study. . . . This survey is concerned instead with systems that attempt to go beyond the text itself, to represent the 'meaning' of legal documents."

14 *See, e.g.*, Berg, A., Hård, L., Docherty, P. *PLUTO – Handling Social Assistance Using Combined DP and KBS Techniques* (1988).

In this context it must be also noticed that opposing interests may appear in various groups outside the organisation for which the AI-support is contemplated (e.g. customers, clients, business partners). Some people may react positively to the notion of "intelligent" autonomous devices in the field of law, e.g. as sentencing support systems. Others may be sceptical towards such solutions and in some cases it may be even impossible to introduce legal decision support systems for psychological or ethical reasons.[15]

As a final comment on these aspects, it may be argued that the problems originating from differences in attitudes between lawyers and technicians, as well as between practically oriented and theoretically inclined contributors, must not be overestimated. At least this is a valid conclusion from the stand-point of the theoretically inclined researcher. That is to say that although conflicting interests may create practical problems in actual system development projects, it must be recognized at the same time that the existence of various approaches can be often regarded as a positive factor for the discipline of AI and law taken as a whole, in the sense that different contributions supplement each other.[16] It is also clear that the apparent conflicts among various contributors can be often solved if one looks upon the practical concerns as short-time objectives and on the theoretically defined goals as long-term objectives. Noticeable is also that in many projects several objectives may be approached simultaneously.[17]

6.2.3 Domain and Task

In a discussion concerning the potentialities of AI-development in law it must be acknowledged that computer technology is not yet so advanced that various methods and products may be employed without regard taken to certain initial considerations about the general characteristics of the

[15] The recent and vivid debate on the mass media in Sweden on these matters concerns the intended elaboration of computer systems for social security offices. The debate was related to the issues of personal integrity, security, and vulnerability in relation to the possible misuse of the systems. The technical aspects were given relatively little attention. The discussion ended with a governmental decision (1992) according to which the project had to be abandoned.

[16] Susskind *supra* chapter 2 note 98, at 19 "Blinkered pragmatism and detached purism are the Scylla and Charybdis of the murky and substantially uncharted (sic) waters of AI and law. A safe channel through requires purism as the vessel within pragmatism can be contained."

[17] Explicitly so in Simon, Gaes *supra* chapter 1 note 24, at 197.

domain. At the present stage of development it must be also admitted that the process of selecting a problem is of crucial importance for the prosperous outcome of an AI-system development project.

As to the nature of the domain, it is thereby obvious that a basic presupposition in AI-system development is that relevant sources of knowledge can be identified and that the materials included in problem solving are possible to delimit. From this also follows that the knowledge and the methods of reasoning that are applied in the field must have reached a certain degree of sophistication and not be based on common sense only.[18]

A likewise distinct conclusion of relevance to the possibilities of developing workable solutions is that it must be able to define and delimit the task that is selected for AI-support in a clear way.[19] In other words, the issue that is selected must not be too complicated in the sense that it is an unique or extremely rare event that is part of a constantly changing process. A problem suitable for AI-technique should not be too easy, on the other hand.[20] In such a case a system that is implemented in order to supplement practical work runs the risk of not being used. It has been furthermore suggested that the AI-technique may be suitable in cases when the knowledge concerning the approached issue is difficult to hold together, or when it is difficult to update the knowledge.[21] From this follows that if the problem can be described in terms of numerical data or algorithms, then the conventional computer technology is to be presumably preferred.[22] It has been also underlined that the problem should be related to the necessity of combining different sorts of elements and that system development is suitable for domains where difficult decisions must be made rapidly.[23]

18 *Cf.* Hayes, Roth *supra* chapter 1 note 2, at 160.

19 *Id.*, Harmon, King *supra* chapter 3, note 97, at 198 *and* Susskind, R.E. *Expert Systems in Law: Out of the Research Laboratory and Into the Marketplace*, 5 (1987).

20 The general criteria for determining how difficult a problem is are, however, not very well articulated, but often the time span needed for solving a problem is referred to as a factor to consider in the analyses of this kind. *See, e.g.*, Hayes, Roth *supra* chapter 1 note 2, at 160, Harmon, King *supra* chapter 3, note 97, at 198.

21 Harmon, King *supra* chapter 3, note 97 *and* Hägglund *supra* chapter 3 note 122, at 15.

22 Harmon, King *supra* chapter 3, note 97.

23 Hägglund *supra* chapter 3 note 122, at 15.

Moreover, it must be kept in mind that AI-system development is a time-consuming activity and that development projects must not therefore focus on problems occurring only sporadically. This is a partly economic aspect in the sense that the invested resources must be made worth-while, but it is also a factor which is related to the way in which a support system will be used. That is to say that if the users have a reason to approach the system only occasionally, there is a risk that they will never become accustomed to the way in which it operates. In this respect, it has been claimed that AI-systems are suitable for routine work of a non trivial nature.[24]

A relevant presupposition for KBS development is also that it is interesting to spread the knowledge within the organization, among one's associates, colleagues, and customers etc. The knowledge – the expertise – must be considered, in other words, as a resource that is difficult to access. The requirements in this respect can be determined in various ways. An important indication at the organizational level is the existence of different personnel categories, working with more or less specialized tasks. One similar implication is that several persons occasionally have to get together to solve frequently occurring problems. The need for the spreading of knowledge may be also perceived in the fact that some key-persons (experts) are constantly occupied with helping others to solve specific tasks.[25]

It is finally important to note that when potentialities of AI-systems in a certain domain are analysed the major parts of the knowledge may be imbedded in the way in which people work. The factors which are related to successful system development are therefore connected not only with the possibilities to interview domain experts but also with being able to study people in realistic work situations as well as cooperating with and actively engaging domain experts during the construction phase.

[24] *Id.*, *Cf. also*, for a discussion of the suitability of AI-techniques for different types of legal decisions, Bench-Capon, T.J.M. *Deep Models, Normative Reasoning and Legal Expert Systems* (1989).

[25] Harmon, King *supra* chapter 3, note 97, at 198.

6.2.4 Acceptance

Another important aspect to consider when analysing the potentialities of AI-technique in a certain domain are the attitudes of the prospective users of the technique. A system development project must therefore consider the question of whether any difficulties concerning the acceptance of the project are likely to appear. Furthermore, if such difficulties can be predicted, then also the possibilities and ways to bring about the understanding of the AI-system implementation must be addressed.

As regards the methods of gaining acceptance, it should be underlined that the objectives of a system development project must be determined at an early stage. That is to say that the potential users of the system as well as the tasks which the system is to perform must be identified and analysed as soon as possible. In the early stages of system development projects it is also advisable to present the technique to the potential users in a realistic way. In this way, many misunderstandings and unrealistic expectations may be avoided.[26] Noticeable in this respect is also that one must try to establish a certain degree of consensus on what is to be considered as relevant knowledge and on how the problems of the domain ought to be addressed. Alternatively, it is advisable that the knowledge of the domain is of an authoritative nature.[27]

In order to establish the preconditions in this respect, the investigation must consider and analyse a number of factors. What are, for example, the presuppositions concerning the organizational and administrative environment? How will the intended system be used? Will it be possible for psychological reasons to integrate the technique with the present form of the organization, or, if not, how difficult will it be to change the presuppositions in this respect?[28] Other important characteristics to observe in the initial stages of a system development project are the requirements of the organization taken as a whole and of the people involved.

A relevant and frequently used motive for the introduction of AI-systems is that the problems approached by the automation project are of

26 Hamfelt, Wahlgren *supra* chapter 1 note 21, at 44 *and* Thompson, Feinstein *supra* note 3, at 114-15.

27 Wahlgren *supra* chapter 1 note 42, at 24 and 57 *and* Hamfelt, Wahlgren *supra* chapter 1 note 21, at 19-20.

28 Wahlgren *supra* chapter 1 note 42, at 23-26 and 54-58.

importance to the persons involved in the matter. It is important here that all the people who will be affected by the final implementation of the system share a conviction that the efforts are worth-while. Even the attitudes of the persons outside the developing organization that that may be affected by a project (e.g. customers and business partners) are of relevance for the achievement of feasible, successful solutions.

In this context it may be noticed that a general presupposition of the suitability of the technique concerning domain and task, viz. the existence of experts, may be also an impeding factor. That is to say that many people may be content with their present professional status and therefore not so eager to accept changes. This is not seldom the case in the legal profession, where the ability to obtain the position of an independent decision maker may be an important goal in the carrier of many lawyers. In consequence, some individuals will hardly welcome the idea of the integration of support systems into legal reasoning. In a polarized perspective the import of AI-devices may be even interpreted as a threat to one's professional status, apprehended as a development entailing a degradation into the role of a button-pushing administrative clerk. Similar reactions may be revealed, of course, not only by legal decision makers but by any category of employees whose work situation is affected by the technique.

The final aspect related to acceptance is that it should be possible to evaluate the systems by testing and comparing their result with the results of work done with other kinds of methods. To have access to such experimental data and constant documentation is therefore important in all system development projects. It should be also noted that this kind of information may have to be collected not only during the development of the project, but even before the practical work actually commences.

6.2.5 Summary

The overview of the general aspects which should be considered in initial stages of the AI-system development indicate that a number of things must be taken into consideration when an automation project is contemplated.

The first obvious observation is that the relevant factors to be investigated will vary from case to case, depending, for example, on the type of project as is the case of a commercial project vs. a long-term research project. In the short-term perspective a number of factors of primarily economic nature may have to be taken into consideration. In a commercial project it is also clear that the suitability of the approached domain and of the selected task must be analysed. Likewise, a lot of effort may have to go into explaining and obtaining approval by the people involved in the intended project. This type of analysis may not only provide important indicators as to when automation projects may be financially profitable, but will also make that the objectives of the project are defined at an early stage.[29] In this context the importance of the ability to develop a *domain specific* cost/benefit analysis must be underlined.

In the scientifically oriented, long-term perspective, on the other hand, other considerations may have to be reflected over. Economic factors, important as they may be are of a different kind. It may be also argued that the limitations originating from the characteristics of the approached domain and the selected task have a less decisive influence here. In the long-term oriented research projects it may be argued, on the other hand, that those limitations should be given high priority when research objectives are contemplated. Likewise, it is obvious that discussions concerning motivations and goal conflicts ought to be performed at a different level and include other kinds of arguments.

Thus, the background considerations of a general nature that may help to understand how to approach a certain task and estimate the possibilities to achieve feasible solutions may be summarized in the following way:

• What does the project aim to achieve? Is the problem to be approached of a computational or of a legal nature? Is it a project approaching long-term, theoretical objectives or short-term, practical goals?

• What economic resources are available for the project? How well can the cost and benefit factors be estimated?

• What is the structure of the organization involved in the intended development project and how does it operate? Can one expect any costs or benefits of an indirect nature and what factors can be affected in this connection?

29 Authentic and elaborated cost/benefit analysis of KBS-implementation in law are few *but see*, for an attempt to identify adequate factors and an estimation of cost benefit aspects related to the VF system, Dahnell *supra* chapter 1 note 44.

• Do the addressed issues reflect a suitable grade of complexity and are the issues sufficiently important to the persons involved?

• Are there any experts in the domain in question and are they unanimous about how problems in the domain ought to be resolved? Alternatively, is the knowledge of the domain of an authoritative nature?

• Can the experts be approached continuously during the development of the project?

• What are the attitudes of the persons that may be affected by the implementation of the system?

• Is the knowledge of the domain of such a nature that it will be possible to evaluate the performance of the AI-systems?

• What are the relations to the groups outside the organization that may be affected by the development project?

6.3 Knowledge Acquisition

6.3.1 General Remarks

The process of knowledge acquisition has been relatively well analysed in the AI-literature[30] and a number of methods have been developed. It should be noted at the start that the common way of procedure is to decompose the knowledge acquisition process into phases[31] in order to delimit the domain and identify the problem. In the initial stages of this work also the relevant sources of knowledge, as well as the group of persons that may be affected by the intended system implementation must be identified.

[30] *See*, generally on knowledge acquisition techniques, Welbank, M. *A Review of Knowledge Acquisition Techniques for Expert Systems* (1983), Kidd, A.L. ed. *Knowledge Acquisition for Expert Systems* (1987) *and* Diaper *supra* chapter 1 note 32.

[31] *See, e.g.*, Jackson *supra* chapter 3 note 96, at 191. Various approaches to knowledge eliciting have also been described as unstructured, semi structured or highly structured, Cordingley, E.S. *Knowledge Elicitation Techniques for Knowledge-Based Systems*, 103-04 (1989).

In the next step – the knowledge elicitation[32] – the substantial material that is going to be implemented should be identified and extracted. As regards the elements of substantial nature, in most cases it is of crucial importance to analyse all the available written material on a given issue. This may be necessary, for example, when specific terminology is to be adopted, when central concepts are to be recognized, or when the basic organization of the underlying knowledge structures is to be explored. In this phase also the individuals that actually are going to participate during the system construction must be approached. In connection to this, and in order to be able to select appropriate methods for future analysis, one should also try to estimate whether or not and to what extent the relevant knowledge is of an inarticulated and covert nature. In this respect the way in which knowledge elicitation will proceed will depend to a large extent on the nature of the knowledge that can be obtained. If the knowledge is vague and fragmented, the elicitation process may prove to be a very complicated one, and vice versa.

In the succeeding work a number of more or less formal methods may be employed, depending on the nature of the issue. In some domains, for instance, it may be feasible to use logical analysis in order to clarify the structure of the knowledge. In other fields of knowledge, mathematical and statistical methods may be more effective in determining frequencies, performance, default probabilities and similar aspects.[33]

Simultaneously, when extracting knowledge imbedded in organizational structures and individuals' experiences, a number of sociological methods (for example, interviews, observations, and active participation of the knowledge engineers) may be put into practice. Undertakings of the latter kind will usually imply the use of a number of technical tools and methods, e.g. video and audio recordings.

Knowledge elicitation is also a process that necessarily interacts with the organization of the extracted knowledge and it is therefore also an undertaking that is integrated with knowledge representation activities.

32 Cordingley *Id.* at 93 "Knowledge eliciting is those activities undertaken by a person, the knowledge elicitor, to – obtain material from any relevant source, – analyse and interpret that material, and – put in a pre-encoded form which, while useful to those who will encode the knowledge in the KBS language, also allows it to be scrutinised by all parties interested in KBS development."

33 *See*, for a tabulated overview of various knowledge acquisition techniques and their suitability for different types of knowledge (e.g. facts, conceptual structures, rules, etc.), *Id.* at 158.

That is to say that in the process of knowledge elicitation it may be feasible to utilize *preliminary knowledge representations*. Representations of a tentative nature may be useful not only for the analysis and the organization of the components of the extracted knowledge, but they may be also of value in the process of eliciting more detailed information, as well as in the fine-tuning of the extracted knowledge. In such work, preliminary representations may be gradually elaborated through systematical reformulations. In practice this may be accomplished by means of regular discussion seminars attended by both knowledge engineers and domain experts, when e.g. graphical representations reflecting general knowledge structures are discussed.

It should be also mentioned that for some tasks computers can be used in the knowledge elicitation process. In other words, potential users and domain experts may be given opportunities to evaluate and criticise succeedingly elaborated representations that have been encoded in a computer programming language. This so called *rapid prototyping* is a method that makes it possible to confront the user with system prototypes at an early stage of system development[34] and is therefore also an effective method of spotting weaknesses in the representation.

6.3.2 Legal Knowledge Acquisition

In law, like in any other domain, it is apparent that authentic studies of individuals' background knowledge representations face various practical problems. Considerable parts of the knowledge become internalized in the minds of the lawyers and such internal representations are, for obvious reasons, difficult to observe. At the same time it must be remembered that the understanding of the human memory organization is still rather poor.[35]

Methodological difficulties related to the possibilities of studying the actual legal background knowledge do not, however, make studies on legal knowledge representations impossible. On the contrary, concepts and notions that are frequently employed in the legal order almost certainly play an important role also in the background knowledge of lawyers.

[34] *See, e.g.*, on rapid prototyping, Diaper *supra* chapter 1 note 32, at 25-28.

[35] *Cf.* Harmon, King *supra* chapter 3, note 97, at 24 "[T]here are competing hypothesis about what the elementary symbols are and how they arrange themselves."

From this also follows that the development of a support system should benefit from the investigation of the existing representations of legal knowledge.[36] In other words, it may be assumed that the observable representations of legal knowledge, as well as the acts performed by lawyers, will to some extent constitute *reflections* of internal representations.[37]

The close relationship between form and substance in legal knowledge implies that considerable parts of legal knowledge appear in written form. From this in turn follows that legal knowledge elicitation as compared to knowledge elicitation in other domains may be a relatively uncomplicated undertaking.

Another conclusion is that in many legal domains it is also possible to identify the relevant sources that may have to be approached. This follows from the principles of predictability and equality before the law which imply that it is very seldom necessary to go beyond the written forms of representation when substantial law is to be extracted. Likewise, it can be concluded that the existence of the doctrine of legal sources implies that the various kinds of material that have to be considered in a system development project are relatively well known. In this respect, it may be also noticed that the way legal work is organized (and institutionalized) often makes it possible to identify the methodological rules as well as the persons possessing the expert knowledge on a certain issue. Examples of legal knowledge sources are shown in figure 6.1:

36 Contributions focusing on the nature of mental representation in law are few, *but see,* Walter, Parks *supra* chapter 2 note 13 *and,* for collections of articles approaching the physical - and much debated - nature of mental representations on a general basis, Blakemore, C., Greenfield, S. eds. *Mindwaves* (1987) *and* Minsky *supra* chapter 3 note 31.

37 This hypothesis is supported among other things by introspection. *Cf. also,* on mental representation in general, e.g. Rosch, E. *Classification of Real-World Objects: Origins and Representations in Cognition,* 219 (1976) ''For most domains . . . categories probably form in accordance with the perceived correlational structure of the environment, prototypes developing at the same time as categories through principles similar to those governing the formation of the categories.'' *and,* especially on legal representation and on the reasons why it may be feasible to study written court decisions although they are sometimes suggested to be merely façade legitimations, McCormick, Summers *supra* chapter 5 note 45, at 17 ''[I]t is a mistake to suppose that, even in those cases where the psychological motivations diverge from the stated justification, the alleged 'façade' that results is itself somehow unreal. The alleged façade is in fact worthy of study itself, since at the very least it represents an effort at self-conscious public justification. Thus it enables us to understand what are regarded as satisfactory and publicly acknowledged grounds for decision making.''

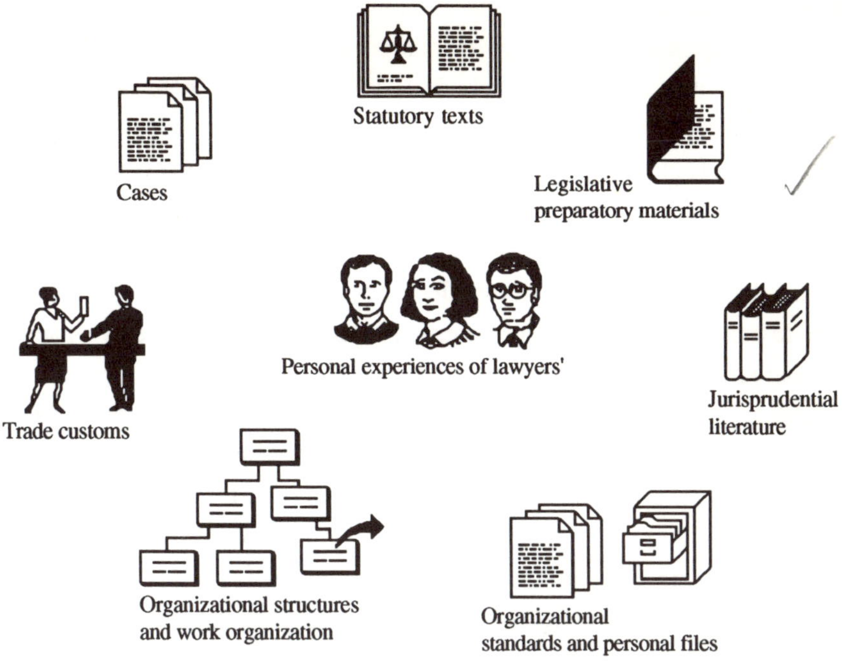

Figure 6.1 Examples of sources and structures that may have to be approached and analysed in the process of legal knowledge elicitation. The doctrine of legal sources and the principles of predictability and equality indicate that the relevant legal sources may be established, in most cases, in an authoritative way – although the identity of the sources, naturally, vary between various fields of the law.

As to the practical experiences of legal knowledge elicitation in this work, the NCA project includes, in addition to the analysis of written material, observations of actual proceedings in a district court, discussion seminars with a reference group consisting of judges, and thinking-aloud sessions with highly experienced judges.[38] In the succeeding VF project, structured interviews, oral presentations by two experienced lawyers, as well as confrontation methods, i.e. discussion sessions including confrontations and evaluations of increasingly elaborated (transcribed, graphically depicted, and finally computerized) representations came into practice.[39] During the

38 Wahlgren *supra* chapter 1, note 42.

39 Hamfelt, Wahlgren *supra* chapter 1 note 21.

first months of the project the sessions were recorded and transcribed. The transcriptions were then discussed in the succeeding sessions. The project group met once a week, initially for two to three hour sessions. These gatherings were later extended into half day meetings as the work came to focus on more specific issues. The prototyping phase encompassed approximately 125 discussion hours. It was completed by a three day intensive tuning session.

Similar methods of legal knowledge elicitation have been described by, for instance, Waterman and Peterson who report in one early project interviews focusing on hypothetical cases where computer programs incorporating models of rule-based cases were used during the interviews. As a ''powerful means for conducting controlled research on negotiating, for organizing the complex information involved, and for testing hypothesis'' the authors suggest ''gaming research;'' i.e. observations of lawyers' actions and strategies in controlled conditions.[40]

Experiences of knowledge elicitation have been reported also by e.g. O'Neil who mentions the analysis of recorded and transcribed ''thinking aloud'' protocols of previously unseen cases and pointed questioning on ''conceptual topics'' from the protocols in order to clarify the ''importance, depth and conceptual relationships of knowledge structures''. O'Neil also refers to instances in which the lawyer ''was asked to respond with free associations to words, phrases, and multiple phrases chosen from the domain'', and, furthermore, to acknowledge the use of information obtained from an expert seminar and from the analysis of textbook material.[41]

A less structured approach illustrating the close similarities between knowledge acquisition and traditional legal analysis is described by *Phillip Capper* and Susskind:

> The expert systems literature is replete with discussions of sophisticated knowledge acquisition techniques. Some knowledge engineers seem, as a matter of course, to record their discussion sessions with their experts and many take video recordings of the ordeal. Some use computer systems to assist in the articulation of knowledge (employing 'rule induction' methods,

40 Waterman, D.A., Peterson, M.A. *Models of Legal Decision Making*, 24, 30 (1981).

41 O'Neil, *supra* chapter 2 note 10, at 53.

> for instance). Others bring to bear recently perfected techniques of cognitive psychology in the quest for draining the expert of every ounce of his expertise . . . We found it sufficient to use rather more prosaic techniques, unexciting perhaps for the AI-scientist, but commensurate with the nature of the activity with which we were involved. We used the techniques of traditional legal research and legal debate; extensive, penetrating, interactive and Socratic dialogue was central to the sessions.[42]

The fact that traditional jurisprudential analysis is a very effective knowledge elicitation method was also clearly indicated in the practical work that was completed in this study. A conclusion that can be drawn from the NCA and VF projects concerning the practical utility of more or less sophisticated knowledge elicitation techniques is nevertheless that of the various methods employed each may play an important role during different phases of the process. Furthermore it is clearly indicated that the knowledge elicitation process requires careful planning. Discussion sessions which had for some reason not been prepared carefully enough from the system developer's point of view tended to focus on the issues that happened to be of particular interest at the time from the point of view of the domain experts.

As regards the difficulties experienced in legal knowledge elicitation, the fact that there existed different opinions about the relative importance of various components among the domain experts was not realized all too often. Another conclusion is that in most cases it was possible to obtain a consensus on the debated issue when various standpoints had been formulated and discussed. A side effect of this was that the persons involved in the discussions often experienced that their knowledge of the issue grew more sound as the project developed.

It must be noted, however, that the consensus was reached among lawyers with a common perspective on the issue. This does not imply that other categories of lawyers would come to the same conclusions. It is, for instance, obvious that lawyers working for a trade union would sometimes prefer a different interpretation than lawyers working for an employers' organization. Even so, however, it would be probably possible to obtain a

[42] Capper, Susskind *supra* chapter 1 note 14, at 57. *See also,* for more structured approaches, Smith, Deedman, *supra* chapter 2 note 48, at 92 and Oskamp *supra* note 2.

consensus on a large percentage of the approached issues on which the legislation is clear and the court practice stable. In this respect it may be also suggested that the sometimes vividly debated issues related to knowledge acquisition, e.g. the relation between knowledge engineers, experts, and users, competing sources of legal doctrine, and so forth, foremost are reflections of competing interests and goal conflicts. Difficulties related to knowledge acquisition are not necessarily reflections of methodological shortcomings.

6.4 Legal Knowledge Representation

6.4.1 Introduction

Knowledge representation is doubtless one of the most problematic and at the same time central aspects of AI with a large number of techniques at its disposal. Many of these techniques have been tested for a relatively long time now and given rise to various commercial products in the form of computer programming languages, computers specially designed for AI-system development and the so called expert system shells. Knowledge representation is also an intensive field of research with many of its aspects given extensive attention in various development projects.

The diversification of the knowledge representation techniques is reflected in the field of AI and law, making that the large number of the existing approaches may be quite bewildering to begin with. A close investigation reveals, however, several explanations for the many, seemingly incompatible solutions. The existence of numerous methods is for one thing explained to a large extent by the fact that various phases of the system development process are supported by different techniques. In addition, several suggestions should be looked upon as complements to each other in respect of that they are intended to support the representation of different aspects of the knowledge (e.g. vagueness, negation, etc.). Likewise when research and development efforts are scrutinized, it is obvious that some contributions should be looked upon as long-range research projects, while other undertakings are intended to solve practical problems in the already operating systems. Right from the start it is, however, also possible to see that competing, alternative models of legal reasoning, as well as various legal knowledge representation approaches, exist in the field of AI and law.

The manifold nature of legal knowledge representation requires that an investigation must take a number of things into consideration. For this reason, the following sections approach the issue from several, somewhat different, but complementary perspectives.

Firstly, sections 6.4.2 - 6.4.4 concentrate on the issue concerning the feasibility of general, authentic models of legal reasoning. The discussion provides further analysis of the arguments claiming that in addition to rules law depends also on principles. Likewise some complementary comments on the notion of legal realism are provided. The intention of these sections is hereby to provide the analysis of some foreseeable criticism of the possible weak spots of the jurisprudential model of legal reasoning (JLR).

Thereafter, in section 6.4.5, some of the most significant knowledge representation approaches as well as the underlying models of the reasoning process that have been articulated in the field are identified and related to the JLR. Simultaneously, the various representation techniques tested in the NCA and the VF projects are illustrated and evaluated. In this way, it is demonstrated how different kinds of representations can complement each other during the actual system development process. Finally, section 6.5 provides an overview of the possibilities of integrating the various solutions and techniques.

6.4.2 Traditionalism vs Creativity

Perhaps the most devastating objection concerning the practical value of models like the JLR is the suggestion that jurisprudential descriptions of legal reasoning are unnecessary in projects related to automation. One underlying reason for such arguments is that to copy natural processes when technical solutions are being developed is not always a very efficient way of tackling the problem. Illustrations of this can easily be found in almost any field. It is, for example, obvious that aeroplanes are able to fly efficiently without flapping their wings. Arguments in this direction have been submitted also in the field of AI and law.[43] From this line of reasoning it may be even argued that models like the JLR may have a hampering

43 *See, e.g.*, Koers, Kracht, Smith, Smits, Weusten *supra* chapter 1 note 48, at 30.

effect on the development by blocking the way towards more creative efforts.

Support for undertakings with authentic models of legal reasoning can be found, on the other hand, in the fact that substantial improvements based on alternative solutions can be accomplished only after the underlying principles of the addressed processes have been understood. The hypothesis that authentic models like the JLR may be feasible for the development of AI-systems in the legal domain is then strengthened by the fact that a deep understanding of the legal reasoning process as well as truly intelligent systems in the field of law are still lacking.

In this context, arguing in defence of a conventional, jurisprudential model of legal reasoning, it must be mentioned that in many juridical systems the strong *methodological tradition* is an important factor to consider. Within jurisdictions based on legal positivism, among other things, these traditions suggest that lawyers are trained to analyse and systemize legal knowledge in a rule-like fashion.[44] It is equally important that lawyers trained in a positivist tradition are taught not to present legal arguments without being prepared to make explicit references to the related legal rules and explain the reasons why a proposed conclusion is relevant by means of giving references to the accepted methods of legal reasoning. In practice, this has come to mean that the ability to relate one's argumentation to legal rules is a necessary element of legal reasoning of high quality. Conversely, to suggest that a lawyer trained in a positivist tradition should avoid the use of rules in his argumentation is much the same thing as to ask him not to utilize the major parts of his legal knowledge.[45] In this respect, it is important to observe also that jurisprudential models of legal reasoning lean on a long *historical and social tradition* in which a great number of legal concepts and institutions have been developed and elaborated during a period stretching over

44 MacCormick, Summers *supra* chapter 5 note 45, at 471 "It is apparent that systemic arguments based on general legal principles (substantive harmonization) are deployed very extensively and, indeed, developed to a high art in all countries except for the U.K. and the U.S.A."

45 In order to describe how deeply rooted the notions of legal rules and accompanying concepts are within the positivist tradition it is probably rather uncontroversial to claim that for many lawyers it is difficult to conceive a legal order without rules. To illustrate this it may be mentioned that a recent Swedish dissertation in civil law labels the approach in which formulation of general principles (concerning damage law) are avoided as the *non-intellectual approach*. Kleineman, J. *Ren förmögenhetsskada*, 19 (1987), (original in Swedish).

several hundred years. This means, among other things, that considerable portions of the accumulated bulk of legal knowledge have been integrated into ordinary language and in the organization of public authorities.

6.4.3 Generality vs Formalism

Another general limitation concerning the feasibility of the JLR model and similar approaches is that the model is rather superficial. From this follows that it cannot be used in any realistic system development project without extensive elaborations and specifications.

From the position adopted in this study it may be argued, however, that any objection based on the fact that the model is too general is irrelevant. This is simply because the aim of the JLR model is not to provide a description that is intended to be directly adaptable to formalization projects. The primary intention with the JLR is of a different kind, namely, to provide an *intermediate* model of legal reasoning, that would bridge the gap between the conventional jurisprudential descriptions and the formal, computational models of the law that so far have been submitted in the field of AI and law. In this context it should be recalled that the ambition of the JLR model is to include all the relevant aspects of the legal reasoning process and to describe them in an authentic fashion, elucidating sequences and their relations to various kinds of legal knowledge and inferences. (This is also the reason why explicit references to more or less obvious aspects of the process have been included.)[46] In this respect, the JLR model differs in many ways from the traditional jurisprudential contributions in which the legal reasoning process is often described in a more or less epic form, with little or no attention given to overall sequences and relations between various functional aspects of the law and sub-processes in legal reasoning.

Another argument supporting the assumption that models of legal reasoning presented in natural language (in contrast to formalized descriptions) are important is that human intelligence is a faculty of a very special kind as compared to any other subject matters that have been the object of automation. This is reflected, among other things, in the fact that

46 This aspect, which may surprise advanced scholars of legal philosophy exploring the field of AI and law, has been commented on by Susskind *supra* chapter 1 note 9, at 109 "No matter how prosaic or commonplace a rule that experts follow might be, it must be represented explicitly in a legal knowledge base if it is to be followed by an expert system."

no indisputable first-hand observations of the involved mechanisms exist and that natural language descriptions provide essential parts of the knowledge that is available.

From this latter aspect it follows that there will always be a need to relate the mechanical processes emulating human intelligence to natural language descriptions. It may be also argued that it is particularly important to maintain this relationship in the legal domain, where elaborated descriptions of appropriate methods of reasoning are of crucial importance for the upholding of the principles of predictability, equality, and similar aspects. In other words, it is easy to foresee that any proposal concerning automation that cannot be related to acceptable methods of legal reasoning in an explicit manner will encounter serious problems with satisfying the conditions for being accepted.

Hence, the JLR model should be looked upon as a complement to formal and traditional descriptions of legal reasoning – not as an ultimate specification that can be directly translated into a final formalization. In this latter aspect no immediate correspondence is suggested. Instead the JLR model is intended (which is in line with the overall objectives of the study) to be useful for the identification of authentic requirements and proper formalization methods. The ambition is also that the model should be able to provide support in the evaluation and understanding of the ways in which more formal models and AI techniques can complement legal reasoning. Some ways in which this may be accomplished are illustrated in the remaining part of this study.

6.4.4 The Notion of Principles

As earlier illustrated, the JLR is founded on the conviction that legal rules are the essential components of the process of legal reasoning. From this also follows that it is assumed that legal reasoning is of a deductive nature. However, as already mentioned in chapters 2 and 5, it must be admitted that many legal philosophers consider this issue rather controversial.

Fresh material for the debate as to whether or not it is appropriate to accept that law is a system of rules, was contributed by Dworkin in the late 1960s and the 1970s who argued that there existed a difference between legal rules and *legal principles*. He also suggested that the distinction was of a logical nature.[47] Legal principles and similar concepts have been thereafter elaborated upon by many contributors. Possibly the most elaborated example in Scandinavian jurisprudence has been provided by Sundby who devotes more than 100 pages of his major work to the analysis of the corresponding concept *retningslinjer.*

The idea that principles are of a different logical nature as compared to legal rules is not considered to be relevant from the perspective adopted in this study. That is to say that from the adopted point of view rules (i.e. conditional if-then relations) provide the best available description of how we believe we think. Legal principles may nevertheless appear to constitute a certain challenge not only to the JLR model but also for logical, rule-based computational models of legal reasoning. In consequence, there are reasons for the analysis of the suggested distinction.

Dworkin went on elaborating the notion of principles in several succeeding works. It may be recalled that the principles were described in Dworkin's work as a set of "standards that do not function as rules".[48] Besides this comparison it is noticeable, however, that Dworkin did not present any explicit definition of legal principles. Instead, he made several comments on how principles differ from rules. In a comparison between the notion of principles (and retningslinjer) in the writings of Dworkin and those of Sundby, *Henning Berger Herrestad* provides a summary of these statements:

> 1. Rules, but not principles, allow normative consequences to be drawn deductively.
>
> 2. Rules determine a solution to a normative problem, while principles only point out factors to be considered in the process of solving a normative problem.
>
> 3. Rules are applicable in an all-or nothing fashion, while principles may be more or less relevant.
>
> 4. Conflict between rules is solved by giving one rule priority, while conflict between principles is solved by taking into account the relative weight of each principle.

47 Dworkin, R.M. *Is Law a System of Rules?* 37 (1968).

48 Dworkin *supra* chapter 2 note 38, at 22.

5. In theory it is possible to make a complete list of all the exceptions to a rule and include them in a more complete statement of the rule, while the counter-instances to a principle are not even in theory subject to enumeration.[49]

As pointed out by several authors, each suggested difference between principles and rules may be easily criticised.[50] To start with, the first argument is very vague and does not explain in any way *how* legal principles can affect the outcome of legal decisions. It is only implied that the influence of legal principles is of such a nature that deduction would not be an appropriate method of inference. As far as can be concluded from the works of Dworkin and Sundby, however, any alternative inference mechanisms appear not to have been elaborated upon.

The second argument appears in turn to be based on the false assumption that legal rules determine the solution of legal problems. That this is not always the case is clearly shown by the JLR model in which methods of interpretation and processes of evaluation are held to be necessary ingredients for the solution of legal problems. From the point of view adopted in this study it would be instead more correct to use in this particular respect Dworkin's statement in which legal principles are described as units only "point[ing] out factors to be considered in the process of solving a legal problem" as a description of legal rules. Thus, although legal principles still appear as only vaguely defined, much of what seems to provide the basis for the suggested logical distinction between legal principles and legal rules can be rather easily discarded.

As to the third argument, it appears to be based on the same assumption about legal rules as the previously mentioned one, viz. that rules are of a rigid, predefined nature. From the theory supporting the JLR model it cannot be, however, inferred by any means that the components of legal rules cannot be the object of e.g. supplementary interpretation, in such a way that only parts of a certain rule may apply. On the contrary, it must be clearly stated that, depending on the circumstances, predefined legal

49 Herrestad *supra* chapter 2 note 82, at 40 with further references to Dworkin *supra* note 47, at 37-40, Dworkin *supra* chapter 2 note 38, at 81 *and* Sundby *supra* chapter 5 note 3, at 198-273.

50 *See, e.g.*, on the analysis and criticism of legal principles, MacCormick *supra* chapter 2 note 2, at 152-94, Herrestad *supra* chapter 2 note 82, at 39-43, Frändberg *supra* chapter 5 note 71, at 41-42 *and* Klami *supra* chapter 2 note 16, at 75.

rules may be more or less relevant. As a consequence, no significant difference between legal rules and legal principles can be detected here.

The fourth argument is, again, rather vague. It does not say anything, for instance, about the grounds on which a certain rule is given priority in cases of conflict. Naturally, it is sometimes possible to find explicit rules governing rule conflicts, but this is not always the case and in instances of the latter kind choices must be made by means of applying some (methodological) rule of evaluation at a higher level of the rule hierarchy. The main point, however, is that it must be assumed that also choices between legal principles must be made in a similar way, i.e. by means of employing some more or less well-defined evaluation rule defining "the relative weight of each principle". If not – choices between principles would have to be made at random.

The fifth proposition, finally, appears to be a reflection of the assumption that rules can be defined in advance. In consequence, the objection to this argument is similar to the ones challenging the second and third arguments, namely, that it is not possible to form complete statements of rules and their exceptions. In a piece of legislation, the rule to be applied, as well as its exceptions, will depend to a great extent on the interpretation and the evaluation that are conducted in each upcoming case and cannot therefore be always possible to predicted in advance.

To summarize, it can be said that although the analysis of rules and principles could easily be extended, it may be argued quite convincingly that no *logical* difference of any relevance exists between legal rules and legal principles.

This does not mean, however, that the notion of legal principles should be considered to be totally irrelevant. On the contrary, differences between legal principles and legal rules can be perceived also from the position adopted in this study. These differences are, however, of a different kind than those suggested by Dworkin and Sundby. It is also important to notice that these differences are in no way in conflict with the JLR model.

The most obvious distinction to be made here is thereby that rules and principles appear at different levels of the rule-hierarchy and that they influence different sub-processes of legal reasoning. As regards principles, these appear to be instruments of a more general nature, whose function is to facilitate the interpretation and/or systematization of legal rules. In this respect and in relation to the discussion in chapter 5 it is clear that the notion of principles is very similar to that of rules of evaluation (canons of interpretation) appearing at the intermediate level in the rule hierarchy.

From this point of view it becomes quite obvious that principles function not as alternatives, but rather as complements to legal rules.[51] For this reason it would be therefore meaningless to suggest that there is a logical difference between legal rules and principles. A more realistic approach would be to look upon rules and principles as if-then structures that may be linked to each other in a hierarchical way so that the consequents of rules (or of compiled groups of rules) in instances of uncertainty will eventually appear as antecedents in principles. An example from criminal law may illustrate: Conflict between rule consequents may for instance occur when a certain criminal act due to its severity according to rule X should be followed by imprisonment. Many legal systems will however also contain a rule Y imposing that no persons under a certain age should be sent to prison. In some instances, i.e. when a severe crime is committed and the perpetrator is very young both these rules may apply. In such instances of rule-collision, when both the propositions "send to prison" and "do not send to prison" have been instantiated, it would then be appropriate to activate e.g. the legal principle *in dubio mitius* imposing that when there is doubt about sentencing the judge should chose in favour of the defendant.

Another conclusion that can be drawn about the JLR model is also that legal principles alone do not constitute conclusive elements in legal reasoning. That is to say that although legal principles may be of value in the application of legal rules, they may also clash with each other at times, which is why evaluative elements at an even higher level may have to be consulted.[52]

6.4.5 Computational Models of Legal Knowledge

Elaborated descriptions of legal reasoning only seldom appear in contributions originating from the field of AI and law. Underlying assumptions

[51] *Cf.* MacCormick *supra* chapter 2 note 2, at 156-57.

[52] *Cf. Id.* at 161 "[T]he appeal to a general principle is . . . not of itself conclusive. The need may be for further evaluative argument in favour, without which a sufficient justification for the decision applying the principle will not be made out, or for contrary evaluative reasons and (as it may be) rebuttal thereof".

about the nature of legal reasoning are often described in an abstracted or fragmented way and in some cases it is not possible to find any references at all to the legal reasoning process. The contributions may for example solely concentrate on some formal representation problem and the relevance of the issue is more or less taken for granted. As mentioned, however, it is obvious that different assumptions about the nature of legal reasoning exist among contributors in the field of AI and law. Likewise it is possible to follow a continuous debate concerning the utility of various approaches with formalization.

To a large extent the diversified picture reflects the various assumptions concerning legal reasoning that are present within jurisprudence. This interdependence is clearly illustrated in a number of system development projects which have been initiated either in a case-based or a rule-based paradigm, with little or no comments on why a certain approach has been chosen. A natural consequence of this is that a number of seemingly more or less incompatible solutions have been presented and in the accompanying discussions on the advantages and disadvantages of various approaches many of the old arguments originating from the comparatively old positivist – realist discussion have been rediscovered and utilized in a new context. Rule- and case-based models are however not the only approaches that appear in the field of AI and law and in the following sub-sections a number of additional models are identified and described.

It should be observed, however, that the following sections do not provide a complete inventory of suggested approaches concerning computational models of legal knowledge. Several interesting and potentially important proposals have been left out. The reason for this is that the submitted suggestions have not yet generated any practical results, and also that the time and space allotted for this study have been rather limited.[53] The fact that different suggestions have reached various degrees

[53] Appropriate to mention in this context are, for instance, proposals for representations based on concept prototypes and deformations of such prototypes, e.g., McCarty, L.T., Sridharan, N.S. *The Representation of an Evolving System of Legal Concepts: II. Prototypes and Deformations* (1981); suggestions based on theories of neural networks, e.g., Warner, *supra* chapter 2, note 14, *and* Warner, D.R. *A Neural Network-Based Law Machine: Initial Steps* (1992); representations reflecting multilayer legal knowledge with the use of metalogic programming, e.g., Hamfelt *supra* chapter 2 note 4 *and* Hamfelt, A. *Metalogic Representation of Multilayered Knowledge* (1992); and attempts to represent natural language (in law), e.g., Haft, F., Jones, R.P., Wetter, T. *The LEX Project* (1987) *and* Lehmann, H. *Legal Concepts in a Natural Language Based Expert System* (1990). Significant are also several contributions concerning the ways in which to represent time in law. Recent articles are thereby provided by e.g., Mackaay, E., Poulin, D., Frémont, J., Bratley, P., Deniger, C. *The Logic of Time on Law and Legal Expert Systems* (1990) *and* Karpf, J. *The*

of sophistication and produced more or less tangible results are, however, not the only criteria that have influenced the selection of the material that has been included in the following discussion. Of equal importance has been the degree of attention accorded to different theories by the AI and law society. The latter is simply to say that some theories have drawn so much interest that it has been necessary to include them in the discussion. It should be explicitly stated, however, that this does not mean that the proposals which have been omitted are necessarily less significant or promising in the long-term perspective.

6.4.5.1 Logical and Rule-Based Models

The most common approach in undertakings concerning the formalization of legal knowledge in AI-applications is to utilize various forms of rule-based methods. Rule-based formalisms are the essential ingredients of most KBSs, not only in the legal field. Underlying this approach is a process in which various forms of legal knowledge are transformed into a *logical model*. In such a model the relations between various entities and propositions are described by means of utilizing formal languages encompassing logical connectives and relations such as "and", "or", "not", "if . . . then". In a logical model rules may be also related to each other in a so called decision tree (to be illustrated). It is thus possible to reflect intricate relations between large number of rules by means of using graphical representations and various computer programming languages.

It should be mentioned that the utility of logical models is by no means limited to computer related projects. As mentioned in section 2.6 above, Layman Allen suggested as early as 1957 that formal languages based on logic could be of assistance in the drafting of legal documents and in interpretation activities. In Sweden, in 1969, Tore Strömberg developed a graphical representation of a central part of civil law. Strömberg argued thereby that the graphical representation made it possible to achieve results in a safer and faster way. It was also concluded that graphical representations facilitate the identification of logical contradictions in written legislation.[54]

Future and Other Time Issues in Legal Representation (1989). *See also*, for a more comprehensive comparative study on various representation approaches for law, Sergot *supra* chapter 1 note 50.

54 Strömberg, T. *Lathund för lagläsare*, 201 (1969).

6.4.5.1.1 The British Nationality Act as a Logic Program

In the field of AI and law the most frequently quoted work based on the use of logical models is probably the experimental formalization of the British Nationality Act of 1981, undertaken by the Logic Programming Group of the Imperial Collage of London.[55] In this project the legislation was translated into a representation based on a sub-set of predicate logic, the so called extended Horn clause logic. Horn clauses are rules of the form A *if* B_1 and B_2 and . . . B_n. "Each such clause has exactly one conclusion A, but zero or more conditions B_i, each of which is an atomic relationship among individuals. Definite Horn clauses are invoked or queried by means of conjunctions of atomic relationships such as

B_1 and B_2 and . . . B_n?

These can be regarded as degenerate 'rules' that have no conclusion."[56] The project group also illustrated that logical models of this kind can be easily represented in the computer programming language Prolog. The rules, such as

> "A person born in the United Kingdom after commencement shall be a British citizen if at the time of birth his father or mother is
> (a) a British citizen; or
> (b) settled in the United Kingdom."

was represented after the transformation in the form (condition a):

> "x is a British citizen
> if x was born in the U.K.
> and x was born on date y
> and y is after on commencement
> and z is a parent of x
> and z is a British citizen on date y."[57]

[55] Sergot, M.J., Sadri, F., Kowalski, R.A., Kriwacznek, F., Hammond, P., Cory, H.T. *The British Nationality Act as a Logic Program* (1986).

[56] *Id.* at 372.

[57] *Id.* at 372 ("After commencement" in the rule means after or on the date on which the act comes into force.)

The experiment did not contain complete formalization of the whole act. Of some 73 pages of text containing some 500 rules approximately 150 were reported to have been implemented in a computer.[58] The presented conclusion was, nevertheless, quite firm and stated that "[a]lthough Prolog logic is severely restricted, it proved to be sufficiently high level so that our implementation could resemble the style and structure of the actual text of the act." It was furthermore underlined that the use of logical representation and deductive inference for knowledge processing provided a number of general advantages. It was thereby mentioned that such a representation

> "• is easy for both naive users and experts to understand;
> • is easy to modify (e.g., to correct errors, to enhance, and to reflect changes that occur over time);
> • allows the inference procedure to interact naturally with the human user and to explain its conclusions."[59]

An important advantage of logical models is also that the representation makes it easy to separate between the object level (the knowledge, the axioms of the domain) and the meta level (the knowledge of how to make inferences in the domain). As described in section 3.7, in a KBS these aspects of knowledge are normally divided into a knowledge base containing the rules about the objects of the domain and an inference engine storing the search patterns, i.e. the knowledge about the kind of objects (conditions) that must be investigated in order to determine e.g. whether or not an individual is a British citizen. According to the logic programming group the use of Prolog programming implies that "any logical consequence of the axiomatization can, in theory, be derived by means of a complete mechanical theorem prover." A support system based on these principles may then elicit facts about the encountered situation by means of confronting the user with yes/no questions in an interactive dialogue. Alternatively, the system may use menues or fill-in

58 *Id.* at 383.

59 *Id.*

questions. Many systems operate in this way by backward chaining, i.e. the conclusions (as whether or not someone is a British citizen) are arrived at by means of systematic investigation of interrelated conditions.

The characteristics of the formalization of the British Nationality Act are in principle of the same kind as the work that has to be done in any development of expert systems or KBSs. The only significant difference of the project that has been reported – as compared to KBS development in general – concerned the fact that the work done here concentrated solely on written legislation. This in turn made it possible to avoid any complications connected with knowledge elicitation.[60]

Other examples of logical and rule-based models of law and legal reasoning in the field of AI and law appear in many shapes. The Logic Programming Group mentions in their comparison of related work McCarty's *TAXMAN I*[61] and Waterman and Peterson's *ROSIE*.[62] Rule-based models appear also to have been essential for, e.g., *The Nervous Shock Advicer* described by *J. C. Smith* and *Carl Deedman*.[63] Another recent, well documented example is *The Latent Damage System* developed by Capper and Susskind.[64] The list of related projects can be, however, easily extended.

6.4.5.1.2 The NCA and VF Projects

Further illustrations of rule-based models are provided in the form of practical experiments undertaken in the NCA and VF projects. The NCA project focused on sentencing rules. The main objectives here were to examine the possibilities of developing a computer-based system that would be capable of assisting judges in their sentencing and to investigate whether such a support system would allow for and facilitate a more uniform practice. On the practical side the experiment came to

60 *Id.*

61 McCarty *supra* chapter 4, note 78 *and* McCarty L.T. *The Taxman Project* (1980).

62 Waterman, Peterson *supra* chapter 4, note 82 *and* Waterman, D.A., Jody, P., Peterson, M.A. *Expert Systems for Legal Decision Making* (1987).

63 Smith, Deedman *supra* chapter 2, note 48.

64 Capper, Susskind *supra* chapter 1 note 14.

concentrate on sentencing in relation to crimes of assault and battery. This meant that a number of various statute rules had to be combined with the practice reflected in case law.

From the perspective of the NCA one underlying reason for the choice of this particular issue was that the Swedish legal system experiences problems with non-uniform practices evolving in different courts and between different judges. In addition, in the Swedish legislation identical sentencing rules apply to a large extent common to all crimes. It was thereby assumed that a system development project focusing on sentencing should be able to generate conclusions valid also for undertakings concerning other kinds of crimes. It was moreover noticed right from the start that cases of assault and battery encompass a comparatively large number of facts and therefore provide good opportunities to try out knowledge methods in realistic and rather complicated situations.

The succeeding VF project was undertaken in an area of a different kind and set up in order to analyse a significant case-based field of law. The issue that was selected was the concept of *fair ground* applied in dismissal situations. In the Swedish jurisdiction "fair ground" is a concept whose meaning can be only extracted through an extensive analysis of interrelated cases and non-statutory material. From the point of view of the VF organization this particular issue was of primary interest due to the fact that problems connected with the establishment of fair ground quite frequently give rise to various questions and require therefore setting up of heavy resources from the part of the negotiating lawyers. From the VF organization it was also indicated that certain questions concerning fair ground in dismissal cases were considered to be some of the most complicated issues that the lawyers in the organization had to deal with.

From the IRI's side, one conscious motive that influenced the selection of this particular topic was that the domain, as compared to the previously investigated sentencing rules, was of a distinctly different nature and that it provided opportunities to try out knowledge methods on a different kind of material. A positive factor here was thereby that the experiment with the concept of fair ground would make it possible to try out the technique in a significantly case-dominated domain. Fair ground, being a classical example of a vague legal concept, also indicated that it would be possible to arrive at some conclusions as regards the possibilities of minimizing problems connected with the representation of vagueness. From the IRI's point of view an additional aim of this sub-project was to develop a more or less complete support system in a limited domain for demonstration purposes.

In the initial stages of organization and systematization of the domain knowledge the work progressed largely in the same way in both sub-projects. In the initial phase this came to include the development of various kinds of graphical overviews. In the NCA project, involving several statute rules and numerous cases, a number of succeeding representations concentrating on various more or less detailed issues were thus developed. The complicated nature of the issue made it also necessary to develop several conceptual graphs – so called decision trees – in order to establish the sequences of the reasoning process by means of determining the order in which various kinds of rules (or groups of rules) may influence the process.[65] In this work it soon became possible to establish several, rather distinct phases in which various kinds of legal material became relevant. In this phase of the work it was also possible to identify various disqualifying facts that could rule out whole groups of rules such as, for instance, that the low age of the perpetrator could make the whole set of rules about imprisonment irrelevant, and so forth.

65 *See, e.g.*, on graphical representations for the representation of knowledge, Jackson *supra* chapter 3 note 96, at 52-56 and *passim, and* Brachman, Levesque *supra* chapter 5 note 82.

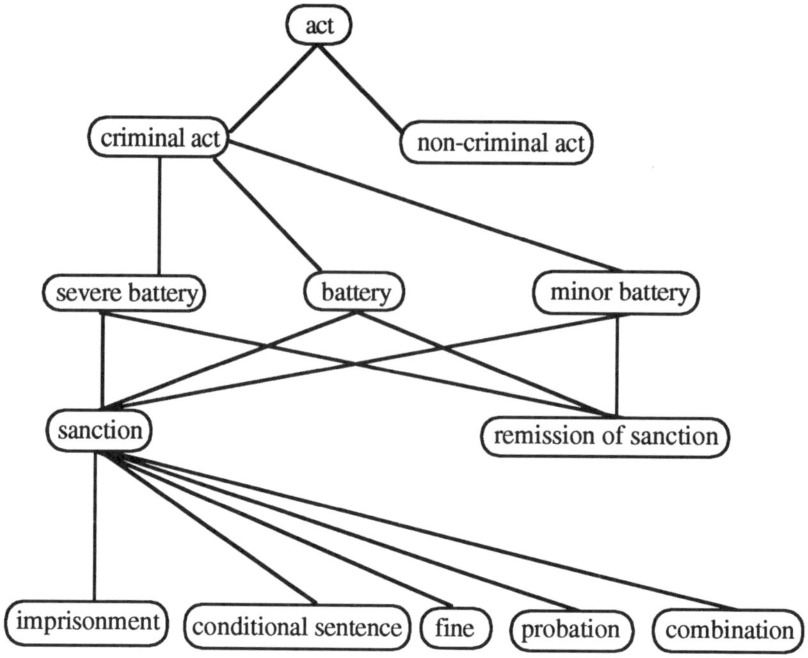

Figure 6.2 Overview of general phases in the sentencing process, each necessarily involving the activation of several interrelated rules. At each level in the hierarchy the lawyer must make a decision about various options. In the NCA project several graphs of this kind were developed.

In the VF project, concentrating on one crucial concept, the repeated use of graphical representations was less frequent and basically only one comprehensive graph was developed. The graph was elaborated for several weeks as the various methods of knowledge elicitation came into practice. The analyses came thereby to focus on components and sub-concepts of fair ground of increasing detail.

In this work it became apparent right from the beginning that the issue of fair ground could be decomposed into a number of primary causes, each of which could constitute the grounds for fair ground, such as e.g. loss of working capability, abuse of alcohol or drugs, misbehaviour, criminal acts and disloyalty. The work came to concentrate on cases of misbehaviour, and more precisely misbehaviour concerning unauthorised absence. Although many cases were left out in this way a very large number of possible instances of fair ground still remained to be analysed. One major issue to be identified and analysed was, for instance, the issue of possible combinations of various kinds of unauthorized absence (for example, late arrivals, absence periods ranging from some minutes up to several hours, longer periods of absence extending over several days, various combinations of late arrivals, short periods and long periods of absence, and so forth).

One additional aspect that had to be clarifyed concerned *mitigating circumstances* – a sub-concept which comprised in turn a large number of factors that could be relevant in various combinations, including among other things, non-functioning public transport, malfunctioning day care facilities for children, illness, alcoholism, family problems, etc.

The third aspect of fair ground that turned out be of a rather comprehensive nature concerned the measures previously taken by the employer to solve the problems connected with unauthorized absence. The issues to be investigated in this respect were such as, for example, whether or not the employer had previously warned the employee in a similar situation, whether any contacts had been taken with the employee's union and so forth.

An in-depth analysis of these aspects, as well as that of a large number of additional factors, eventually made it possible to arrange the understanding of the domain in a hierarchic and logical order, so that instances of fair ground could be easily recognized by means of investigation of only a few interrelated concepts. During this work the graph was reformulated several times as the understanding of the domain increased. Some of the sub-concepts that had been thus identified soon stood out as disqualifying factors that could be successfully applied at different levels of the hierarchy. In this respect, the most noticeable fact was that in many cases it became quite obvious that it was sufficient to investigate whether or not the intended dismissal was preceded by a warning or some other kind of action on the part of the employer. If this was not the case the rule of fair ground did not apply. The analytical work that was undertaken in this phase of the system development was essentially of the same kind as the work that must be done in traditional jurisprudential analysis. The project group experienced no practical problems in gaining acceptance for the methodology based on the reformulation and the organization of the case-based knowledge into a hierarchically ordered chain of ''if-then- rules'', logically related to each other and using the "and" and "or" relations. The only noticeable difference as compared to the traditional jurisprudential analysis was the orderly and the comprehensive use of methods, such as graphical representations, recorded discussions, etc.

Eventually, the graphical representation came to comprise more than ten hierarchical levels and about a hundred logical connections. Each node in the graph provided thus a potentially relevant element to the concept of fair ground, accompanied by references to authentic cases, or by hypothetical situations based on interpretations of available decisions concerning related issues.[66] In the end, the graph was so elaborate that it was possible to relate all the known cases of *fair ground* due to unauthorized absence that the domain experts held to be relevant[67] to a certain node in the representation.

In the graph describing *fair ground* in the VF project the Boolean relations were expressed as in figure 6.3. The principles of the graphical representation are illustrated in figure 6.4.

Figure 6.3 Graphical representations of the Boolean operators "and", "or".

66 *Cf.*, For a similar, complementary approach based on statutory material, Sergot, Sadri, Kowalski, Kriwacznek, Hammond, Cory, *supra* note 55, at 371 "[W]hen imprecision or ambiguity did exist, it was usually possible to identify the intended interpretation with little difficulty."

67 There was a general consensus on the fact that some inconsistent cases were never cited, *Cf.* Smith, Deedman *supra* chapter 2, note 48, at 92 "[D]ecisions which may not fit the analysis . . . can be assumed at this point to be wrongly decided."

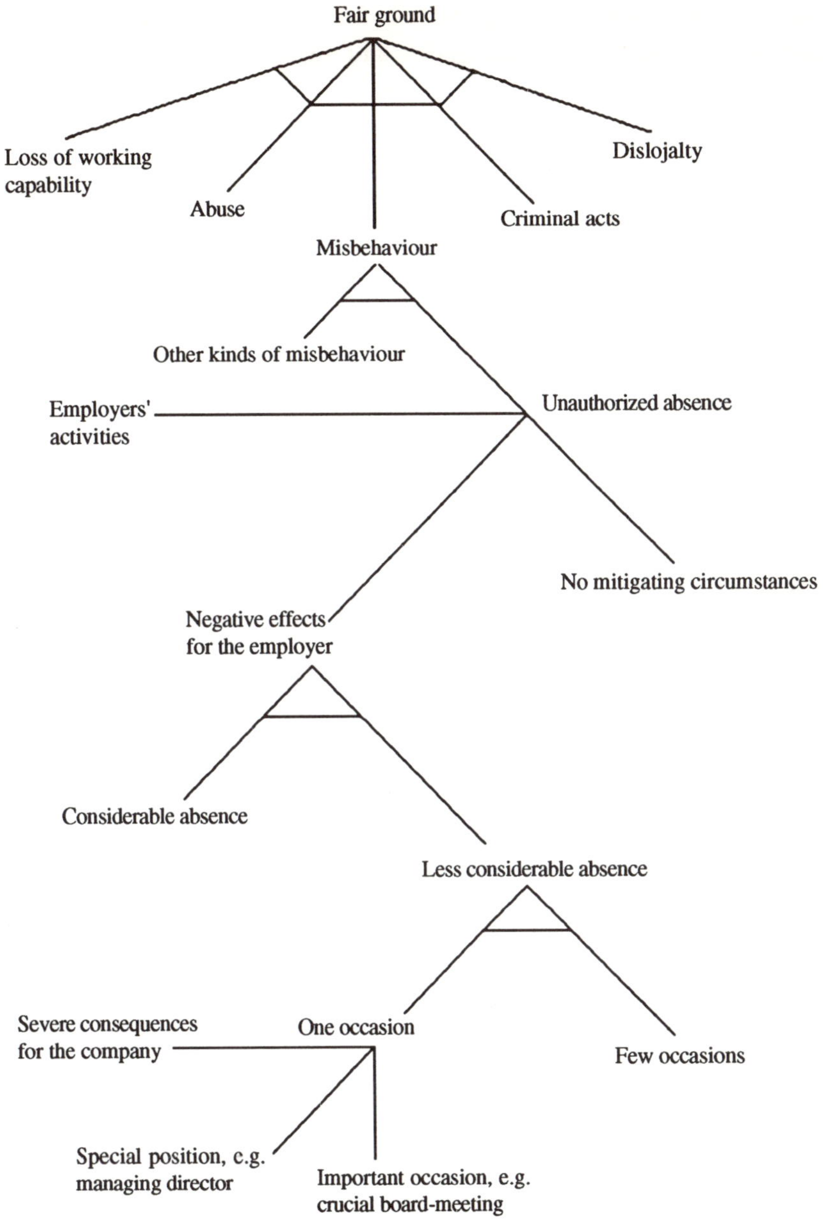

Figure 6.4 (Simplified) fraction of a graphical illustration of elements and relations constituting fair ground

In the next step, the knowledge reflected in the graphic representation was transformed into if-then sentences and represented in a Prolog programming language. It should be mentioned, however, that the work with the graphical representation and the computer program was by no means strictly sequenced. To a considerable extent the work with the various representation forms consisted of parallel and interactive operations.

The transformation of knowledge into computer program was rather simple in this phase, owing to the fact that the most relevant relations had been identified and represented in the graph. The conceptual graph served thus as a blueprint in the construction of the knowledge base. In this way, the representation of fair ground eventually took the shape that is depicted in figure 6.5.

```
;;principal part
(defpred if-then
 ((if-then principal-rule-1
    (misbehaviour)
    (fair ground)))
 ((if-then principal-rule-2
    ((other kind of misbehaviour)
     or
     (unauthorized absence ))
    (misbehaviour)))
 . . .
 ((if-then inexcusable -absence-rule
    ((general introduction)
     and
     ((inexcusable unauthorized absence)
     or
     (inexcusable less comprehensive absence)))
    (inexcusable absence)))
 . . .
     ((if-then rule-solely-short-or-combination-short-long
    ((not (is it solely a case of continuous absence exceeding half a day))
       and
     ((inexcusable number of short absences)
```

or
(combination of long and short absences)))
(solely short or combination)))

Figure 6.5 Fractions of Prolog program developed in the VF project (the original in Swedish).

In the NCA project a similar transformation was completed, although on a more limited material. The NCA project employed a different computer programming language, viz. Lisp, in this phase. The formalization performed in the NCA project was also supported in part by a more powerful computer, a so called workstation which had been especially designed in order to support the AI-system development (as compared to the VF project which was developed on Macintosh computers). Workstations may be able, for instance, to automatically generate graphical representations from computer program code and be able to provide support for various aspects of the programming.[68] Workstations are also significantly more powerful than ordinary computers.

6.4.5.1.3 Logical Models and Legal Reasoning

Logical, rule-based models of law have in several ways been criticised. Likewise, various difficulties related to the representation of legal knowledge have been reported. It has been argued, for instance, that logic is not a very adequate representation language for law because it is (i) truth functional and does not allow for the measurement of the relative weight of conflicting principles; (ii) monotonic, i.e. it does not make it possible to take new information into consideration; and (iii) because it does not allow for meta levels, i.e. ''explicit statements about its own rules''.[69]

A number of limitations have been also suggested to originate from ''the indeterminacy of law'', i.e. the fact that there exist acceptable legal arguments to support both sides of many important issues. Complications

[68] *See, e.g.* for a theoretical description of various tools for the construction of KBSs, Jackson *supra* chapter 3 note 96 chapter 12 *and*, for an overview of commercial products, Morris, Reed, *supra* chapter 3 note 111.

[69] Berman, Hafner *supra* chapter 1 note 37, at 3.

in this respect have been said to originate from e.g. (iv) the existence of conflicting rules and precedents, (v) the ambiguity and imprecision of natural language and (vi) the need for evolution in the legal system in order to adapt to a changing world.[70] In addition, difficulties with (vii) the representation of negation, and (viii) disjunctive and negated conclusions have been reported.[71] The latter arises from the fact that only antecedents but not consequents of rules in Horn clause logic can contain disjunctive and negative connectives. Additional complications (ix) have been related to the fact that changes in the representation becomes increasingly cumbersome as the size of the knowledge-bases increases.[72]

Many of the issues that have been raised no doubt represent intriguing and controversial research problems. An important observation, however, is that many of the issues appear to be essentially theoretical and that several problems that have been discussed do not necessarily reflect practical difficulties of any great significance. Extending this line of argument it may be claimed even that in this respect it is sometimes possible to perceive a gap between the practical feasibility of logical rule-based representations and vivid argumentations about various detailed representation difficulties and suggested shortcomings.[73] One other way of saying this is that it is beyond doubt that logical rule-based representations can be the basis for well functioning AI-systems in the field of law.

In practical system development, problems concerning negation, for instance, can be resolved, to a large extent, with the help of a methodology known as *negation by failure*, i.e. by means of adopting an approach in which anything that is not familiar from previous cases is assumed to be false. In a KBS-session, negation can be thus established by means of posing questions to the user about all previous, known instances of a certain fact. If none of these instances apply in the current case, the fact is assumed to be false. This methodology can be refined in various ways and in the VF project it was found, for example, that it was feasible

70 *Id.* at 1.

71 Sergot, Sadri, Kowalski, Kriwacznek, Hammond, Cory, *supra* note 55, at 379-82.

72 *Id.* at 382.

73 *See*, for a discussion, Bench-Capon *supra* note 24.

to complement all the interrogation sequences of this kind with a final question to the user as to whether there was anything in the situation that reminded him any of the familiar elements elements of the case.[74] To recall in this context is also the nature of choices between principles that is discussed in section 6.4.4 above. It is there argued that from the jurisprudential point of view it is difficult to acknowledge that there exist any logical difference between rules and principles, or that conflicting rules and principles provide any serious problems in the process of legal reasoning, except on rare occasions. In connection to this it should also be made explicit that if from the stand point adopted in this study there is little reason to suggest that the law is truth functional (the reasons for this are elaborated on in section 6.4.5.4 *infra*).

However, although many problems appear to be of a significantly theoretical nature, it is of course not possible to discharge the whole discussion about the usefulness of logical rule-based models by means of referring to practical feasibility. On the contrary, when research problems related to logical representations are discussed, there is naturally also a critical relationship between the levels of ambitions and the proposed problems. That is to say that if it is accepted that it is sufficient to be able to represent the law *de lege lata*, it can be convincingly concluded that rule-based models provide a feasible technique and that no serious limitations have been detected. If, on the other hand, it is implied that the aim is to create a representation of the law as it may develop in the future, or, if the aim is to create more or less autonomous reasoning systems, the task becomes more complicated. In this respect problems with indeterminacy, natural language understanding, meta-level representations, and a large number of additional research problems may become relevant. But again, trying to adopt a critical attitude to the criticism, one important issue that may be raised here is whether many of the suggested problems necessarily have anything to do with the feasibility of logical, rule-based models as such. As an alternative it may well be argued that logical rule-based models – limited as they may be – can be complemented with theories operating at different levels of abstraction, reflecting, e.g., modules of legal knowledge. This is simply to say that it

74 *See*, for further elaborations about problems and ways of avoiding difficulties with negation, Kowalski, R. *The Treatment of Negation in Logic Programs for Representing Legislation* (1989).

may turn out that the problems related to changes in the law, indeterminacy and similar aspects have very little to do with how the different components of law actually are represented. Instead, the crucial problem may be to understand the ways in which different components can be related to each other in an intelligent manner. (A further elaboration of a suggestion in this direction is outlined in chapter 7 of this study.)

In summary this means that it can be concluded that logical, rule-based models are by no means in conflict with the JLR model and that although logical models do not provide an exhaustive theory for the representation of legal knowledge, the rule-based approach very much resembles the traditional jurisprudential way of understanding the law. The feasibility of logical, rule-based models for the representation of law is well documented in many system development projects. In this respect the NCA and the VF projects that have been completed during this project also illustrate the ways in which legislation, case law, and vague concepts, as well as combinations of legislation and case law including various kinds of methodological rules and rules of formality, can be represented in a logical, rule-based fashion. Numerous other projects, of which several have been put into day-to-day use, also show that rule-based representations can be efficiently employed in many areas of law and that, provided the computer system is supplemented with sufficient input data, complex rule-based inferences can be simulated.

One must note in this context also that in the VF project several subsections concentrating on the definition of more or less interdependent concepts in the main graph have been developed. In this respect the technique of relating sections, or modules, of interrelated sub-rules in a hierarchic representation of this kind makes the integration of various kinds of rules possible. There are, for instance, no obstacles to the inclusion of one or several introductory modules encompassing the rules of formality concerning a certain issue. Such modules may then be activated in order to investigate e.g. the presuppositions related to jurisdiction, the competence of the user, and so forth. In the same way, there are no severe difficulties related to the inclusion of supplementary rules that have been developed through intentional interpretation, processes of evaluation, etc. The crux of the matter is the extent to which it is possible to accomplish consensus over the suggested representations.

6.4.5.2 Inductive Case-Based Models

In the field of AI and law several examples of case-based (inductive, example-based) knowledge representation methods have been elaborated. Some of the models have originated in the North American sphere and have been no doubt, influenced by the tradition of legal realism. The underlying assumption here is that the acute problem in legal reasoning is to find the precedent that is most similar to the encountered case.

> "Case-based argument plays an essential role in legal argument. An attorney's law school training and legal practice inculcate standards of legal argument, and those standards strongly prefer arguments whose conclusions are justified by citing precedents (prior legal cases)."[75]

6.4.5.2.1 HYPO – A Case-Based Approach

A recent example of a computer system designed for case-based reasoning is HYPO, a program developed for trade secrets law. HYPO is a system that can support the analysis of the encountered cases and also retrieve similar precedents from a case knowledge base. The methodology is based on case-fact analysis, where various factors that have been found relevant in the previously reported cases are utilized in order to analyze the encountered problem situations.[76] The factors function thereby as sets of prerequisites that can be used to test the ways in which an encountered situation matches the known precedents. The factors are grouped together and represented in so called dimensions. This classification is based on various kinds of legal claims that have been identified and on whether the factors appear to be favourable or unfavourable for the outcome of a particular case.

[75] Ashley, K.D. *Modeling Legal Argument*, 9 (1990).

[76] *Id.* It should be mentioned that case-fact analysis as a method for the prediction of the outcome of legal decisions has been discussed in the jurimetrical tradition for a rather long time. *See, e.g.*, for an overview Tyree, A.L. *Fact Content Analysis of Case Law: Methods and Limitations* (1981). Tyree also observes that there is no principal contradiction between the analysis and the predictions of legal decisions by means of employing mathematical methods, *Id.* at 4. This fact seems to have been given relatively little attention, however, and there are surprisingly few cross-references between works on case-fact analysis submitted in the field of AI and law and previous works in the jurimetrical tradition.

> Dimensions encode domain knowledge that certain groups of operative facts and features derived from them enable one to make certain arguments or address a case in a certain way.[77]

The program uses a ''case frame language'' for the representation of the facts and the user of the system must be able to state his problem in this language. At a finer level factors ''have magnitudes to reflect the fact that a particular case may be a more or less extreme example of the factor.''[78] It is mentioned, for example, that unauthorised disclosure to one hundred people is considered to be a more serious offence than than disclosure to six outsiders. After identifying the stated problem the program is also capable of giving references to ''most-on-point'' cases, by posing cases as counter-examples, and by making suggestions (hypotheticals) about the ways of weakening and strengthening the arguments. It is reported that the HYPO case-knowledge base contains 30 cases and that thirteen dimensions have been implemented. The representation of the dimensions appears in the following form:

NAME: Secrets-Volutarily-Disclosed
SHORT-TITLE: Secrets-Disclosed-Outsiders
CLAIMS: Trade Secrets Misappropriation
PREREQUISITES:
There is a corporate plaintiff
There is a corporate defendant
Plaintiff makes a product
Plaintiff and defendant compete
Plaintiff has product information
Plaintiff made some disclosure to outsiders
FOCAL SLOT PREREQUISITE
Plaintiff made some disclosures to outsiders
FOCAL SLOT
Plaintiff's product: Number of disclosures
RANGE
0 to 10.000.000

[77] Skalak, D.B., Rissland, E.L. *Using Case-Based Reasoning to Extend the Expertise of Expert Systems*, 682 (1989).

[78] Ashley *supra* note 75, at 27.

COMPARISON TYPE:
Greater-than versus Less-than
PRO-PLAINTIFF DIRECTION: Less-than[79]

The theory behind HYPO, so called ''adversarial case-based reasoning'' is argued to be a general kind of reasoning. It is also suggested that this kind of reasoning ''is not just for attorneys'' but that ''[i]t applies to a variety of domains where experts argue with or extrapolate from case examples.''[80] The conclusions lead up to far reaching speculations about the feasibility of the methodology. It is among other things suggested that ''the research demonstrates a new, contemporary medium for doing jurisprudence'' and that it ''contributes to research in artificial intelligence not only as an example of a case-based reasoner that works but as an example of an expert system that (1) presents alternative answers, not just the one 'right' answer, (2) argues in favor of the alternatives, and (3) models intelligent behavior in a messy domain that lacks a strong theoretical model.''[81]

6.4.5.2.2 NCA – A Numerical Approach

A sketchy illustration of how a case-based methodology of a somewhat different kind may be developed was presented in the NCA project. The formalization concentrated solely on the factors that were found to have a decisive influence on the severity of the crime (assault and battery). The objective of the project was to investigate the extent to which it was possible to facilitate uniform sentencing with this kind of methodology.[82]

In the first place, in order to understand the ways in which various components actually determined the outcome of sentencing, a collection of

[79] *Id.* at 109.

[80] *Id.* at 250.

[81] *Id.* at 250-51, 253.

[82] To some extent this approach is similar to work that has been undertaken with sentencing guide-lines using severity levels. *See, e.g.*, Jareborg, von Hirsch, Hanrahan *supra* chapter 5 note 132 *and* Knapp, K.A., *Minnesota Sentencing Guidelines and Commentary* (1985). *Compare also*, the comprehensive documentation of a Norwegian project, Hansen, J. *Et system for analyse av rettslige avgjørelser* (1981) *and* Hansen, J. *SARA* (1985).

case abstracts on assault and battery was examined.[83] A total number of 42 cases were scrutinized. The investigation revealed 45 explicitly mentioned factors which could be identified as relevant to the outcome of the decisions. The factors could be classified in various ways. For instance, 21 of them could be related to the perpetrator, while 23 were related to the act itself. In addition, general prevention seemed to constitute a factor of general relevance with regard to the outcome.

Some of the factors could be immediately categorized as aggravating or mitigating in terms of their relation to the outcome of the sentencing. The fact that the perpetrator was very young was, for instance, easily identified as a mitigating circumstance. Other kinds of factors were found to be either mitigating or aggravating, depending on the situation they appeared in. To illustrate this, it may be mentioned that a crime of assault and battery must be always geographically located. In many cases this "location-aspect" is of little or no relevance. In other cases, however, the location-aspect may be an aggravating factor. This may be, for instance, the case if a crime of assault and battery has been committed in a place where the victim had no chance of escape. One could also notice was also that some factors adopted at times neutral values.

By means of analysing each factor it was eventually possible to develop a tabulated overview including all the facts that – within the selected set of cases – had been held relevant to the outcome in the issues of assault and battery. The factors were arranged in two columns, one for mitigating circumstances, and the other for aggravating circumstances. Some examples are given below:

Aggravating	*Mitigating*
criminal history/prognosis	criminal history/prognosis
relation to the victim	social situation
resulting injuries	age
location	abuse
situation	situation
type of violence	etc.
etc.	

83 Brattgård, E. *Något om hovrättens påföljdspraxis i misshandelsmål* (1985) The Brattgård case abstract collection was at the time of the NCA project rather extensively used as a reference document at one of the Swedish appeal courts. In a authentic system implementation project, however, a much larger number of cases must be included in the analysis.

In the second phase, various instances of each fact were identified and related to each other. Here the method made use of numerical values. The element "relation to victim" may serve as an example.

The preliminary analysis concluded that the existing relationship between the perpetrator and the victim was a basically negative factor as far as the severity of the crime of assault and battery was concerned. On some occasions, however, it may be appropriate not to pay any special attention to the relation between the persons involved in the act. The factor "relation to victim" is held to be neutral on such occasions. In practice this means that it will not be explicitly mentioned in the case description. On the other hand, in the cases where the factor appeared, one could clearly see that certain kinds of relations between the perpetrator and the victim were considered to be of a more serious kind. The close study of the factors and their instances resulted in comprehensive and meticulous descriptions of the factors considered as relevant in assault and battery cases. The analysis of court decisions made it also possible to attach a number of instances to each factor. In the experiment three common instances of the "relation to victim" factor were specified as "known", "spouse" and "unknown". Each instance was then given a value, "known" = 1, "spouse" = 3, and "unknown" = 5. In other words, it was found that the crime of assault and battery is considered to be very serious if committed against the perpetrator's spouse and that it is even worse when done to a totally unknown person.

Naturally, all these relations can be discussed and it should be underlined that no detailed analysis was performed concerning the assessment of the various instances in an authentic application. The ambition of the project was merely to illustrate the methodological aspects of a case-based support system, and not to make statements on how various factors ought to be evaluated in actual sentencing. It should be also mentioned that only a small fraction of the prerequisites and facts that are held to be relevant in assault and battery cases was actually implemented in the computer program.

When all the identified factors had been analysed in this manner and when a reasonable number of usually re-occurring situations had been evaluated, it became possible to develop more or less elaborate formulas in order to compute the material.

The simplest way to do this is to just add up all the negative factors and thereafter subtract the sum of the positive factors. That is to say that if all the aggravating factors supporting the arguments against the defendant are denoted as X_1, X_2, X_3, . . . X_n and all mitigating factors supporting arguments in favour of the defendant are denoted as Y_1, Y_2, Y_3 . . .Y_n, this gives the following

$$(X_1 + X_2 + X_3 + \ldots X_n) - (Y_1 + Y_2 + Y_3 + \ldots Y_n) = Z$$

The possible values for X and Y must be then adjusted on a scale, where sum Z indicates the severity of the sentence. If Z turns out to have the value between 10 and 14 this may indicate, for instance, that one month of imprisonment is appropriate. Z between 15 and 20 may indicate two months of imprisonment, and so forth.

Addition is the simplest possible solution. There are, however many other ways of developing more sophisticated formulas in order to establish even more refined values of Z. This may be the case, for instance, when various groups of Xs and Ys, which are for some reason considered to be of a particularly aggravating character, must be handled separately. Likewise, it is possible to let the occurrence of certain instances automatically generate suggestions of various specified kinds (the fact of abuse may be related, for instance, to suggestions concerning treatment). All the cases in the case abstract collection could be classified in the following way:

> Perpetrator – male, aged 23 (Y_1) fell into dispute with working companion (X_1). The perpetrator hit his victim four times with his fist (X_2) in the face (X_3) (Bleeding wound that needed stitching (X_4), swelling, headache, difficulties to move his jaws for some weeks (X_5)). The perpetrator had no previous criminal record (Y_2). The district court came to the conclusion that the attack was unprovoked (Y_3) and that with respect to general prevention (X_6) the perpetrator should be sent to prison for six months. The appeal court found that it could not rule out the possibility that the perpetrator felt that he had been provoked (Y_3) due to the fact that the victim was much bigger than the perpetrator and in connection with the fact that the perpetrator had no pre-

vious criminal record and had a socially acceptable position (Y_4) the sentence was reduced to a fine combined with a probation period.[84]

The case description contains the following factors

Aggravating		*Mitigating*	
X_1	Relation	Y_1	Age of P
X_2	Violence	Y_2	Criminal history
X_3	Aim of attack	Y_3	Situation
X_4	Need of medical care	Y_4	Social situation of P
X_5	Injury		
X_6	Need of general prevention		

Tabulated instances of these factors may be (randomly selected values):

X_1		X_2		X_3	
known	= 1	minor	= 1	body	= 1
spouse	= 3	severe	= 3	head	= 5
unknown	= 5	major	= 6	eyes	= 7

X_4		X_5		X_6	
none	= 1	none	= 1	none	= 1
some	= 3	passing	= 2	some	= 3
considerable	= 7	long-time	= 3	great	= 5
		chronic	= 7		

Y_1		Y_2	Y_3
$P \leq 18$	= 3	no history = 3	provoked = 3
$18 \leq P < 21$	= 2	one incident = 1	fight = 0
$P > 21$	= 1	several incidents = 0	unprovoked = - 1
			revenge = -3

Y_4	
residence	= 1
occupation	= 3
both	= 5

84 Example from *Id.* at 3, case abstract 1.1 (original in Swedish).

The district court's decision

$$(X_1 + X_2 + X_3 + X_4 + X_5 + X_6) - (Y_1 + Y_2 + Y_3) = Z$$
$$(1 + 3 + 5 + 3 + 3 + 3) - (1 + 3 ((-1)) = 15$$

The appeal court's decision

$$(X_1 + X_2 + X_3 + X_4 + X_5 + X_6) - (Y_1 + Y_2 + Y_3 + Y_4) = Z$$
$$(1 + 3 + 5 + 3 + 3 + 3) - (1 + 3 + 3 + 5) = 6$$

The severity levels of the crime in relation to the severity of punishment

Z = 1 - 14 = probation in combination with fines

Z = 15 - 25 = imprisonment 1 month

As indicated above, the theory underlying the methodology that is described here is in several respects similar to the theory underlying the use of sentencing guidelines in the U.S.A. In this context it should be also mentioned that several applications of sentencing guide-lines have been implemented in computer programs, and that some of them have been put into practical use. For example, the previously mentioned sentencing system ASSYST is reported to relate its output to a table in the form of a "sentencing-grid", reflecting 43 levels of crime seriousness and six categories of criminal history. Each "cell" in the grid prescribes a specific sentence-length, as well as a possible range of discretion of 25% in either direction (or 6 months, whichever is larger). "If the sentence handed down is outside the prescribed guideline range, the offended party may appeal, solely on those grounds".[85]

[85] Simon, Gaes, *supra* chapter 1 note 24, at 195-96. *See also, e.g.*, Fino, S.P. *Microcomputers and Criminal Sentencing*, 421 (1987) "At that time the judge must justify any departures from the sentencing range prescribed by the guidelines and give the reasons in the final sentence report."

6.4.5.2.3 Case-Based Models and Legal Reasoning

There is little doubt that the case-based models of the kind illustrated in this section to a large extent can be used in order to represent legal knowledge in a very detailed form. It should be noticed, however, that there exists a limit for the utilization of case fact analysis as a purely inductive instrument in law. The reason for this is simply that any classification of precedents which originates solely from the analysis of facts represents a bottom-up approach which may easily generate results which will be in conflict with legal rules at a higher level of the rule hierarchy (or, with rules operating on different sub-processes within legal reasoning). From the point of view of the JLR it is apparent that projects based on fact-content analysis focus primarily, and often solely, on issues related to the processes of identification and search. Important elements of legal reasoning, such as intentional interpretation, rule-application, and evaluation of intended decisions, are entirely neglected in many contributions. This is illustrated by the theory underlying the development of HYPO-program which, although it is claims to be able to define "relevant similarities and differences among cases" and "most analogous precedents" appear to operate solely with knowledge elements on the level of fact:

> "According to the theory, an arguer justifies a decision in a new case by citing a precedent with the desired outcome and as close to the same factors and magnitudes as possible. The precedent justifies resolving the problem's conflicting factors in the same way that they were resolved in the precedent."[86]

Since many of the aspects of legal reasoning that are neglected by this methodology will often have a decisive influence on the outcome of a legal decision, it is clear that in many situations a case-fact analysis can only provide support of a fragmented and preliminary kind (default suggestions). Complications may, however, arise for several reasons, e.g. when previously neglected facts appear. Such an event may easily lead up to a solution that may challenge any kind of a previously conducted fact-

86 Ashley *supra* note 75, at 249.

content analysis. Devastating effects may follow, for instance, when a previously overlooked disqualifying fact suddenly appears. One sole factor may then cancel out all the relevant similarities with the previous cases. From all this follows that it can be concluded that a representation based on case-fact analysis primarily has to be looked upon as a methodology for the representation of existing law. In addition, it is evident that case-fact analysis can be efficient for the *recognition* of novel facts. To rely on case-fact (similarity) analysis when novel situations containing previously unidentified facts are to be decided, however, seem to be an all too hazardous approach.

The development of practicable solutions based on case-fact analysis depends also, naturally, on the fact whether the cases and the facts can be identified and described in a unbiased manner. Likewise, the number of cases that provide the basis of any case-knowledge base must be of a certain magnitude and must reflect a certain degree of uniformity as regards the outcome of the decisions.[87] In this context it may be recalled also that the discussion seminars held during the NCA project indicated the existence of a general consensus about the need to establish all kinds of numerical fact-values, and formulas operating on such values, through legislation.

Despite these restrictions, there are instances where methods originating from the attempts to formalize case-based reasoning may be also useful in the framework of the JLR. An important conclusion from the NCA and VF projects that must be mentioned here is the fact that there exist important differences between various kinds of legal decisions. An additional finding is that an investigation of the similarities at the case-fact level can be sometimes isolated. This is possible, e.g., in instances when the obligatory evaluations of the rule-application process have been already completed in a indisputable way. The most striking example of this are criminal court decisions which can be divided into two separate parts. In criminal court decisions the court (or the jury) must first determine whether or not a crime has been committed and whether or not the accused person should be sentenced. This first conclusion that must be reached in such a reasoning process is in principle, just like any other

[87] *Cf.* Karpf, J. *Inductive Modelling in Law*, 303 (1991) "The judgement must be adequately circumscribable.", "The judgements must have a sufficient practice."

legal decision as regards the fact that it may include recurrent processes of identification, search, and interpretation. In the succeeding phase, however, when it has been decided that a crime has been committed the court has to decide on an appropriate sentence. At this stage of the process it is only the set of facts in the already defined situation that is relevant. In such instances, the principle of equality will frequently be the only rule of evaluation that has to be taken into consideration and on such occasions it may therefore also be motivated to rely on similarity analysis.

Similar preconditions may appear in e.g. damage law when damages are to be estimated, or in stable fields of law, where it can be determined in advance that the facts that can be related to a certain indisputable and relevant consequence are of a restricted number. From this point of view it is also clear that the inductive method can be applied on some occasions at a more detailed rule level.[88]

6.4.5.3 *Associative Models*

In an article published in 1945, *Vannevar Bush* makes some preliminary comments concerning the associating inference technique, in connection with criticism levelled at the conventional methods of information processing.

> When data of any sort are placed in storage, they are filed alphabetically or numerically, and information is found (when it is) by tracing it down from subclass to subclass. It can be in only one place, unless duplicates are used; one has to have rules as to which path will locate it, and the rules are cumbersome. Having found one item, moreover, one has to emerge from the system and reenter on a new path.
>
> The human mind does not work that way. It operates by association. With one item in its grasp, it snaps instantly to the next that is suggested by the association of thoughts, in accordance with some intricate web of trails carried by the cells of the brain. . . . Man cannot hope fully to duplicate this mental process artificially, but he certainly ought to be able to learn from it. . . . Selection by association, rather than by indexation may yet be mechanized.[89]

88 *Cf.* Karpf, *Id.*, who in a discussion on technical/feasibility criteria for inductive modelling in law suggests that "The judgement must have a precise normative location."

89 Bush *supra* chapter 4 note 3, at 54.

In the accompanying discussion Bush outlines an alternative method for information processing. The article was written without special references to computers. What Bush had in mind, was an advanced microfilm retrieval tool which he labelled MEMEX.

The introduction of computers made that Bush's ideas have found several practical areas of application. The technique presently known as hypertext (the term coined some twenty years after Bush's publication[90]), originating form the ideas presented by Bush, is now looked upon as one of the cornerstones of modern theories on the storage and representation of knowledge.

6.4.5.3.1 Hypertext

Hypertext is used as a collective name for a number of methods for knowledge management. A hypertext application may be described as flexible cross referring of a web of knowledge storage units, which may be used as both a storage tool and a retrieval system. The technique makes it possible to process, store and retrieve texts, graphics, sounds, motion pictures, and combinations of different forms of knowledge.

As a point of terminology it should be mentioned in this context that the technique which is often referred to as *hypertext* is of a general nature. That is to say that, despite the inclusion of the word ''text'' the technique is not restricted to the management of written material or text documents. On the contrary, the technique makes it possible to combine various types of knowledge items with each other, regardless of whether they are represented in texts or not. It is, for instance, possible to specify the storing units for antecedents and consequents, and also to relate such components to each other in a logical manner. The generality of this technique is the reason for using the term ''associating program'' in the remaining part of this study as a synonym to ''hypertext''. Furthermore, it may be noticed that the word ''unit'' is preferred as a generic term denoting components (''data-blocks'') used to represent knowledge in hypertext programs. It should be noticed, however, that alternative names appear in different commercial products. Examples of synonyms that sometimes appear also

90 Nelson, T.H. *The Hypertext* (1965), Nelson, T.H. *Getting it out of our System* (1967).

in this study are "cards" and "documents". The use of the word "document" in this context should not be, however, interpreted as an indication that hypertext is a technique that is restricted only to text management or document retrieval. Nor is it appropriate to look upon programs of hypertext nature primarily as complements to conventional information retrieval systems.

In an associating computer program the knowledge may be represented at several, more or less specific levels and the user of the system may choose the level from which he would like to approach the system, the order in which he would like to investigate the knowledge, and the way in which the knowledge should be presented. Associating programs connects elements of knowledge through links. A word in a text, a field in a document, details in a picture, symbols and other subject matters that have been presented, may be all used as links. The user is able to retrieve units by indicating the appropriate link. The most feasible way to do this is by using a mouse (moveable function key) controlling a cursor on the computer screen.

A knowledge storing unit may have one or several links to other units. The organization of the units, or the design of the links, need not be pre-described, i.e. the user may decide and adjust the methods to the current type of knowledge. The point of departure can be, for instance, a picture. An element of the picture may be linked up with a text. In the text the maker of the picture may be described. The description may be linked up with other texts, footnotes, tables of different kinds, and other pictures etc. The designer of the picture may be linked up with other designers, and the concepts expressed in the text can be expressed in several other ways in other texts. Applications may be comprehensive – intended to be used by several employees in an organization - or selective for specific purposes and individual use. Changes of the structure, creation of new units and updating of the existing ones, as well as the storing of knowledge may be conducted by means of centralized control, or else on a decentralized basis with the individual users performing these tasks. Applications of hypertext may be thus designed for the use in distributed systems via terminals, or for the use in personal computers.

The hypertext methods make it also possible to consider the sequence aspects. In many situations it may be necessary, for instance, to approach knowledge concerning a certain subject in a specific order. Time aspects, hierarchical, statistical, functional or procedural relations may be the reason for this. With hypertext, such knowledge may be conserved by means of linking several units together in a certain order. A hypertext base may thus contain pre-defined default search paths. Moreover, in order to facilitate the retrieval of information and to be able to gain from previous experience, search paths may be logged. In addition, the users may easily add notes or mnemonic symbols to the existing units. Alternatively, new unit may be added.

The questions about what to store, and how the material should be structured, are sometimes answered best only after authentic work situations have been investigated. The knowledge that is requested in different situations may be of a more or less specific character, depending partly on the identity of the user, partly on the nature of the current problem. A hypertext base may, nevertheless, fulfil several functions and a number of knowledge structures may be stored in a parallel way. Several structures may also support and interact with each other.

A further application may be also developed which combines hypertext techniques with other search functions. The basis for conventional IR and Boolean operators, may, for instance support the technique of linking text elements together. Smaller hypertext applications may be connected with conventional IR-systems and through links with remote databases external documents or very large collections of data may be accessed. The amassed knowledge may then be amplified by the user, and eventually communicated to others through a computer network. It is also practicable to combine local and general access with different parts of a hypertext system. Isolated units, or groups of units, may be divided by means of access codes. Computer programs which use hypertext or similar techniques may be used in order to combine several media, e.g. video, projectors, computers and sound-systems. The technique is then often called hypermedia – sometimes the label multimedia is used instead.

The future vision of the possibilities connected with hypertext application methods is rather far-reaching. Alongside with the more obvious possibilities of knowledge storage, hypertext has been recommended as a universal medium. Extensive applications have been suggested, including literature of different kinds, research libraries in full text, and so forth.[91]

[91] *See, e.g.*, Parsaye, K., Chignell, M., Khoshafian, S., Wong, H. *Intelligent Databases* (1989).

6.4.5.3.2 The VF Project

A practical experiment with the hypertext technique has been performed in the VF project. The experiment was conducted with a standard program, viz. *Apple HyperCard*.[92] The project group had had, when the work was initiated, some experience with the program. Generally speaking, the program is quite easy to learn and in several respects self-instructive. In consequence, after a short introduction most users with some computer experience would be able to construct their own hypertext knowledge-bases of the kind that is presented here.

The aim of the VF project was, firstly, to see if the technique worked at all. In addition, the project was meant to investigate whether or not the methods were suitable for legal material. Since this was the first experiment, there were not so many aspects to be considered as regards the content of the application. The only criterion that had to be fulfilled was that the content should be related to the rule-based decision support system that was being constructed simultaneously (described in section 6.4.5.1.2 supra). The field of law was thereby limited to labour law, or more precisely, to the problems concerning dismissal of employees owing to misconduct in the form of unauthorized absence. As illustrated, in its dialogue with the user the decision support system operated at the conceptual level, i.e. the questions that were put forward to the user were normally about one isolated (and more or less decomposed) labour-law concept. Hence, it was also natural to start the development of the hypertext application from the conceptual level. The future, integrated system would then be able to guide the user in his in-depth search for definitions, illustrations and examples of concepts in the dialogue with the decision support system. Regarding this aim, and in order to integrate the two systems, the hypertext application was developed around the concept of the employee's illness.

To construct hypertext databases with the help of the selected program implies that units, (cards) which are linked together in adequate and rational ways, must be created. The first unit which was created in the database was given the name *Main text* and contained, besides a definition of the relevant concept of illness, also an overview of the knowledge-base.

92 *See*, for an elaborated description, Goodman, D. *The Complete HyperCard Handbook* (1987).

The definition was formulated with the help of quotations from the literature, case decisions and from other legally relevant material. The contents directory listed the different types of units that were present in the application.

Some words in the overview in the main text unit served as links, i.e. if they were indicated with the mouse, the system immediately presented a unit with the corresponding name and content. All activated words, i.e. word that could be used as links, were framed. It should be stressed, however, that the designer, or even the user of a hypertext database, can decide himself how the links should be indicated. Framing words is by no means the only possible solution. The choices are numerous. Links may be designed as pictures of buttons, or as symbols, or they may be hidden. In the latter case, for instance, words, or fields in a document, may act as hidden links.

This particular application was, however, intended to be used by several different persons. Many of them would probably not need to approach the system very often. Therefore, it was found appropriate to let the user see when a link was present. However, when this kind of computer systems become more widespread, this strategy may have to be changed. In future, users of computer systems may assume that central concepts and important words will have been defined for a given text and exemplified at several levels, and automatically indicate them any time they want additional information. In many kinds of applications it will be probably also quite natural for the user to change the form of the links or to hide them away in the system.

After the initial unit giving the definition of the main concept had been created, more units, one after the other, were added to the knowledge-base. The new units were then linked in various ways with the previous ones.

In all the units identically outlined fields for headlines and buttons were defined. The headline field stated that the unit was a part of a system dealing with employees' illness. It also contained the name of the current unit. The names of the units were selected in such a way as to be as content-descriptive as possible. The button fields contained links to other units. The links were marked by button symbols. Each unit contained between five and ten button symbols which were arranged in a similar way in all the units.

The two fields for headlines and buttons, later received a standardized, uniform form for most of the units in the knowledge base. Thus the user always knew were to look on the screen to find information about the current unit. At the same time he could also see what other units were directly available. The technique of using the so called ''ever present maps'' may also be important, especially in more in complex applications, in helping the user to retrace his search paths.[93]

In order to make the hypertext base self-instructive, two units containing explanations of the technique were created. Together with the introductory unit, the explanatory units formed an introduction module in the database. The introductory unit functioned as a start up screen and it was also the unit appearing on the screen as soon as the user left the hypertext base. The first explanatory unit showed examples of links, in the form of words and buttons. The user was given an opportunity to try out the technique by means of indicating any of the links. If he did so, the other explanatory unit, in turn linked him back with the first one. The introductory module also provided an opportunity of trying the scrolling functions and the Boolean search functions.

93 *See,* generally on presentation techniques in hypertext applications, Kindborg, M. *Visual Techniques for Orientation in Hypermedia Structures* (1991).

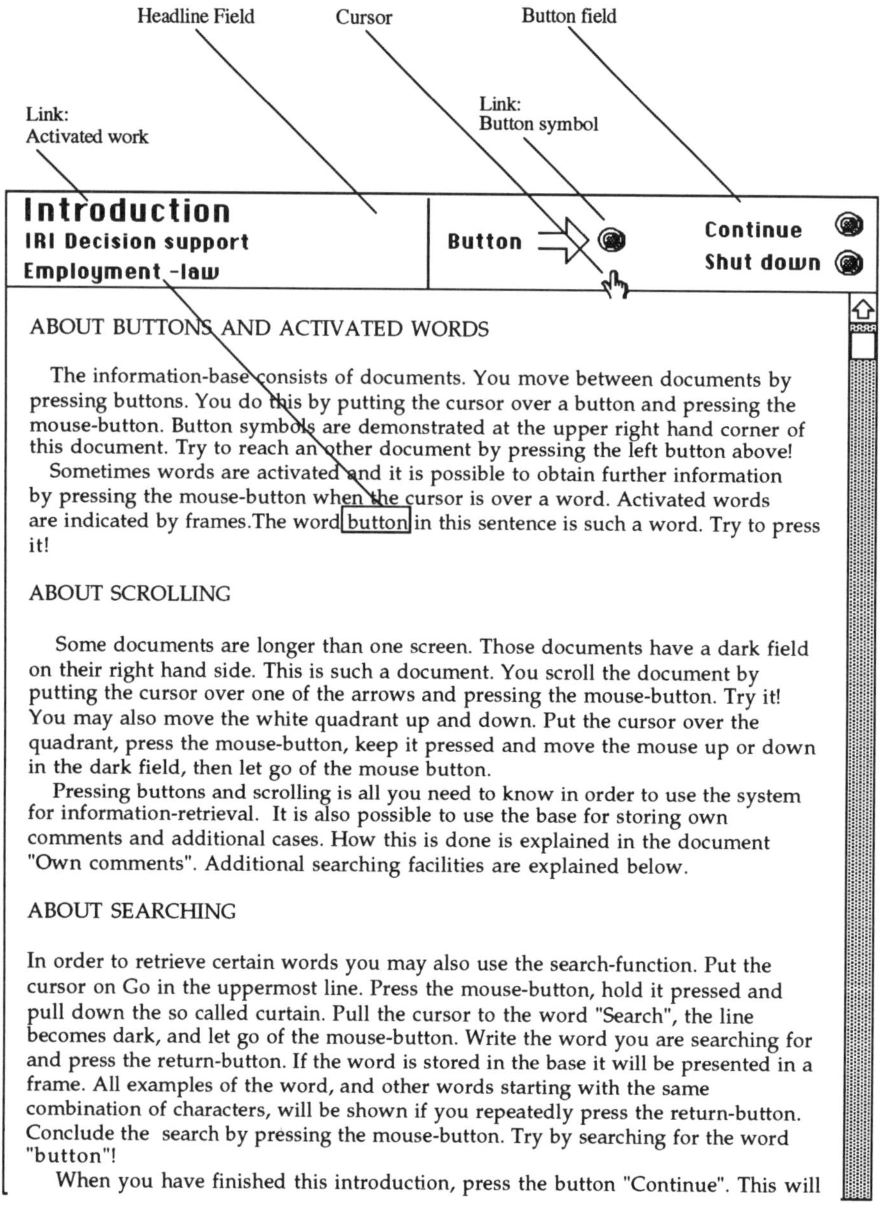

Figure 6.6 Introductory unit in hypertext-base.

The hypertext-base came to include, in addition to the introductory module, two other types of units; text documents and picture units. The text documents were in turn of two kinds, overview documents and full text documents. The overview documents fulfilled the function of being indexes and tables of contents, listing cases, headlines, index words and literature quotations from the base. In the overview documents, headlines and case labels were linked with the full text documents. Different texts were included. In addition to the main text unit, cases in the original text form, cases in the form of abstracts, quotations from labour law literature and from legislative preparatory works, as well as units intended for the user's own commentaries were defined.

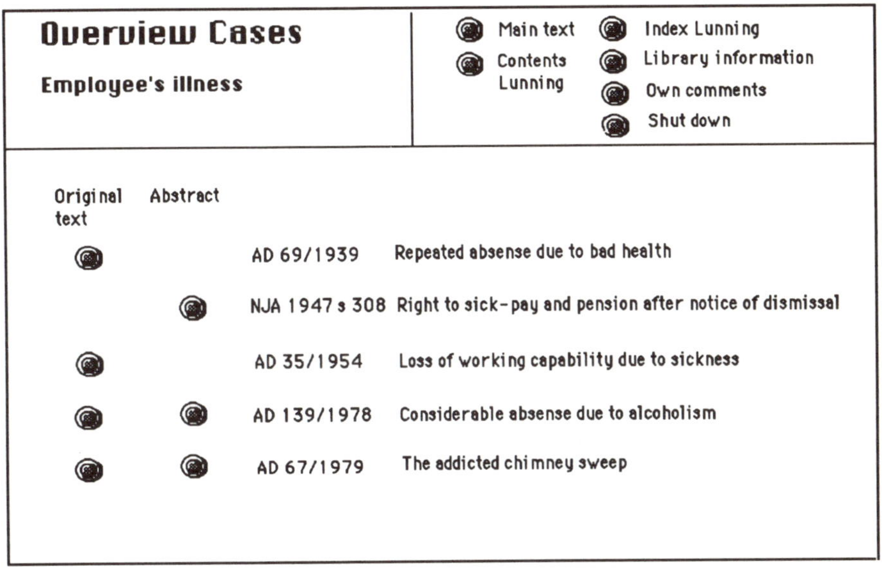

Figure 6.7 Overview document

Only two picture units were created, not counting the start up screen. The first presented an imaginary map of a labour law library. From this unit it was possible to reach text units through book-symbol links. The library unit also contained a link to the communication unit with an image of a telephone with dial-up facilities, showing, among other things, the telephone number to the labour law library. The communication unit was intended to act as a link with the library and/or with other sources of information. Although the actual communication facilities were not implemented at the experimental stage, in other experiments IRI has connected Macintosh computers with similar programs to remote databases.

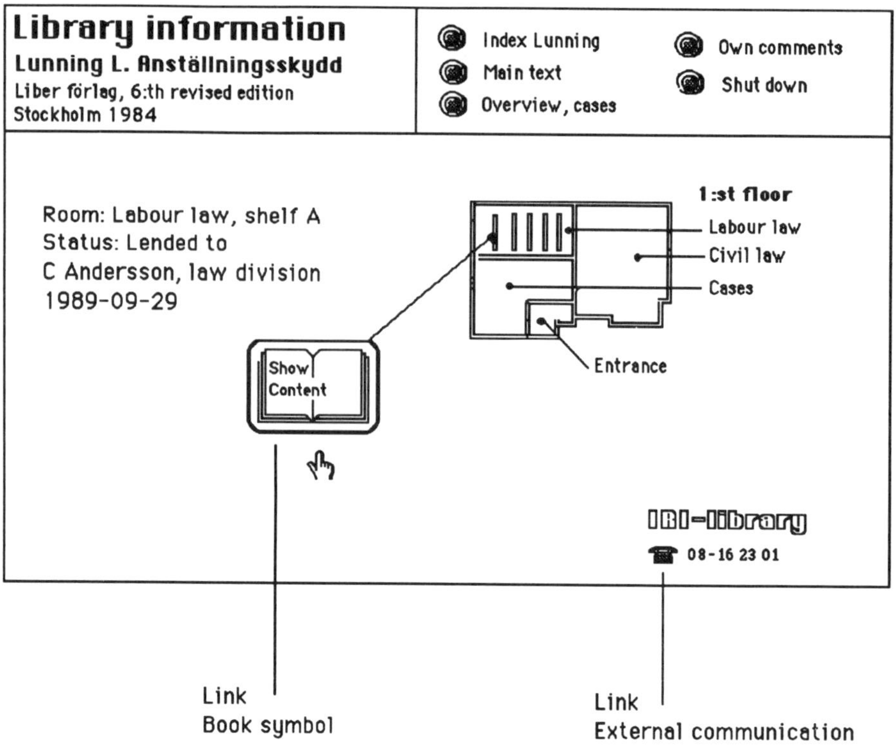

Figure 6.8 Library unit.

In addition to the predefined units, the hypertext base included a unit for the user's own comments. This unit was intended to function as a note pad to use when new, unstructured information was to be included. In practice such units would have the function of collecting and dispersing new information of common interest among the VF lawyers. In our application the comment unit was perceived as a communication facility for forwarding experiences of immediate interest arising from negotiations in various geographical places. Unit of this type were simultaneously conceived for the VF library in order to herald the new literature and other kinds of information.

The program product used included advanced word processing facilities, drawing facilities and several other possibilities. It should be also mentioned that the program makes it possible to divide the users into different categories. For different reasons it may be necessary to deny access to certain units to some users. This is especially valid for legal texts, such as statutes, case decisions, etc. where for many important reasons it may be necessary to preserve and protect these units from unauthorized changes. In the version of the program we used there are several possibilities of protecting a certain type or group of units from changes. It is also possible to qualify the access of different users in such a way that e.g. some users may only have permission to use the system for information retrieval, others may be authorized to write in some units, still others may be authorized to write in all units; some may have the right to draw, to open new units, make changes in the existing ones or delete links.

The hypertext database became finally relatively complex, containing about 30 cross-referring units concerning the concept of employees' illness. The various units and the links between them are illustrated in figure 6.9. It should be mentioned in this context that several researchers have reported problems with the maintenance of large hypertext bases due to the fact that units and links are to numerous.[94] The number of units and links reflected in this project was, however, not a significant problem.

94 *See, e.g.*, on problems with so called "hyperspagetti", Greenleaf, G., Mowbray, A., Tyree, A. *The DataLex Legal Workstation – Integrating Tools for Lawyers*, 217 (1991) *and* on ways of avoiding it, Kindborg *Id.*

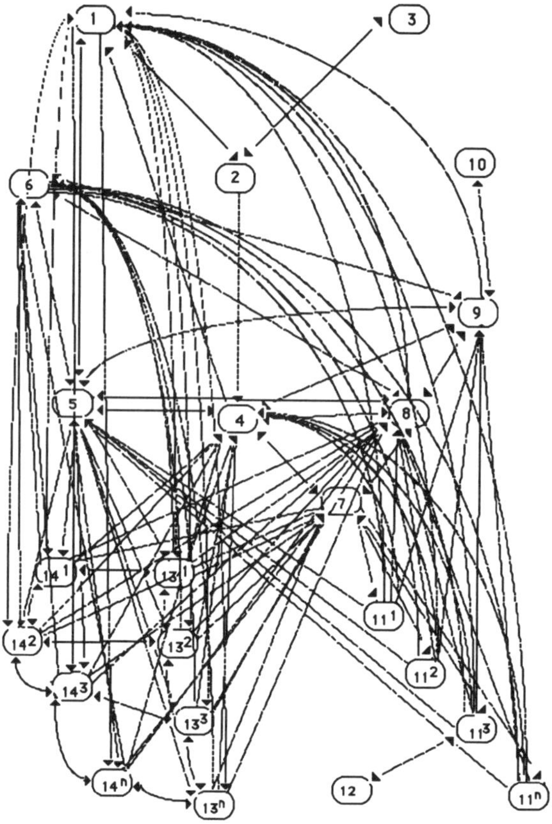

Figure 6.9 Units and relations in hypertext database. Each node represents a knowledge storing unit. The numbers are explained below.

1	Presentation and exit unit.
2	Explanatory unit.
3	Explanatory unit.
4	Main text: Definition of concept.
5	Overview cases.
6	Own comments.
7	Index of subjects in Lunning, L. *Anställningsskydd: Kommentar till anställningsskyddslagen.*
8	Table of contents in Lunning, L. *Anställningsskydd: Kommentar till anställningsskyddslagen.*
9	Library information.
10	Telephone and external communication.

11^1 - 11^n	Citations from Lunning, L. *Anställningsskydd: Kommentar till anställningsskyddslagen.*
12	Legislative preparatory material: Proposition 1974:174 p 55.
13^1 - 13^n	Case abstracts (*Svenska arbetsgivareföreningen* loose-leaf files, *Arbetsdomstolens domar. Anställningsskyddslagen.*
14^1 - 14^n	Cases in original text.

6.4.5.3.3 Associative Models and Legal Reasoning

Associative representation and hypertext are by no means in conflict with the JLR. The fact that the associating technique would be of interest to lawyers was predicted by Bush already in his article from 1945[95] and, as illustrated in chapter five, it is clear that the essential parts of the legal reasoning process are aimed at establishing and relating knowledge segments to each other, e.g. concepts, rules, cases, jurisprudential literature, and so forth. Recently also, several suggestions concerning the ways of utilizing this technique in the legal domain have been presented.[96]

As regards the possibilities of applying the hypertext techniques to legal AI-systems it is quite apparent that the hypertext technique can serve as a basis for the development of elaborated support systems in the identification and search-process. It should be underlined, however, that the feasibility of the application of the associating technique into legal knowledge representation is not only restricted to search and retrieval. The close relationship between form and substance in law makes that a support system for legal reasoning may benefit from a technique which can link elements with each other during the whole process by means of providing the user with, e.g., explanations during the interpretation and rule-application phases. The VF experiment also illustrates that the hypertext technique may be of great value for the presentation and management of various kinds of legal material. The flexibility of the technique which makes it possible to make changes and additions in the

95 Bush *supra* chapter 4 note 3.

96 *See, e.g.*, on the drafting of legal documents, Wilson, E. *Drafting Legal Documents With Justus' Clerk* (1989) *and*, on hypertext as a potential tool in legal education, Painter, D. *Hyperlaw* (1990). It can be mentioned also that presently (winter 1991/92) IRI in the LexLab project is conducting hypertext experiments with rule-representations in a KBS-like fashion.

applications in an individual manner also means that the technique may be very effective in providing support for learning. As will be illustrated in chapter 7 it is also possible to conceive central and important tasks for associating methods in future AI-systems of a more complex kind.

6.4.5.4 Deontic Models

A discussion examining computational models of legal reasoning must not overlook deontic models of law, i.e. descriptions utilizing deontic logic. The reason for this is simply that several researchers have suggested that deontic logic is a necessary component of any undertaking dealing with with AI and law.[97] As mentioned before, deontic logic is quite a broad term concerned with a number of issues of various kinds. In a recent contribution the following aspects have been found to be the major issues of concern:

> (i) analysing the difficulties to which the use of truth-functional connectives give rise . . .; (ii) characterizing the negation of (sentences expressing) legal norms . . .; (iii) providing a suitable account of the notion of permission . . .; (iv) investigating the notion of deontic necessity . . .; (v) testing whether how to deal with conflicts of norms and gaps is a matter of logical principles rather than a matter of legal metanorms . . .; (vi) figuring out a new formal treatment of deontic conditionals.
>
> Much attention is also devoted to the question as to whether deontic logic is to be conceived as a logic of (sentences expressing) legal norms rather than as a logic of descriptive sentences concerning norms.[98]

In works concentrating ~~on~~ on deontic logic it is furthermore noticeable that conflicting opinions are not infrequent. The various discussions do not only concern themselves thereby with the ways of dealing with detailed formalization problems, such as those exemplified above,[99] but

[97] *See, e.g.*, McCarty, L.T. *Permissions and Obligations* (1983), Susskind *supra* chapter 1 note 9 at 225, Jones, A.J.I. *Deontic Logic and Legal Knowledge Representation* (1990) *and* Jones, A.J.I., Sergot, M. *Deontic Logic in the Representation of Law: Towards a Methodology* (Forthcoming).

[98] Mazzarese, T. *Guest Editor's Preface,* at i (1991).

[99] Åqvist is remembered for stating that "It is tempting to answer that it [deontic logic] is a field with the property that there is virtually no single issue in it upon which a settled consensus has been reached." *Id.*, with reference to Åqvist, L. *Deontic Logic* (1984).

also with the more crucial question of whether deontic logic is a useful approach at all.[100]

The arguments submitted in this work concern solely the latter issue, with no attempt to go into any details of various research approaches, concerning, e.g., the logical form of deontic sentences. The reason for this is simply that nothing of what has been undertaken in this study indicates that deontic logic has any practical significance in the context of automation of legal reasoning. Neither in the theoretical description of law and legal reasoning undertaken in chapter 5, nor in the practical and theoretical system development approaches that are described in this part of the study have any requirements concerning deontic logic been detected.[101] For many reasons it is also possible to arrive to the conclusion that the assumptions leading up to the formation of deontic logic are to some extent inconsistent with the assumptions underlying the JLR model.

In order to further explain this, perhaps surprising, conclusion a number of general observations should be made explicit. The ambition is that this undertaking can help to shed some light on the seemingly incompatible presuppositions prevailing in the field. It is important to underline, however, that the conclusions reached in this study do not say anything about the utility of deontic logic in projects approaching law from alternative directions.[102] It may well be that the jurisprudential perspective outlined in this study in comparison with deontic theories may turn out to be too poorly developed, or even incorrect, and that deontic models may eventually obtain a crucial position in the legal theory. Nor is anything said about the possibilities of forming logically consistent

100 Mazzarese *Id.* "Notwithstanding the apparent – i.e. both manifest and pretended – double bind between deontic calculi – which, at least implicitly, aims at being logic of (sentences expressing) norms – and the search for formal tools enabling a logical analysis of legal language, it is doubtful whether deontic logic (in spite of its manifold developments since 1951) does in fact provide a suitable account of the logical behaviour of (sentences expressing) legal norms."

101 This is probably not a unique experience. As yet no implemented systems appear to be based on deontic models. *See, e.g.*, Bench-Capon, T.J.M. *Deep Models, Normative Reasoning and Legal Expert Systems,* 38 (1989) "If we look beyond academic systems to the current work being done in legal expert systems, . . . we find that it is largely based on shallow systems using at most first order predicate calculus as the underlying logic." *and* Jones, Sergot *supra* note 97, at 2 "The deontic logic . . . has not been employed in any application as far as we know."

102 *See, e.g.*, for a recent suggestion of more limited functions, von Wright, G.H., *Is There a Logic of Norms?*, 282 (1991). *Compare* Jones, Sergot *supra* note 97 *and* Herrestad *supra* chapter 2 note 82, at 62-63.

systems reflecting the relations between deontic concepts. It is in other words accepted that it it may be possible to construct one or several such systems. What is suggested here is merely that the possibilities of enhancing the understanding of legal reasoning by means of employing components such as permissions, obligations, rights and similar concepts at the present level of understanding must be looked upon as a still unproved hypothesis. In other words, the crucial issue is whether it is possible to find practical applications of deontic logic without challenging basic jurisprudential presuppositions.

6.4.5.4.1 A Normative Perspective

One reason behind the divergent views concerning the feasibility of deontic logic lies, no doubt, in the different perception of the functions of the law. This may be illustrated by the *normative* perspective recently articulated by *Andrew J. I Jones* and *Marek Sergot*. In this approach deontic logic "needs to be taken seriously whenever it is necessary to make explicit, and then reason about, the distinction between what ought to be the case and what is the case, or as we say, between the ideal and the actual."[103] It is furthermore suggested that "Norms lay down constraints by specifying how agents ought to behave and how they are permitted to behave."[104]

From the point of view of the lawyer trying to reach a legal decision, as well as from the point of view of the lawyer describing legal reasoning and the function of law, however, it is difficult to accept this description. In other words, from the perspective of the JLR model it appears to be uncertain, and often even questionable, to what extent law aims to define "ideal" situations. It may also be put in question to what extent the critical issue in legal reasoning is to investigate whether agents *violate* logically established, required and/or permitted behaviour patterns, except perhaps in certain situations where it can be concluded that the relevant rules form a more or less closed and predefined system. Instead, in almost all processes of legal reasoning it must be taken into consideration that law is a flexible system providing legal descriptions – a set of propositions at

103 Jones, Sergot *supra* note 97 at 1.

104 *Id.* at 7.

various levels of abstraction that may be used to reflect situations occurring in reality – and that in cases when the actual situations (or the intended actions) can be subsumed under these descriptions, then the law may apply. Conversely, if the situations (actions) cannot be subsumed (eventually through the utilization of acknowledged methodological rules) the law will not apply, and for a number of reasons – most of them concerning the principles of predictability and legality – there can be no in-between choice. If for some reason the law is found to be *inappropriate* (i.e. if the law cannot fulfil its *underlying function*) it may have to be changed. This can be only done, however, in a formalized process of legislation and the changes can only affect situations that have not yet occurred. This "descriptive" or "definitional" stand point can be contrasted with the normative perspective in which it appears as if the formation of a consistent and complete rule system appears to be the focal interest.

> But if agents cannot be assumed to behave flawlessly, or if there are *unregulated extraneous factors*, then there is also the possibility of deviation from this ideal, or what we have called violation. And typically it is necessary to go further, to specify what other norms come into force in the case of such violations: not necessarily in order to punish, or to display a stick to encourage ideal behaviour, but because *to leave the resulting behaviour completely unregulated is just not acceptable.*[105]

6.4.5.4.2 Changes in the Law

Admittedly, both the JLR model and the normative perspective assume that legal propositions must be adjusted in order to fit situations incorporating previously undefined (unregulated) factors. The important differences appear to originate, however, from the assumptions about the accomplishments of these adjustments.

The deontic model appears to assume that it is possible to find indications on how changes may be accomplished, solely by means of investigating the logical relations between the legal components at the level of rules, or by means of elaborating a logic of sentences expressing legal rules.

105 *Id.* at 7 (Italics added). *Compare,* for discussion about a descriptive view of the law, , *e.g.*, Kelsen *supra* chapter 2 note 70, at 73, Hedenius, I. *Om rätt och moral,* (1941), Strömholm, *supra* chapter 1 note 29, at 95-96 *and* Hamfelt *supra* chapter 2 note 4, at 19.

According to the jurisprudential approach elaborated in chapter 5, however, it is very difficult to accept a logic, or even discussions about changes in law, that focus solely on the components at the level of rules.

From the jurisprudential point of view – when novel situations are encountered – it is instead appropriate to assume that a large number of legal components (e.g. the definition of a legal concept, the application area of a legal rule, or the interpretation of formal rules of competence, etc.) can be adjusted in accordance with the requirements of the situation and the legal order. It is also obvious that law provides a large corpus of knowledge describing the ways in which such transformations can be accomplished. With the use of a slightly different terminology (as a comment on point (v) of the initial citation of section 6.4.5.4) this means that conflicts of norms and gaps are dealt with by means of applying legal metanorms (various kinds of methodological rules of a legal nature).

When these aspects are discussed it is important to mention that all changes of the law may bring about conflict of interests. It is also obvious that it is not always easy to determine whose side the law should support or defend. In this respect, law is not a system that can be observed only from the point of view of the legislator. Nor can it always be assumed that legal decision makers are prepared to share the intentions of the legislator. In line with this it is also clear that the utilization of a gap in a rule system does not have to be looked upon as a violation. On the contrary, from the point of view of e.g. the actor in a certain situation the fact that there is a gap in the system may be considered as an ideal situation.

6.4.5.4.3 Permissions and Obligations

The classification of legal rules according to the deontic logic appear to a large extent to be dependent on whether the rules (or the sentences expressing rules) describe, e.g., permissions, obligations or prohibitions and similar relations (vis-à-vis a certain legal agent).

Such a classification raises problems of acceptance. The difficulties that occurs here is a consequence of the general difficulty mentioned above, namely that in legal reasoning conflicts of interests and gaps between the rules are dealt with by means of applying various kinds of methodological rules. Of equal importance in this respect is the fact that the various types of methodological rules operate on different sub-processes which are necessarily interrelated with each other.

In other words, this means that the formation of a rule in the process of legal reasoning can be never solely dependent on its logical relations with other rules. That is to say that if it is accepted that the function of (sentences expressing) rules is to provide a means of classification during the identification process, it must be also accepted that this aspect of legal reasoning is necessarily interrelated with the activation of legal knowledge of different kinds, e.g. for rule application and evaluation. When it comes to the possibilities of using the concepts like permissions, obligations and prohibitions it is quite obvious that a legally defined act may be either prohibited or permissible, depending on the context in which the issue is to be decided. Likewise, a legal rule may have to be adjusted in accordance with the interpretation of the interrelated elements occurring in a certain situation, whereas formal and evaluative rules may have to be modified to conform to social changes, and so forth. (The requirements will in this respect ultimately reflect the acceptable standards for legal decision making for a society at a given point of time). It can be also concluded that in many instances the nature of a permission or a prohibition can be affected by the ways in which elements (e.g. concepts making up prerequisites in the antecedents) are interpreted at a lower level of abstraction.

In practice, this appears to indicate that the possibilities of forming a logic at the levels of rules categorized into permissions, obligations and other similar concepts are strictly limited. Or, to be more cautious, that the possibilities of developing a logic from such components that reflect *authentic* relations appearing in law and legal reasoning are strictly limited.

In this respect, as an alternative to this normative understanding of the concepts of permission and obligation, it may be argued that the function of such components is of a different nature – viz. that they may be perceived as vehicles of inferences which may be used in order to tie together sets of rules and concepts concerning substantial matters in a convenient manner, e.g. in order to facilitate communication. In the perspective underlying this study, however, trying to isolate the level of rules would appear irrational. Likewise it would be incorrect to assume the existence of logical or even stable relations between rules reflecting permissions and obligations.

6.4.5.4.4 Paradoxes

In a discussion concerning the possibilities of describing logical relations in rule systems it is also important to note that legal systems contain numerous paradoxes and contradictions. Some of them may be accidental and – as indicated above – occur as a result of new presuppositions and changes in the law. It is important to note, however, also that gaps and paradoxes may be intended by the legislator for practical or political reasons, e.g. in order to give room to developments in the rapidly changing fields of society or simply because no consensus can be reached. One example of this is provided by the Swedish penal code in which it is stated that in the process of sentencing a judge must take into consideration also what is best from the point of view of the criminal (which implies an obligation to facilitate resocialisation by means of deciding about appropriate support). Simultaneously, however, it must be understood that the legal code assumes also that the lawyer will apply the sentencing rules – which implies an obligation to punish. In order to solve such dilemmas, a lawyer must chose between incompatible obligations. This can only be done by means of decomposing the components making up the various rules, in order to find more detailed regulations indicating that situations of certain kinds ought to be managed in a certain way. Alternatively, a lawyer in this situation may have to generalize from one or several legal propositions in order to find additional support for his decision (e.g. an *intentional law fragment* (*cf.* section 5.4.2.2. *supra*) that will enable him to construct a high level rule indicating how to chose between incompatible obligations in criminal law).

Also in this respect it is obvious that it makes little sense to see law as a set of rules appearing at one distinct level of generality. On the contrary, from the point of view of the practicing lawyer it is obvious that legal reasoning assumes that in many fields of law it is possible to actively form individual solutions by means of combining legal components from different levels of abstraction.

6.4.5.4.5 Truth-Related Connectives

Some comments should be also made on the much discussed issue of the so called truth-related connectives (deontic conditionals), i.e. the fact that legal propositions may take the form of e.g. "if (a) then it *may be* the case that (b)'', ''if (a) then it *ought to be* the case that (b)'', or ''if (a) then it *must not be* established that (b)'', etc.

Connectives of this seemingly vague nature appear in many forms and are sometimes understood to be related to the nature of the conclusions that can be drawn from such statements – especially when more complex rules of inference are to be applied. This seems, in turn, to be one of the major reasons underlying the assumption that classical logic is inadequate and that in order to properly reflect the language of law a formal system must include operators such as P for permission (denoting it may be, e.g., established that), O for obligation (denoting it must be, e.g., established that), and Ph (denoting that it is prohibited), (e.g. a —> P(b), b —> O(c)). From this in turn follows, it has been argued, that the laws of inferences as known from classical logic (as e.g. the previously mentioned law of hypothetical syllogism ((a —> b) & (b —> c)) —> (a —> c)) lose much of their clarity and that alternative relations must be identified and elaborated.[106] This has lead to attempts to find and describe relations such as *if* O(a) *then* ~ Ph (a) and so forth.

In contrast to this, however, it may be argued that – provided that a legal rule (or a sentence expressing a legal rule) is valid according to the doctrine of legal sources – it would be pointless to suggest that it is untrue. Nor does it make any sense to suggest that a rule application can be true in varying degrees. From the point of view of the practicing lawyer – as well as from the objective point of view – it is obvious that legal rules that are valid according to the doctrine of legal sources – disregarding the kind of connectives they may contain – can be applied to situational facts and also that the conclusions which can be drawn from such a process are of a substantial (true) nature, provided no formal rule concerning, e.g., jurisdiction, validity in time and competence of the decision maker is violated. To suggest otherwise would be very much the same as to claim that there can be no legal system.

In this perspective – and this is the crucial point – it is also clear that the so called truth-related connectives do not say anything about the strength of the logical relation between the antecedent and the consequent in a conditional statement. Instead, from the legislators' point of view, the use

106 *See, e.g.,* Susskind *supra* chapter 1 note 9, at 230 ''The problem, then, concerns the extent, if any, to which we can chain together or conjoin statements with deontic content in the process of legal reasoning.''

of various kinds of connectives is the usual way of indicating that there may exist additional sub-rules defining the facts related to the situation. In this way, the use of the phrase "ought to" (and similar, on the surface seemingly ambiguous, notions) in legislation is simply a way of indicating that a description of the accompanying situation may contain exceptions (often defined in interrelated sub-rules) and that the question of whether or not the rule should be applied depends on the applicability of those sub-rules. Alternatively, if no such rules can be found, the appearance of various connectives indicates that the issue may be open to interpretation, i.e. that methodological rules may have to be employed. In this respect, (following the terminology introduced by Sundby) modal connectives function primarily as "assessment markers" (*avveiningsmarkører*),[107] i.e. as components of textual representations of law, helping the lawyers to find their way in complex rule systems.

6.4.5.4.6 Concluding Remarks

In summary, when comparing the basic assumptions underlying this study with the projects concerning deontic models, we can see that the latter reflect a different way of looking at legal reasoning and the function of law. From the point of view adopted in this work, law appears by necessity to be of too dynamic and open a nature to allow for the existence of logical relations between components, such as permissions and obligations, except in closed sets of rules (or sets of sentences expressing rules). In this perspective, the only possible practical significance of a logic based on deontic operators appears to be in whether it can be established that the intended legislation does not contain contradictions with respect to permissions and obligations. One important question remains still, and that is why permissions, obligations and similar concepts should be looked upon as components of any particular significance. Any legal system contains innumerable legal concepts, as well as general descriptions of agents, objects, legal positions, acts, intentions, functions, objectives, time aspects, events, and so forth, which in many fields of law play a much more important role than permissions and obligations in legal reasoning. Furthermore, as regards the issue concerning difficulties

[107] It should be noticed however that Sundby uses the term *avveiningsmarkører* in a broader meaning, Sundby *supra* chapter 5 note 3, at 200-22.

connected with the so called deontic (modal) connectives and truth values, it may be surmised that much of the discussion reflects a different understanding of the function of assessment markers that appear in textual representation of legal rules.

As a consequence, in the search for a methodology (and practical applications) for deontic logic it appear as if several, more or less tacit assumptions, need further attention and clarification. Is it, for instance, (apart from the suggested existence of the so called deontic conditionals) possible to observe any attributes supporting the theory of truth-related normative functions? In what sense and for whom is law a normative system? Whose ideal is it that is expressed and in which ways does this ideal influence different agents' lines of reasoning? Are there any empirical studies supporting the theory that a normative, rule-oriented perspective is a reasonable way of perceiving legal reasoning, or any authentic function of law?

6.4.5.5 Conceptual Models

In the field of AI and law several theories concerning *conceptual models*[108] or *deep conceptual models*[109] in law have been submitted. Most often such proposals imply that entirely different components, as well as different kinds of relations, must form the basis of any representation of the law. The analysis of the existing descriptions of the conceptual models of law shows, however, that such models are rather fragmentary and quite vague. Except for a large number of detailed technical descriptions of how relations between some components may be expressed in a formal logic or in a computer programming language, general explanations as to why certain components have been chosen and how the proposed relations are relevant to the process of legal reasoning are to a large extent lacking.[110] This state of the matter has met with surprisingly little debate.

108 *See, e.g.*, Biagiole, C., Mariani, P., Tiscornia, D. *ESPLEX: A Rule and Conceptual Based Model of Representing Statutes* (1987).

109 McCarty, L.T. *Intelligent Legal Information Systems: Problems and Prospects* (1984).

110 Exceptions in this respect are provided by a number of suggestions on conceptual IR. *See, e.g.*, Hafner, C.D. *Conceptual Organization of Case Law Knowledge Bases* (1987), de Bessonet, C.G., Cross, G.R. *An Artificial Intelligence Application in the Law: CCLIPS, A Computer Program That Processes Legal Information* (1987), Bing, J. *Designing Text Retrieval Systems for Conceptual Searching* (1987).

The issue has been addressed, however, by Susskind who concludes that "their results are not universalizable in so far that they do not seem to be offering any coherent guidance regarding the development of conceptual models in other legal domains. . . . The crucial question . . . is this: what might a conceptual model be like?"[111] Thereafter, in his own discussion Susskind submits the following suggestion:

> "It is clear that its function will be to fill the gaps in rule-based legal knowledge bases . . ., but it is far less clear, on a general level, what the nature of the representation form will be. It is tentatively submitted (in the light both of relevant writings on AI and legal reasoning, and on expert systems in general), that a conceptual model in law will consist of a theoretical representation of the specific area of law in question involving a model of its characteristic reasoning process, the structure of its legal statements, and denotations of all the central entities involved. Descriptions of all the relations between all the components will also be encoded, for which purpose a rich theory of deontic logic will be required . . . ."[112]

One of the original adherents of conceptual models in AI and law, *L. Thorne McCarty*, in one of the probably most elaborated and ambitious proposals in this direction – "a language for legal discourse" – remarks upon the criticism concerning vagueness and claims that "the basic idea behind a deep conceptual model is easy to state" arguing that:

> [t]here are many common sense categories underlying the representation of a legal problem domain: time, space, mass, action, permission, obligation, causation, purpose, intention, knowledge, belief, and so on. The idea is to select a small set of these common sense categories, the ones that are most appropriate for a particular legal application, and then develop a knowledge representation language that faithfully mirrors the structure of the set. The language should be formal: it should have a compositional syntax, a precise semantics and a well-defined inference mechanism. The semantic interpretation of the common sense categories should be intuitively correct, that is, it should generate exactly those entailments that ordinary people (and ordinary lawyers!) generate in similar situations. The inference mechanism for the language should be complete and

111 Susskind *supra* chapter 1 note 9, at 153.

112 *Id.*

> sound, in principle, but in practice, completeness and soundness would be sacrificed for computational tractability, just as they are in ordinary human (and ordinary legal!) reasoning.[113]

Thereafter, McCarty sets out to illustrate the ways in which various components and relations may be represented in a computer programming language. The following components have been selected: "sorts and subsorts", "count terms and mass terms", "horn clauses" "negations and embedded implications", "default rules and default proofs", "prototypes and deformations", "time", "events and actions", "permissions and obligations". The underlying model of legal reasoning or a more detailed theory concerning the nature of various kinds of legal components, or of the relations between them, is nevertheless not addressed further and, as yet, no complete solutions seem to have been presented, let alone implemented. It is therefore difficult to evaluate the approach from the practical point of view. The references to "a legal problem domain" and a "particular legal application" nevertheless imply that the solution may turn out to be of a restricted generality.

The search for categories of a common nature appears, nevertheless, to be an important and even necessary task, if AI-applications in the field of law are ever to reach beyond the level of small-scale support systems. A promising aspect of a project like the one concerning the development of a language for legal discourse is thereby that it accepts the relevance of a large number of entities – this in contrast to many undertakings which focus solely on, e.g., deontic aspects such as permissions and obligations. An approach of equal interest would in this respect be the one taken by *Stig Kanger, Lars Lindahl* and others, who using deontic concepts, try to investigate the possible *positions* of an *agent* or a pair of *agents*, that are logically valid in a normative environment.[114] (The works in this tradition are still however mostly philosophical investigations without any explicit references to the work done in the area of AI.)

113 McCarty, L.T. *A Language for Legal Discourse: I. Basic Features* (1989).

114 Kanger *supra* chapter 2 note 77, Lindahl *supra* chapter 2 note 77.

6.4.5.5.1 Conceptual Models and Legal Reasoning

From the perspective based on the JLR model no objection can be raised against the fact that an authentic representation of law must include a large number of categories. The ability to manipulate conceptual structures is crucial, for instance, for the identification and search processes. A theoretical difficulty that must be mentioned here is, however, that the conceptual modelling of common-sense categories – similarly to setting up proposals based on case-based reasoning – reflects a bottom-up approach. As indicated above, this may easily create problems, at least if any kind of generality is intended. This is simply because the entities, as well as the connections that can be established between various entities in a situation, will depend on the nature of the issue and the available legal propositions. Likewise, it must be remembered that the context of the situation will often play a crucial role in the evaluation of legal decisions. As pointed out by several researchers, complications may also arise due to various traditions of normative, ethical, or sociological nature, which may affect the kind of conceptual model that can be developed and accepted.[115] In consequence the questions whether or not categories that are common to more than limited domains of the law exist, and what the general relations between such categories may be, are still questions open to debate. From this follows that the possibilities of formulating sound models of a general, non domain-bound nature solely by means of manipulating the various components at the conceptual level are uncertain and would have to be investigated in a long-time research project.

One other plausible assumption concerning deep conceptual models would be that beyond the decomposition into structures consisting of such components as concepts, rules, rule-systems, texts (representations) and documents it is not possible to find entities of a truly general nature. That is to say that even if notions such as obligations and rights may be proved to be relevant for some domains, it would be rather far-fetched to assume that they will have any practical significance in, e.g. the part of the road traffic legislation whose primary function is to provide definitions of various kinds of vehicles – disregarding the kind of sophisticated normative theory that one might want to develop. Likewise, it would be too

[115] *See, e.g.*, Sergot *supra* chapter 1 note 50, at 63-64.

much to assume that a theory on agent positions is of any practical significance in such a field of law.

Nevertheless, assuming that the objective of the research is to develop more advanced systems capable of reasoning about law and supporting legal work, it seems that various kinds of conceptual models must be integrated, one way or another. In this respect conceptual models are not in conflict with the JLR. Instead they seem to provide necessary complements to the rule-based, case-based and associative models. As a consequence, chapter 7 of this study illustrates how such an integration can be accomplished.

6.5 Integrated Solutions

6.5.1 Introduction

The future of DSSs in the field of law is heavily dependent on the possibilities of combining various AI-methods with each other and incorporating them into other kinds of computer applications. The reason for this is simply that the use of legal DSS in any professional situation will constitute a part of a work process in which various kinds of requirements are present and also because many aspects of legal work are already more or less dependent on various forms of computer support.

From this in turn follows that all legal AI-systems must be designed in such a way as to be able to function in combination with e.g., communication systems, legal IR-systems, administrative systems, and so forth. From the practical point of view it is therefore also necessary to investigate the ways in which methods originating from various AI models can be integrated with each other and combined with other kinds of techniques.

It deserves to be mentioned that also various kinds of conventional computer technologies can be integrated with each other in order to meet the complex requirements of legal work. The investigation of all the ways in which this can be accomplished is not a major objective of this study, but a couple of examples may illustrate how this could be accomplished. One early illustration in this respect is the ABF project, developed and documented by *James Sprowl,* with the focus set basically on formulation (assembling of legal documents) by means of the integration of the administration of client data, mathematical computation, word processing, and retrieval and selection of predefined text paragraphs.[116]

Another example of a legal tool capable of integrating several functions by the use of conventional computer technology is the Swedish *Pacta* – a commercially available on-line system for the drafting of commercial agreements. Through hierarchically ordered menus Pacta provides predefined default text-paragraphs of relevance for a large number of commercial agreements. In relation to contract clauses the system also provides commentaries authored by legal experts in the field. The users of the system are able to select among and individualize (and print out) the retrieved texts (contract clauses) by means of employing word processing facilities in their interconnected personal computers. Pacta thus provides support during the search, the interpretation, and the formulation phases.[117]

In this context, it should be also noticed that further extensions of the information retrieval technique have been explored with the help of various research-approaches.[118] Examples can be found in various projects on automated indexes[119], document weighting[120], linguistic research[121] and the elaboration and indexing of various concepts.[122] This parallel development makes that to uphold the distinction between AI-components and other kinds of computer technologies may be sometimes perceived as not very appropriate.

116 Sprowl, J.A. *The Automated Assembly of Legal Documents* (1980).

117 Westin, G. *Pacta avtalsdatabas – ett datoriserat system för avtalsskrivning och förhandling* (1987).

118 *See, e.g.*, for overviews, Oddy, R.N., Robertson, S.E., van Rijsbergen, C.J., Williams, P.W. eds. *Information Retrieval Research* (1981) *and* Bing *supra* chapter 4 note 1.

119 *See, e.g.*, Seipel, P. *Informationssystem för rättsväsendet: Projekt index* (1976).

120 *See, e.g.*, Salton, G., McGill, M.J. *Introduction to Modern Information Retrieval* (1983).

121 *See, e.g.*, Fjeldvig, T. *Effektivisering av tekstsøkesystemer: Utvikling av språkbaserte metoder* (1987), Brodda, B. *Gimme More O' That* (1990).

122 *See, e.g.*, Hafner *supra* note 110, Ciampi, C., Pirro, D.E., Elio, F., Trivisonno, G. *THES/BID: An Expert System for Constructing a Computer-Based Thesaurus for Legal Informatics and Computer Law* (1985), *and* Gelbart, D., Smith, J.C. *Beyond Boolean Search: FLEXICON, A Legal Text-Based Intelligent System* (1991).

6.5.2 Integration of AI-Techniques

Many of the methods originating from the computational models described in section 6.4 above can be integrated into more complex systems. Some combinations are for practical reasons more interesting to study than others and one obvious object of interest is to investigate how logical and case-based methods can be made to work together.

An early illustration of this requirement was given in the NCA project, where it was found that for case-fact analysis it would be feasible to combine a logical rule-based model with a numerical method and that it was therefore desirable to integrate two different computer modules. Although only a small fragment of the material was actually implemented it can be nevertheless concluded that from the computational point of view an integration of such a kind creates little or no practical difficulties.

The link that is needed between the modules in such an application is uncomplicated and of a basically straightforward nature. That is to say that if through the consultation of the rule-base the user arrives at the conclusion that sentencing should be done, he is then in a position where it is appropriate to start up the module for fact examination. In the tuning of the decision it may be necessary to consult the case fact modules repeatedly, but there will be little or no need for interactive inspections of the various modules in different phases of the rule-based dialogue.

Several commercial products which allow for the interactive integration of rule-based and inductive methods exist and, as shown in several projects, it is also possible to develop customized solutions in which the systems can be shifted between the various modes in a more or less unrestricted way.

A similar approach from the functional point of view is illustrated by the American system labelled CABARET. This system is reported to be based on a system design combining a rule-based reasoner, which is a redesigned standard expert system, and a case-based component modelled on the previously described HYPO case-based reasoning system and another related system labelled TAX-HYPO. The case-based reasoning component of CABARET appears thus, as compared to the NCA project, to be less dependent on a numerical approach. CABARET also encompasses ''an agenda-based controller using heuristics to post and order interpretation tasks and subtasks''.[123] The controller determines what kinds of reasoning tasks the system should perform on the basis of the states of the rule- and case-based reasoning components. The apparent difference of CABARET as compared to the NCA approach is thereby that the practical possibilities of introducing various combinations of rule-based and inductive reasoning appear to be unrelated to the jurisprudential frameworks that are provided by various types of legal decisions.[124] Instead, the developers report that they have ''gathered a collection of some 30 or so heuristics that we belive experts use for controlling and interleaving reasoning with rules and reasoning with cases.''[125] The work has recently been extended and the authors report the development of a theory

> ''of how arguments can be created in complex domains that require both rule-based and case-based reasoning. The theory depends in identifying argument strategies, which arise from one's viewpoint toward a rule-governed conclusion. The theory specifies how a strategy may be effected through tactics called 'moves'. Moves are accomplished by retrieving cases that satisfy certain requirements as to disposition and rule satisfaction and applying primitive arguments techniques such as analogizing or distinguishing, to compare these precedents with the problem situation.''[126]

A different kind of integration is exemplified by the VF project in which a logical model was integrated with an associating hypertext program. In the first version of the system each question that was posed before the user in the fact elicitation dialogue was accompanied by a text document providing explanations and references to different kinds of material that could be used in order to facilitate the interpretation of the issues under discussion. The documents were in no way static and the user, depending on his own requirements, could delete, change and add references or other kinds of text-material.

123 Rissland, E.L., Skalak, D.B. *Interpreting Statutory Predicates*, 48 (1989).

124 The distinction between various kinds of legal decisions in this respect was first observed in the NCA project, Wahlgren *supra* chapter 1 note 42. The implications as to the possibilities to include inductive methods are discussed in Hamfelt, Wahlgren *supra* chapter 1 note 21, at 47-48, 53-54. *See also* section 6.4.5.2 *supra*.

125 Rissland, Skalak *supra* note 123, at 49.

126 Skalak, D.B., Rissland, E.L. *Argument Moves in a Rule-Guided Domain*, 10 (1991).

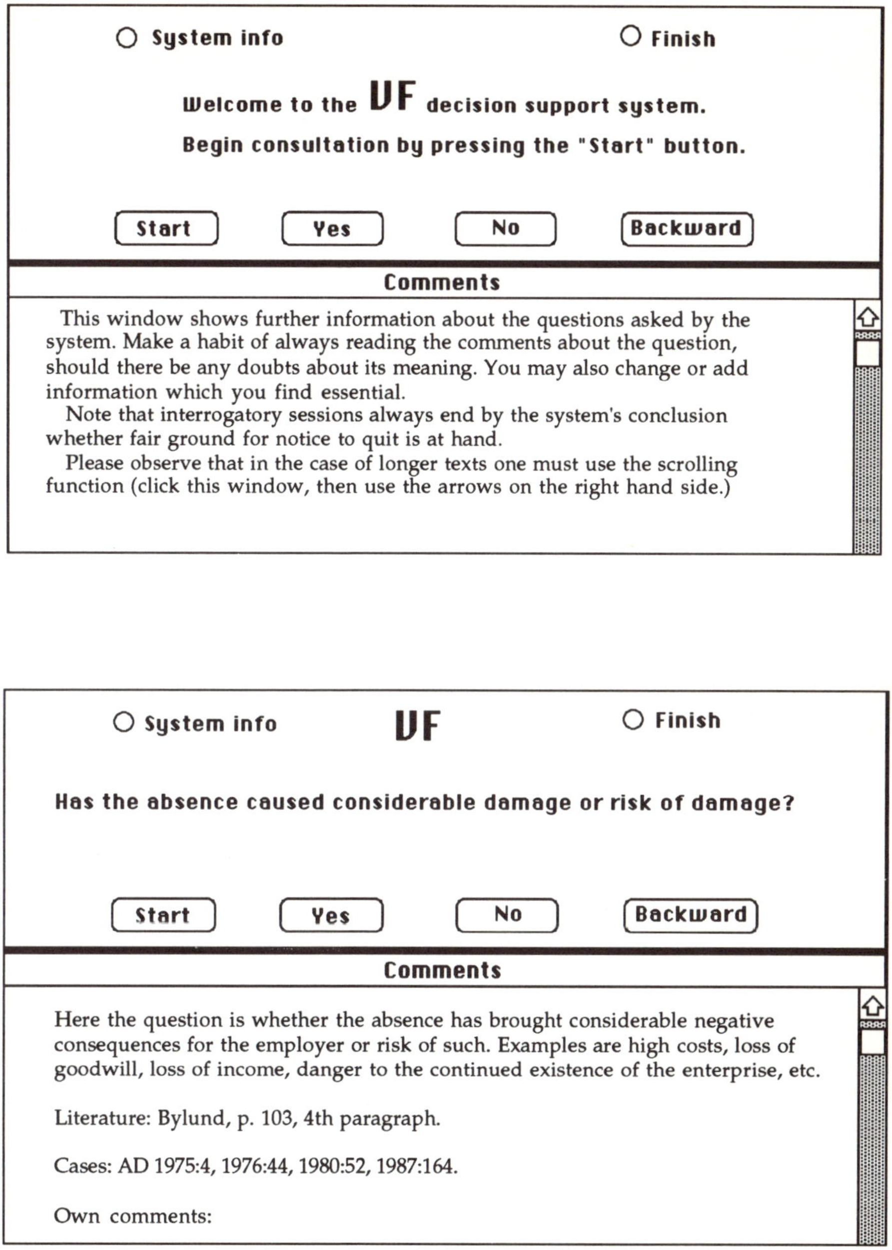

Figure 6.10 Interface of VF system consisting of a dialogue window and a comment window.

In an elaborated prototype the rule-base was related to a hypertext program.[127] The principle behind such a design is that from every node in the rule-representation it is possible to activate a number of associating links and reach a set of related units for in-depth investigations. When such an excursion is completed, the user can easily return to the interactive dialogue and continue the session from the point at which he left it. As he moves on to the next question he gets access to a new set of units. Although this was not a primary research objective in this project, it is important to note in this context that the combination of an associating program and a logical model can to a large degree eliminate problems with maintenance related to all too complex and extensive hypernets (''hyperspagetti''). The architecture can be illustrated as in figure 6.11.

127 Hamfelt, A., Barklund, J. *An Intelligent Interface to Legal Data Bases Combining Logic Programming and Hypertext* (1989).

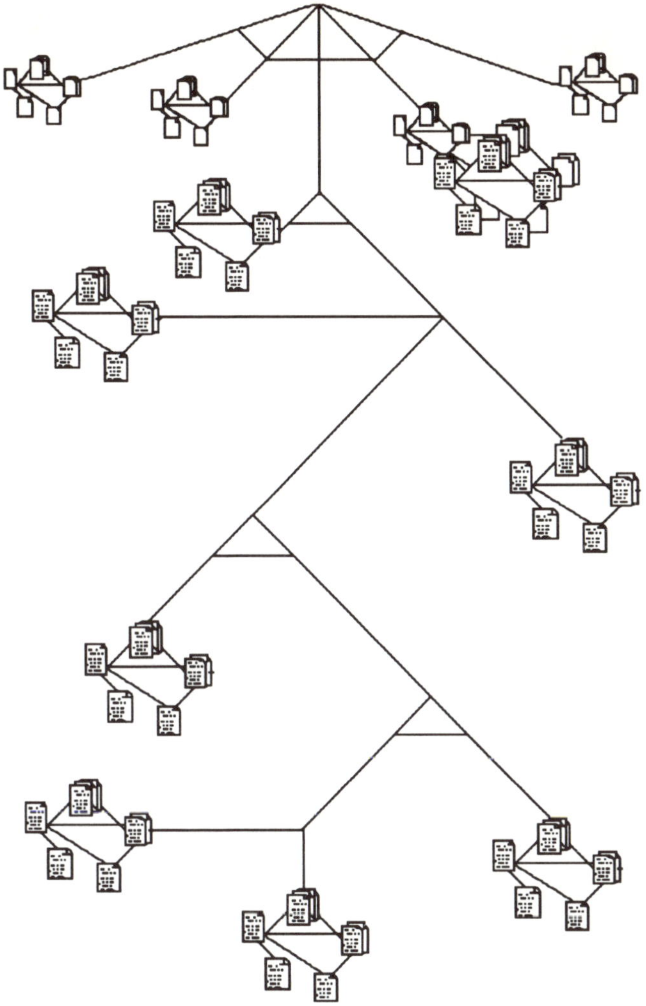

Figure 6.11 Elaboration of concepts in a logical model by the use of hypertext technique.

The VF system provided also support for formulation and when the system reached a conclusion the user would gain access to examples of letters concerning warnings, etc., to a dismissal form, and to various notes giving instructions on how to fill in the form correctly. By means of employing word processing facilities at this stage of the consultation the user could elaborate or adjust these text units in an individual manner (figure 6.12). In addition, as mentioned above in the description of the hypertext part of the system, it is also possible to augment this kind of systems with links to communication facilities, such as electronic-mail, fax machines and telephones.

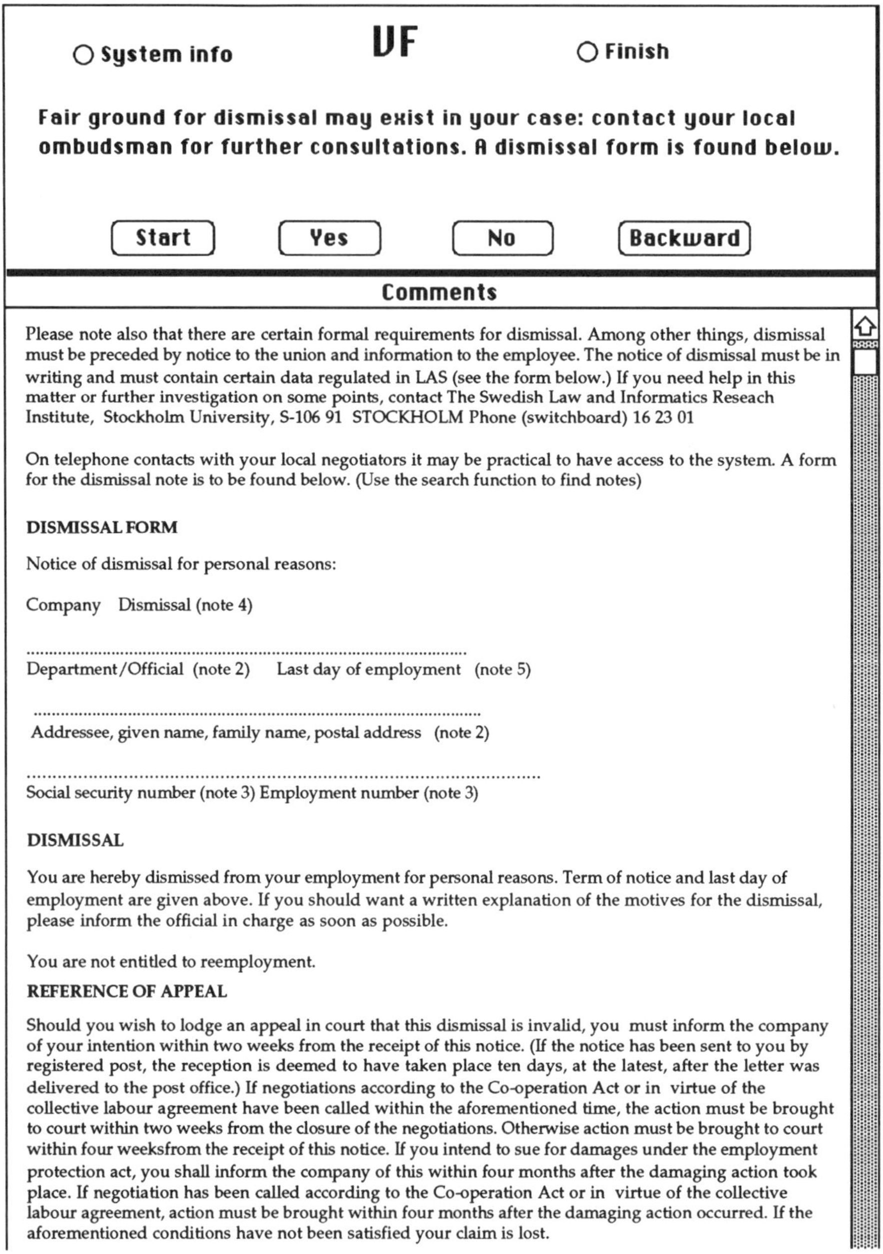

System info VF Finish

Fair ground for dismissal may exist in your case: contact your local ombudsman for further consultations. A dismissal form is found below.

Start Yes No Backward

Comments

Please note also that there are certain formal requirements for dismissal. Among other things, dismissal must be preceded by notice to the union and information to the employee. The notice of dismissal must be in writing and must contain certain data regulated in LAS (see the form below.) If you need help in this matter or further investigation on some points, contact The Swedish Law and Informatics Reseach Institute, Stockholm University, S-106 91 STOCKHOLM Phone (switchboard) 16 23 01

On telephone contacts with your local negotiators it may be practical to have access to the system. A form for the dismissal note is to be found below. (Use the search function to find notes)

DISMISSAL FORM

Notice of dismissal for personal reasons:

Company Dismissal (note 4)

....

Department/Official (note 2) Last day of employment (note 5)

....

Addressee, given name, family name, postal address (note 2)

....

Social security number (note 3) Employment number (note 3)

DISMISSAL

You are hereby dismissed from your employment for personal reasons. Term of notice and last day of employment are given above. If you should want a written explanation of the motives for the dismissal, please inform the official in charge as soon as possible.

You are not entitled to reemployment.

REFERENCE OF APPEAL

Should you wish to lodge an appeal in court that this dismissal is invalid, you must inform the company of your intention within two weeks from the receipt of this notice. (If the notice has been sent to you by registered post, the reception is deemed to have taken place ten days, at the latest, after the letter was delivered to the post office.) If negotiations according to the Co-operation Act or in virtue of the collective labour agreement have been called within the aforementioned time, the action must be brought to court within two weeks from the closure of the negotiations. Otherwise action must be brought to court within four weeksfrom the receipt of this notice. If you intend to sue for damages under the employment protection act, you shall inform the company of this within four months after the damaging action took place. If negotiation has been called according to the Co-operation Act or in virtue of the collective labour agreement, action must be brought within four months after the damaging action occurred. If the aforementioned conditions have not been satisfied your claim is lost.

Figure 6.12 Dismissal form in VF system

6.5.3 Legal Workstations

As a further extension, systems integrating logical, case-based and associating models can be easily integrated with IR-systems for full text retrieval of legal documents. How this can be accomplished is illustrated in an Australian project named DataLex. DataLex is a system developed for educational purposes and commercial applications, combining "expert systems, hypertext, and free text retrieval into one general purpose tool" The workstation combines functions from six separate programs, an expert system shell, a free text retrieval system, a text animation package, an automated document generator, a hypertext engine and an example-based shell for modelling legal precedents.[128] A similar approach, although on a smaller scale basis, is being elaborated in the LexLab experiments at Stockholm University. In this project it has been illustrated, among other things that through the development of so called macro-functions it is possible to efficiently combine logical models and hypertext with IR-facilities. (A macro function is built up from a number of serially interlinked sub-functions. It can be used, for instance, to start up an IR-system or to activate Boolean search-functions. A macro function can be triggered off in several ways, e.g. through the indication of a button-symbol) In such an environment a concept encountered e.g. in an interactive dialogue in a rule-base or in an explanatory text, may be used more or less immediately as a search query in a remote database, containing e.g. full text legal cases. At the same time, the user suffers very little from the fact that the system is made up of different geographically dispersed modules.

The DataLex and the LexLab projects illustrates the ways in which AI-techniques and other forms of computer applications can be combined together to form more complex legal workstations. For many reasons it can be also concluded that the future of AI-technology in law must be seen in this perspective. In this context, it may be also recalled that a distinction between various forms of computational representations makes little or no sense from the jurisprudential point of view. In the perspective of the JLR, for instance, it is obvious that an advanced DSS should provide facilities for text and document retrieval. Likewise, a practicing lawyer,

128 Greenleaf, Mowbray, Tyree *supra* note 94.

will find no reason in most cases to make a difference between various forms of representation techniques as long as the results are usable in a practical sense. From the point of view of a professional lawyer it is more relevant to be able to evaluate proposed solutions by means of scrutinizing functional aspects, i.e. the ways in which systems can integrate various forms of decision support.

The necessity to include the whole work process in an analysis concerning decision support systems became apparent in the previously described NCA project. The project group here had to take into consideration the fact that the courts were already in the process of receiving support from other kinds of computer systems. This, among other things, made it necessary to develop a scenario in which a contemplated KBS was integrated not only with the work process as such, but also with additional computer systems. In this way the system-design came to embrace a KBS incorporating a logical and a case-based module (as described above for identification and sentencing support), which was integrated with the Swedish national legal IR-system, *Rättsbanken,* and with the existing administrative system for case-management, *Kanslidatorsystemet* that is presently being implemented in Swedish courts. Rättsbanken is a conventional IR-system (as described in section 4.3 above) providing support for legal document retrieval. The system contains the major parts of official legal documents, e.g. statutes, international agreements, cases, legislative preparatory work, etc. The administrative system provides storing and retrieval functions for case related data, word processing functions, decision formulation assistance, decision support for form dispatching, and also furnishes time respite control, and similar functions.[129]

In the scenario-sketch various parts of the computer system were related also to the types of data appearing in the court process and, for pedagogical reasons, to the various functions and work-phases that could be detected in the present organisation of the courts.

129 Domstolsverket. *Utvärdering av försöket med datorstöd vid avdelningskansli i tingsrätt* (1987).

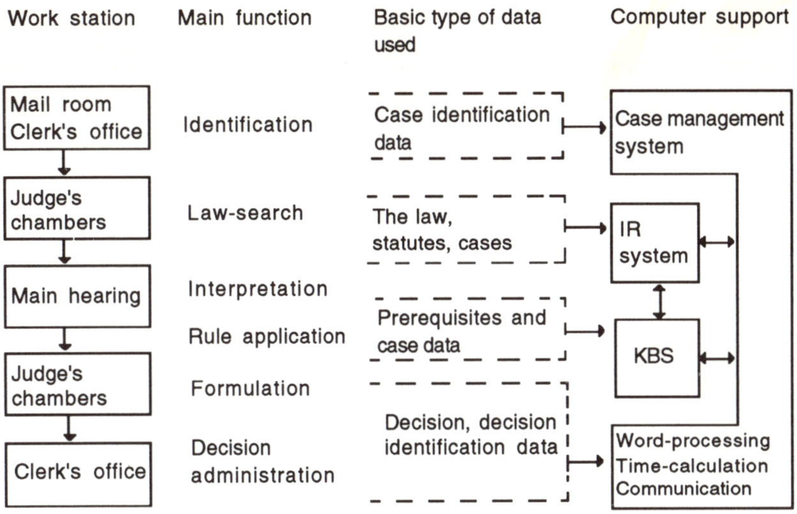

Figure 6.13 Sketch of a support system for criminal court proceedings in a Swedish district court. The design encompasses support functions for all phases of the process. The case management system and the IR-system are existing applications. Decision support functions are presently available for some kinds of civil law decisions only. (Reviewed version of scenario sketch in Wahlgren *supra* chapter 1 note 42 at 72.)

A number of other projects aiming to provide support for legal reasoning processes through the integration of various forms of computer technology have been presented in Sweden. One example is provided by SAFAD that has developed PLUTO – a support system for social workers handling social assistance applications.[130] The system is based on a knowledge based system shell written in Lisp, combined with six main data processing modules written in Pascal (programming language). The different modules support various functions, ranging from data collection, calculation and information retrieval to document management (word processing).[131] The result is an integrated support tool, combining conventional data processing facilities and knowledge-based techniques. At the time when the system was presented, the development group

130 Statskontoret *supra* chapter 3 note 124.

131 *Id.*

underlined that PLUTO differs from conventional expert systems in that it encompasses support for the whole work process. PLUTO has been tested at a district social services office and is being presently (winter 1991/92) being evaluated. The project group has explained that in the future suitable system architectures, interfaces with existing systems, communication facilities with external data bases and system maintenance should be studied. Another future goal that has been mentioned is also to create a tool that would help the local social security authorities to update the system and make alterations to it.

The strategy of approaching legal and administrative work from a uncloven perspective has been also elaborated in a later SAFAD study on the development of a system for managing financial support for foreign students.[132]

A description of various kinds of legal workstations can be easily extended. It is, however, impossible to describe all the ways in which various kinds of computer support systems can be integrated with each other. The requirements will vary, no doubt, with respect to how the work is organized around different issues in various organizations. As a conclusion it can be, nevertheless, positively stated that the above mentioned projects clearly illustrate that there are no technical or computational obstacles to the integration of different kinds of KBS-techniques into more complex systems. Likewise, it can be maintained that methods originating from AI-models can be integrated with conventional computer systems in various ways.

132 Statskontoret. *Verktyg för handläggare*, 46-47 (1990). *See,* for further illustrations of such broad approaches, Oskamp, A., Vandenberghe, G.P.V. *Legal Thinking and Automation* (1985), Koers, Pelger *supra* chapter 1 note 28, Council of Europe *supra* chapter 1 note 28, Greenleaf, Mowbray, Tyree *supra* note 94 *and* Sprowl, J. *Assembling Standardized Legal Documents in a Semiautomated Fashion with a Rule-Based Expert System* (1989).

7 Prospects

7.1 Basic Presuppositions

One definite conclusion that can be drawn from this investigation so far is that the limitations of automation are not concentrated to computational restrictions or problems connected with detailed knowledge representation. Likewise, it is apparent that the question as to whether or not it is possible to develop functioning legal decision support systems is no longer a serious research problem. Primary issues revolve around the ways in which the generality and autonomy of the applications may be increased – how to reach beyond the level of small scale support systems. Thus, the most apparent limitation of legal AI is the fact that the available systems are of a significantly domain-specific nature and that they are cumbersome to develop and maintain. In addition, several other features, such as e.g. the fact that the systems often fail when it comes to coping with changes in the law, that the systems are dependent on interactive dialogues with users, and the fact that all the results which are based on something else than the manipulation of familiar factors must be evaluated by a lawyer, may appear strikingly primitive. As a result of this, the remaining part of this investigation is devoted to the elaboration of a design strategy for more general legal AI-systems. (General, in the sense that they are able to support several functions, but not necessarily in the sense that they must encompass many different fields of law.) The approach is based on a further analysis of law and legal reasoning and starts from the modularization of the legal reasoning process that has been outlined in chapter 5.

An important assumption for the design strategy that is outlined here is thereby that an adequate (functional) decomposition of legal reasoning makes it possible to identify and categorize factors influencing the ways in which each sub-process is operated. This assumption follows from the discussion in chapter 5, from which it can be concluded that a considerable number of factors governing the legal reasoning process can be found within the legal system. It is thereby obvious that legal propositions exerting crucial influence on the process appear both in the form of substantive law and as various kinds of methodological and formal rule structures. An illustration of how various legal components are related to the modules of the JLR model is given in figure 7.1.

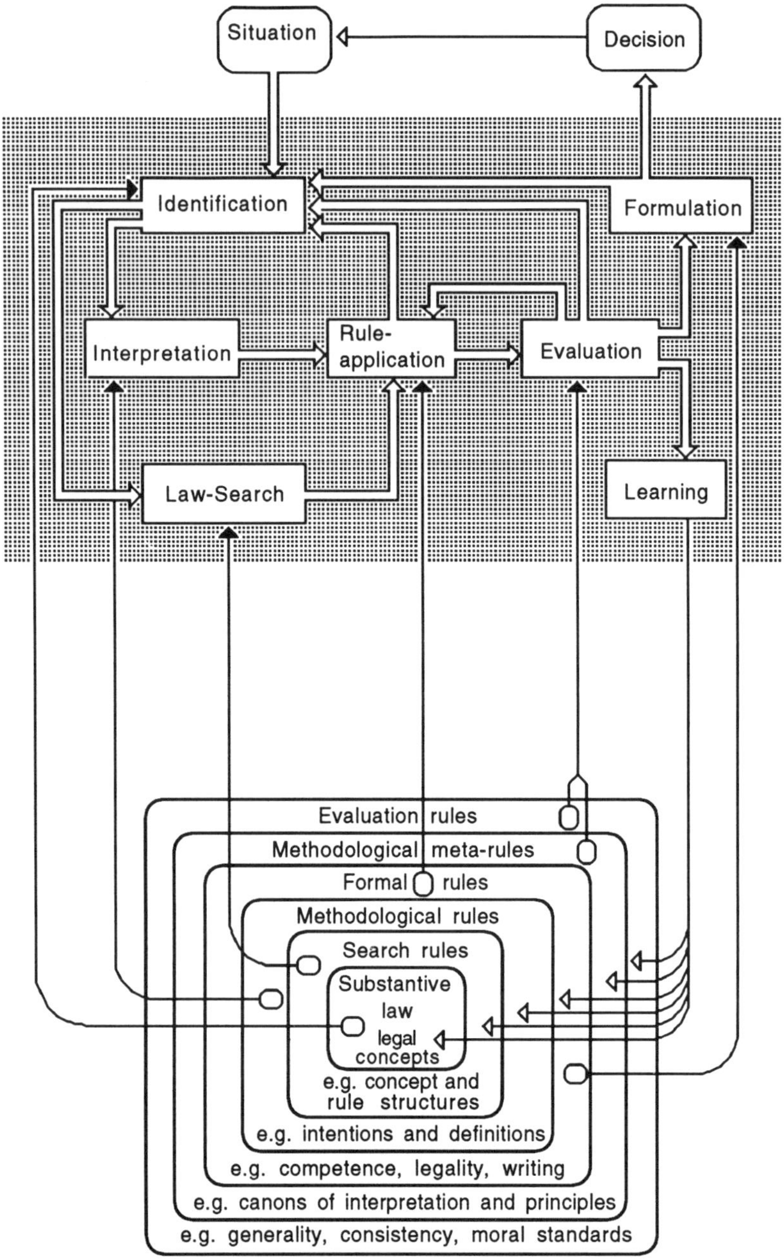

Figure 7.1 The operation of various mechanisms in legal reasoning is determined to a large extent by different types of legal knowledge structures and various established methods of inference making.

A likewise important assumption for the development of the theory outlined here is that legal reasoning is to a large extent a domain-dependent activity. That is to say that in terms of generality, extensiveness, etc. the nature of the relevant legal propositions varies not only with respect to the different fields of law and the nature of the issues that are approached, but also in relation to their various functions vis-à-vis the legal reasoning process. To illustrate this, it should be noticed that some of the knowledge components in figure 7.1 (e.g. the concept and rule structures supporting search for legal propositions) will be strictly domain- and situation-dependent at any actual instance of legal reasoning, whereas others (formal rules and methodological rules) are of an extended generality and will thus be valid for several kinds of legal decisions (determining e.g. the jurisdiction of a court or how to complete sentencing in criminal cases). Yet other components (e.g. the generality and consistency rules operating on evaluation), as well as the general inference methods making the navigation within and between different knowledge structures possible (e.g. backward and forward chaining), are *prima facie* generally valid for all types of legal decisions.

The varying degree of domain dependence of crucial legal components naturally limits the possibilities of developing general legal AI-systems based on some fundamental concepts, common to all fields of the law. It is equally important, however, that the functional decomposition of law and legal reasoning indicates that it is possible to make extensive generalizations as regards different types of legal rules and components.

A further elaboration of the functional perspective justifies the assumption that it appears to be feasible to extract legal knowledge structures from the corpus of legal knowledge with a more or less decisive influence on each vital part of the legal reasoning process. For instance, the analysis of legal reasoning undertaken in chapter 5 and figure 7.1 show that legal concepts and rules of a substantial nature function as classification schemes in initial instances of identification and that formal rule structures affect the rule application process, and so forth. The reason for the perhaps more far-reaching hypothesis that all crucial aspects of legal reasoning to some extent must be reflected in the law is simply that if some *vital* sub-process was totally neglected by the legal order, the whole process of legal reasoning could turn out to be of an arbitrary and non-legal nature. The crucial influence of various types of legal knowledge in this respect is among other things illustrated by the fact that many factors that affect the legal reasoning process are of a mandatory nature, i.e. a failure to observe them may cause that the effects of legal decisions will be invalidated. An additional assumption following from this perspective is thereby that it would be possible to construct a more advanced AI-system by means of elaborating a flexible representation reflecting various functionally decomposed portions of legal knowledge.

At this point it should be underlined, however, that the conclusion stating that all vital aspects of the legal reasoning process are reflected in the corpus of legal knowledge is not the same thing as the claim that the outcome of legal reasoning is predictable from the substantial point of view. What is assumed is merely that all kinds of significant, legal *requirements* that the lawyer is faced with in the legal reasoning processes must be reflected, at least to some extent, in the *functions* of various types of legal knowledge.

7.2 A General Legal AI-System

7.2.1 Introduction

In this section a sketch of a design strategy for a more general support tool for legal reasoning is outlined. The strategy is based on the approach outlined above and on a combination of principles which may be described as *functional decomposition*, *technical integration*, and *structural integration*. Each of these design principles is motivated by the functions as well as the attributes of legal knowledge and AI-methods that have been identified in chapters 5 - 6.

The design strategy assumes the application of AI-technology on small, functionally decomposed portions of legal knowledge. The modularization of legal knowledge starts from the components identified in relation to the JLR model, reflecting a number of complementary decompositions. It is furthermore assumed that a large number of small-scale KBSs, each with a limited function, can be integrated into a more general system. In its knowledge representation requirements the design strategy reflects and combines notions originating from rule-based, case-based, associative and conceptual models. It is also assumed that the system can be integrated with various forms of conventional computer technologies and IR-systems. The approach can be illustrated in the following way.

7.2.2 Design for the Representation of Substantive Law

7.2.2.1 Functional Decomposition

In the initial identification of relevancy the lawyer must be able to establish an adequate legal domain. From the discussion on the nature of legal identification in chapter five it can be thus concluded that some kind of legal knowledge must be present to make it possible to recognize adequate legal domains. Aid for the legal classification of the encountered situations is also quite easy to find in the corpus of legal knowledge. Components supporting the initial processes of the identification of relevancy and law-search are, for instance, a taxonomy of legal domains, and general descriptions of subject-matters appearing in various legal fields, e.g. types of agent, acts, issues, legal institutions and general legal concepts.

In the succeeding sequence the lawyer must be able to identify an adequate sub-domain and a relevant legal situation. From the basic assumption that law functions as a scheme of classification follows in turn that there must exist some kind of legal knowledge that makes it possible to elicit additional facts and identify adequate legal situations. Also this somewhat more detailed knowledge is often easily identified. Components supporting these aspects of legal reasoning are for example sets of hierarchically ordered sub-domains, types of transactions and more detailed issues, legal institutions and legal concepts.

There is little doubt that legal components and legal knowledge structures supporting the requirements in the initial stages of the identification and search processes can be elicited and represented. Functional taxonomies of the law of a very general kind, as well as hierarchically ordered sub-divisions of legal domains, can be unfolded from works of jurisprudence, the structures of legislation, the classification of issues in courts and public authorities, the organization of legal-libraries, and so forth. It is also clear that each sub-domain of law consists of – or is actually defined by – a limited number of legally relevant agent types, legal concepts and legal issues – each represented by (or capable of being reflected in a representation of) legal rules. Tax law, for instance, can be decomposed into rule systems concerning taxation of individuals, and taxation of corporations, taxation of capital, etc. Family law can be decomposed into sub-domains, such as divorce law, inheritance law, adoption law, for example.

Admittedly, the legally relevant situations that can be identified and incorporated in the general knowledge structure are more or less dependent on how well the law is developed in each domain. In some domains, as e.g. in criminal law and inheritance law, it may be assumed that virtually all kinds of legally relevant acts and agent constellations are rather well defined. In such domains a trained lawyer may be able to immediately recognize factors of relevance for a given legal situation. In other fields of law, it may be difficult to recognize any specific situations at all. The VF project illustrates, nevertheless, beyond doubt that by means of traditional jurisprudential analysis and in combination with structured knowledge acquisition, it is possible to identify and define legal type-situations also in case-based areas originating from vague legal concepts. A similar conclusion is possible to draw from the NCA experiment in which it was shown that it was possible to identify various kinds of situations reflecting assault and battery by means of extracting and analysing material from cases.

From the assumption that general classification schemata, as well as more detailed taxonomies for the identification of sub-domains and situations can be represented follows that in principle there is no obstacle to the development of a rule based KBS supporting the identification of legally relevant situations. Or, at least, admitting that the great number of legal domains and sub-domains can make such a project impractical, in principle it should be possible to develop one KBS (labelled G for general) capable of recognizing different legal domains, and a number of additional KBSs, (labelled D for domain) each capable of recognizing sub-domains and situations in various domains. It is also obvious that the recognition of a certain legal domain (e.g. X) by the KBS(G) can be related to the activation of a KBS(D(X)) for the identification of an appropriate sub-domain and relevant situation within X.

The identification of a legally relevant situation makes it often possible to single out the legal rules of a substantial nature that may affect a legal decision. This is for instance the case in the many legal domains in which the law merely provides authoritative descriptions of how certain issues or objects should be defined. Law provides in such cases an uncontroversial set of prerequisites that may be checked against the situation.

Uncomplicated processes of identification occur in situations where the number of possible (legally relevant) requirements for the legally defined agents is low and where these are easy to identify right from the start. Or, which is another way of saying this, when the functions of law are few and easily identified. This is for instance the case in numerous situations in which law provides instructions only for the ways in which a process should be completed. Similarly, less problematic situations occur in domains where the rules and the court practice are stable and indisputable. A KBS(D) can in such domains contain all the substantive legal knowledge of relevance for the identification of the current situation. A KBS(D) may thus also provide sufficient support for additional fact elicitation and law search that may have to be carried out.

In many legal domains, however, it is possible to establish the identity of rules and facts that may be relevant in different ways. A significant feature of such domains is that various agents may want to use the material in lines of reasoning reflecting different objectives. The different requirements may concern here details, but they may also reflect comprehensive lines of reasoning which stand in opposition to each other.

A lawyer as well as any legal reasoning system must have access in such cases to additional support in order to be able to select the appropriate set of rules and prerequisites. This may be sometimes problematic but the difficulties must not be exaggerated. In conventional situations of legal reasoning the choice between possible alternatives is often done unconsciously and constitute a trivial part of the identification process. In other words, in each actual case of e.g. dismissal it will be rather obvious whether the lawyer should try to identify rules and factors supporting the employer or those supporting the employee. In such cases the lines of legal reasoning of possible relevance are strictly limited, as the identity of the client indicates immediately which side of the dispute is to be defended. In other cases, on the other hand, the process of finding the relevant legal presuppositions may be very complicated. This may occur for instance in planning sessions or in situations involving a large number of various organizations and complicated transactions. In such cases a lawyer may have to investigate a large number of objectives, legal functions, and definitions of various agent types in order to identify an adequate line of reasoning and find the appropriate set of rules.

In all situations involving a choice between multiple (legally acknowledged) functions of the law – and disregarding the fact that identification of an appropriate line of reasoning may be more or less problematic depending on the case – this ''agent-requirement-aspect'' adds one layer of extra difficulty to the design of a general AI-system for legal reasoning. In practice this means that in many domains a truly general AI-system would have to be complemented with a mechanism that enables it to determine the identity and the objectives of the user.

Taken as a whole, the agent requirement together with the functional aspect of law constitute an intricate problem, difficult to ignore. When the legal order is decomposed into small domain portions, however, it appears that there are no methodological or jurisprudential obstacles to the identification and elicitation of various legally relevant lines of reasoning in each domain. In this respect it is obvious that each legal domain recognizes only a limited number of generally defined agent types. Likewise, it appears indisputable that each different domain of the law can fulfil only a limited number of legally relevant functions. The identification of the sub-domain defined by the rules concerning the *sale of goods* in civil law, for instance, makes it possible to identify the legally relevant agents (e.g. buyers, sellers, and authorized representatives). The identification of an agent makes it in turn possible to identify a limited number of legally relevant requirements (e.g. the law may contain rules that may help buyers to obtain the goods, to cancel contracts and so forth).

Naturally, depending on the nature and quality of the law in different domains, the identification of legally relevant agents and requirements may be a more or less cumbersome task. Moreover, great differences between different legal cultures as regards the nature of work that has to be completed may also prevail. In a positivist environment encompassing an elaborated corpus of legal rules the identification of legal knowledge of this kind may be a rather straight-forward undertaking in many subdomains. In other kinds of jurisdiction in which the formulation of general principles and general concepts has had a low priority for a long time – as well as in any case-based area within a positivist jurisdiction – the identification of agents and requirements of a general nature may be a time-consuming project. It should also be kept in mind that it may be difficult to detect general components of this kind due to the fact that some of the cases appearing in certain areas are extremely rare.

Despite the fact that the identification of relevant agents and the legally acknowledged requirements may be complicated, it must be noticed that the suggestion that in each domain it should be possible to identify legally acknowledged agents and the accompanying lines of reasoning is nothing more than to say that in principle it must be always possible to describe and represent the law *de lege lata* in a functional perspective.

A further examination of this aspect of law makes it reasonable to believe that knowledge about agent-related requirements – i.e. "argumentative knowledge" could be reflected in a KBS(D), or, for reasons to be explained, could be represented in a large collection of small scale domain-dependent KBSs (labelled A for agent-argument-aspect). It is also reasonable to assume that the identification of a certain sub-domain or situation by a KBS(D) could lead to the activation of the relevant KBS(A) for the identification of the agent and the relevant requirement that has been previously reflected in the corpus of legal knowledge in that particular domain. From a general point of view it can be thus concluded that an interrelated set of KBSs(D) and KBSs(A) would be able in most cases to help to identify the most specific problem situation and the adequate line of reasoning vis-à-vis the current issue.

In many domains it is possible to incorporate all the relevant rules of a substantial nature (or, more precisely, it is possible to incorporate all the rules of a substantial nature that have been previously found relevant in similar situations) into a KBS(A). This is no more than what has been accomplished in numerous existing domain-dependent KBSs and in this respect the VF project illustrates again how a certain situation in a (to a large extent) uncodified area of law can be identified and represented in a logical rule-based model. In the functional perspective, the representation in the VF system reflects a legally defined requirement (the support for dismissal) of a legally defined agent (the employers' organization).

An additional illustration of the ways in which factors of a substantial nature can be related to various requirements, using a somewhat different methodology, is the development of so called "dimensions" in the HYPO experiment described in chapter 6. It should be also mentioned that although the factors in HYPO's dimensions and the logical rule-based model in the VF project have been extracted from cases, the same kinds of functionally composed lists of prerequisites can be obtained from statute rules, as well as from combinations of cases and rules. From this perspective, it is also obvious that there is a close similarity between factors and dimensions in the HYPO project and between prerequisites and rules that can be extracted through conventional jurisprudential analysis. Factors and prerequisites indicate here the elements that in previous situations have been found relevant, while dimensions and rules provide inference patterns for various situations.

Another, perhaps trivial conclusion following from the assumption that legally relevant agents and requirements are possible to identify and describe is that in principle – whenever the need arises and when the issues are frequent enough – it would be possible to develop a large number of small-scale KBSs (labelled S for substantive law), each reflecting one reasonable requirement of substantial law de lege lata vis-à-vis each agent. The identification of the agent *employers' organization* with the help of a KBS(A) in the domain of labour law could thus be linked up with the activation of any of the several KBS(S)s containing legal knowledge of a substantial nature about the prerequisites related to employment, dismissal, social security issues, pension plans, etc. (Such an extension based on the modularization of the requirements of the employers' organization was actually discussed when the economical prospects of the VF system were investigated.)[1]

7.2.2.2 Structural Integration

In many domains, most of the knowledge relevant to the legal identification of a certain situation could be undoubtedly incorporated in only a few KBSs. Hence, a decomposition of the material into a set of KBSs (G), (D), (A), and (S) may seem unnecessary. At this point of the description it should be underlined, therefore, that one important reason for the elabo-

[1] Hamfelt, Wahlgren *supra* chapter 1 note 21 *and* Dahnell *supra* chapter 1 note 44.

ration of various functionally defined, small-scale KBSs is that eventually – as the various small-scale systems are linked up into a more integrated system – also the sub-systems and the relations between the sub-systems will form a classification structure of significant importance. In other words, it is possible to take advantage of the fact that a consistent set-up of interrelated, small-scale KBSs reflects the structure of legal concepts, situations, agents etc., and that in this way it is possible to build a conceptual model of the law.

Thus, a large number of interrelated KBSs (G), (D), (A), and (S) can provide an extended and flexible scheme for legal identification. In such a design the KBS(S) reflects the lowest level in a hierarchy of KBSs, structured in such a way as to meet the requirements concerning identification and law-search. In this architecture the various KBSs reflect legal concepts supporting the identification of relevancy, and when activated, each KBS provides support for the identification of supplementary facts. The primary objective of KBSs(S) in this set up is thus to provide support for the identification of low-level concepts and detailed prerequisites. KBSs (G), (D), (A), and (S) are in the following referred to as KBSs of type (I), where "I" stands for identification. The principle of the organization of KBSs(I) is illustrated in figure 7.2.

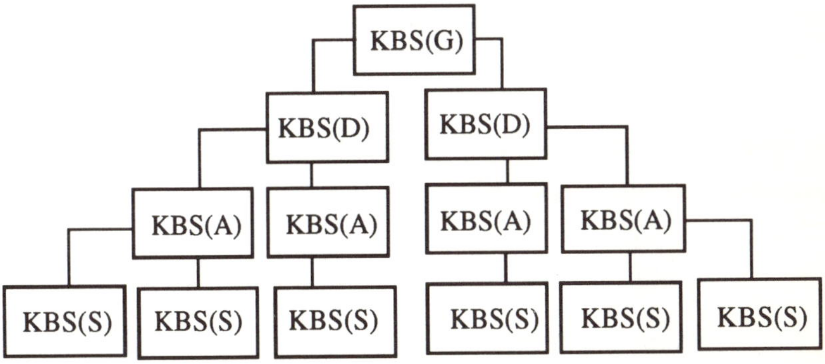

Figure 7.2 Organizational principle for the arrangement of KBSs(I), i.e. subsystems providing support for legal identification.

Within the sub-systems type (I) logical, rule-based models constitute the basis of the representation of substantive legal knowledge. An associative computer program that can manage predefined links between the logical, rule-based models is sufficient in order to combine and start up the various sub-systems. (In a small-scale LexLab experiment an extended version of the HyperCard program has been used for this function.)

In this context it should be also mentioned that the user of a system encompassing a large number of KBSs(I) should not be restricted by a certain, pre-designed order of investigation for a given system. That is to say that although it may be natural to arrange the sub-systems in an hierarchical structure from the point of view of the user the set-up should exhibit maximal flexibility and should be approachable at any level. The user who immediately recognizes the relevant legal agent or the relevant legal concept should thus be able to instantly select the adequate KBS(A), (D) or (S) for further investigation. From each instantiated KBS it should be also possible to generalize or specify by means of activating links with the related sub-systems. Ideally, the system should be able to manage the transition between the sub-systems without any particular effort on the part of the user who should be permitted to concentrate on the substantial content of the systems. The design should furthermore allow for tentative identification by means of successive inspections of the various sub-systems. From this follows that the model should be also complemented with one or several graphic representations depicting the represented concepts and the relations between the various KBSs. In addition, in order to support low-level concept identification within the various types of sub-systems the design should be equipped with one or several index files reflecting the content of each KBS.

7.2.3 Design for Methodological Legal Knowledge

7.2.3.1 Technical Integration

At our present level of understanding it appears obvious that it is not possible to elaborate some general mechanism in such a way that it could resolve problems concerning interpretation of concepts in different areas of law. This is simply to say that also various forms of methodological legal knowledge (i.e. knowledge about the ways in which substantial legal knowledge can be adjusted and/or complemented) will in each actual instance of legal reasoning appear to be of a distinct, domain dependent nature. This is perhaps most apparent when various forms of support for *contextual interpretation* (cf. section 5.4.2 supra) are scrutinized. In practice, this means that the methodological support that can be obtained from the legal system is often restricted to the existance of a definition of some subject matter in a case description (e.g. a low level legal concept), and that the fact interpretation procedures reflected in a civil law statute, for example, may be irrelevant when issues concerning administrative or criminal law are to be decided. Likewise, as when *intentional support* is present, an explicitly mentioned purpose is often valid only for the issues regulated in a specific field of law. In the same way, it is obvious that various fields of law acknowledge different combinations of rules regarding the priority in which material from various legal sources may be comprised.

The domain-dependent nature of methodological legal knowledge has implications for any AI-system development. The most apparent consequence is that the most efficient way of incorporating methodological knowledge in any KBS reflecting substantial legal knowledge – disregarding whether it is a part of a general AI-system or not – is often to complement the representation of substantial law with various forms of contextual and supplementary material of a domain-dependent nature.

The requirements concerning knowledge representation following from this desire to combine different forms of methodological legal knowledge with various kinds of KBSs do not raise insurmountable obstacles to a further elaboration of a general legal AI-system. In many cases it is thereby obvious that methodological knowledge in the form of extended definitions of interrelated legal concepts that can be extracted from case law, from interpretations of contextual intentions in jurisprudential literature, and so forth, should be integrated with the logical rule-based models representing the original substantial material that can be found in e.g. a statute. Likewise, it is clear that a doctrine of legal sources determining the hierarchical order of the legal material can be recasted and represented in a rule-based representation and thus imbedded in a KBS. A further examination of the need to represent, e.g., rules of priority during the interpretation phase shows that in this context the possibilities of reflecting disqualifying facts and sequences of fact-elicitation in logical rule-based models should be also recalled. Illustrations of how this can be done can be seen in any legal AI-system development-project. That is to say that each existing legal KBS which does not reflect purely legislative material only will actually incorporate various kinds of general and interpretive knowledge, e.g. in the form of hypothetical examples explaining the intentions of a certain rule, an explicit definition of a legal concept, the arrangement of the material in an order reflecting the usual knowledge elicitation procedure used by some legal expert, and so forth.

The fact that different types of legal knowledge can be transformed and represented in logical rule-based models does not, however, satisfy all the requirements following from the existence of various kinds of domain-dependent methodological material. In many cases the most adequate way of representing methodological knowledge in a KBS would be by means of complementing the rule-based models with explicit text descriptions and with various kinds of secondary components providing overviews, of e.g. the written material on a certain issue. In some instances there may be also room for inductive methods and different kinds of numerical and statistical procedures for the identification and interpretation of particular aspects. In yet other cases, in order to facilitate the resolution of uncertainty, it may be feasible to incorporate synonym dictionaries, term lists, and so forth. Furthermore, it is clear that each KBS reflecting substantial and methodological legal knowledge should be linked up with an IR-system encompassing the original legal documents.

From all this follows that each KBS encompassed in a more general AI-system for law should be able to integrate and manage various computational techniques. How this can be accomplished is illustrated by numerous KBS development projects, of which several have been described in section 6.5, showing among other things some different ways in which case-based and logical rule-based models, as well as of numerical and logical rule-based models can be combined. Furthermore, the use of associative hypertext techniques in the VF project, as well as the integration of logical rule-based models, hypertext, and IR in the DataLex project and the LexLab experiments shows that it is possible to represent legal knowledge supporting the interpretation process with various complementary methods, including the use of full text documents. The VF project shows furthermore that logical rule-based models combined with hypertext programs allow for the amendment of personal comments, which makes that in principle it is also possible to include methodological knowledge of a subjective nature.

7.2.3.2 Functional Decomposition

Domain-dependency of methodological legal knowledge is not absolute. Different types of methodological, or, to be more exact – generally applicable, legal knowledge exist in many shapes. In its simplest form, general legal inference patterns appear as rules or definitions of concepts that can be applied in a number of situations, i.e. as components of a number of lines of reasoning. Somewhat more complex patterns are provided by rules that may function in combination with different prerequisites. Examples of the latter kind derived from the domain of criminal law would be a set of rules that may be employed in order to define *criminal intent* and the previously described procedure of comparing mitigating and aggravating circumstances, related to the establishment of appropriate sentencing.

Legal components which may influence the legal reasoning process at an even higher level of generalization in a greater or smaller degree appear in the shape of elaborate descriptions of complex situations that can be applied in many different kinds of cases. One example of the above is provided by the Swedish Contracts Act of 1915 which stipulates default definitions and descriptions of actors, types of messages, time limits, powers, and grounds for the violation of certain acts that can be in principle used in any situations concerning commercial agreements, except for certain explicitly defined exceptions. Knowledge of this kind can be employed not only by several agents debating one distinct objective but it can be also be used in order to evaluate the argumentation and the positions of the opposing parties, and to define concepts of a common kind at a high level of abstraction, etc.

In addition, it should be mentioned that extensive methodological knowledge that can be applied to several different cases can be also found in various procedural codes regulating e.g. knowledge elicitation procedures, message exchange guidelines, definitions of valid claims and so forth. Furthermore, descriptions of general procedures appear as various kinds of more or less purified methodological rules and sometimes also as rules specifying exceptions to methodological procedures. Examples of the former are the previously described inferences of analogy and e contrario which may be reflected in rather simple search and inference patterns which may apply at both a detailed concept/prerequisite level as well as in the identification of complicated situations. A rule of the latter kind may prescribe, for instance, that inferences of analogy are excluded in cases when extensions of prerequisites in criminal law are contemplated, on account of the principle of legality.[2]

The fact that one may find in the corpus of legal knowledge reflections of a variety of more or less generally applicable inference patterns means that within any large set of KBSs(I) it will be possible to find components common to more than one system. From this follows in turn that the decomposition of legal knowledge can be extended and that in principle it is possible to identify and extract generally applicable portions of legal knowledge that can be represented in KBSs designed especially for this purpose. In consequence, in a discussion of elements that ought to be included in a general AI-system for law another class of KBSs (labelled Gc for general component) can be introduced.

In the domain of criminal law, for instance, it may be desirable to elaborate one KBSs(Gc) containing legal knowledge about criminal court proceedings, sentencing, the establishment of intent, and so forth. A set of KBS(Gc) of this kind can be then combined with any set of KBS(S) reflecting various crimes, as well as with a large number of KBSs(A) reflecting the requirements of various agents. Likewise, in the domain of employment law it is apparent that e.g. definitions concerning the employees' illness easily could form the basis of a KBSs(Gc) in the VF system, with the function of supporting several different lines of reasoning and useful not only to the employers' organizations but also to e.g. the employees' unions, the courts, the social security officers, etc.

[2] In some instances such a rule may have to be also complemented with further exceptions. *Cf.*, on *camouflaged analogies*, Frändberg *supra* chapter 2 note 80, at 125.

Different types of legal knowledge can be, no doubt frequently, identified and demarcated so that a KBS(Gc) reflecting a given type of legal knowledge can function in different domains. An example of the latter is provided by the high level definitions of various concepts that can be found in the previously mentioned Contracts Act.

In this context it should be noticed that one crucial aspect concerning the degree to which legal knowledge should be looked upon as being of a substantial or methodological nature is the level of generality that can be reached from the functional point of view. From this follows that the components of general knowledge may appear as both definitions of subject matter and as descriptions of procedures. It should be likewise noted that in its original representation knowledge of a general kind is often closely interrelated with the representation of domain-dependent substantial material. Among other things this means that some components will be mentioned explicitly in the legislative material but it also means that similarly to substantive law, legal knowledge of a general nature may be dispersed and that it can be perceived only through juxtaposition of e.g. case-law precedents. Moreover, it is obvious that various kinds of general legal knowledge may appear in in works of jurisprudence or that they may be simply reflected in the methods employed by individual lawyers and in organizational structures.

It may be also observed that the demarcation line between various forms of substantial and methodological legal knowledge is not embedded in the internal logical structure of the different legal components (or in the structure of the sentences representing these components). This can be illustrated by the previously mentioned rules on criminal intent. The inference patterns reflected in these rules will frequently appear in the reasoning of several different agents (e.g. judges, prosecutors, counsellors) concerning various kinds of crimes and they may therefore more or less automatically acquire the status of general or methodological legal knowledge. Simultaneously, however, very similar and explicitly defined legal rules that must be applied in order to determine e.g. the will of a testator and which can be only used in very specific and rare situations will be normally looked upon as peripheral pieces of substantial knowledge making up inheritance law.

From the fact that significant differences between various kinds of legal knowledge lies primarily in the different functions of the knowledge (and not in the nature of the representation) follows that with respect to formalization no special kinds of representation methods appears to be required for the development of KBSs(Gc). In practice, this means that logical rule-based, case-based, and associative models may be sufficient for basic knowledge representation also in this case. It may be furthermore observed that several already operating systems of the type KBS(Gc) are already in existence. One illustration of such a system, providing support for several agents engaged in various issues is the previously mentioned ASSYST operating with sentencing guidelines. The system was originally developed for the U.S. probation offices but it has been reported to have "proliferated throughout the Federal criminal justice system."[3]

7.2.4 Design for Formal and Evaluative Knowledge

7.2.4.1 Functional Decomposition

In the same way in which substantial and methodological components can be identified, formal knowledge structures can be also distinguished in the corpus of legal knowledge. This is illustrated by the existence of numerous rules and rule systems of different form, e.g. concerning the competence of legal agents, the temporal validity of statutes and the definitions of various jurisdiction, which are more or less firmly related to certain fields of law, situations and issues. In their conventional textual representations formal components are integrated with the material reflecting substantial and methodological aspects, just like any other type of legal knowledge. It is also noticeable that formal components appear at several levels of generalization and that they are domain-dependent in various degrees. As compared to the methodological components it is significant, however, that in many jurisdictions (as e.g. in the Scandinavian countries) formal rule-structures are more often explicitly represented and that in written material they frequently appear under certain headings and sometimes

3 Simon, Gaes *supra* chapter 1 note 24, at 195.

even in especially elaborated procedural codes. This no doubt the result of the fact that in order to fulfil their function of providing frameworks and basic presuppositions for legal decision making the formal aspects of law require in many cases explicit and unambiguous formulations.

A similar continuum of more or less general components can be perceived in legal knowledge structures which may help the lawyer to evaluate a contemplated solution. As indicated in chapter 5, it may be also assumed that to some extent portions of legal knowledge which may help to evaluate legal decisions in different domains can be represented in hierarchical structures. In this context it may be recalled that evaluative support appears often in the form of so called canons of interpretation, which may be supported in turn by legal principles and, at the highest level of generalization, by rules of evaluation used to examine among other things, generality and consistency aspects. (In figure 7.1 this relationship is reflected in the demarcation between methodological meta-rules and evaluation rules.) In addition to the existence of more clearly demarcated knowledge structures reflecting evaluative rules at high levels of generalization it should be also noticed that rules of an evaluative nature are integrated in various ways with substantial material at a distinct sub-domain or situational level. Examples may be found in the Swedish family law, where among the rules relating custody there exist an evaluation rule indicating that a decision must be adjusted to what is best from the point of view of the child. Another example appears in the set of rules on divorce issues where it is explicitly stated that the way in which property is divided should be depending, among other things, on the length of marriage.

The fact that formal and evaluative legal components are to a large extent explicitly represented in written legal material (as well as described in works of jurisprudence) validates the conclusion that formal and evaluative legal knowledge can be represented in KBSs. The elicitation of knowledge that must be performed in the process of developing KBSs encompassing this kind of knowledge is in principle nothing more than what has to be done before any jurisprudential description of law de lege lata can be worked out. It can be also assumed that extensive representations can be developed without any special requirements concerning representation techniques and that at least the same degree of detail that can be detected in conventional textual representations of law can be reflected in a representation using well-established knowledge-based methods. In other words it can be argued that logical rule-based models in combination with other kinds of previously described AI-techniques and traditional computer techniques are sufficient for the representation of formal and evaluative legal knowledge, as we presently understand and describe them. Illustrations of the ways in which this can be accomplished can be found in many AI-systems in the legal field, where formal and evaluative material is included.

In this context it should be explicitly stated that the recurring suggestion proposing that the established knowledge representation methods are sufficient to reflect knowledge contained within the various sub-systems is by no means equivalent to the suggestion that further research into knowledge representation is unnecessary. On the contrary, it should be obvious that access to more efficient and elaborate representation methods is (and probably always will be) an important presupposition for further advancement in all undertakings related to AI. In this respect, the design strategy outlined here constitutes no challenge to further research into more detailed formalization problems. Instead, the outlined design strategy may (if it turns out well) provide a *complement* to undertakings of a more specific nature by means of showing that it is actually possible to model and represent legal knowledge also at levels which have been previously given little attention.

Thus, what is suggested here – and what may be new from the point of view of the legal system development theory – is that various types of legal knowledge, such as rule-systems making up formal and evaluative components can be eventually separated from substantial and methodological material. Likewise, it is assumed that formal and evaluative legal components can be reflected in separately defined, small-scale KBSs – very much in the same manner as hypothesized that it is possible to decompose and represent different kinds of substantive and methodological rules.

Whether or not an elaboration of specifically demarcated KBSs representing formal and evaluative components is a worthwhile enterprise will be determined in each case by the level of generalization that can be detected in the material. If the formal and evaluative components are of a distinct, domain-dependent nature, as e.g. in the case of the evaluative rule related to custody mentioned above, or, as would be the case with a formal rule of an ad hoc nature regulating the competence of some individual in a very special situation (e.g. the authority that can be drawn from a specific power of attorney) there would be, of course, little sense in separating the substantial and the formal material.

On other occasions, however, i.e. when the formal and evaluative knowledge is of such a nature that it is possible to use it in different cases, a demarcation between different kinds of material can no doubt increase the flexibility of the representation. Examples concerning formal rules, e.g. about jurisdiction, are obvious and as for evaluation aspects it may be sufficient to mention the similarity rules exerting influence in e.g. damage law.

In this way the generality of formal and evaluative material leads to a conclusion that in many cases it may be practical to develop several small-scale KBSs, one type for each kind of knowledge. In a design of a general AI-system for law it is feasible to introduce in this way a set of KBSs(F) managing legal rules of formality, and a set of KBSs(E) managing rules of evaluation.

7.2.4.2 Structural Integration

The discussion concerning a further elaboration of general legal AI-systems presented in this chapter has so far outlined a perspective in which the corpus of legal knowledge can be decomposed into several components. It has been furthermore suggested that the decomposition should be based on the functions of the material that can be detected. In addition it has been suggested that each class of components that has been identified can be represented by a set of small-scale KBSs.

One foreseeable advantage following from the elaboration in the outlined direction has been already mentioned, viz. that the development of a large number of KBSs(I) makes it possible to elaborate and represent conceptual models of law, providing in-depth knowledge about various kinds of legal concepts which can be approached and investigated in different ways. From this point of view it is also obvious that a further decomposition of the material into sets of KBSs (Gc), (F) and (E) reflecting general components, formal rules, and evaluative material will lead to a further refinement of conceptual structures by means of increasing the preciseness and the number of components that can be approached for in-depth investigations.

The possibilities of refining conceptual structures are, however, not the only advantages brought by a further elaboration in this direction. In the design of a more general AI-system for law it should be also noticed that the elaboration of small-scale KBSs reflecting various kinds of legal knowledge makes it possible to enhance the flexibility of the system by means of linking up the different components with each other. Most importantly, because of the domain-dependent nature of various types of methodological, formal, and evaluative knowledge one will be able to link up the various sub-systems with each other so that the instantiation of a set of KBSs(I) will lead to the activation of a set of KBSs (Gc), (F) and (E). In this way, the identification of a certain legal domain and the substantial material concerning a given legal issue will make it possible to automatically delimit more or less extensive sets of formal, methodological and evaluative rules.

Criminal law may serve as an illustration. Here, the nature of the domain immediately indicates that inferences of analogy may have to be excluded when prerequisites of substantive nature are to be established. In addition, certain formal rules of (e.g. territorial) jurisdiction become relevant. Simultaneously, the principle of equality will indicate that similarity is an important aspect in the evaluation of sentencing, and so forth. In consequence, the activation of a set of KBSs(I) for criminal law may automatically activate one or more KBSs(Gc) reflecting sentencing procedures, one or more KBSs(F) reflecting jurisdiction, and one or more KBSs(E) reflecting evaluation rules. An identical, or similar, combination of various types of legal knowledge may be appropriate to activate when various kinds of tax-issues are to be dealt with. If the domain is family law, on the other hand, a different set of formal rules defining personal jurisdiction may become relevant. Inferences of analogy may be admitted and the set of rules related to evaluation may be of a different kind, etc.

To summarize the discussion so far it can be claimed that the outlined design strategy provides the necessary features and components (in comparison with the conventional KBS development) to explicitly represent one additional layer of legal knowledge. That is to say that the decomposition and the integration of components representing different functions of legal knowledge will make it possible to describe the legal system not only at the levels reflecting legal rules and concepts but also – with the help of the terminology introduced in chapter 5 – at the *rule-system level.* It can be furthermore argued that such a representation is a crucial ingredient in the development of more advanced legal AI-systems by means of increasing the flexibility and generality of the design. It is also important to mention, however, that development in the indicated direction does introduce complications, as well as further possibilities. Some of these aspects are discussed in the next sub-section.

7.2.5 Design for Legal Reasoning

In a general AI-system for law of the kind outlined here each class of KBSs will include large volumes of sub-systems. This in turn makes it possible to foresee problems similar to those encountered in the development of large applications of hypertext nature, i.e. problems with so called hyperspagetti, which are due to the fact that the number of components and links in those systems are too numerous to control. In the design of a general AI-system for law based on a large number of small-scale KBSs it must be therefore observed that some kind of control structure must be set up also at the level of rule-system representation. (Some of the ways in which difficulties with complex hypernets can be tackled are illustrated in sections 6.4.5.3.2 and 6.5.2.)

In order to outline a theory on how various knowledge components can be made to function together in a meaningful way, or, by a more provoking expression, to describe the ways in which control structures for legal reasoning can be developed, it may be appropriate to recall the description from section 7.2.2.2 concerning the ways in which KBSs forming type (I) can be linked up hierarchically. From this follows that the activation of a KBS can be made dependent on the activation of the interrelated KBSs. Hence, from the functional point of view it is relevant to observe the control function of the links between the various systems, i.e. that the activation of a link, e.g. from a high level KBS(A), controls the activation of interrelated lower levels KBSs(S) and vice versa. From this follows in turn that it is actually possible to develop logical models describing the ways in which small-scale KBSs can be related to each other.

To notice in the design of a general AI-system for law is furthermore that the technique of interrelating various KBSs to each other is not restricted to various KBSs(I) and that in each actual instance of legal reasoning it is also possible to describe the ways in which other kinds of subsystems can interact. This conclusion is based on the assumption that the corpus of legal knowledge will by necessity contain several more or less hierarchically (or sequentially) ordered structures exercising control over the ways in which different kinds of legal knowledge can be combined. (This is of course nothing more than a natural consequence of the fact that the legal reasoning process actually in practical situations can show great flexibility and yet be looked upon as legal reasoning.) It may be furthermore assumed that if the nature of and the relations between these control structures can be identified it is also possible to develop a meta-theory on how legal reasoning may function.

A further elaboration of the functional representation of legal knowledge shows clearly that the already outlined components of formal and evaluative nature play distinct roles. Before the roles of these components are discussed in more detail a further decomposition of the material described in connection with the outline given on the KBSs(Gc) must be, however, introduced. To explain this it may be recalled that generally applicable legal knowledge appears in many shapes and that it is in principle possible to specify various types or sub-classes of general legal knowledge. The ways in which the corpus of legal knowledge can be decomposed are numerous and the attained level of detail will no doubt be a reflection of the characteristics and of the number of agents operating in various legal domains. It is for instance possible to perceive a particularization based on the explicit representation of the material in various procedural codes and on the generally applicable components in various statutes. Alternatively, the material can be decomposed in such a way that it will satisfy the requirements originating from the process sequences of various activities from the point of view of the courts (or other organizations), and so forth. It should be also underlined that an important aspect determining the ways in which legal knowledge can be decomposed is the extent to which law has been developed in different areas. The latter is simply a reflection of the fact that legal knowledge is often of a fragmented nature and that in many cases an in-depth jurisprudential analysis can enhance the possibilities of the identification of various kinds of generally applicable components.

The variety of ways in which feasible solutions can be developed indicates that more distinct statements on how general legal components ought to be defined and classified from the functional point of view may require further research. However, in this context in which the outline of a design strategy where the identification of control structures that are essential to legal reasoning is the primary objective, it is possible to tentatively suggest at least two general types of knowledge that can form the basis for a further elaboration of a general legal AI-system, viz. *legal rules* and *legal situations*. As a consequence, at this point of the description, two additional components of a more general AI-system for law can be introduced, namely KBSs(R) and KBSs(Si). In a more elaborate system these latter components sometimes replace KBSs(Gc).

The theory underlying the development of KBSs(R) assumes more specifically that it is sometimes possible to extract and isolate inference patterns operating on various prerequisites and/or inference patterns that can be utilized by different agents in different situations. It is further assumed that the extracted inference patterns can be (and sometimes actually are) described in conditional form i.e. as rules, or as rules linked up with each other in lines of reasoning. It is also assumed that inference patterns can be represented in logical rule-based models. Likewise, it is hypothesized that the possible combinations of prerequisites, rules, and agent requirements that have previously been described in the corpus of legal knowledge can be reflected in links between the various types of KBSs. From the functional point of view it is thus appropriate to look upon KBSs(R) as control structures able to identify and combine various valid constellations of KBSs(A) and (S).

To illustrate: if the issue that has been identified by a KBS(D) is a sale of goods and the agent requirement identified by a KBS(A) is the one of the buyer trying to cancel a contract (e.g. due to the fact that the vendor has not delivered the goods), it would be possible to decompose the representation of legal knowledge in such a way that the KBS(A) would only contain the knowledge structures necessary for the recognition of the (legally acknowledged) requirements of buyers in general terms (e.g. to obtain goods, to cancel contracts, etc.) and the KBSs(S) would only reflect the prerequisites which have been previously related to these kinds of requirements. If such a decomposition is done in a consistent manner – and provided that the representation is broad, i.e. that it covers a large number of legally acknowledged requirements and a large number of substantial definitions of prerequisites – it would be possible to eventually let the user of the system (within reasonable limits and to various extent with regard to the nature of the domain, no doubt) try out novel combinations of KBSs(A) and KBSs(S). In such a set-up the role of a KBS(R) would be to provide knowledge about the various types of KBSs(A) and KBSs(S) that have been previously acknowledged as valid combinations. The KBSs(R) should be naturally also equipped with procedures for similarity analysis so that they are able to compare the suggested combinations and recognize and indicate the most similar combinations. With an example taken from chapter 6 this could mean, for instance, that the combination of prerequisites (e.g. type of violence, location, etc.) used in order to instantiate a certain rule describing a criminal act can be selected so as to fit the current situation. In such a process the user may chose between various KBSs of the (S) type and also introduce new components. It should be noticed, however, that a formalization of this kind would make it also possible to approach an issue not only from the point of view of the requirements placed by legal agents but also from the ''bottom-to-top'' approach by means of trying out various combinations of prerequisites and through the inspection of interrelated KBSs(R) find links to various agent requirements. In such a system it would also be desirable to allow for the user to chose among and replace KBS(A) components. In relation to the above mentioned issue about sale of goods, for example, this would enable the user to combine a set of prerequisites that previously have been related to the requirements of buyers with the requirements of renters by means of replacing the KBS(A) component. (In the Swedish legal system this would reflect a well known and widely accepted inference of analogy).

To summarize this approach, it can be predicted that in some domains KBSs(R) would solely reflect knowledge of the ways in which different combinations of KBSs the (S) type can function together (i.e. indicate the ways in which prerequisites have been previously related to each other) e.g. as aggravating and mitigating elements. In other situations, however, KBSs(R) would no doubt reflect knowledge of the ways in which KBSs(A) and (S) can function together (i.e. indicate the ways in which agent requirements and combinations of prerequisites have been previously related to each other).

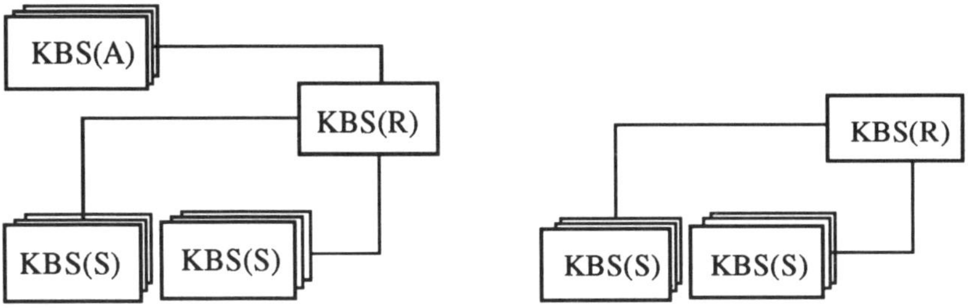

Figure 7.3 Examples of the organizational principles of the KBSs type (A), (S) and (R).

The flexibility of legal reasoning cannot be explained only by the fact that various prerequisites and agent requirements can be combined into rules that previously have not been described. An advanced AI-system for legal reasoning would need to allow for flexibility at several levels of generality. What is most obvious in this respect perhaps is that a general legal AI-system must have access to some kind of device indicating the ways in which new combinations of rules and different types of agent requirements may be combined. In this context it is thus relevant to introduce the KBSs(Si).

As compared to KBSs(R), the KBSs of (Si) type reflect legal knowledge which may support inference patterns at a higher level of generalization. A higher level of generalization in this context means that many of the components in the representation are of a more complex kind in the sense that they can be decomposed into more specific factors. An important presupposition for the formation of KBSs(Si) is therefore the existence of high-level descriptions for various kinds of legal situations and legal actions, e.g. various types of economic transactions, loans, set-offs, taxation, inheritance, different kinds of court proceedings, etc., each reflecting combinations of components – legal rules and legal agents – originating from levels of descriptions of a more detailed character.

In consequence, a basic feature of a KBS(Si) would be to link up different kinds of KBSs type (A) and (R) in such a way that they were able to reflect the ways in which different rules and agent requirements have been related to each other in previous (legally) described situations. If this is performed in a consistent manner it will be eventually possible to let the activation of a KBS type (R) or (A) lead to the activation of a KBS(Si) which could, in turn, indicate links to additional systems of the (A) and (R) type reflecting the ways in which valid combinations of rules and agent requirements have been previously formed.

KBSs(Si) should not however only possess knowledge about the ways in which individualized legal components of more a specific character can be combined. It is equally important that the systems of the (Si) type can provide knowledge about the ways in which various *classes* of KBSs(A) and (R) can be combined and in this way furnish the features that will make it possible to try out novel combinations. An important feature in this respect is that the (Si) component could carry information about various legal domains and thus indicate the cases when inferences of analogy, i.e. replacements of lower-level components would be acceptable and vice versa. At this level it is also obvious that the system design could benefit from elaborated methods for consistency analysis of various kinds. In addition, (Si) components could be augmented by supplementary knowledge, e.g. explicit information about the objectives of the legislation in various domains, and so forth.

To illustrate: if a KBS(Si), e.g. concerning bankruptcy proceedings, is activated by a substantial rule concerning the liquidation of companies, the KBS(Si) can automatically indicate the legally relevant agents and agent requirements (e.g. those of the enforcement officer or the manager of the company), the additional rules that have to be instantiated in order to identify the situation (e.g. concerning the estimation of assets and establishment of insolvency), as well as other components that have been found legally relevant in other similar situations. At this level a KBS(Si) could also (in the interest of creditors and as a reflection of the principle of prediction) prohibit e.g. the replacement of components affecting the definition of economic factors.

Admittedly, in many domains situational descriptions of law – as they have been outlined here – may be poorly developed. It can be therefore predicted that any broad representation (i.e. any representation covering many fields of law) may require comprehensive jurisprudential analysis. This is not however a serious obstacle to system development activities. On the contrary, from the jurisprudential point of view it may well be argued that the efforts to develop descriptions of this kind may provide excellent opportunities for the elaboration of the legal system in many fields of the law. It is also clear that each jurisdiction based on a positivist tradition will actually provide a rich variety of descriptions reflecting different kinds of legal situations of more complex kinds. In this context it may be also recalled that law was once perceived as a taxonomy of *actiones* and that it was assumed that each new upcoming case could be related to one of the previously known issues. In ancient Roman law actiones could originate from e.g. things, actions, agreements, etc.[4]

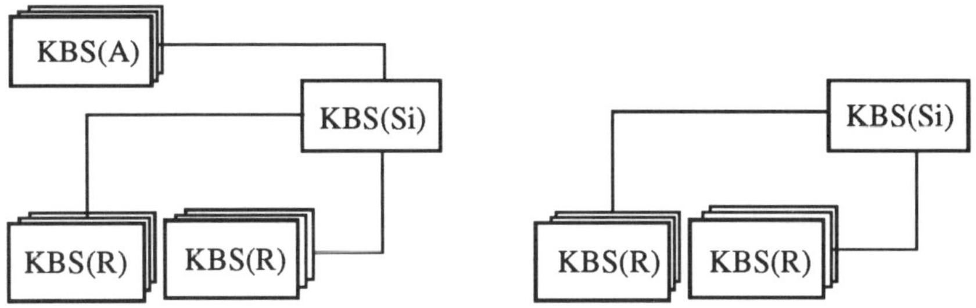

Figure 7.4 Examples of organizational principles for (A), (R) and (Si) KBS types.

[4] *See, e.g.*, for an overview of ancient Roman law, Daube, D. *Collected Studies in Roman Law* (1991) *and*, for a discussion of the relevance of this perspective to the AI and law enterprise, Samuel, G. *The Challenge of Artificial Intelligence: Can Roman Law Help us Discover Whether Law is a System of Rules?* (1991). The parallels between the design approach outlined above and the Roman way of perceiving legal reasoning are interesting and further investigations appear to be motivated. To illustrate this it may be mentioned that Samuel, among other things, submits that "[F]ormal reasons for a decision were referable to sets of formalized self-referencing categories: sets of factual alternatives were matched to sets of interrelating reference categories." and that "Roman legal reasoning involved the creation of a series of conceptual networks within which any particular rule or principle was fitted only as part of a system." Quotations from pages 44 and 45.

The possibilities of forming novel combinations of legal rules and agent requirements clearly explain much of the flexibility that can be achieved in legal reasoning. In the legal reasoning process legal descriptions of situations constitute therefore a necessary complement to legal rules of a substantial nature. At the same time, it is obvious that the flexibility of the legal reasoning process cannot be solely explained by the fact that various sub-components can be combined into more complex situations according to some well-formed rules describing the possible combinations of such components. That is to say that a flexible system for legal reasoning must allow also to some extent for novel combinations of components at a situational level.

In other words, it is clear that there must exist knowledge structures at a higher level of generalization, indicating the ways in which complex legal situations can be comprised and adjusted. From this point of view it seems quite clear that the function of formal legal knowledge will in many cases be to demarcate valid and invalid combinations of e.g. legal agents, legal rules and legal situations. From this in turn follows that in a more complex AI-system for law the previously described KBSs of the (F) type could play a distinct role by means of identifying valid combinations of the (A), (R) and (Si) type. A KBS(F), for example, in the field of family law could thus more or less automatically check out the possibilities of combining the requirements of an agent with rules of a certain kind by means of investigating the validity of law from the point of view of time, jurisdiction and the formal aspects (competence required for agents operating in the domain, the form of the claim, etc.) that must be established in order to realize valid legal decisions. It should be observed that systems of the (F) type need not only be restricted to the task of recognizing valid combinations of interrelated sub-systems. Systems type (F) could naturally also contain additional, in-depth knowledge reflecting more detailed aspects of competence, various types of qualifications, time aspects, jurisdiction, etc.

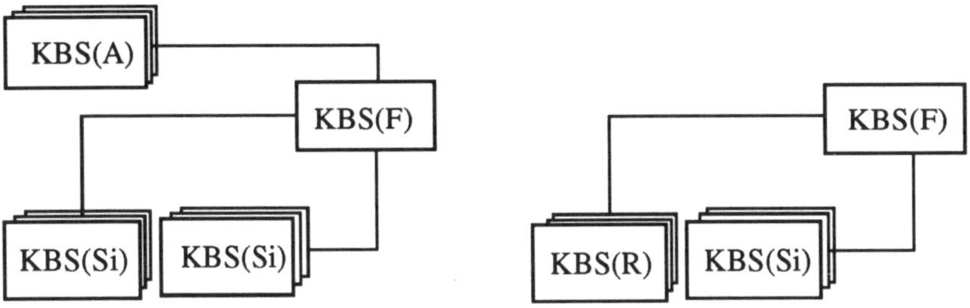

Figure 7.5 Examples of organizational principles of KBSs (R) (Si), (A) and (F).

Pursuing this line of thought further, and as illustrated in the elaborated JLR model, occasionally there will also be reasons for the invalidation of rules of formality if acceptable legal decisions are to be reached. In consequence, in an advanced AI-system for legal reasoning there will eventually appear a need for supplementary control structures that would be able to indicate the ways in which valid combinations of legal situations, agent requirements and formal rules can be formed in a legally acceptable manner.

In this context it is therefore also possible to establish a distinct function for the previously introduced sub-systems type (E). That is to say, it can be suggested that eventually it may be possible to understand and describe the knowledge related to the evaluation of legal decisions in such a way that KBSs(E) will be able to recognize, or, at least, support the recognition of valid combinations of sub-systems of the (A), (Si) and (F) type. The relations between sub-systems of the (A), (Si), (F) and (E) type can thus be depicted as in figure 7.6.

The evaluation of legal decisions is, however, not always a reflection of valid combinations of the legal knowledge components. Evaluation will in many cases also depend on the knowledge about non-legal factors and on the understanding of what is acceptable in a society at a certain point of time. At this level there exists therefore a borderline as to the kind of knowledge that is possible to identify and extract from the legal domain. For this reason, sub-systems of the E type should naturally, in addition to logical rule-based models indicating valid combinations of sub-systems, be also augmented with texts giving suggestions for and against various solutions in a well-balanced manner. Thus a KBS(E), e.g. in a legal office of a commercial company, could supply knowledge about corporate policies, trends in legal dispute settlements, long-term objectives, etc. It can be also stipulated that KBSs(E) – despite the lack of formalized rules concerning substantial matters – can be useful to the user of the system in various ways in reminding him of appropriate questions that must be posed in any process of legal reasoning, e.g. questions related to consistency, similarity, etc.

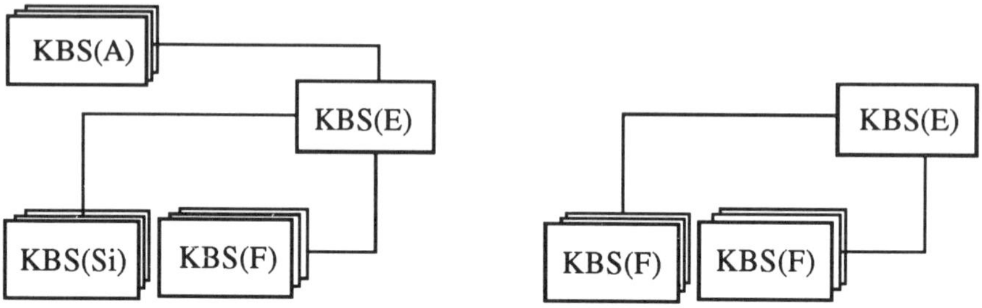

Figure 7.6 Examples of organizational principles of KBSs (E), (F), (A) and (Si).

The design approach outlined here leads to the conclusion that eventually it would be possible to elaborate general AI-systems for law based on the integration of different kinds of computational techniques, functional decomposition of legal knowledge, and structural integration of different kinds of small-scale legal knowledge based systems. In legal AI-systems based on these principles it can be argued that the systems of the (R), (Si), (F) and (E) type may be looked upon as components that can be used in order to recognize and support the identification of valid combinations of sub-systems. They may therefore be referred to as KBSs(C) where "C" indicates functions related to control. It can be furthermore assumed that various KBSs(C) can be arranged in such a way that they each operate on different material (i.e. different types of sub-systems). Presumably – as indicated in the overview of legal reasoning submitted in chapter 5 – it will be also possible to find a hierarchical or sequential order in which these control-structures can be made active in order to best support the process of legal reasoning.

The perspective outlined here indicates furthermore that the method of linking up sub-systems with each other will eventually make it possible to minimize the number of questions that have to be posed to the user by means of letting the system automatically draw many of the inferences originating from the fact that various kinds of legal knowledge are activated. It may be even argued that the methodology submitted here makes it possible (at least in theory) to actually represent the links between portions of knowledge, which, if properly combined, could facilitate the support of inferences of analogy. This can be accomplished by means of classifying and linking up the sub-systems with similar functions, and (during consecutive consultations) by letting the user at each stage of the process more or less freely replace one or several KBSs of the same type. The combinations formed in this way are then evaluated by the higher level systems of the (C) type in the succeeding sequence.

To some extent it can be also hypothesized that the design will enable the lawyer to describe the possible relations between various types of sub-systems in terms of disjunctive and conjunctive relations. That is to say, it is reasonable to assume that law can be actually understood in the way which makes it possible to postulate that a line of reasoning in a certain field of law (e.g. x) must include components reflected in the sub-systems e.g. of type (D_x) *and* (S_x) *and* (R_x) *or* (Si_x) *and* (F_x) and so forth. Existing knowledge of this kind may be found, e.g., in procedural codes stating that a lawyer must present a written power of attorney (F-component), that the claim (A-component) should be explicit and that it should be accompanied by references concerning the grounds for the claim (Si-component) as well as by the evidence supporting the claim (S-component).

From the method of linking up portions of legal knowledge reflecting the various functions, it also follows that it may be argued that it will be possible to elaborate legal AI-systems so that they could be employed in a large number of tasks. This follows from the fact that if the decomposition of legal knowledge and the integration of the sub-systems are carefully performed, it will be also possible to obtain decision support not only for issues of substantial nature but also for the management of problems related to legal methods, legal rules of formality, and evaluative issues. The design will thus make it possible to start an interrogatory session from any of the integrated KBSs and, by means of investigating the links between the sub-systems, try out different combinations in a tentative way. This may be done, for example, in order to see in which domains and situations a certain general component (e.g. the definition of intent) appears, or in which domains a certain formal rule structure (e.g. concerning personal jurisdiction) applies, or in which domains various rules of evaluation (e.g. including economic factors) have been employed, and so forth. The fact that the system should ideally contain knowledge of relevance for different agents will naturally also make the investigation of alternative ways of reasoning possible, for example in planning sessions.

In a general AI-system for law it can be also suggested that the integration of the various components should be monitored by a module able to keep track of and store knowledge about the combinations of KBSs that have been employed in successful lines of reasoning. A sketch of a general system based on these principles is given in figure 7.7.

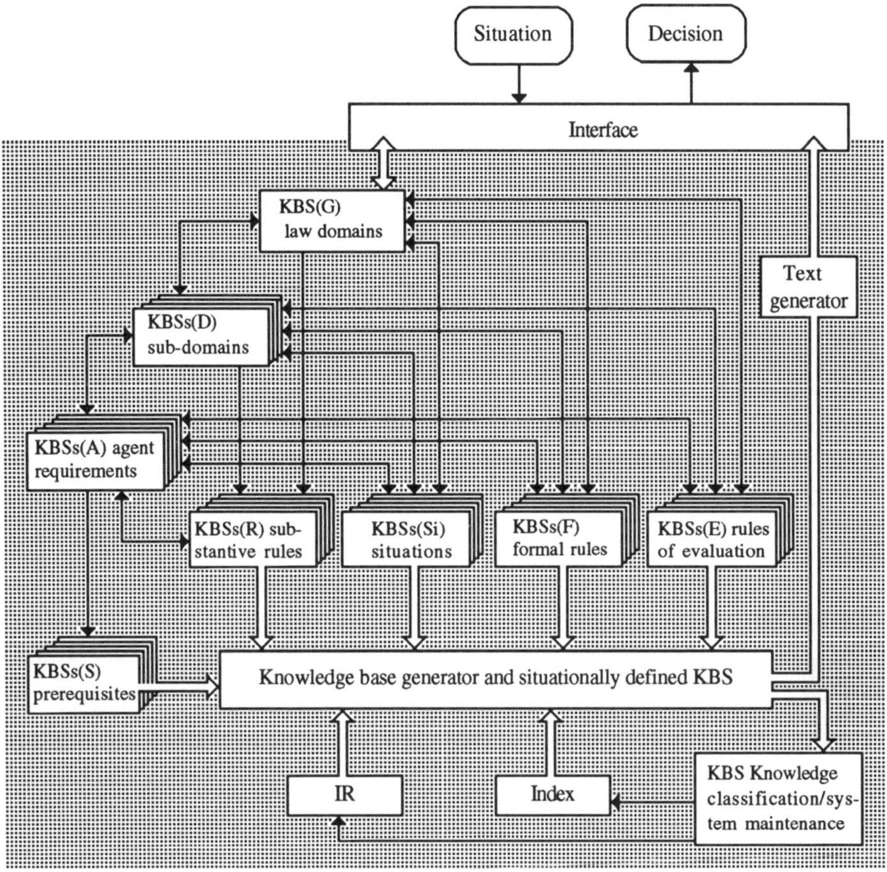

Figure 7.7 Sketch of a general legal AI-system based on the modularization of legal knowledge. The modules reflect functionally decomposed portions of legal knowledge and are defined and restricted by the levels of generality that can be identified in different kinds of legal material. In the system, the modules are each operated by a KBS. The user of the system can either approach any of the sub-systems in order to obtain detailed knowledge about the reflected component, or use the system for consultation by means of activating the KBSs for identification, i.e. sub-systems of the (G), (D), (A) and (S) type, containing substantial knowledge. In instances of the latter kind, by means of relying on the KBSs for control, i.e. on the sub-systems of the (R), (Si), (F), and (E) type, the system allows the user to try out various novel combinations of legal knowledge.

7.2.6 Concluding Remarks

The identification and representation of legal knowledge in the way which has been outlined here constitute admittedly a complicated and cumbersome task. The realization of a general AI-system with the help of the suggested design approach represents therefore a long-term research goal. The approach is, however, by no means unrealistic. The design strategy is intended to function also on limited portions of legal knowledge. Likewise, it is assumed that the development of a general AI-system can proceed in a modularized manner so that an increasingly number of components can be included. To keep in mind in this respect is also the fact that if the material is decomposed into small domain portions, it is obvious that an extensive jurisprudential analysis will make the identification of various functions of the legal material possible. It is equally clear that the large majority of the sub-systems of the kind outlined here will be very small as regards the size of the knowledge bases that must be developed. It can be therefore assumed that the work to be performed must be of a manageable size.

In this context, it may be also argued that the functional representation like the one outlined here provides also an efficient means for the updating and adjustment of the material. Likewise, it may be suggested that the design strategy provides an efficient and elaborated structure for the understanding of how such changes will affect the system. This simply because it is comparatively easier to update and change small-scale KBS modules, as compared to more complex systems. It is important to mention also that the decomposition and the integration of the material has advantages in the respect that the knowledge components can be utilized in many different situations and that the knowledge representation effort that is required in the development of KBSs can be minimized.

One natural limitation is, however, the fact that in many fields of law further decompositions beyond the level of KBSs(A) and (S) will make little sense. This is for instance the case in many fields of law, where the existing legal knowledge is of a detailed, uncontroversial, and indisputable domain-dependent nature. In such domains the existing rules and the defined prerequisites are best reflected in an integrated representation. The decomposition of the material into prerequisites and rules, situational descriptions, and formal and evaluative components is motivated, in other words, only when the legal knowledge components are of such a nature that they can be used in many different situations or by different agents in their various lines of reasoning. In an attempt to develop more advanced, general AI-systems for law it may be, nevertheless, suggested that the investigation of whether or not a separation between agent requirements, rules, prerequisites, and so forth can increase the flexibility of the system should be a standard procedure.

As regards the requirements concerning knowledge representation it should be also emphasized that the above outlined design requires no special forms of logic or other novel kinds of knowledge representation techniques in order to reflect the material within the different sub-systems. None of the sub-systems outlined here, nor the integration of the systems, appear to require any form of representation that has not been already utilized, e.g. in the VF project. In other words, it should be possible to start developing systems of the suggested kind with the help of established KBS-methods in combination with conventional computational techniques.

To suggest that it is possible *to start* more advanced system development projects with the use of current knowledge representation methods is, of course, not the same thing as to claim that all knowledge representation problems have been solved. What is proposed here is little more than to claim that it would be possible to utilize and combine the existing knowledge representation methods in the ways that would better reflect the various layers of knowledge which actually are present within the domain. It may be, however, also suggested that such an approach may result in the fact that some problems which have so far appeared as central may be avoided, or, at least, looked upon from a different perspective. It must be noticed, nevertheless, that the elaboration of system development projects of the kind proposed here will doubtless give rise to other, new knowledge representation problems. Many of them will probably also be very difficult to solve, and, as mentioned above, more efficient methods of knowledge representation with high level of complexity will be always crucial for further developments of AI.

As a final comment it should be also observed that the possibilities of the identification of the relevant components that can be utilized in a legal reasoning process do not depend solely on legal knowledge. On the contrary, in the process of the identification of the components which can be combined into functionally meaningful lines of reasoning several other control structures obviously exercise influence on the process. As for the future, it may be therefore also hypothesized that each component in a legal AI-system can be augmented with other kinds of knowledge, e.g. knowledge of a linguistic nature concerning the ways in which to recognize different kinds of functions from text structures making it possible to classify the encountered components in a rational and consistent manner.

8 Summary and Conclusions

8.1 Introduction

Section 8.2 of this closing chapter provides a summary of chapters 1 - 7. In section 8.2 also some distinct conclusions related to the issues approached in the various chapters are submitted. Thereafter, sections 8.3 – 8.5 provide some concluding remarks on the main questions raised in chapter 1. Finally, in section 8.6, a number of research objectives and legal issues that must be given high priority in future work are identified.

8.2 Summary

Chapter 1 presents the general objective of the study, which is to investigate the prospects of the integration of AI and law. The objective is related to a number of alternative motives for the undertakings in the field. It is also emphasised from the start that the task is approached from a jurisprudential perspective. Thereafter the more detailed aims of the study – (i) to investigate the extent to which AI-applications may support legal work, (ii) whether, and if so, the extent to which AI-methods may be of value for the legal method, and (iii) whether, and if so, the extent to which jurisprudential theories may provide valuable knowledge for AI – are described. The objectives are then related to the method of the study, which is to approach the topic from the point of view of the legal reasoning process. Furthermore, some limitations and practical intentions are articulated. Among other things, it is emphasised that one further aim of the work is to facilitate the elimination of the commonly encountered problems concerning conflicting jurisprudential and/or computational models by means of articulating basic presuppositions.

Chapter 2 – structured so as to meet the requirements of the non-legal reader – provides an overview of some commonly accepted jurisprudential notions concerning the nature of law and legal reasoning. The description encompasses a number of jurisprudential approaches and relates them to the historical development of legal realism and legal positivism. It is concluded that jurisprudential theories on legal reasoning are often intricately interwoven with discussions of the foundations of legal systems, the nature of law and similar matters, and that pure studies of legal reasoning are rare. It is finally suggested that anyone undertaking a study of legal reasoning must be prepared to admit the relevancy of different methodological approaches, such as the manipulation of formal logic, sociological methods and system analysis.

Chapter 3 – structured so as to meet the requirements of the reader without technical background – describes the development of AI. The initial sub-sections offer an overview of philosophical notions and scientific theories of relevance for the concept of intelligence. Thereafter, the historical development of the basic components of AI, such as electronic computers and formal logic, is characterized. In addition, the formation of a uniform discipline of AI is mentioned. Finally, some important ingredients of the study, such as decision support systems and AI-system development methods are introduced.

Chapter 4 describes the development of the two disciplines – computers and law, and AI and law. The early predictions as well as the related development in the field of jurimetrics are reviewed. In this chapter a description of an early but still the most wide spread computer application within law – viz. information retrieval systems – is also given. In the light of the historical perspective it is suggested that the emerging concept of AI and law reflects more a terminological evolution than a technical revolution. It is also observed that as yet the majority of contributions within AI and law are rather technically oriented and that comparatively little attention has been given to jurisprudential presuppositions.

Chapter 5 provides an analysis of legal reasoning. The task is accomplished by means of providing the outline of a model of legal reasoning based on the distinguishing of six sub-processes – identification, law-search, interpretation, rule-application, evaluation and formulation. The sub-processes, as well as the relations between them, are thereafter analysed in-depth. Simultaneously different types of legal knowledge influencing each sub-process are identified. In addition some comments concerning the related learning process are given. It is concluded that a large number of factors influencing the legal reasoning process can be found within the legal system. It is furthermore established that many factors are of a mandatory nature and that a violation of any of these factors may lead to the invalidation of the result of the reasoning process.

A firm conclusion of chapter 5 is also that many factors influencing the legal reasoning process are of a distinct, domain-dependent nature.

Chapter 6 analyses various experiments conducted in the domain of legal AI. Initially, some non-technical aspects that must be given attention to in any project concerning the introduction of AI-techniques into the legal field are discussed. Thereafter, the issue of knowledge acquisition is analysed in the light of the experiences gathered from two system development projects, completed in the current investigation. In the accompanying subsections various computational models that have been suggested for legal knowledge are related to the jurisprudential model of legal reasoning outlined in the preceding chapter. Five AI-related knowledge representation approaches are identified and exemplified – logical rule-based, inductive case-based, associative, deontic and conceptual models. In this context, also the system development projects undertaken in this study are described.

It is concluded that methods originating from logical rule-based, inductive case-based and associative models meet the requirements and standards distinguishable from the jurisprudential perspective in various degrees. As for deontic models, it is argued that presently it is difficult to perceive any corresponding notions or distinct requirements from the practical or jurisprudential point of view. It is also stated that as yet no practical applications based on deontic logic seem to have been presented. The latter is found also true for conceptual models which for the time being appear to be too poorly developed in order to reach any practical significance. It is suggested, however, that conceptual models are necessary ingredient of the development of more advanced computer systems and that various kinds of conceptual models ought to be further elaborated upon.

It is finally underlined that from the practical point of view the different AI-methods must be looked upon as components which will be integrated with each other in the future and that also various kinds of conventional computational techniques must be included in a discussion of the automation of legal reasoning. For this reason some experiments integrating different AI-methods are presented.

Chapter 7 addresses the prospects of more advanced AI-tools in the field of law. The discussion starts from the conclusions arrived at in chapters 5 and 6. It is thereby suggested that at present the limitations of further development do not primarily lie in computational restrictions. It is likewise hypothesized that knowledge representation methods originating from logical rule-based, inductive case-based, and associative AI-models in combination with conventional computational methods are sufficient for the initiation of the development of much more general and flexible AI-systems in law, as compared to those that have been so far presented. It is furthermore argued that virtually all the factors of vital importance for legal reasoning must be reflected per definition in the corpus of legal knowledge and that the crucial issue for further advancement in the area is a better understanding and characterization of law and legal reasoning from the functional point of view.

In the accompanying sections an outline of a design strategy for a more advanced AI-system is submitted. The design strategy is based on the development of a large number of small-scale, interrelated KBSs, each reflecting different functions of law vis-à-vis legal reasoning. The various KBSs form a conceptual model of law founded on the functional classification of legal knowledge. The design reflects thereby the various forms of legal knowledge identified in chapter 5, as well as additional decompositions. During a consultation, the user of the system may approach each of the KBSs with the help of an index or graphical representations for further, in-depth consultations and/or for the inspection of the relations between various forms of legal knowledge. Each KBS of the set up contains a logical rule base and is, depending on the nature of the domain knowledge, augmented by various forms of associating and inductive methods. An associating computer program is used to link up the various KBSs.

Two main groups of KBSs – systems for identification, KBSs(I), and systems for control, KBSs(C) – are specified. In addition, a knowledge-base generator (a situationally specified KBS) and a number of additional features are included, such as an IR-system containing full-text legal documents, an index module, and a knowledge classification/maintenance module. The KBSs(I) are arraigned hierarchically and reflect domains, sub-domains, agents, requirements and prerequisites in various legal fields. The system is flexible in the way that it allows the user to activate and combine different kinds of KBSs(I).

Each KBS(I) is related to one or several KBSs(C) encompassing control structures, such as legal rules, legal descriptions of situations, formal rules and evaluative rules. During a consultation the activation of a certain set of KBSs(I) thus activates a set of KBSs(C). The knowledge-base generator synthesizes material from valid combinations of KBSs and is able to extract and construct situationally defined knowledge-bases from rule modules contained in the various KBSs. Through a dialogue with the user the system is also able to support the elaboration of old and the construction of new rules. This is accomplished by the activation of various general mechanisms for rule-search, inductive and interpretative support.

In the final section some advantages as well as limitations concerning the construction of a general legal AI-system are discussed. It is admitted that the development of a system of the kind outlined here is a difficult task. It is also explicitly stated that such an enterprise will give rise to many new intricate research problems, concerning, e.g., the functions of legal reasoning, adequate knowledge representation, etc. It is, however, simultaneously suggested that the effort required for the updating and maintenance of the conventional representation of legal knowledge is of a comparative degree of difficulty. It is therefore hypothesized that an extensive use of KBSs, as compared to the conventionally represented legal system, will eventually turn out to be more efficient for the individual users, as well as for the legal domain as such. Likewise, it is suggested that knowledge-based representation will eventually prove to be less cumbersome as regards up-dating and easier to embrace. The study makes it possible to formulate the following conclusions.

8.3 AI-Applications in Law

The investigation of AI-technologies shows that in the light of the requirements which can be detected from the decomposition of the legal reasoning process the possibilities to represent various kinds of legal entities are well developed. That is to say that if the relevant entities can be described in a sufficiently elaborate manner, it is perfectly possible to reflect all of them in a computer program. It may be also hypothesized that if the relevant relations between the components can be described in a general way, also the inference patterns operating on such entities may be represented by means of logical programming and the use of associating techniques. Moreover, the experiments undertaken in this study indicate that there are no technical obstacles to the integration of various kinds of representation methods into operating systems. Different kinds of components may be thus reflected in e.g. associated texts and logical rule-based models which can be activated in a dynamic manner. As illustrated, various kinds of AI-applications may be also integrated with IR-systems and administrative computer systems. Experiments reported indicate furthermore that within limited fields of law AI-systems are able to provide legal support at a level surpassing human experts.[1] In addition, the model of a more general AI-system for law outlined in section 7.2 indicates extensive possibilities of increasing the generality and flexibility of the systems by means of integrating various kinds of small-scale KBSs into them.

For these reasons the initially posed question as to whether AI-applications are suitable for the legal domain may be answered in the affirmative. It can be firmly concluded that the techniques that have been discussed here can take over a large number of tasks that a few years ago were possible to solve only by means of using a trained legal intellect. It is also adequate to foresee a further development that will make it possible to elaborate systems that can perform several tasks that today require the attention of trained legal minds. It can furthermore be concluded that the introduction of legal AI systems can bring about effects that are positive from the jurisprudential point of view. In other words, there is no doubt that a more extensive use of AI-technology in legal work can increase the quality of legal decisions and legal advice in terms of equality, predictability, etc. Likewise it is obvious that the technique in comparison with conventional methods for the managing of legal knowledge offers better possibilities of handling complex material in an efficient and simultaneously flexible manner. It can be also concluded that the potentialities in this respect are considerable.

As regards the possibilities of the application of AI-systems to practical work situations, the premises will differ, however, depending on the field

[1] *See, e.g.*, Bench-Capon *supra* chapter 6 note 24, at 43.

of law and the issues that are approached. From this point of view, it is likely that a systematic investigation of the non-technical factors performed in a pre-project feasibility study will result in many fields of the law in a combination of positive and negative indicators as regards the possibilities of successful completion of a system development project. Factors of this kind have not been investigate in any great depth in this study, but the discussion in chapter 6, as well as the experiences from the NCA and VF projects, indicate that difficulties concerning acceptance may arise and that they may be reflected in goal conflicts between the various groups of persons affected by a legal AI-system. Another factor that may impede a direct extensive use of AI-technology in law is that the development of elaborate systems represents still a rather cumbersome and expensive undertaking.

In the long-term perspective, on the other hand, it may be assumed that many of the problems related to acceptance will dissolve as education and information about the technique and its presuppositions will increase the computer readiness. Likewise, goal conflicts may become a less important problem in future, as the understanding of how to build flexible applications increases. It should be furthermore kept in mind that the strength of AI-applications, and that of computer applications in general, lies in much in the possibilities of increasing the efficiency of legal work. For economical reasons, this will in turn motivate further work on various kinds of computer-applications in law. The flexibility of AI-technologies and of the ways in which they can be integrated into the existing computer applications of a more conventional kind constitutes in this respect a vital factor indicating excellent prospects of further development in the area. In addition, as mentioned in the introduction, several factors integrated to the legal system, such as the principles of equality and prediction, will provide natural motives for further research in the foreseeable future.

As a consequence, it is realistic to predict that in future the legal domain will rely rather heavily on various forms of computer technologies, including different methods originating from AI-research. The incorporation of a more advanced technology into the area will not be completed, however, overnight. On the contrary, it is possible to foresee a slow but steady development in which a growing number of aspects of legal work will obtain computer support. By the same token, various kinds of computer-based functions will become successively more integrated as the development continues. In this perspective, it is for many reasons not possible to concentrate on AI-methods alone and, from the point of view of both the users and the system developers a more sound approach should also include components originating from the conventional computer technology.

As integration and technical development continue, the systems will be able to support increasingly complex tasks. One can therefore foresee that the AI-systems will reflect a higher degree of independence from human agency. In this perspective it may be even argued that there are no *technical* obstacles to autonomous computer-based systems within limited fields of law. (Autonomous in the sense that the systems will be able to operate solely with data obtained from the interrelated computer-systems without human involvement.) Such computer applications – though still rather primitive – exist already, e.g. in the form of pay-roll systems that can deduct taxes, calculate sick-leave allowance and overtime adjustments, etc. From the technical point of view it is rather obvious that also computer systems managing more complex data obtained solely from interlinked computer systems can be developed. As an illustration, computer applications of this kind can be perceived e.g. for the management of various kinds of applications, administrative law issues, debt collection, tax issues, sentencing in petty crimes, and so forth. Interconnected computer-systems can be managed in such cases by administrative officers, debt collectors, tax-law officers, prosecutors, counsellors, etc. Naturally, one can also predict a development in which various autonomous computer systems are linked up with each other. From this perspective, for many kinds of legal problems the issue of whether autonomous systems will come into practical use is basically a question of the nature of competence that a society or an organization is prepared to assign to computer systems. The limit is not of a primary technical character.

Autonomous legal reasoning systems cannot, however, provide standard solutions for the legal domain. For a large number of legal issues a more reasonable future scenario will be the one in which AI-applications will be used to provide support for the users. A number of reasons speak for this assumption, one of them being the fact that many issues do not appear frequently enough to motivate system development of full coverage. On other occasions the applicable law may be unstable and controversial. Likewise, it is obvious that many domains are of too dynamic or political a nature to allow for any autonomous system. In such cases one would expect instead a development of legal workstations able to augment the creative and interpretational skills of the users by means of providing extensive methodological support and domain-knowledge about the ways in which similar issues have been managed in in the past. Such systems will be able to provide in future intentional and definitional support, communication facilities, support for rule-construction, and formulation assistance, among other things. It will be also possible to use the systems in an individual manner and to adjust them to various tasks in different domains. A possible design approach for a general and an advanced system of this kind is illustrated in chapter 7 of this study.

As regards the prospects concerning the development of advanced systems it is certainly also possible to imagine a development of systems that would be capable of identifying and managing routine cases in a more or less autonomous way, while more complex cases would be sorted out and assigned to a legal workstation for further investigation in an interactive dialogue with a lawyer. The identification of complicated cases of the latter kind can be related, for instance, to the recognition of conflicting material, the activation of certain constellations of sub-systems, the recognition of unusual levels of particularisation of the input-data, etc.

As to the possibilities of increasing the availability of legal knowledge, it seems rather clear that many legal workstations will be for obvious reasons designed and developed in such a way as to meet the requirements of professional lawyers. The generality of the technique and the possibilities of combining various kinds of knowledge in conceptual structures indicate, however, that there are not any major obstacles to the development of various kinds of systems also for the use of non-lawyers. Such a scenario was outlined in the VF project, where the final system was intended to function as a filter between the employers organization and the various enacted companies. The idea was to reduce the VF lawyers' workload, by giving the personal managers of medium and large companies access to the system for a first consultation. It was hypothesized that such a strategy would make that a large number of trivial questions which could obvious not lead to further legal action were immediately sorted out.

8.4 AI-Methods in Law

The second question this study set out to investigate, as to whether AI-methods may be useful for legal work in a more general way, may be also answered in the affirmative. In other words, there is little doubt that an extensive use of the knowledge elicitation and the knowledge representation methods that have been described in this study can increase the understanding of the material in many fields of law. It is also clear that such development can be of practical value for the legal domain even without any connection to computer-system development projects. There are several ways in which this can be accomplished. Perhaps the most obvious depends on the fact that AI-methods originating from logical rule-based models can be efficient in the analysis and the formulation of rule-systems. The focus is then set on the legal text and the legal rules which may be transformed and re-formulated in order to enhance the consistency of the material. In this respect, the potentialities in connection to legislative drafting processes and contracting, for example, were described a long time ago.[2]

When thinking about the ways in which legal work is often organized, it is further possible to perceive several future application prospects for various kinds of knowledge representation methods, e.g. at an individual level – by means of supporting a more structured problem analysis, or as a method that can be employed in order to explore various lines of legal reasoning. It has been also suggested that AI-related logical rule-based methods can be used as a support device in policy making,[3] and that they can be used in order to facilitate predictions about the effects of changes occurring in complex rule systems.[4]

2 *See, e.g.*, Allen *supra* chapter 2 note 79 and Allen L.E. *Language, Law and Logic: Plain Legal Drafting for the Electronic Age* (1980).

3 Bench-Capon, T.J.M. *Support for Policy Makers* (1987).

4 *Cf.* McCarty, L.T. *The Taxman Project* (1980).

Positive conclusions as regards the prospects of the incorporation of AI-methods into legal work can be also arrived at in regard of associating techniques. In this context it may be recalled that associating methods had been recommended to be used as a support device in the storing and retrieval of legal knowledge already before computers came into practical use. It is also rather uncontroversial to assume that many of the insights about legal structures that may emerge from the management of legal knowledge with associating computer programs can bring positive results – for example at an organizational level, by means of increasing the awareness of how legal knowledge can be decomposed and how legal work processes can be best organized.

In an inventory of prospective uses of AI-methods it must be also mentioned that various procedures for case-fact analysis can be employed in the legal field, provided the context and presuppositions have been satisfactorily established. This has been shown in the rather extensive literature on sentencing guidelines. Sentencing guidelines were originally designed for manual use. It is however no doubt that experiences and methods originating from the development of computer programs make it possible to elaborate the methodology extensively. It is equally safe to suggest that an extensive use of carefully worked out knowledge acquisition methods can complement other approaches and be of use in many instances of conventional legal work.

The inclusion of elaborated AI-methods in law and legal reasoning is, however, not a very straightforward process and despite a number of obvious potentialities it is clear that outside the field of AI and law few methods originating from research in the field of AI have yet achieved any practical significance within the legal community. The restrictions in this respect seem, however, to be based not so much on the problems concerning acceptance or on the encountered shortcomings. They are rather a reflection of the fact that AI and law still represent two, noticeably different "cultures" showing very little interaction with each other. In this respect, the situation very much resemblances the fate of the proposals originating from the fields of research known as logic in law and jurimetrics. In these traditions, methods which are closely related to the ones that are now being put forward in the field of AI and law have been developed and promoted for a long time. Yet, most of them have despite their obvious potentialities, received very little attention from the professional, non-academic legal society.

Seen from this perspective, and assuming that difficulties related to the acceptance of alternative methods are to a large extent a reflection of a lack of communication between theoretically and practically inclined legal professionals, it appears, however, that the prospects of AI-related methods in law are more promising as compared to the earlier methodological suggestions. The reason for this postulate is simply the belief that computers can illustrate the ways in which alternative methods can be used in more unambiguous manner. In addition, it is obvious that any comprehensive method which can be related to and illustrated by computers can reach a much larger group of persons, as compared to, e.g., proposals publicized solely in the field known as logic in law.

As regards the future, it may be furthermore hypothesized that increased computer readiness will enhance the understanding of the potentialities that are related to the adoption and assimilation of the underlying principles. Legal education may constitute in this respect an important factor, taking an active part in the introduction and exemplification of the ways in which knowledge based methods can be employed in legal work. Illustrations of how this can be accomplished are provided by the previously mentioned LexLab computer laboratory for legal education and other similar initiatives. LexLab will certainly affect the students' perception of law and legal problem solving in the future by means of introducing law students to logical rule-based and associating techniques and, as an obligatory element, by teaching them the ways to design small-scale logical rule-based and associative models with the use of knowledge based methods. In this context it should be also noted that the development of various kinds of legal workstations will in many situations affect the ways in which the non-computerized aspects of legal work are organized and understood.

From this point of view it may be also assumed that the phenomena described in this study will affect not only various specific aspects of legal work but that, on the contrary, in the long-term perspective computerization (including the methods originating from AI) and functional perspective (like the one outlined in chapter 7) will also affect the basic understanding of law. It is thus possible to foresee a development in which several complementary legal taxonomies will emerge, designed to facilitate the development of various kinds of support systems for legal reasoning and whose side-effect may very well be a more general transition in the perception of law. It can be moreover hypothesized that such a process will favour a perspective in which various functions of law vis-à-vis legal reasoning will play a predominating role. Simultaneously, it may be speculated that taxonomies reflecting various forms of publications and fragmentations (such as e.g. rules and cases) will loose some of their importance. This can eventually lead to the rapprochement and merging of the sometimes apparent discrepancies between the basic presuppositions that are reflected in various legal traditions. This is simply to say that from the functional point of view there is little sense in arguing over the question as to whether law consists of rules or cases. What is important, instead is that law should provide as efficient classification structures for legal identification as possible.

In this respect in the long-term perspective the future of jurisprudence appears to be not only a question of incorporating new methods into the discipline. The development will also reflect to a considerable extent the adoption of a different perspective and a transformed conceptual theory. From all this follows that although the development will not bring about a complete revolution of the legal method, it can well be argued that computer science and AI can induce a considerable modernization of the content in the analytical tool-box for legal problem solving.

In this process it is also necessary to note that AI-systems for knowledge management, and computerization as such, will necessarily affect the ways in which intellectual work will be understood and described on a broader basis in other domains outside law. For this reason it may be hypothesized that the development will eventually set new standards also for legal decision making and that it in the future it may be difficult to avoid the incorporation of elaborated methods into legal work e.g. by means of referring to the fact that legal decisions are too complicated and that they must include a certain degree of discretion. This being very much the state of the matter in contrast with the present situation.

8.5 *Jurisprudence for AI*

Jurisprudence is essential for the development of AI and law in many ways. The most obvious point is of course the fact that legal knowledge incorporated in any legal AI-system intended for practical use must be of high quality in terms of completeness, authenticity and actuality, and that the only way of accomplishing this is by means of developing representations that will faithfully reflect the original jurisprudential material. One should furthermore recall here that any law system contains not only written material but also a number of principles which are sometimes reflected only in the ways in which the work is organized.

Summing up the role of jurisprudence in the field of AI and law, it is also important to notice that jurisprudential principles and the nature of the legal material delimit the ways in which AI-methods can be employed. Examples are provided by the principles of predictability, legality and equality, which no doubt impose certain restrictions on the possibilities to use inductive and statistical techniques in several fields of law. Likewise, legal rules concerning directness, freedom of information, the right to oral proceedings, and so forth, affect the prospects of rationalization and the introduction of computerized methods in many different ways. It should be also observed that many of the standards imposed by jurisprudence are of absolute nature. That is to say that if the jurisprudential standards cannot be defended, it may well be argued that no other motives will suffice for the introduction of automated or computerized procedures in the legal domain. From the stand-point adopted in this work it is therefore also appropriate to suggest that the law should provide frameworks for the development. A further effect of this is that it can be argued that jurisprudence and jurisprudential models of legal reasoning can be used to some extent, as illustrated in chapter 6, for the evaluation of various computational models and automation projects.

In this context it should be also recalled that the vindication of jurisprudential principles is not always an easy and uncontroversial task. The fundamental jurisprudential standards are often hidden from the outside viewers and, as a consequence, their importance is not always obvious to system developers concentrating on substantial and explicit legal knowledge. This is reflected e.g. in the frequently reported difficulties concerning knowledge acquisition and in the managing of the so called tacit knowledge. The ability to develop adequate representations of various types of legal knowledge is nevertheless for natural reason crucial and it can be assumed that one reason that so many projects concerning AI-techniques in the field of law have failed is that many of the underlying jurisprudential principles have not been observed or given sufficient attention in the initial stages of the system development.[5]

Difficulties related to the preservation of jurisprudential standards may also arise from the fact that economic factors, attempts of rationalization, and practical difficulties connected with knowledge representation may sometimes constitute a challenge to the aspects of legal quality. In this way a number of problems may arise as the development process forces the involved parties to articulate their different perspectives. The experiences gained from this project makes it nevertheless justifiable to claim that it is by no means impossible to maintain legal standards in AI-system development projects. In connection with this it can be recalled that in the system development projects that were completed during this study (in which the responsible knowledge engineers were lawyers) knowledge acquisition and knowledge representation constituted no serious problems.

The supply of the original material to be incorporated into knowledge bases and the facilitation of the evaluation of computational models are not, however, the only functions of jurisprudence where it meets with AI. Jurisprudence may also play an active role in the future development of more advanced systems and in this respect this work has shown that an in-depth analysis of legal reasoning and legal knowledge can, by generating authentic conceptual models, constitute the basis of quite elaborate AI-system architectures. The essence of the outlined theory is thereby based on the fact that legal reasoning can be perceived as a process in which various kinds of substantial, methodological, formal and evaluative knowledge structures are combined in the ways which – at least to some extent – can be described in a general manner. To some extent, it can be also assumed that it is possible to elucidate the functions of various types of legal knowledge in different fields of the law so that system

[5] *Cf.* Magnusson Sjöberg, C. *Rättsautomation* (1992).

architectures for different types of legal reasoning processes can be explored.

Admittedly, the jurisprudential theories adjusted in such a way as to satisfy the requirements of system development need to be refined. A jurisprudentially sound theory of legal AI-system development may therefore require much more research before it (if ever) comes anywhere near completion. An elaboration of the legal theory in the direction indicated in this study appears nevertheless to be the basic foundation for further developments towards more advanced AI-systems (i.e. systems that are able to support a large number of authentic requirements) in the field of law. From all this follows the rather apparent conclusion that future developments in AI and law will in many cases depend on whether the legal community can better articulate the fundamental jurisprudential principles in a manner understandable also to system developers and administrators without legal background.

In this respect it should be also noticed that a more extensive elaboration of the legal theory in the outlined direction may not, however, be crucial only as regards the ability to construct more advanced systems. The elaboration of system development approaches and architectures reflecting jurisprudential notions and theories may also constitute a critical ingredient in an attempt to develop computerized solutions that can be understood and accepted by large groups of the legal profession. This development may of course also bring about new interpretations and transformations of the above mentioned jurisprudential principles.

Speculating further on the role of jurisprudence it may be also hypothesized that an articulation of legal knowledge in this field of work can have a significant impact on the discipline of AI as such. That is simply to say that to some extent it can be assumed that several of the presuppositions that have been outlined in this study are not necessarily limited to the legal domain. In other words, it is not unrealistic to believe that functional models of reasoning originating from the identification of sub-processes, as well as the demarcation of various types of knowledge exerting influence on the different sub-processes can be of value also in a more general sense. From this follows that the JLR model supplied with just a few adjustments could probably serve as a sketch for descriptions of decision making processes also in other domains. To illustrate this point it may be sufficient to mention that the process of relating the upcoming cases to previous descriptions is not unique for law. A physician or a psychiatrist, for instance, may in the course of their work relate the same situation (e.g. a crime of assault and battery) to medically and psychologically important case descriptions. During this process it is relevant to assume that the elements which have been found in the previous descriptions will direct the attention of the decision makers to certain details in the current situation in a similar way in which legal knowledge influences legal identification. The encountered elements will in turn influence the search for additional knowledge that has to be extracted, and so forth. In this way, although the relevant, substantial elements will be different as compared to the legal elements, there are reasons to believe that the *sub-processes* and the *types of knowledge* that must be activated in order to reach a decision in other domains (e.g. a medical or psychological diagnosis) will be to a large extent similar to the the sub-processes and the types of knowledge that must be activated during legal reasoning.

Thus, as a final comment on the role of jurisprudence where if meets with AI it can well be argued that legal science can help not only in bridging the gap between practical legal work and computational models but that it can also constitute a source of inspiration for the continued development of the field of AI. In this respect it is also quite clear that the combination of the fields of AI and law is an area which carries a significant potential for new achievements.

A final glance at the philosophical issue of whether further steps down the avenue of thought described in this study may eventually lead to the development of true, artificial, legal intelligence, shows that issues concerning the limitations of AI will always depend on the ways in which one chooses to define intelligence. Likewise, it is clear that intelligence is a concept that keeps changing its meaning. This is also true for the definition of intelligence based on mental faculties and adopted for this study. This is simply to say that as our knowledge changes various types of faculties have to be supported.

As regards general limitations concerning the possible AI-system performance, it must be also concluded that legal AI-systems will be always to some extent dependent on the interactions with the outside world. No lawyer and no legal AI system will be ever able to perform meaningful tasks in a vacuum. In a general sense one can therefore conclude that intelligence is something that presupposes intelligence. From this also follows that legal AI-systems must be always looked upon as a (more or less vital) part of a larger system encompassing also one or several users (lawyers, clients, students, etc.). Which part of such a system should be eventually looked upon as the primary or the secondary part may be nevertheless open to debate.

8.6 *Future Work*

From the methodological point of view the most obvious task to be approached in future studies is the development of more general KBSs of the kind outlined in chapter 7. Such projects should start from the subprocesses that have been identified in legal reasoning and from the different types of legal knowledge exerting influence over them. The identified types of legal knowledge should then be reflected in a set of small-scale KBSs, each system representing one functionally demarcated type of knowledge. The systems should be designed so that they are able to combine different kinds of AI-methods with conventional computer technology. The elaborated KBSs should be designed in such a way that they can be interrelated to each other in a more integrated set-up.

It should be again explicitly stated that each research project of this kind does not need to aim necessarily at the formalization of very large corpora of legal knowledge or at the formalization of many domains. The approach in which the legal system is decomposed into functional components is of a general kind and can be in principle adopted on any portion of legal knowledge of a non-trivial kind. Provided that the methods and the principles of work are standardized it is also possible to advance such research projects in a modularized way by means of continuously adding and integrating more sub-systems to the set-up as the formalization continues.

Experiments along the lines outlined in chapter 7 will, if properly executed, generate additional knowledge on how adequate conceptual legal models can be worked out and integrated. (''Properly executed'' refers in this context to the demands of careful planning, analysis and documentation with the indicated objective of integration in mind.) Full-scale experiments could also – by means of pointing out practical difficulties – accentuate the need for research on many aspects, such as e.g. how to efficiently interlink rule-modules, how to visually represent interrelated structures of KBSs, new types of knowledge representation problems, maintenance techniques, and so forth.

Alongside the initiation of full-scale construction projects a further elaboration of AI-systems for law will doubtless depend on in-depth theoretical analyses. The objective of such undertakings is to identify and demarcate even more detailed sub-processes in legal reasoning as well as to explore functionally adequate portions of legal knowledge. From this also follows that for several reasons it would be interesting to initiate a large number of system development projects in many different fields of law; this in order to detect similarities and differences that will make it possible to categorize different types of legal reasoning processes, to find out in which situations it may be adequate to combine rule-based representation with inductive or numerical approaches, and so forth. In this way the development poses great and interesting challenges for jurisprudential research, in which respect this study has done little more than to indicate a way in which to approach further studies.

Tasks aiming to increase the abilities to develop more general and advanced AI-systems from the practical and philosophical point of view are not the only aspects of AI and law that must be given attention in future. Equally important are the various implications which a more common use of computers and AI-systems in the legal field may bring about. It is therefore important to underline that a more wide-spread introduction of legal AI-systems will in various ways be dependent on further studies also of substantial matters. At least three additional aspects of the development require extensive attention: standards for system development, standards for system performance, and legal issues related to consequences of legal AI-system use.

The investigation of *standards for system development* is motivated by the need to vindicate the legal aspects during the whole process of the development of legal KBSs. In this respect it should be underlined that choices which are made during the development of legal AI-systems can have far-reaching consequences. Depending on the ways in which the systems become integrated with legal work, it is not unrealistic to predict that the content of legal AI-systems may receive a status similar to the one held by legislation. It is also important to notice that the transformation of original textual material into knowledge-based representations may bring about transitions of the original meanings and the intended functions of the material. Thus, the introduction of AI-systems can challenge the lawyers' privilege of controlling the central phases of decision-making. In a computerized environment several issues related to interpretation will be allocated for instance to the system development phase. A number of crucial questions appear: who is best suited to decide about the content of the system and the issues that have to be taken up as regards interpretation – the knowledge engineer, the project administrator, the expert who participated in the developing process, the employer, or the user? The important issues in such studies are in other words related to how to balance the influence of various user groups, system administrators, knowledge engineers, and so forth. Should, for instance, some issues be decided solely by knowledge engineers trained in computer science? Alternatively, is it possible to develop a methodology in which various kinds of competence support each other? Among other things it is thereby also important to clarify the issues related to the competence of the individuals who should have the right to determine or affect the content of legal knowledge bases.

In a somewhat more general perspective, this indicates that the development of legal AI-systems should be eventually accompanied by the development of explicit standards for the transformation of legal rules into logical models, legal inference making, and the identification and demarcation of the material (the legal sources) that should be included in different types of knowledge bases. Perhaps the most crucial issue in this respect is the question as to whether it is possible to find system development methodology that would satisfy also the jurisprudential concerns.

The elaboration of *standards for system performance* is necessary if the technique is to reach larger groups and to be accepted as a useful tool that can be employed during legal reasoning processes. Issues related to this aspect are often complicated and it is obvious that a large number of components may require attention as well as standardization.[6]

To exemplify, it is obvious that standardization may have to focus on the content of the systems (regarding among other things authenticity, completeness and actuality) as well as on technical aspects (regarding for instance transparency, computer standards, reliability, communication facilities, etc.). Issues related to the ways in which legal AI-systems ought to function may naturally also originate from organizational matters. In this respect there may be reasons to discuss solutions which make it possible to obtain user influence, acceptable updating and availability, technical maintenance, non-discriminating price policies, etc. Important to notice is furthermore that the nature of the systems one may want to develop will differ depending on the task and the types of issues that are approached. It is therefore also clear that different standards may have to be developed in different areas of the law.

Issues related to the *consequences of system use* in the legal domain are numerous. It is also obvious that many of them are of a very complex nature and that legal rules that may have to be revised can be found in different fields of the law. Initially, it may be also important to recognize the fact that the effects of AI-applications may appear at different levels – social, organizational, individual, etc.

The increasing use of computer technology by the public authorities will, for instance, place new demands on the administrative legislation. More detailed issues may evolve in this respect around freedom of information, changes related to legal decision making, legislation through computer programs, and, in a more general sense, to the upholding of the

[6] Evaluation of legal KBSs is a task that may be approached in different ways. In a summary of a number of pioneering articles in a Dutch publication *empirical validation, formal validation, theoretical validation* and *methodological validation* have been distinguished. Kracht *supra* chapter 1 note 33, at 3. In the various articles the different types of validation have been elaborated on. During formal validation the focus is set on specifications of programs and formalisms. Schmidt, A., van den Herik, J. *How to validate a Legal Knowledge Based System*, 62 (1990) and de Vey Mestdagh *supra* chapter 1 note 50, at 100. Empirical validation is conducted by means of relating "implemented theory (or program behaviour) of an actual world to observable actual world behaviour." A KBS can thus be evaluated by a forum of experts or by experiments. Schmidt, van den Herik *Id.* at 62-63. During theoretical validation applications are looked upon "with respect to the underlying theory" (e.g. the theoretical description of the material system). Methodological validation focuses on "the methods and instruments used in the information systems cycle." de Vey Mestdagh *Id.* (*Cf.* standards for system development *supra*.)

rule of law. What is for instance the legal status of decisions produced by AI-systems? What is the legal status of interpretations that are made during a process in which several systems interact?

In the long run the technique will also affect the courts and in this respect a number of issues appear: how is it, for instance, possible to vindicate the principles of oral proceedings and directness if prerequisites and other facts are collected from geographically remote computers and when decisions follow as necessary consequences of the program in the central system? How may automatically generated decisions be appealed and how is it possible to have a wrongful decision adjusted in accordance with formal procedure rules during an automatic proceeding? Furthermore, what does a reasonable second trial look like? Is it a manually filed decision, a new fact collection to the machine, or a second processing in a more elaborated computer system?

A likewise important complex of consequences is related to questions about security, vulnerability and surveillance. What risks are, for instance, related to the import of the technique in different kinds of legal work? What happens if systems collapse and when manual routines no longer exist? To what extent is it possible to provide security by means of using physical arrangements, back-up facilities and such, and to what extent is it possible to supplement the protection with legal actions? What happens when several AI-systems start interacting with each other when those who initially had a general overview of the situation no longer are around. Who decides when AI-systems ought to be turned off, elaborated, or adjusted because the development has in some respect moved on? Who understands and evaluates the quality of AI-systems and their legal implications?

A related and almost unexplored complex of questions concerns liability.[7] Who is responsible for choices that are made during system construction? Is is possible to identify specific categories of users, and what are the effects of system introduction in various situations? In short – what does a suitable distribution of liability for legal decision support systems look like?

[7] *See,* for early contributions on liability for AI and expert systems, Cannataci, J. A., *Liability and Responsibility for Expert Systems* (1988) *and* Cole, G.S. *Tort Liability for Artificial Intelligence and Expert Systems* (1990).

The list of the legal issues that are being affected by the development may be easily extended and, broadening the perspective somewhat, it may be appropriate in this context to also mention the shift in perspective that the development may bring about for issues related to intellectual property and patent law.[8]

The manifold nature of the development and the sometimes intriguing questions that may evolve lead up to the most important conclusion of this study, namely that the development described in this book must be properly reflected in legal education. For several reasons proper education is necessary if the joint endeavour of law and AI is to have a fair chance to succeed. Important in this respect is not only to meet the demand for intermediaries (lawyers trained in AI-methods who are able to actively participate in system development projects), but also to bring about a higher level of computer readiness in the legal domain. The latter in order to make it possible for lawyers to critically evaluate the systems and the consequences the technique will bring along.

[8] *See, e.g.*, articles presented at *WIPO Worldwide Symposium on the Intellectual property Aspects of Artificial Intelligence* (1991).

(judicial vs admin — lots done)

continental vs anglo saxon

logical

realistic

practical

ling ? a beyond in

ips ...

fee from agency

what kind of law

do we want ?

rules or fairness ?

access for all a

law shopping

reasoning : goes beyond systems (S

self-rep. in paralegals, divorce,

mental health.

academic AI vs very

academic (validated ?)

rubbish P250

why not steal from

a court problem ?

(adversarial) can procedure be eliminated ?

an 6-7-24 visits about

cts — only tax

role in cts —

lawyers —

can one separate the

logical phase from the

pragmatic phase as W.

does ?

Literature References

See also, for additional information on short forms, List of Abbreviations.

Aarnio, Aulis. *Introduktion*. In Peczenik, Aleksander. Rätten och förnuftet. En lärobok i allmän rättslära. Norstedts förlag, Stockholm, (2:nd ed. 1988) 13-27.

Aarnio, Aulis. *On Legal Reasoning*. Turun Yliopisto, Turku, (1977), (Turun Yliopiston Julkaisuja Annales Universitatis Turkuensis. SARJA-SER. B OSA-TOM. 144).

Aarnio, Aulis, Alexy, Robert, Peczenik, Aleksander. *The Foundation of Legal Reasoning*. (Parts 1, 2, and 3), Rechtstheorie, 12 Band, (1981) 133-58, 257-79, 423-48.

Alchourrón, Carlos E., Bulygin, Eugenio. *Normative Systems*. Springer-Verlag, Wien, . . . (1971), (Library of Exact Philosophy 5).

Alchourrón, Carlos E., Martino, Antonio A. *A Sketch of Logic Without Truth*. Proceedings ICAIL-89, ACM, New York, (1989) 165-79.

Alexy, Robert. *Legal Expert Systems and Legal Theory*. In Fiedler, H., Haft, F., Traunmüller, R. eds. Expert Systems in Law: Impacts on Legal Theory and Computer Law. Attempto Verlag Tübingen, GmbH, Tuebingen University Press, (1988) 67-74, (Neue Methoden im Recht. Band 4).

Allen, Layman E. *Language, Law and Logic: Plain Legal Drafting for the Electronic Age*. In Niblett, B. ed. Computer Science and Law: An Advanced Course. Cambridge University Press, Cambridge, . . . (1980) 75-100.

Allen, Layman E., Caldwell, Mary E. eds. *Communication Sciences and Law: Reflections from The Jurimetrics Conference*. The Bobbs-Merrill Company, Inc., Indianapolis, . . . (1965).

Allen, Layman, E. *Symbolic Logic: A Razor-Edged Tool for Drafting and Interpreting Legal Documents*. Yale Law Journal, Vol. 66, (1956/57) 833-79.

Alpsten, Börje. *ADB-planeringen inom rättsväsendet*. In Wahlgren, P. ed. Det goda kunskapssamhället: Ett perspektiv på rättsinformatiken. IRI, (1988) 43-58, (IRI-rapport 1988:5).

Anners, Erik. *Europas rättshistoria: Några huvudlinjer*. Del 2. AWE/GEBERS, Stockholm, (1972).

Ashley, Kevin D. *Toward a Computational Theory of Arguing with Precedents: Accomodating Multiple Interpretations of Cases*. Proceedings ICAIL-89, ACM, New York, (1989) 93-102.

Ashley, Kevin D. *Modeling Legal Argument*. A Bradford Book, The MIT Press, Cambridge, Massachusetts, (1990).

Baade, Hans W. ed. *Jurimetrics*. Basic Books, Inc., Publishers, New York, . . . (1963).

Bachant, Judith, McDermott, John. *R1 Revisited: Four Years in the Trenches*. AI Magazine, fall, (1984) 21-32.

Barr, Avron, Feigenbaum, Edward A. eds. *The Handbook of Artificial Intelligence*. Vol. I & II. Pitman Books Limited, London, (Vol. I, 1981, Vol. II, 1982).

Bauer-Bernet, Hélène. *Computerised Legal Documentation System of the European Communities (Celex)*. C&L, No. 7, (1976) 2-3.

Bench-Capon, Trevor J.M. *Support for Policy Makers: Formulating Legislation with the Aid of Logical Models.* Proceedings ICAIL-87, ACM Press, New York, (1987) 181-89.

Bench-Capon, Trevor J.M. *Logical Models of Legislation and Expert Systems.* In Fiedler, H., Haft, F., Traunmüller, R. eds. Expert Systems in Law: Impacts on Legal Theory and Computer Law. Attempto Verlag Tübingen, GmbH, Tuebingen University Press, (1988) 27-41, (Neue Methoden im Recht. Band 4) .

Bench-Capon, Trevor J.M. *Deep Models, Normative Reasoning and Legal Expert Systems.* Proceedings ICAIL-89, ACM, New York, (1989) 37-45.

Bennion, Francis A.R. *Computers and Law in Canada.* (Parts 1 and 2), C&L, Part 1 in No. 10, (1976) 8-10, Part 2 in No. 11, (1977) 10-11.

Berg, Anders, Hård, Lars, Docherty, Peter. *PLUTO – Handling Social Assistance Using Combined DP and KBS Techniques.* In Duffin, P.H. ed. Knowledge Based Systems: Applications in Administrative Government. Ellis Horwood Limited Publishers, Chichester, (1988), (Ellis Horwood Books in Information Technology).

Berman, Donald H., Hafner, Carole D. *The Potential of Artificial Intelligence to Help Solve the Crisis in Our Legal System.* Communications of the ACM, Vol. 32, (1989) 928-38.

Berman, Donald H., Hafner, Carole D. *Indeterminacy: A Challenge to Logic-based Models of Legal Reasoning.* In YLC&T, Vol. 3. Butterworths, London, (1987) 1-35.

Beutel, Frederick K. *Some Potentialities of Experimental Jurisprudence as a New Branch of Social Science.* University of Nebraska Press, Lincoln, (1957).

Biagiole, C., Mariani, P., Tiscornia, D. *ESPLEX: A Rule and Conceptual Based Model for Representing Statutes.* ICAIL-87, ACM Press, New York, (1987) 240-51.

Bigelow, Robert P. ed. *Computers & The Law: An Introductory Handbook.* Commerce Clearing House, Inc., New York, . . . (1:st ed. 1966, 2:nd ed. 1969, 3:rd ed. 1981).

Bing, Jon. *Designing Text Rerieval Systems for Conceptual Searching.* Proceedings ICAIL-87, ACM Press, New York, (1987) 43-51.

Bing, Jon. *Rettslige kommunikasjonsprocesser: Bidrag til en generell teori.* Universitetsforlaget, Oslo, . . . (1982), (Noris 30).

Bing, Jon. *Three Generations of Computerized Systems for Public Administration and Some Implications for Legal Decision-Making.* RJ, Vol. 3, (1990) 219-36.

Bing, Jon. *Legal Decisions and Computerized Systems.* In Seipel, P. ed. From Data Protection to Knowledge Machines: The Study of Law and Informatics. Kluwer Law and Taxation Publishers, Deventer, . . . (1990) 223-50, (Computer/Law Series 5).

Bing, Jon. *Legal Information Services: Some Trends and Characteristics.* In Campbell, C. ed. Data Processing and the Law. Sweet & Maxwell, London, (1984) 29-45.

Bing, Jon. *Om tolkning av enkeltord – særlig i lovtekst.* In Bratholm, A., Opsahl, T., Aarbakke, M. eds. Samfunn, Rett, Rettferdighet: Festskrift till Torstein Eckhoffs 70-årsdag. Tano, Norway, (1986) 131-43.

Bing, Jon. *Rettsutdannelse och rettsdannelse på tyvehundretallet.* In Wahlgren, P. ed. Det goda kunskapssamhället: Ett perspektiv på rättsinformatiken. IRI, (1988) 85-88, (IRI-rapport 1988:5).

Bing, Jon. *Fra problem til resultat: Modell av den juridiske beslutningsprosess.* Jussens venner, bind X, (1975) 1-32. (Reprinted in Thrap-Meyer, R. ed. Utvalgte emner i rettsinformatikk. NRCCL/Tano, Oslo (1988) 3-34, (Complex 1/88)).

Bing, Jon ed. *Handbook of Legal Information Retrieval.* North-Holland Publishing Company, Amsterdam, . . . (1984).

Bing, Jon, Harvold, Trygve. *Legal Decisions and Information Systems.* Universitetsforlaget, Oslo, (1977), (Publications of NRCCL No. 5).

Biunno, Vincent P. *History of Electronic Methods for Legal Research.* M.U.L.L. Vol. 60S, (1960) 99-102.

Bjarup, Jes. *Skandinavischer Realismus: Hägerström – Lundstedt – Olivecrona – Ross.* Verlag Karl Alber Freiburg, München, (1978), (Alber Kolleg Rechtstheorie, Band III, 1).

Blakmore, Colin, Greenfield, Susan eds. *Mindwaves: Thoughts on Intelligence, Identity and Consciousness.* Basil Blackwell, Oxford, (1987).

Blume, Peter. *Jurauddannelsen og retsinformatikken – nu og i fremtiden.* In Wahlgren, P. ed. Det goda kunskapssamhället: Ett perspektiv på rättsinformatiken. IRI, (1988) 153-58, (IRI-rapport 1988:5).

Bolding, Per Olof. *Rättssociologin i den nya juristutbildningen.* In Festskrift till Per Stjernquist. Juridiska föreningen i Lund, (1978) 127-35, (Acta Societatis Juridicae Lundensis no 24).

Boole, Georg. *An Investigation of the Laws of Thought.* London, (1854).

Boole, Georg. *The Mathematical Analysis of Logic.* Cambridge, (1847).

Boston University Law Review. *Symposium: Probability and Inference in the Law of Evidence.* Vol. 66, (1986) 377-952.

Bowden, B.V. ed. *Faster than Thought: A Symposium on Digital Computing Machines.* Sir Isaak Pitman & Sons, Ltd., London, (1953).

Brachman, Ronald J., Levesque, Hector J. eds. *Readings in Knowledge Representation.* Morgan Kaufmann Publishers, Inc., Los Altos, (1985).

Bratt, Percy, Tiberg, Hugo. *Domare och lagmotiv.* SvJt, (1989) 407-25.

Brattgård, Erik. *Något om hovrättens påföljdspraxis i misshandelsmål.* Svea hovrätt, Stockholm, photoreprint, (1985).

Brodda, Benny. *Gimmie More O' That.* In Seipel, P. ed. From Data Protection to Knowledge Machines: The Study of Law and Informatics. Kluwer Law and Taxation Publishers, Deventer, . . . (1990) 251-70, (Computer/Law Series 5).

Brownlie, Ian. *Principles of Public International Law.* Clarendon Press, Oxford, (3:rd ed. 1979).

Bruun, Niklas, Wilhelmsson, Thomas. *Rätten, moralen och det juridiska paradigmet.* SvJt, (1983) 701-13.

Buchanan, Bruce G., Headrick, Thomas E. *Some Speculation About Artificial Intelligence and Legal Reasoning.* Stanford Law Review. Vol. 23, (1970) 40-62.

Buchanan, Bruce G., Sutherland, G., Feigenbaum, Edward. A. *Heuristic Dendral: A Program for Generating Explanatory Hypotheses in Organic Chemistry.* In Meltzer, B., Michie, D., Swann, M. eds. Machine Intelligence 4. Edinburgh University Press, Edinburgh, (1969) 209-54.

Burks, Alice R., Burks, Arthur W. *The First Electronic Computer: The Atanasoff Story.* The University of Michigan Press, Ann Arbor, (1988).

Bush, Vannevar. *As we may Think.* The Atlantic Monthly, Vol. 176, (1945) 101-08. (Reprinted in Pylyshyn, Zenon W. ed. Perspectives on the Computer Revolution. Prentice-Hall, Inc., Englewood Cliffs, (1970) 47-59.)

Buxton, Harry W. *Memoir of the Life and Labours of the Late Charles Babbage Esq., F.R.S.* The MIT Press, Cambridge, Massachusetts, . . . /Tomash Publishers, Los Angeles, . . . (1988), (The Charles Babbage Institute Reprint Series for the History of Computing. Vol. 13).

Campell, Colin ed. *Data Processing and the Law.* Sweet & Maxwell, London, (1984).

Cannataci, Joseph A. *Liability and Responsibility for Expert Systems.* NRCCL/Tano, Oslo (1988), (Complex 5/88).

Capper, Phillip, Susskind, Richard E. *Latent Damage Law – The Expert System.* Butterworths, London, (1988).

Cardozo, Benjamin N. *The Nature of the Judicial Process.* Yale University Press, New Haven, . . . (1921).

Chandler, James P. *Computers and Case Law.* RJCL, Vol. 3, (1974) 202-18.

Ciampi, Constantino. *Artificial Intelligence and Legal Information Systems.* In Proceedings of the 6:th Symposium on Legal Data Processing in Europe. Thessanoliki, 1-3 July 1981, Council of Europe, Strasbourg, (1982) 159-70, (CJ-IJ symp (82) 1).

Ciampi, Constantino ed. *Artificial Intelligence and Legal Information Systems.* North-Holland Publishing Company, Amsterdam, . . . (1982), (Edited Version of Selected Papers from ICLID-81).

Ciampi, Constantino, Pirro, Deirdre Exell, Fameli, Elio, Trivisonno, Giuseppe. *THES/BID: An Expert System for Constructing a Computer-Based Thesaurus for Legal Informatics and Computer Law.* In Walter, C. ed. Computing Power and Legal Reasoning. West Publishing Company, St. Paul, . . . (1985) 375-412.

Cohen, L. Jonathan. *The Probable and the Provabel.* Clarendon Press, Oxford, (1977).

Cole, George S. *Tort Liability for Artificial Intelligence and Expert Systems.* Computer/Law Journal, Vol. X, (1990) 127-231.

Comte, Auguste. *Discours préliminaire sur l'esprit positif.* Paris, (1844), (Swedish ed: Om positivismen. Bokförlaget Korpen, Göteborg 1979).

Cordingley, Elizabeth S. *Knowledge Elicitation Techniques for Knowledge-based Systems.* In Diaper, D. ed. Knowledge Elicitation: Principles, Techniques and Applications. Ellis Horwood Limited Publishers, Chichester, (1989) 89-175, (Ellis Horwood books in information technology).

Cotterrell, Roger. *The Sociology of Law.* Butterworths, London, (1984).

Council of Europe. *Recommendation no. R(80) 3 of the Committee of Ministers to Member States Concerning Teaching, Research and Training in the field of "Computers and Law".* Council of Europe, Strasbourg, (1980).

Council of Europe. *Systems Based on Artificial Intelligence in the Legal Field.* Council of Europe, Strasbourg, (1991), (Proceedings of the 9:th Symposium on Legal Data Processing in Europe, Bonn, 10-12 October 1989).

Council of Europe. *Artificial Intelligence and Linquistic Problems in Legal Data Processing Systems.* Council of Europe, Strasbourg, (1982), (Proceedings of the 6:th Symposium on Legal Data Processing in Europe, Thessanoliki, 1-3 July 1981), (CJ-IJ Symp (82) 1).

Council of Europe. *Integrated Work Stations in the Legal Sector and Decision Support Systems.* Council of Europe, Strasbourg, (1989), (Proceedings of the 7:th Colloquy on the use of computers in the administration of justice, Lisbon, 11-13 October 1988).

Coval, Samuel Charles, Smith, Joseph C. *Law and its Presuppositions: Actions, Agents and Rules.* Routledge & Kegan Paul, London, . . . (1986), (International Library of Philosophy).

Cowan, Jack D., Sharp, David H. *Neural Nets and Artificial Intelligence.* In Graubard, Stephen R. ed. The Artificial Intelligence Debate: False Starts, Real Foundations. The MIT Press, Cambridge, Massachusetts, . . . (1988) 85-121.

Craik, Kenneth J.W. *The Nature of Explanation.* Cambridge at the University Press, (1943, reprinted 1952).

d'Entrèves, A.P. *Natural Law: An Introduction to Legal Philosophy.* Hutchinson & Co. (Publishers) LTD., London (1951, 2:nd revised ed. 1971), (Hutchinson University Library).

Dahnell, Olof. *Ekonomiska aspekter på ett beslutstödsystem.* IRI, (1990), (IRI-rapport 1990:3).

Daube, David. *Collected Studies in Roman Law,* Vittorio Klostermann, Frankfurt am Main, Vol. 1 and 2 (1991), (Studien zur Europäischen Rechtgeschichte 54, eds. Cohen, D., Simon, D.).

Davis, Richard P. *LITE: Legal Information Through Electronics.* M.U.L.L. Vol. 65S, (1965) 138-40.

De Salvo, Daniel A., Liebowitz, Jay, eds. *Managing Artificial Intelligence & Expert Systems.* Yourdon Press, Englewood Cliffs, (1990), (Yourdon Press, Computing Series).

de Vey Mestdagh, C.N.J. *How Artificial Should Artificial Intelligence Be?* In Kracht, D., de Vey Mestdagh, C.N.J., Svensson, J.S. eds. Legal Knowledge Based Systems: An Overview of Criteria for Validation and Practical Use. Koninklijke Vermande BV, Lelystad, (1990) 93-104.

deBessonet, Cary G., Cross, Georg R. *An Artificial Intelligence Application in the Law: CCLIPS, A Computer Program that Processes Legal Information.* HTLJ, Vol. 1, (1987) 329-409.

Dewdney, A.K. *The Turing Omnibus: 61 Excursions in Computer Science.* Computer Science Press, Rockville, (1989).

Diaper, Dan ed. *Knowledge Elicitation: Principles, Techniques and Applications.* Ellis Horwood Limited Publishers, Chichester, (1989), (Ellis Horwood books in information technology).

Dickerson, Reed. *Some Jurisprudential Implications of Electronic Data Processing.* Law and Contemporary Problems, Vol. 28, (1963) 53-70.

Dickinson, John. *Legal Rules: Their Function in the Process of Decision.* University of Pennsylvania Law Review, Vol. 79, (1931) 833-68.

Docherty, Peter, Loman, Lars. *Personalinflytande och datorisering.* Ekonomiska forskningsinstitutet vid Handelshögskolan i Stockholm i samarbete med privattjänstemannakartellen, Stockholm, (1983).

Domstolsverket. *Utvärdering av försök med datorstöd vid avdelningskansli i tingsrätt.* DV, Jönköping, (1987), (DV rapport nr 1987:4).

Domstolsverket. *Rättsväsendets informationssystem: Bestämmelser om avfattning av dom och slutligt beslut i brottmål m.m., (Tingsrätt).* DV, Jönköping, (1986), continuously updated loose leaf file).

Domstolsverket. *ADB inom domstolsväsendet: Studiematerial.* DV, Jönköping, (1985).

Dorn, Phil H. *Commercial Data Processing: A Brief History.* In Bruhn, E. ed. EDB Historik – i nordisk perspektiv. DATAaktieselskabet af 2. april 1971. n. p., (n. d.) 13-29.

Dreyfus, Hubert L. *What Computers Can't Do: A Critique of Artificial Reason.* Harper & Row, Publishers, New York, . . . (1972).

Duda, R., Gaschnig, J., Hart, P.E. *Model Design in the PROSPECTOR Consultant System for Mineral Exploration.* In Michie, D. ed. Expert Systems in the Micro-Electronic Age. Edingburgh University Press, Edingburgh, (1979) 153-67.

Duffin, Paul H. ed. *Knowledge Based Systems: Applications in Administrative Government.* Ellis Horwood Limited Publishers, Chichester, (1988), (Ellis Horwood Books in Information Technology).

Duggan, Michael A. *Legal Research Projects.* M.U.L.L. Vol. 65J, (1965) 83-86.

Duggan, Michael A. *Legal Research Projects: Supplement.* M.U.L.L. Vol. 66J, (1966) 97-99.

Dworkin, Ronald. *Taking Rights Seriously.* Harvard University Press, Cambridge, Massachusetts, (1977).

Dworkin, Ronald M. *Is Law a System of Rules?* In Summers, Robert S. ed. Essays in Legal Philosophy. University of Carlifornia Press, Berkely, . . . (1968) 25-60.

Dyer, Michael G., Flowers, Margot. *Toward Automating Legal Expertise.* In Walter, C. ed. Computing Power and Legal Reasoning. West Publishing Company, St. Paul, . . . (1985) 49-68.

Ebersole, J. L., Hall, J. A. Jr. *COURTRAN: A Modular Management Information and Research System for the Judicial Process.* RJCL, Vol. 3, (1973) 83-127.

Eckert, J. Presper. *The ENIAC.* In Metropolis, N., Howlett, J., Rota, G.C. eds. A History of Computing in the Twentieth Century. Academic Press, New York, . . . (1980) 525-39.

Eckhoff, Torstein. *Rettskildelære.* Johan Grundt Tanum Forlag, Oslo, (1971).

Eckhoff, Torstein. *Feedback in Legal Reasoning and Rule Systems.* In Schmidt, F. ed. Scandinavian Studies in Law. Vol. 22, SISL, Stockholm, (1978) 39-51.

Eckhoff, Torstein, Sundby, Nils Kristian. *Rettssystemer: Systemteoretisk innføring i rettsfilosofien.* Tanum-Norli, Oslo, (1976).

Eek, Hilding. *Folkrätten.* Norstedts förlag, Stockholm, (3:rd ed. 1980), (Institutet för rättsvetenskaplig forskning LI).

Ehrlich, Eugen. *Grundlegung der Soziologie des Rechts*. Duncker & Humblot, Berlin, (1913, 3:rd ed. 1967).

Ekelöf Per Olof. *Om värdering av strukturala bevis*. In Klami, H. T. ed. Rätt och Sanning: Ett bevisteoretiskt symposium i Uppsala 26-27 maj 1989. (1990) 22-30.

Ekelöf, Per Olof. *Rättegång. Fjärde häftet*. Norstedts förlag, Stockholm, (4:th revised ed. 1977), (Institutet för rättsvetenskaplig forskning XXXVIII).

Ekelöf, Per Olof. *Teleological Construction of Statutes*. SISL/Almqvist & Wiksell, Stockholm, (1958) 75-117 (Scandinavian Studies in Law, Vol. 2).

Ekelöf, Per Olof. *My Thoughts on Evidentiary Value*. In Gärdenfors, P., Hansson, B., Sahlin, N-E., eds. Evidentiary Value: Philosophical, Judicial and Psychological Aspects of a Theory. C. W. K. Gleerups, Lund, (1983) 9-26, (Library of Theoria No. 15).

Ekelöf, Per Olof. *Är termen rättighet ett syntaktiskt hjälpmedel utan mening?* SvJt, (1952) 546-59.

Evans, Jim. *Statutory Interpretation: Problems of Communication*. Oxford University Press, Oxford, . . . (1988).

Expertech. *Employment Law: Clarifying Dismissal*. photoreprint, n.p. (1987).

Farnsworth, E. Allan. *An Introduction to the Legal System of the United States*. Oceana Publications, Inc., London, . . . (2:nd ed. 1983).

Feigenbaum, Edward A., Buchanan, B. G., Lederberg, J. *On Generality and Problem Solving: A Case Study Using the DENDRAL Program*. In Meltzer, D., Michie, D. eds. Machine Intelligence 6. Edinburgh University Press, Edinburgh, (1971) 165-90.

Feigenbaum, Edward A., Feldman, Julian. *Computers and Thought*. McGraw-Hill Book Company, New York, . . . (1963).

Feigenbaum, Edward A., McCorduck, Pamela, Nii, H. Penny. *The Rise of the Expert Company: How Visionary Companies are using Artificial Intelligence to Achieve Higher Productivity and Profits*. MacMillan London Limited, London, (1988).

Fiedler, Herbert. *Rechtsinformatik*. In Ergänsbares Lexikon des Rechts, 32, vom 29, Luchterland, (1988) 1-11.

Fiedler, Herbert, Haft, Fritjof, Traunmüller, Roland eds. *Expert Systems in Law: Impacts on Legal Theory and Computer Law*. Attempto Verlag Tübingen, GmbH, Teubingen University Press, (1988), (Neue Methoden im Recht. Band 4).

Fino, Susan P. *Microcomputers and Criminal Sentencing: Michigan as a Case Study*. RCTLJ, Vol. 12, (1987) 407-32.

Fjeldvig, Tove. *Effektivisering av tekstsøkesystemer: Utvikling av språkbaserte metoder*. NRCCL, Universitetsforlaget, Oslo, (1987), (Complex 13/87).

Flavius, Gnaeus J. (pseudonym for Kantorowicz, Herman Ulrich). *Der Kampf um die Rechtswissenschaft*. Carl Winter's Universitätsbuchhandlung, Heidelberg, (1906).

Fleck, Glen ed. *A Computer Perspective*. Harvard University Press, Cambridge, Massachusetts, (1973).

Fleming, John G. *The Law of Torts*. The Law Book Company Limited, Sydney, (6:th ed. 1983).

Flodin, Mats. *On Valid Law and Valid Moral Norms.* Author, Stockholm, (1986), (Doctoral dissertation. Department of Law, Lund University).

Forslund, Anne Louise. *Vad är rättssociologi?* Liber Förlag, Jurist och samhällsvetareförbundets förlags AB, Stockholm, (1978).

Frank, Jerome. *Courts on Trial: Myth and Reality in American Justice.* Princeton University Press, Princeton, (1950).

Frank, Jerome. *Law and the Modern Mind.* Coward-McCann, Inc., New York, (1930, 6:th printing 1949).

Frankel, Marvin E. *Criminal Sentences: Law Without Order.* Hill and Wang, New York, (1973).

Franken, H. *The Expertise Centre for Juridical Software.* In Kracht, D., de Vay Mestdagh, C.N.J., Svensson, J.S. eds. Legal Knowledge Based Systems: An Overview of Criteria for Validation and Practical Use. Koninklijke Vermande BV, Lelystad, (1990) 5-7.

Freeman, Paul R.W. *Expert Systems and the Law.* C&L, No. 47, (1986) 9-12.

Frändberg, Åke. *Om analog användning av rättsnormer: En analys av analogibegreppet inom ramen för en allmän juridisk metodologi.* Norstedts förlag, Stockholm, (1973).

Frändberg, Åke. *Om rättsordningars giltighet.* In Bratholm, A., Opsahl, T., Aarbakke, M. eds. Samfunn, Rett, Rettferdighet: Festskrift till Torstein Eckhoffs 70-årsdag. Tano, Norway, (1986) 323-34.

Frändberg, Åke. *Rättsregel och rättsval: Om rättsliga regel- och systemkonflikter i tid och rum.* Norstedts förlag, Stockholm, (1984).

Frändberg, Åke. *Till frågan om de juridiska begreppens systematik: En studie i juridisk begreppsbildning.* Tidsskrift for rettsvitenskap, (1985) 79-116.

Gardner, Anne von der Leith. *An Artificial Intelligence Approach to Legal Reasoning.* The MIT Press, Cambridge, Massachusetts, . . . (1987).

Gelbart, Daphne, Smith, Joseph C. *Beyond Boolean Search: FLEXICON, A Legal Text-Based Intelligent System.* Proceedings ICAIL-91, ACM, New York, (1991) 225-34.

Genesereth, Michael R., Nilsson, Nils J. *Logical Foundations of Artificial Intelligence.* Morgan Kaufmann Publishers, Inc., Los Altos, (1987).

Gold, David I., Susskind, Richard, E. *Expert Systems in Law: A Jurisprudential and Formal Specification Approach.* Preproceedings ICLID-85 IDG, Florence, (1985) 305-16.

Goldberg, Steven P. *On Legal and Mathematical Reasoning.* JJ, Vol. 22, (1981) 83-91.

Golding, Martin P. *Legal Reasoning.* Alfred A Knopf Inc., New York, (1984), (Borzoi Books in Law and American Society).

Goodman, Danny. *The Complete HyperCard Handbook.* Bantam Books, Toronto, . . . (1987).

Gottlieb, Gidon. *The Logic of Choice: An Investigation of the Concepts of Rule and Rationality.* Georg Allen and Unwin Ltd., London, (1968).

Gratte, Ingvar, Månsson, Erik. *Datorer? – att leva med datorer.* Studentlitteratur, Lund, (2:nd ed. 1985).

Graubard, Stephen R. ed. *The Artificial Intelligence Debate: False Starts, Real Foundations.* The MIT Press, Cambridge, Massachusetts, . . . (1988).

Greenleaf, Graham, Mowbray, Andrew, Tyree, Alan. *The DataLex Legal Workstation – Integrating Tools for Lawyers.* Proceedings ICAIL-91, ACM, New York, (1991) 215-24.

Greenleaf, Graham, Mowbray, Andrew, Tyree, Alan. *Legal Expert Systems: Words, Words, Words. . . ?* In YLC&T, Vol. 3. Butterworths, London, (1987) 119-35.

Grossman, Garry, S., Solomon, Lewis D. *Computers and Legal Reasoning.* ABAJ, Vol. 69, (1983) 66-70.

Göranzon, Bo. *Det praktiska intellektet: Datoranvändning och yrkeskunnande.* Carlsson Bokförlag, Stockholm, (1990).

Hafner, Carole D. *An Information Retrieval System Based on a Computer Model of Legal Knowledge.* University of Michigan, photoreprint, (1978).

Hafner, Carole D. *Conceptual Organization of Case Law Knowledge Bases.* Proceedings ICAIL-87, ACM Press, New York, (1987) 35-42.

Haft, F., Jones, R.P., Wetter, Th. *A Natural Language Based Legal Expert System for Consultation and Tutoring – The LEX Project.* Proceedings ICAIL-87, ACM Press, New York, (1987) 75-83.

Hall, A.D., Fagen, R.E. *Definition of System.* In Buckley, W. ed. Modern Systems Research for the Behavioral Scientist. Aldine Publishing Company, Chicago, (1968) 81-92.

Hall, Jerome. *Foundations of Jurisprudence.* The Bobbs-Merrill Company Inc., Indianapolis, . . . (1973).

Hamfelt, Andreas. *The Multilevel Structure of Legal Knowledge and its Representation.* IRI, (1990), (IRI-rapport 1990:2).

Hamfelt, Andreas *Metalogic Representation of Multilayered Knowledge.* UPMAIL, Uppsala (1992), (Uppsala Theses in Computing Science 15).

Hamfelt, Andreas, Barklund, Jonas. *An Intelligent Interface to Legal Data Bases Combining Logic Programming and Hypertext.* UPMAIL, Uppsala, (1989), (UPMAIL Technical Report No. 60).

Hamfelt, Andreas, Wahlgren, Peter. *Datorstödda beslut: Artificiell intelligens och juridik.* IRI, (1988), (IRI-rapport 1988:4).

Hansen, Johannes. *Et EDB-system for analyse av rettslige avgjørelser.* Institutt for privatrett, avdeling for EDB-spørsmål, Universitetsforlaget, Oslo, (1981), (Complex 1/81).

Hansen, Johannes. *SARA: Brukerveiledning og programdokumentasjon.* Noris (49) NRCCL, Universitetsforlaget, Oslo, (1985), (Complex 7/85).

Hansen, Johannes. *Simulation and Automation of Legal Decisions.* NRCCL, Norwegian University Press A/S, Oslo, (1986), (Complex 6/86).

Harmon, Margaret. *Stretching Man's Mind: A History of Data Processing.* Mason/Charter Publishers Inc., New York, (1975).

Harmon, Paul, King, David. *Expert Systems: Artificial Intelligence in Business.* John Wiley & Sons, Inc., New York, . . . (1985).

Hart, H.L.A. *The Concept of Law*. Oxford University Press, Oxford, . . . (1961), (Clarendon Law Series).

Hart, H.L.A. *Positivism and the Separation of Law and Morals*. Harvard Law Review, Vol. 71, (1958) 593-629.

Hayes-Roth, Frederick., Waterman, Donald A., Lenat, Douglas B. eds. *Building Expert Systems*. Addison-Wesley Publishing Company, Inc., Reading, . . . (1983), (Teknowledge Series in Knowledge Engineering. Vol. 1).

Heather, Michael A. *A Demand-Driven Model for the Design of a "Half Intelligent" Common Law Information Retrieval System*. In Walter, C. ed. Computing Power and Legal Reasoning. West Publishing Company, St. Paul, . . . (1985) 69-103.

Hedenius, Ingemar. *Om rätt och moral*. Tidens förlag, Stockholm, (1941).

Hellner, Jan. *Lagstiftning inom förmögenhetsrätten*. Juristförlaget, Stockholm, (1990).

Hellner, Jan. *Arbetsgruppen för ADB och juridik*. Cir. no. 1, 15 October 1968, photoreprint, (1968).

Hellner, Jan. *Rättssociologisk undersökning av skadeståndsrätten*. Stockholm, (1969), (SOU 1969:58).

Hellner, Jan. *Rättsteori: En introduktion*. Juristförlaget, Stockholm, (1988).

Herrestad, Henning Berger. *Norms and Formalization*. NRCCL/Tano A.S., Oslo, (1990), (Complex 12/90).

Heuman, Lars. *Rättspraxis*. In Bernitz, U., Heuman, L., Löfmark, M., Roos, C. M., Seipel, P., Victorin, A. Finna rätt – Juristens källmaterial och arbetsmetoder. Juristförlaget, Stockholm, (2:nd ed. 1988) 109-38.

Hillis, W. Daniel. *Intelligence as an Emergent Behavior; or, The Songs of Eden*. In Graubard, Stephen R. ed. The Artificial Intelligence Debate: False Starts, Real Foundations. The MIT Press, Cambridge, Massachusetts, . . . (1988) 175-89.

Hilpinen, Risto ed. *Deontic Logic: Introductory and Systematic Readings*. D. Reidel Publishing Company, Dordrecht, . . . (1971, 2:nd printing 1981).

Hiselius, Patrik. *The Institute for Legal Documentation (IDG)* IRI, (1991), (IRI-PM 1991).

Hodges, Andrew. *Alan Turing: The Enigma*. Simon & Schuster, Inc., New York, (1983).

Hofstadter, Douglas R. *Gödel, Escher, Bach: An Eternal Golden Braid*. Penguin Books Ltd. Harmondsworth, (1979).

Hofstadter, Douglas R. *Metamagical Themas: Questing for the Essence of Mind and Pattern*. Basic Books, Inc., Publishers, New York, (1985).

Hohfeld, Wesley Newcomb. *Fundamental Legal Conceptions As Applied in Judicial Reasoning and Other Legal Essays*. Yale University Press, New Haven, (1923), (Edited version of essays originally published in 1909-17, edited by Cook, W.W.).

Holmes, Oliver Wendell. *The Path of the Law*. Harvard Law Review, Vol. 10, (1897) 457-78.

Holmes, Oliver Wendell Jr. *The Common Law*. Little Brown and Company, Boston, (1881), (Reprinted: Macmillan, London, . . . 1968).

Hoppenfeld, Ellias, C. *Law Research Service/Inc.* M.U.L.L. Vol. 66M, (1966) 46-52.

Hynynen, Raija, Salokivi, Jouni. *Datorprogrammet Aatu hjälper.* Kommuntidningen no. 10, (1988) 30-32.

Hägerström, Axel. *Inquiries Into the Nature of Law and Morals.* Almqvist & Wiksells, Uppsala, (1953), (Edited version of essays originally published in 1917-39, edited by Olivecrona, K.).

Hägglund, Sture. *Datorstödda kunskapssystem i framtidens kontor.* Teldok, televerket, Stockholm, (1986), (Teldok rapport 26).

Jackson, Kevin T. *Definition in Legal Reasoning.* JJ, Vol. 25, (1985) 377-86.

Jackson, Peter. *Introduction to Expert Systems.* Addison-Wesley Publishing Company, Workingham, . . . (1986).

Jansson, Carl-Gustaf, Wahlgren, Peter. *Expertsystem för juridik: Ett försök med avtalslagen.* IRI, (1985), (IRI-rapport 1985:12).

Jareborg, Nils. *Värderingar.* Norstedts förlag, Stockholm, (1975).

Jareborg, Nils. *Kriminalisering.* In Heckscher, S., Snare, A., Takala, H., Vestergaard, J. eds. Straff och rättfärdighet. Norstedts förlag, Stockholm, (1980) 33-46.

Jareborg, Nils, von Hirsch, Andrew, Hanrahan, Kathleen J. *Påföljdsbestämning i USA.* BRÅ, Stockholm, (1984), (BRÅ Forskning 1984:4).

Johnson-Laird, P. N., Wason, P.C. eds. *Thinking: Readings in Cognitive Science.* Cambridge University Press, Cambridge, . . . (1977).

Jones, Andrew, J.I. *Deontic Logic and Legal Knowledge Representation.* RJ, Vol. 3, (1990) 237-44.

Jones, Andrew, J.I., Sergot, Marek. *Deontic Logic in the Representation of Law: Towards a Methodology.* Forthcoming in Artificial Intelligence and Law, Kluwer Publ. Co., (1992).

Jones, Edgar A. Jr. *Foreword.* In Communication Sciences and Law: Reflections from the Jurimetrics Conference. Allen, L.E., Caldwell, M.E. eds. Bobbs-Merrill Company Inc., Indianapolis, . . . (1965) ix-xi.

Jurimetrics Journal. *Education in Jurimetrics.* JJ, Vol. 13, (1972) 69-107.

Jurimetrics Journal. *Education in Jurimetrics: Supplement.* JJ, Vol. 14, (1974) 166-71.

Jørgensen, Jørgen. *Imperatives and Logic.* Erkenntnis, Vol. 7, (1937/38) 288-96.

Kanger, Stig. *New Foundations for Ethical Theory. Part 1.* Stockholm (1957), (Reprinted in Hilpinen, R. ed. Deontic Logic: Introductory and Systematic Readings. Dordrecht (1971) 36-58).

Kantorowicz, Herman Ulrich. *See* Flavius, G. J.

Karpf, Jørgen. *A Contribution to a Classification of Legal Models.* Paper presented at ESL-89, Bologna, (1989).

Karpf, Jørgen. *The Future and Other Time Issues in Legal Representation.* Paper presented at ESL-89, Bologna, (1989).

Karpf, Jørgen. *Danish Expert Systems in Law: Overview of 12 Danish Systems.* Technical University of Denmark/Copenhagen University, photoreprint, Preliminary version, (1991), (Jurimatrics no. 16).

Karpf, Jørgen. *Inductive Modelling in Law: Example Based Expert Systems in Administrative Law.* Proceedings ICAIL-91, ACM, New York, (1991) 297-306.

Karpf, Jørgen. *Modularization of Legal Expert Systems.* Preproceedings ICLID-89, Vol. 1, IDG, Florence, (1989) 381-409.

Kelsen, Hans. *Essays in Legal and Moral Philosophy.* D. Reidel Publishing Company, Dordrecht-Holland, (1973), (Weinberger, O. ed. Synthese Library).

Kelsen, Hans. *Reine Rechtslehre.* Verlag Franz Deuticke, Vienna (2:nd ed. 1960), (English ed: Pure Theory of Law. University of California Press, Berkley, . . . 1970).

Kelsen, Hans. *The Pure Theory of Law.* (Parts 1 and 2), Law Quarterly Review, Part 1 in Vol. 50 (1934) 474-498, Part 2 in Vol. 51, (1935) 517-35.

Kelso, Louis O. *Does the Law Need a Technological Revolution?* Rocky Mountain Law Review. Vol. 18 (1946) 378-92.

Kidd, Alison, L. ed. *Knowledge Acquisition for Expert Systems: A Practical Handbook.* Plenum Press, New York, . . . (1987).

Kindborg, Mikael. *Visual Techniques for Orientation in Hypermedia Structures.* Stockholm University/The Royal Institute of Technology, Department of Computer & Systems Sciences, Stockholm, (1991).

Klami, Hannu Tapani. *Föreläsningar över juridikens metodlära.* Iustus förlag AB, Uppsala, (2:nd ed. 1989).

Klami, Hannu Tapani. ed. *Rätt och sanning: Ett bevisteoretiskt symposium i Uppsala 26-27 maj 1989.* Iustus förlag AB, Uppsala, (1990).

Kleineman, Jan. *Ren förmögenhetsskada: Särskilt vid vilseledande av annan än kontraktspart.* Juristförlaget, Stockholm, (1987).

Kluwer Academic Publishers. *Artificial Intelligence and Law: An International Journal.* Information leaflet, Dordrecht, (1990).

Knapp, Kay A. *Minnesota Sentencing Guidelines and Commentary.* West Publishing Company, St. Paul, . . . (1985).

Knight, Max. *Translator's Preface.* In Kelsen, H. Pure Theory of Law. University of California Press, Berkley, . . . (1970) v-vi.

Knuth, Donald E., Trabb Pardo, Luis. *The Early Development of Programming Languages.* In Metropolis, N., Howlett, J., Rota, G.C. eds. A History of Computing in the Twentieth Century. Academic Press, New York, . . . (1980) 197-273.

Koers, A. W., Kracht, D., Smith, M., Smits, J.M., Weusten, M.C.M. *Criteria for the Classification of Legal Knowledge Systems: Advisory Systems on Legal Questions.* In Kracht, D., de Vay Mestdagh, C.N.J., Svensson, J.S. eds. Legal Knowledge Based Systems: An Overview of Criteria for Validation and Practical Use. Koninklijke Vermande BV, Lelystad, (1990) 23-35.

Koers, A. W., Pelger, W.D. *Information Technology and Court Administration.* In Wedekind, W. ed. The Eight World Conference on Procedural Law: Justice and Efficiency: General Reports and Discussions. Kluwer Law and Taxation Publishers, Deventer, . . . (1989) 407-30.

Kowalski, Robert. *The Treatment of Negation in Logic Programs for Representing Legislation.* Proceedings ICAIL-89, ACM, New York, (1989) 11-15.

Kowalski, Robert, Sergot, Marek. *The Use of Logical Models in Legal Problem Solving.* RJ, Vol. 3, (1990) 201-18.

Kracht, D., de Vey Mestdagh, C.N.J., Svensson, J.S. eds. *Legal Knowledge Based Systems: An Overview of Criteria for Validation and Practical Use.* Koninklijke Vermande BV, Lelystad, (1990).

Lacock, Darrel D. *The Relevance of Logic to Law.* M.U.L.L. Vol. 64J, (1964) 13-23.

Lawlor, Reed C. *What Computers Can Do: Analysis and Prediction of Judicial Decisions.* ABAJ, Vol. 49, (1963) 337-44.

Lawlor, Reed C. *Stare Decisis and Electronic Computers.* In Schubert, G. Judicial Behavior: A Reader in Theory and Research. Rand McNally & Company, Chicago, (1964) 492-505.

Lee, Keekok. *The Positivist Science of Law.* Avebury, Gower Publishing Company Ltd. Aldershot, . . . (1989), (Avebury Series in Philosophy).

Lehmann, Hubert. *Legal Concepts in a Natural Language Based Expert System.* RJ, Vol. 3, (1990) 245-53.

Leith, Philip. *The Computerised Lawyer: A Guide to the Use of Computers in the Legal Profession.* Springer-Verlag, London, . . . (1991).

Leith, Philip. *Legal Expert Systems: Misunderstanding the Legal Process.* C&L, No. 49, (1986) 26-31.

Levi, Edward, H. *An Introduction to Legal Reasoning.* The University of Chicago Press, Chicago, (1949).

Lewis, Clarence Irving, Langford, Cooper Harold. *Symbolic Logic.* Dover Publications Inc., New York, (1932, 2:nd ed. 1959).

Lindahl, Lars. *Definitioner, begreppsanalys och mellanbegrepp i juridiken.* In Rationalitet och emperi i rättsvetenskapen. Stockholms universitet, Stockholm, (1985) 37-49 (Juridiska fakulteten i Stockholm, skriftserien nr. 6).

Lindahl, Lars. *Position and Change: A Study in Law and Logic.* D. Reidel Publishing Company, Dordrecht-Holland, (1977), (Synthese Library/Vol. 112).

Lindell, Bengt. *Sakfrågor och rättsfrågor.* Iustus förlag, Uppsala, (1987), (Skrifter från juridiska fakulteten i Uppsala 11).

Lindgren, Michael. *Glory and Failure: The Difference Engines of Johann Müller, Charles Babbage and Georg and Edvard Scheutz.* Department of Technology and Social Change-Tema T, Linköping University, (1987), (Linköping Studies in Arts and Science 9 and Stockholm Papers in History and Philosophy of Technology 2017).

Llewellyn, Karl N. *The Bramble Bush: On our Law and its Study.* Oceana Publications, New York, (1930, 3:rd printing 1960).

Llewellyn, Karl N. *The Common Law Tradition: Deciding Appeals*. Little, Brown and Company, Boston, . . . (1960).

Llewellyn, Karl N. *Remarks on The Theory of Appellate Decisions and the Rules or Canons About how Statutes are to be Constructed.* Vandebilt Law Journal, Vol. 3, (1950), 395-406.

Loevinger, Lee. *Jurimetrics: The Methodology of Legal Inquiry.* In Baade, H. W. ed. Jurimetrics. Basic Books Inc., Publishers, New York, . . . (1963) 5-35.

Loevinger, Lee. *Jurimetrics: The Next Step Forward.* Minnesota Law Review, Vol. 33, (1949), (Reprinted: JJ, Vol. 12, (1971) 3-41).

Losee, John. *A Historical Introduction to the Philosophy of Science*. Oxford University Press, London, . . . (1972, 2:nd ed. 1980).

Lovelace, Ada A. *Translators Notes to Menabrea, L. F. Sketch of the Analytical Engine Invented by Charles Babbage, Esq.* (1842), (Reprinted in Bowden, B. V. ed. Faster than Thought. Sir Isaak Pitman & Sons, Ltd., London, (1953) 341-408).

Luhmann, Niklas. *Rechtssoziologie*. Rowchlt Taschenbuch Verlag GMbH, Reiinbek bei Hamburg, (1972), (English ed: A Sociological Theory of Law, Routledge & Kegan Paul, London, . . . 1985).

Lukes, Steven, Scull, Andrew, eds. *Durkheim and the Law*. Martin Robertson & Co. Ltd., Oxford, (1983).

Lund, Jörgen. *Från kula till data.* Gidlunds bokförlag, (1988).

Lunning, Lars. *Anställningsskydd. Kommentar till anställningsskyddslagen.* Allmänna förlaget, Stockholm, (7:th revised ed. 1989).

Lübcke, Poul ed. *Filosofilexikonet*. Bokförlaget Forum AB, Stockholm, (1988).

Löf, Staffan. *The POLYTEXT/ARBIT Demonstration System.* The National Defence Research Institute, Umeå, (1980), (FOA 4 rapport C 40121-M7).

M.U.L.L. *Cumulative Index 59S-63S*. Vol. 63D, (1963).

MacCormick, Neil. *Legal Reasoning and Legal Theory.* Oxford University Press, Oxford, . . . (1978), (Clarendon Law Series).

MacCormick, Neil D., Summers, Robert S. eds. *Interpreting Statutes: A Comparative Study.* Dartmouth Publishing Company Limited, Aldershot, . . . (1991).

MacCormick, Neil, Weinberger, Ota. *An Institutional Theory of Law: New Approaches to Legal Positivism.* D. Reidel Publishing Company, Dordrecht, . . . (1986), (Law and Philosophy Library).

Mackaay, Ejan, Poulin, Daniel, Frémont, Jacques, Bratley, Paul, Deniger, Constant. *The Logic of Time in Law and Legal Expert Systems.* RJ, Vol. 3, (1990) 254-71.

Mackintosh, Allan R. *Dr. Atanasoff's Computer.* ScAm, Vol. 259, No. 2, (1988) 72-78.

Maggs, Peter B., deBessonet, Cary G. *Automated Logical Analysis of Systems of Legal Rules.* JJ, Vol. 12, (1972) 158-69.

Magnusson, Cecilia. *New Roles in the Shaping of the Law*. In Seipel, P. ed. From Data Protection to Knowledge Machines: The Study of Law and Informatics. Kluwer Law and Taxation Publishers, Deventer, . . . (1990) 135-65, (Computer/Law Series 5).

Magnusson Sjöberg, Cecilia. *Rättsautomation: Särskilt om statsförvaltningens datorisering.* Stockholm, (forthcoming, Norstedts juridikförlag, Stockholm, 1992).

Marshall, Catherine, C. *Representing the Structure of a Legal Argument.* Proceedings ICAIL-89, ACM, New York, (1989) 121-27.

Martino, Antonio A. ed. *Deontic Logic, Computational Linguistics and Legal Information Systems.* (Edited Versions of Selected Papers from ICLID-81). North-Holland Publishing Company, Amsterdam, . . . (1982).

Martino, Antonio A., Socci Natali, Fiorenza. eds. *Automated Analysis of Legal Texts: Logic, Informatics, Law.* (Edited Versions of Selected Papers from ICLID-85). North-Holland Publishing Company, Amsterdam, . . . (1986).

Mathiesen, Thomas. *Rett og samfunn: Utkast til en rettssosiologi.* Pax Forlag A/S, Oslo, (1977).

Mauchly, John W. *The ENIAC.* In Metropolis, N., Howlett, J., Rota, G.C. eds. A History of Computing in the Twentieth Century. Academic Press, New York, . . . (1980) 541-50.

Mayer, Richard E. *Thinking, Problem Solving, Cognition.* W.H. Freeman and Company, New York, (1983).

Mazzarese, Tecla. *Guest Editor's Preface.* RJ, Vol. 4, (1991) i-iii.

McCarthy, John. *Mathematical Logic in Artificial Intelligence.* In Graubard, Stephen R. ed. The Artificial Intelligence Debate: False Starts, Real Foundations. The MIT Press, Cambridge, Massachusetts, . . . (1988) 297-311.

McCarty, L. Thorne. *Intelligent Legal Information Systems: Problems and Prospects.* In Campbell, Colin, ed. Data Processing and the Law. Sweet & Maxwell, London, (1984) 125-51.

McCarty, L. Thorne. *Reflections on TAXMAN: An Experiment in Artificial Intelligence and Legal Reasoning.* Harvard Law Review, Vol. 90, (1977) 837-93.

McCarty, L. Thorne. *A Language for Legal Discourse: I. Basic Features.* Proceedings ICAIL-89, ACM, New York, (1989) 180-89.

McCarty, L. Thorne. *The TAXMAN Project: Towards a Cognitive Theory of Legal Argument.* In Niblett, Bryan, ed. Computer Science and Law: An Advanced Cource. Cambridge University Press, Cambridge, . . . (1980) 23-43.

McCarty, L. Thorne, Rissland, Edwina L. *Series Foreword.* In Gardner, A. v. d. L. An Artificial Intelligence Approach to Legal Reasoning. The MIT Press, Cambridge, Massachusetts, . . . (1987).

McCarty, L. Thorne. *Permissions and Obligations.* Proceedings of the Eight International Joint Conference on Artificial Intelligence, Karlsruhe, (1983), (Reprinted: Preproceedings ICLID-85, IDG, Florence, (1985) 103-25).

McCarty, L Thorne, Sridharan, N.S. *The Representation of an Evolving System of Legal Concepts: II. Prototypes and Deformations.* Rutgers University (1981), (Rutgers University Laboratory for Computer Science Research, Technical Report LRP-TR-11).

McCorduck, Pamela. *Machines Who Think: A Personal Inquiry Into the History and Prospects of Artificial Intelligence.* W.H. Freeman and Company, San Francisco, (1979).

McCulloch, Warren S., Pitts, Walter. *A Logical Calculus of the Ideas Immanent in Nervous Activity.* Bulletin of Mathematical Biophysics. Vol. 5, (1943) 115 -33.

Mehl, Lucien. *Automation in the Legal World: From the Machine Processing of Legal Information to the "Law Machine"* . Symposium on Mechanization of Thought Processes. National Physical Laboratorium, U.K., (1958) 757-79.

Meldman, Jeffrey A., Holt, Anatol W. *Petri Nets and Legal Systems.* JJ, Vol. 12, (1971) 65-75.

Meldman, Jeffrey, A. *A Structural Model for Computer-Aided Legal Analysis.* RJCL Vol. 6, (1977) 27-71.

Michaelsen, Robert H. *An Expert System for Federal Tax Planning.* Expert Systems Vol. 1, (1984) 149-67.

Minsky, Marvin. *The Society of Mind.* Simon & Schuster Inc., New York, . . . (1985).

Mollenhoff, Clark R. *Atanasoff: Forgotten Father of the Computer.* Iowa State University Press, Ames, (1988).

Morris, Anne, Reed, Anne eds. *Directory of Expert Systems Tools.* Learned Information (Europe) Ltd. n.p., (1989).

Morrison, Rees W. *Market Realities of Rule-Based Software for Lawyers: Where the Rubber Meets the Road.* Proceedings ICAIL-89, ACM, New York, (1989) 33-36.

Nagel, Ernest, Newman, James R. *Goedel's Proof.* In Newman, James R. ed. The World of Mathematics. Vol. 3, Simon and Schuster, New York, (1956) 1668-95.

Navarro, Joseph A., Taylor, Jean G. *Data Analyses and Simulation of a Court System for the Processing of Criminal Cases.* JJ. Vol. 9, (1968) 101-26.

Nelson Theodor H. *The Hypertext.* Paper presented at 1965 Congress of the International Federation for Documentation, Washington D.C., (1965).

Nelson, Theodor H. *Getting it out of our System.* In Schecter, G. ed. Information Retrieval. A Critical View. Thompson Book Company, Washington D.C. (1967) 191-210, (Based on the Third Annual Colloquium on IR, Philadelphia, May 12-13 1966).

Newell, Allen, Shaw, J.C., Simon, H.A. *Empirical Explorations with the Logic Theory Machine: A Case Study in Heuristics.* Proceedings of the Western Joint Computer Conference, (1957) 218-39, (Reprinted in Feigenbaum, E. A., Feldman, J. eds. Computers and Thought. McGraw-Hill Book Company, New York, . . . (1963) 109-33).

Newell, Allen, Simon, Herbert A. *Computer Science as Empirical Inquiry: Symbols and Search.* Communications of the ACM, March 1976, (1976) 113-26, (Reprinted in Haugeland, John, ed. Mind Design: Philosophy, Psychology, Artificial Intelligence, The MIT Press, Cambridge, Massachusetts, . . . (1981) 35-66).

Newsweek. *C-3POs for the Display Floor.* Vol. 115, no. 16, April 16, (1990) 49.

Niblett, Bryan. *Expert Systems for Lawyers.* C&L, No. 29, (1981) 2-4.

Niblett, Bryan ed. *Computer Science and Law: An Advanced Course.* Cambridge University Press, Cambridge, . . . (1980).

O'Neil, D. Peter. *A Process Specification of Expert Lawyer Reasoning.* Proceedings ICAIL-87, ACM Press, New York, (1987) 52-59.

O'Shea, Tim, Eisenstadt, Marc eds. *Artificial Intelligence: Tools, Techniques, and Applications.* Harper & Row, Publishers, New York, . . . (1984).

Oddy, R.N., Robertson, S.E., van Rijsbergen, C.J., Williams, P.W. eds. *Information Retrieval Research.* Butterworth & Co. Publishers Ltd., London, . . . (1981).

Olivecrona, Karl. *Law as Fact.* Stevens & Sons, London, (1939, 2:nd ed. 1971).

Oskamp, Anja, Vandenberghe, Guy P.V. *Legal Thinking and Automation.* Preproceedings ICLID-85, IDG, Florence, (1985) 549-59.

Oskamp, Anja. *Het ontwikkelen van juridische expertsystemen (een theoretische beschouwing).* Kluwer, Antwerpen, . . . (1990).

Painter, Desmond. *Hyperlaw.* Law Technology Centre & Bileta Newsletter, Vol. 2, (1990) 88-92.

Parsaye, Kamran, Chignell, Mark, Khoshafian, Setrag, Wong, Harry. *Intelligent Databases: Object Oriented, Deductive Hypermedia Technologies.* John Wiley & Sons, Inc., New York, . . . (1989).

Pattaro, Enrico. *Il realismo giuridico scandinavo.* Cooperativa, Bologna (1974).

Patterson, Edwin W. *Logic in the Law.* University of Pennsylvania Law Review, Vol. 90, (1942) 875-909.

Pear, Charles, E. Jr. *Expert Systems and the Race for Clients.* Preproceedings ICLID-89, Vol. 2, IDG, Florence, (1989) 649-54.

Peczenik, Aleksander. *The Basis of Legal Justification.* Author, Lund, (1983).

Peczenik, Aleksander. *Rätten och förnuftet.* Norstedts förlag, Stockholm, (1986, 2:nd ed. 1988).

Peczenik, Aleksander. *Juridikens metodproblem: Rättkällelära och lagtolkning.* AWE/GEBERS, Almqvist & Wiksell Förlag AB, Stockholm, (1974, 2:nd ed 1980).

Peczenik, Aleksander. *Rättsnormer.* Norstedts förlag, Stockholm, (1987).

Peczenik, Aleksander, Bergholz, Gunnar. *Statutory Interpretation in Sweden.* In MacCormick, Neil D., Summers, Robert S. eds. Statutory Interpretation. Dartmouth Publishing Company Limited, Aldershot, . . . (1991) 311-58.

Penrose, Roger. *The Emperor's New Mind.* Oxford University Press/Vintage, London, . . . (1989).

Popp, Walter, G., Schlink, Bernhard. *Judith: A Computer Program to Advise Lawyers in Reasoning a Case.* JJ, Vol. 15, (1975) 303-14.

Pound, Roscoe. *Mechanical Jurisprudence.* Columbia Law Review, Vol. 8, (1908) 605-23.

Pound, Roscoe. *Jurisprudence.* Vol. 1, West Publishing Co., St. Paul, (1959).

Quinlan, J. Ross. *Fundamentals of the Knowledge Engineering Problem.* In Michie, Donald, ed. Introductory Readings in Expert Systems. Gordon and Breach Science Publishers, New York, . . . (1982) 33-46.

Quinlan, J. Ross, ed. *Applications of Expert Systems*: Based on the Proceedings of the Second Australian Conference. Turing Institute Press in association with Addison-Wesley Publishing Company, Sydney, . . . (1987).

Quinlan, J. Ross, ed. *Applications of Expert Systems.* Vol. 2: Based on the Proceedings of the Third and Fourth Australian Conferences. Turing Institute Press in association with Addison-Wesley Publishing Company, Sydney, . . . (1989).

Randell, B. *The COLOSSUS.* In Metropolis, N., Howlett, J., Rota, G.C. eds. A History of Computing in the Twentieth Century. Academic Press, New York, . . . (1980) 47-92.

Ratio Juris. *Expert Systems in Law.* An International Journal of Jurisprudence and Philosophy of Law, Vol. 3, No.2, (1990) 189-319, (Selected papers from ESL-89).

Raz, Joseph. *The Authority of Law: Essays on Law and Morality.* Clarendon Press, Oxford, (1979).

Raz, Joseph. *The Concept of a Legal System: An Introduction to the Theory of Legal System.* Clarendon Press, Oxford, (1970).

Reeke, George N. Jr., Edelman, Gerald M. *Real Brains and Artificial Intelligence.* In Graubard, Stephen R. ed. The Artificial Intelligence Debate: False Starts, Real Foundations. The MIT Press, Cambridge Massachusetts, . . . (1988) 143-73.

Reid, T.R. *The Chip: How Two Americans Invented the Microchip and Launched a Revolution.* (1984), (Swedish ed: Det fantastiska Chipset: Hur två forskare revolutionerade världen. Bokförlaget Prisma, Stockholm, 1987).

Rissland, Edwina L. *Dimension-Based Analysis of Hypotheticals from Supreme Court Oral Argument.* Proceedings ICAIL-89, ACM, New York, (1989) 111-20.

Rissland, Edwina L. *Artificial Intelligence and Law: Stepping Stones to a Model of Legal Reasoning.* Yale Law Journal, Vol. 99, (1990) 1957-81.

Rissland, Edwina L., Ashley, Kevin D. *A Case-Based System for Trade Secrets Law.* Proceedings ICAIL-87, ACM Press, New York, (1987) 60-66.

Rissland, Edwina L., Skalak, David B. *Interpreting Statutory Predicates.* Proceedings ICAIL-89, ACM, New York, (1989) 46-53.

Robben, F., Herbosch, E., van Buggenhout, B., van Bulck, K. *The Computer Supported Development of Juridical Advice Systems Based on the Decision Table Technique.* In Kracht, D., de Vay Mestdagh, C.N.J., Svensson, J.S. eds. Legal Knowledge Based Systems: An Overview of Criteria for Validation and Practical Use. Koninklijke Vermande BV, Lelystad, (1990) 50-56.

Roos, Carl Martin. *Mot en verklighetsorienterad juridik: Några reflexioner kring Per Stjernquists juridiska författarskap.* In Festskrift till Per Stjernquist. Juridiska föreningen i Lund, (1978) 19-27, (Acta Societatis Juridicae Lundensis, nr 24).

Rosch, Eleanor. *Classification of Real-World Objects: Origins and Representations in Cognition.* In Ehrlich, S., Tulving, E. eds. La memoire semantique. Paris Bulletin de psychologie, (1976), (Reprinted in Johnson-Laird, P. N. ,Wason, P. C. eds. Thinking: Readings in Cognitive Science. Cambridge University Press, Cambridge, . . . (1977) 212-22).

Rosengren, Karl Erik. *Sociologisk metodik.* Scandinavian University Books/ Esselte Studium AB, Stockholm, . . . (1971, 2:nd ed. 1975).

Ross, Alf. *Tû-Tû.* In Borum, O. A., Illum, Knud, eds. Festskrift till Henry Ussing. Juristforbundet/Nyt Nordisk Forlag Arnold Busck, København, (1951) 468-84, (English ed: Harvard Law Review, Vol. 70 (1956/57) 812-25).

Ross, Alf. *Om ret og retfærdighed: En indførelse i den analytiske retsfilosofi.* Nyt nordisk forlag, Arnold Busck, København, (1953).

Ross, Alf. *Directives and Norms.* Routledge & Keagan, Paul, London, (1968).

Rothfeder, Jeffrey. *Minds over Matter: A New Look at Artificial Intelligence.* Simon & Schuster, Inc., New York, (1985).

Rylander, Staffan. *Strömholm och rättssociologin.* SvJt, (1970) 484-88.

Salton, Gerard, McGill, Michael J. *Introduction to Modern Information Retrieval.* McGraw-Hill Book Company, New York, . . . (1983).

Sammet, Jean E. *Programming Languages: History and Fundamentals.* Prentice-Hall, Inc., Englewoods Cliffs, (1969).

Samuel, Geoffrey. *The Challenge of Artificial Intelligence: Can Roman Law Help Us Discover Whether Law is a System of Rules?* Legal Studies, Vol. 11 (1991) 24-46.

SARI. *Straffmätning: Slutrapport.* Justitiedepartementet, SARI, Stockholm, (1980), (Ds Ju 1980:9).

Schank, Roger C. *What is AI, Anyway?* In Partridge, Derek, Wilks, Yorick. eds. The Foundations of Artificial Intelligence. A Sourcebook. Cambridge University Press, Cambridge, . . . (1990) 3-13.

Schmidt, Aernout, van den Herik, Jaap. *How to Validate a Legal Knowledge Based System.* In Kracht, D., de Vey Mestdagh, C.N.J., Svensson, J.S. eds. *Legal Knowledge Based Systems: An Overview of Criteria for Validation and Practical Use.* Koninklijke Vermande BV, Lelystad, (1990) 57-68.

Schmidt, Folke. *Domaren som lagtolkare.* In Festskrift tillägnad Nils Herlitz. Norstedts, Stockholm, (1955) 263-98.

Schmidt, Folke. *The Uppsala School of Legal Thinking.* In Schmidt, F. ed. Scandinavian Studies in Law. Vol. 22, SISL, Stockholm, (1978) 149-75.

Schubert, Glendon ed. *Judicial Behavior: A Reader in Theory and Research.* Rand McNally & Company, Chicago, (1964).

Schwartz, Jacob T. *The New Connectionism: Developing Relationships Between Neuroscience and Artificial Intelligence.* In Graubard, Stephen R. ed. The Artificial Intelligence Debate: False Starts, Real Foundations. The MIT Press, Cambridge Massachusetts, . . . (1988) 123-41.

Searl, John R. *Is the Brain's Mind a Computer Program?* ScAm, Vol. 262, No.1, (1990) 20-25.

Seipel, Peter. *Introducing Law Students to Computers: Swedish Experience.* RJCL, Vol. 1970 Spring, (1970) 88-93.

Seipel, Peter. *Rättsutbildning och informationsteknologi i ett internationellt perspektiv.* In Galtung, A. ed. Internationella aspekter på rättsinformatiken. Norstedts, Stockholm, (1991) 20-36, (NÅR 1991).

Seipel, Peter. *Informationssystem för rättsväsendet: Projekt index. En undersökning av sakregister för juridisk informationssökning.* SARI, Stockholm, (1976).

Seipel, Peter. *LEXLAB: A Computer Laboratory for Legal Teaching and Training.* IRI, (1991), (IRI-PM 1991:3).

Seipel, Peter. *Om användning av automatisk databehandlingsteknik inom juridiken.* (Parts 1 and 2), SvJt, (1970) 257-92, 722-48.

Seipel, Peter. *Computing Law: Perspectives on a New Legal Discipline.* Liber förlag, Stockholm, (1977).

Seipel, Peter ed. *From Data Protection to Knowledge Machines: The Study of Law and Informatics.* Kluwer Law and Taxation Publishers, Deventer, . . . (1990), (Computer/Law Series 5).

Sergot, M.J., Sadri, F., Kowalski, R.A., Kriwaczek, F., Hammond, P., Cory, H.T. *The British Nationality Act as a Logic Program.* Communications of the ACM, Vol. 29, (1986) 370-86.

Sergot, Marek. *The Representation of Law in Computer Programs: A Survey and Comparison.* Department of Computing, Imperial College/NRCCL, Tano, Oslo, (1991), (Complex 1/91).

Sergot, Marek. *Representing Legislation as Logic Programs.* Imperial College of Science and Technology, London, (1985).

Shabtai, Rosenne. *The World Court: What It Is and How It Works.* Martinus Nijhoff Publishers, Dordrecht, . . . (1962, 4:th ed. 1989).

Shannon, Claude E. *A Chess-Playing Machine.* ScAm, (1950), (Reprinted in Newman, James R. ed. The World of Mathematics. Vol. 4, Simon and Schuster, New York, (1956) 2124-33).

Shannon, Claude, E. *A Mathematical Theory of Communication.* The Bell System Technical Journal. Vol. 27, No. 3, (1948) 379-423.

Shelley, Mary C. *Frankenstein: The Modern Promethus.* (1817), (Reprinted: The Bobbs-Merrill Company, Inc., Indianapolis, 1974).

Shortliffe, E.H. *Computer-Based Medical Consultations: MYCIN.* Elsevier, New York, . . . (1976).

Simmonds, Nigel E. T*he Decline of Juridical Reason: Doctrine and Theory in the Legal Order.* Manchester University Press, Manchester, . . . (1984).

Simon Eric, Gaes, Gerry. *ASSYST – Computer Support for Guideline Sentencing.* Proceedings ICAIL-89, ACM, New York, (1989) 195-200.

Simon, Herbert A., Newell, Allen. *Heuristic Problem Solving: The Next Advance in Operations Research.* Operations Research, Vol. 6, (1958) 1-10.

Simon, Herbert, A., Newell, Allen. *Information-Processing in Computer and Man.* The American Scientist, Vol. 52, No. 3, (1964), (Reprinted in Pylyshyn, Zenon W. ed. Perspectives on the Computer Revolution. Prentice-Hall Inc., Englewood Cliffs (1970) 256-73).

SIS-Standardiseringskommissionen i Sverige, ed. *Dataordboken.* SIS, Stockholm, (1989), (SS 01 16 01 Utgåva 4).

Skalak, David B., Rissland, Edwina L. *Argument Moves in a Rule-Guided Domain.* Proceedings ICAIL-91, ACM, New York, (1991) 1-11.

Skalak, David B., Rissland, Edwina L. *Using Case-Based Reasoning to Extend the Expertise of Expert Systems.* Preproceedings ICLID-89, Vol. 1, IDG, Florence, (1989) 671-92.

Slack, Jon M. *Cognitive Science Research.* In O'Shea, Tim, Eisenstadt, Marc eds. Artificial Intelligence. Tools, Techniques, and Applications. Harper & Row, Publishers, New York, . . . (1984) 155-77.

Slayton, Philip. *Electronic Legal Retrieval – The Impact of Electronic Computers on a Profession.* JJ, Vol. 14, (1973) 29-40.

Smith, Brian C. *Prologue to "Reflection and Semantics in a Procedural Language".* MIT, Cambridge (1982), (Ph. D. thesis and Tech report MIT/LCS/TR-272), (Reprinted in Brachman, R. J. Levesque, H. J. eds. Readings in Knowledge Representation. Morgan Kaufmann Publishers, Inc., Los Altos, (1985) 31-40).

Smith, Joseph C., Deedman, Cal. *The Application of Expert Systems Technology to Case-Based Law.* Proceedings ICAIL-87, ACM Press, New York, (1987) 84-93.

Soeteman, Arend. *Logic in Law: Remarks on Logic and Rationality in Normative Reasoning, Especially in Law.* Kluwer Academic Publishers, Dordrecht, . . . (1989), (Law and Philosophy Library).

Sokolowski, Robert. *Natural and Artificial Intelligence.* In Graubard, Stephen R. ed. The Artificial Intelligence Debate: False Starts, Real Foundations. The MIT Press, Cambridge, Massachusetts, . . . (1988) 45-64.

Sowa, John, F. *Conceptual Structures: Information Processing in Mind and Machine.* Addison-Wesley Publishing Company, Inc., Reading, . . . (1984), (The Systems Programming Series).

Sprowl, James A. *Assembling Standardized Legal Documents in a Semiautomated Fashion with a Rule-Based Expert System.* Paper presented at ESL-89, Bologna, (1989).

Sprowl, James A. *The Automated Assembly of Legal Documents.* In Niblett, Bryan, ed. Computer Science and Law: An Advanced Cource. Cambridge University Press, Cambridge, . . . (1980) 195-205.

Squires, Lynn B., Rombauer, Majorie Dick. *Legal Writing in a Nutshell.* West Publishing Co., St. Paul, (1982).

Stamper, R.K., Jones, S., Mason, P.J., Mudarth, P.E. *The LEGOL Project.* C&L, No. 10, (1976) 6-8.

Stamper, Ronald. *Legol: Modelling Legal Rules by Computer.* In Niblett, Bryan, ed. Computer Science and Law: An Advanced Cource. Cambridge University Press, Cambridge, . . . (1980) 45-71.

Statskontoret. *Statskontorets projekt Kunskapssystem –"Växthuset".* SAFAD, Stockholm, photoreprint, (1988).

Statskontoret. *Verktyg för handläggare: En skrift om kunskskapssystem, stordatorer och ärendehantering.* SAFAD, Stockholm, (1990), (Statskontoret rapport 1990:27).

Statskontoret. *Social Assistance and Knowledge-Based Systems: PLUTO – A Support System.* SAFAD, Stockholm, (1988), (Statskontoret rapport 1988:53).

Stevens, Robert. *Two Cheers for 1870: The American Law School.* In Fleming, Donald, Bailyn, Bernard eds. Perspectives in American History. Vol. 5, Law in American History. Harvard University, Cambridge, Massachusetts, (1971) 405-551.

Stjernquist, Per. *En aspekt på rättssociologisk forskning.* Tidskrift för rättssociologi, Vol. 1, (1983/84) 7-17.

Stone, Julius. *Legal System and Lawyers' Reasonings.* Maitland Publications PTY. LTD., Sydney, (1964).

Strömberg, Håkan. *Allmän förvaltningsrätt*. Liber förlag, Malmö (12:th ed. 1984).

Strömberg, Tore. *Lathund för lagläsare*. In Logik, rätt och moral: Filosofiska studier tillägnade Manfred Moritz på 60-års dagen den 4 juni 1969. Studentlitteratur, Lund, (1969) 191-205.

Strömberg, Tore. *Rättsfilosofins historia i huvuddrag*. Studentlitteratur, Lund, (1981, 2:nd ed. 1985).

Strömberg, Tore. *Rättsordningens byggstenar: Om normtyperna i lag och sedvanerätt*. Studentlitteratur, Lund, (1988).

Strömholm, Stig. *Ideer och tillämpningar*. Norstedts förlag, Stockholm, (1978), (Institutet för rättsvetenskaplig forskning XCVI).

Strömholm, Stig. *Allmän rättslära: En första introduktion*. Norstedts förlag, Stockholm, (2:nd ed. 1973).

Strömholm, Stig. *Något om sociologiens betydelse för juridiken*. SvJt, (1970) 97-125.

Strömholm, Stig. *Den juridiska argumentationens relevanskriterier*. SvJt, (1974) 641-68.

Strömholm, Stig. *Genmäle (till Rylander)*. SvJt, (1970) 488-91.

Strömholm, Stig. *Rätt, rättskällor och rättstillämpning: En lärobok i allmän rättslära*. Norstedts förlag, Stockholm, (1981, 3:rd ed. 1988), (Institutet för rättsvetenskaplig forskning CIX).

Summers, Robert S. *Form and Substance in Legal Reasoning*. In Bratholm, A., Opsahl, T., Aarbakke, M. eds. Samfunn, Rett, Rettferdighet: Festskrift till Torstein Eckhoffs 70-årsdag. Tano, Norway, (1986) 700-15.

Sundberg, Jacob W.F. *fr. Eddan t. Ekelöf: Repetitorium om rättskällor i Norden*. Studentlitteratur/Akademisk forlag/Institutet för offentlig och internationell rätt, (1978).

Sundby, Nils Kristian. *Om normer*. Universitetsforlaget, Oslo, (1974), (Fiolosofiske problemer XLIII, Scandinavian Studies in Philosophy, Næss, A. ed.).

Suppes, Patrick. *Introduction to Logic*. D. Van Nostrand Company, Inc., Princeton, . . . (1957), (The University Series in Undergraduate Mathematics).

Susskind, Richard E. *Expert Systems in Law: Out of the Research Laboratory and Into the Marketplace*. Proceedings ICAIL-87, ACM Press, New York, (1987) 1-8.

Susskind, Richard E. *Review of Gardner, A. v. d. L. An Artificial Intelligence Approach to Legal Reasoning*. In YLC&T, Vol. 4. Butterworths, London, (1990) 221-28.

Susskind, Richard, E. *Expert Systems in Law: A Jurisprudential Inquiry*. Clarendon Press, Oxford, (1987).

Susskind, Richard, E. *Pragmatism and Purism in Artificial Intelligence and Legal Reasoning*. Paper presented at ESL-89, Bologna, (1989).

Susskind, Richard, E. *General Survey of the Situation in Europe Concerning Artificial Intelligence Systems in the Legal Field*. In Council of Europe. Systems Based on Artificial Intelligence in the Legal Field. Strasbourg, (1991) 173-90, (Proceedings of the 9:th Symposium on Legal Data Processing in Europe, Bonn, 10-12 October 1989).

Svea hovrätt. *Språket i domar och beslut*. Allmänna förlaget, Stockholm, (2:nd ed. 1987).

Taddei Elmi, Giancarlo. *Origine, sviluppo, attualita' e prospettive dell'informatica giuridica.* Preproceedings ICLID-89, Appendix, IDG, Florence, (1989) 35-73.

Tammelo, Ilmar. *Modern Logic in the Service of Law.* Springer-Verlag, Wien, . . . (1978).

Tapper, Colin. *British Experience in Legal Information Retrieval.* M.U.L.L. Vol. 64D, (1964) 127-34.

Tapper, Colin. *Lawyers and Machines.* The Modern Law Review. Vol. 26, (1963) 121-37.

Tapper, Colin. *Computers and the Law.* Weidenfeld and Nicolson, London, (1973).

Tarski, Alfred. *Symbolic Logic.* In Newman, James R. ed. The World of Mathematics. Vol. 3, Simon and Schuster, New York, (1956) 1901-31.

Thompson, Donna M., Feinstein, Jerald L. *Cost Justifying Expert Systems.* In De Salvo, Daniel A., Liebowitz, Jay, eds. Managing Artificial Intelligence and Expert Systems. Yourdon Press, Englewood Cliffs, (1990) 93-121, (Yourdon Press Computing Series).

Tidskrift för rättssociologi. *Inledning.* Vol. 1, (1983/84) 2-6.

Traunmüller, Roland. *The Entrance of Informatics into the Domain of Law: The Different Faces of Informatics.* In Fiedler, H., Haft, F., Traunmüller, R. eds. Expert Systems in Law: Impacts on Legal Theory and Computer Law. Attempto Verlag Tübingen, GmbH, Tuebingen University Press, (1988) 139-48, (Neue Methoden im Recht. Band 4).

Trautman, Donald T. *The Computer in American Legal Education.* Law Technology Centre & Bileta Newsletter, Vol. 2, (1990) 95-101.

Triangle Books LTD. *Law, Computers and Artificial Intelligence.* Information leaflet, Wallingford, (1991).

Turing, Allen M. *On Computable Numbers with an Application to the Entscheidungsproblem.* Proceedings of the London Mathematical Society, Ser. 2 Vol. 42, 1936/37, (1936) 230-65.

Turing, Allen M. *Computing Machinery and Intelligence.* Mind: A Quarterly Review of Psychology and Philosophy. Vol. 59, (1950) 433-60.

Turkle, Sherry. *Artificial Intelligence and Psychoanalysis: A New Alliance.* In Graubard, Stephen R. ed. The Artificial Intelligence Debate: False Starts, Real Foundations. The MIT Press, Cambridge, Massachusetts, . . . (1988) 241-68.

Turnbull, Herbert Westren. *The Great Mathematicians.* In Newman, James R. ed. The World of Mathematics. Vol. 1, Simon and Schuster, New York, (1956) 75-168.

Tyree, Alan L. *Fact Content Analysis of Case Law: Methods and Limitations.* JJ, Vol. 22, (1981) 1-33.

U.S. Air Force JAG Law Review. Special Issue, *LITE, Legal Information Thru Electronics.* Vol. 8, No. 6, (1966).

University of British Columbia, Faculty of Law. *Law and Computers Project: Law and Artificial Intelligence Research Project and L.I.S.T. Foundation,* UBC, Vancouver, photoreprint, (1989).

van Noortwijk, C. *Criteria in the Juricas Project.* In Kracht, D., de Vay Mestdagh, C.N.J., Svensson, J.S. eds. Legal Knowledge Based Systems: An Overview of Criteria for Validation and Practical Use. Koninklijke Vermande BV, Lelystad, (1990) 36-42.

von Bertalanffy, Ludwig. *General System Theory: Foundations, Development, Applications.* Penguin Books Ltd., Harmondsworth, (1968).

von Jhering, Rudolf. *Der Zweck im Recht,* Vol. 1. Breitkopf und Härtel, Leipsig, (1877, 4:th ed. 1903), (English ed: Law as a Means to an End. The Macmillan Co., New York, 1924).

von Mises, Richard. *Mathematical Postulates and Human Understanding.* In Newman, James R. ed. The World of Mathematics. Vol. 3, Simon and Schuster, New York, (1956) 1723-54.

von Neumann, John. *First Draft of a Report on the EDVAC.* Moore School of Electrical Engineering, University of Pennsylvania, (1945).

von Savigny, Friedrich Carl. *Vom Beruf unserer Zeit für Gesetzgebung und Rechtswissenschaft.* Zeitschrift für Geschichtliche Rechtswissenschaft, (1815), (English ed: Of the Vocation of Our Age for Legislation and Jurisprudence. Littlewood & Co., London, (1831), Reprinted: Arno Press, New York, (1975)).

von Savigny, Friedrich Carl. *System des heutigen Römischen Rechts.* 1 Band, Berlin, (1840).

von Wright, Georg Henrik. *Deontic Logic.* Mind: A Quarterly Review of Psychology and Philosophy, Vol. 60, (1951) 1-15.

von Wright, Georg Henrik. *Is There a Logic of Norms?* RJ, Vol. 4, (1991) 245-83.

Wahlgren, Peter. *AI, kunskapsingenjörer och expertsystem i juridiken.* In Wahlgren, P. ed. Det goda kunskapssamhället: Ett perspektiv på rättsinformatiken. IRI, (1988) 59-67, (IRI-rapport 1988:5).

Wahlgren, Peter. *ADB, telekommunikationer och juridiskt arbete.* IRI, (1983), (IRI-rapport 1983:3 and Teldok Information nr 3).

Wahlgren, Peter. *Beslutstöd för brottmål: En förstudie om kunskapsbaserad systemutveckling.* IRI, (1987), (IRI-rapport 1987:5, and DV rapport 1987:9).

Wahlgren, Peter. *Artificiell intelligens, juridisk metod och nya rättsfrågor.* Juridisk tidskrift, Årgång 1, 1989-90, (1990) 496-512.

Walter, Charles ed. *Computer Power and Legal Language: The Use of Computational Linguistics, Artificial Intelligence and Expert Systems in the Law.* Quorum Books, New York, . . . (1988).

Walter, Charles ed. *Computing Power and Legal Reasoning.* West Publishing Company, St. Paul, . . . (1985).

Walter, Charles, Parks, Michael. *Natural Models of Intelligence.* In Walter, C. ed. Computing Power and Legal Reasoning. West Publishing Company, St. Paul, . . . (1985) 5-27.

Waltz, David L. *The Prospects for Building Truly Intelligent Machines.* In Graubard, Stephen R. ed. The Artificial Intelligence Debate: False Starts, Real Foundations. The MIT Press, Cambridge, Massachusetts, . . . (1988) 191-212.

Warner, David R. *The Role of Neural Networks in the Law Machine Development.* RCTLJ, Vol. 16, (1990) 129-44.

Warner, David, R. *A Neural Network-Based Law Machine: Initial Steps.* RCTLJ, Vol. 18 (1992) 51-63.

Wasserstrom, Richard A. *The Judicial Decision: Toward a Theory of Legal Justification.* Stanford University Press, Stanford, . . . (1961).

Waterman, Donald A., Jody, Paul, Peterson, Mark A. *Expert Systems for Legal Decision Making*. In Quinlan, J. Ross, ed. Applications of Expert Systems: Based on the Proceedings of the Second Australian Conference. Turing Institute Press in association with Addison-Wesley Publishing Company, Sydney, . . . (1987) 23-47.

Waterman, Donald A., Peterson, Mark A. *Models of Legal Decisionmaking: Research, Design and Methods.* The Institute for Civil Justice, Rand, Santa Monica, (1981), (R-2717-ICJ).

Waterman, Donald A., Peterson, Mark A. *Rule-Based Models of Legal Expertise.* In Proceedings of The First Annual National Conference on Artificial Intelligence. Stanford, (1980) 272-75.

Webber, Bonnie Lynn, Nilsson Nils J. eds. *Readings in Artificial Intelligence.* Morgan Kaufmann Publishers, Inc., Los Altos, (1981).

Weinberg, Gerald M. *An Introduction to General Systems Thinking*. John Wiley & Sons Inc., New York, . . . (1975), (Wiley Series on Systems Engineering and Analysis).

Weizenbaum, Joseph. *Computer Power and Human Reason: From Judgement to Calculation.* W.H. Freeman and Company, San Francisco, (1976).

Welbank, Margaret. *A Review of Knowledge Acquisition Techniques for Expert Systems.* Martlesham Consultancy Services, British Telecom Research Laboratories, Martlesham Heath, (1983).

Westin, Göran. *Pacta avtalsdatabas – ett datoriserat system för avtalsskrivning och förhandling.* In Magnusson, C., Torvund, O. eds. Datoriserad rättsinformation. Norstedts, Stockholm, (1987) 75-79, (NÅR 1987).

Weyl, Hermann. *The Mathematical Way of Thinking.* In Newman, James R. ed. The World of Mathematics. Vol. 3, Simon and Schuster, New York, (1956) 1832-49.

Wiener, Norbert. *Cybernetics, or Control and Communications in the Animal and the Machine.* John Wiley & Sons Inc., New York, (1948).

Wiener, Norbert. *The Human Use of Human Beings: Cybernetics and Society.* Houghton Mifflin Company, Boston, (1954).

Wilson, Alida. *The Nature of Legal Reasoning: A Commentary with Special Reference to Professor MacCormick's Theory.* Legal Studies, Vol. 2, (1982) 269-85.

Wilson, Eve. *Drafting Legal Documents With Justus' Clerk.* Preproceedings ICLID-89, Vol. 1, IDG, Florence, (1989) 909-22.

Winograd, Terry. *Frame Representation and the Declarative/Procedural Controversy.* In Bobrow, D. G., Collins, A. M. Representation and Understanding: Studies in Cognitive Science. Academic Press, Inc., New York, (1975), (Reprinted in Brachman, R. J. Levesque, H. J. eds. Readings in Knowledge Representation. Morgan Kaufmann Publishers, Inc., Los Altos, (1985) 185-210).

WIPO. Papers presented at *WIPO Worldwide Symposium on the Intellectual property Aspects of Artificial Intelligence,* Stanford University, WIPO, Geneva, (1991).

Wittgenstein, Ludwig. *Philosophical Investigations.* Basil Blackwell, Oxford, (1953).

Wood, G.D. *On the Classification and Evaluation of Knowledge-Based Systems in Law.* In Kracht, D., de Vay Mestdagh, C.N.J., Svensson, J.S. eds. Legal Knowledge Based Systems: An Overview of Criteria for Validation and Practical Use. Koninklijke Vermande BV, Lelystad, (1990) 9-12.

Zemanek, H. *Central European Prehistory of Computing*. In Metropolis, N., Howlett, J., Rota, G.C. eds. A History of Computing in the Twentieth Century. Academic Press, New York, . . . (1980) 587-609.

Zuse, Konrad. *Some Remarks on the History of Computing in Germany*. In Metropolis, N., Howlett, J., Rota, G.C. eds. A History of Computing in the Twentieth Century. Academic Press, New York, . . . (1980) 611-27.

Åqvist, Lennart. *Kausalitet och Culpaansvar inom en logiskt rekonstruerad skadeståndsrätt: En studie i analytisk rättsfilosofi*. Uppsala, (1973), (Rapport från Riksbankens Jubileumsfonds projekt n:o 68/35 om kausalitetsfrågor inom juridiken).

Åqvist, Lennart. *Towards a Logical Theory of Legal Evidence: Semantic Analysis of the Bolding-Ekelöf Degrees of Evidential Strength*. Preproceedings ICLID-89, Vol. 1, IDG, Florence, (1989) 21-47.

Åqvist, Lennart. *Deontic Logic*. In Gabbay, D., Günter, F. eds. Handbook of Philosophical Logic. D. Reidel Publishing Company, Dordrecht, . . . (1984).

Index

Computer/Law Series

1. Telebanking, Teleshopping and the Law

   Y. Poullet & G.P.V. Vandenberghe (eds.), H.W.K. Kasperen, A.P. Meijboom, A. Oskamp, M. Schauss, C. Stuurman

2. Freedom of Data Flows and EEC Law

   Poul Hansen, José Carlos Moitinho de Almeida, Pierre Catala, James Michael, André Prüm, Martine Briat, Michel Vivant, P.V.U. van Grevenstein, Femke Groustra, Joachim Scherer, William Casey, Patric L. Kelly, David Vaughan

3. Advanced Topics of Law and Information Technology

   Prof. G.P.V. Vandenberghe (ed.), K.D. Ashley, P.H. van den Berg, Prof. J. Bing, H.W.K. Kaspersen, Prof. A.A. Martino, A.P. Meijboom, A. Oskamp, Prof. Y. Poullet, Prof. E.L. Rissland, Prof. J.H. Spoor, C. Stuurman, Prof. M. Vivant, R.F. Walker, P.G.M. Zeinstra

4. Knowledge Based Systems in Law. In Search of Methodologies and Tools

   A.W. Koers, D. Kracht, M. Smith, J.M. Smits, M.C.M. Weusten

5. From Data Protection to Knowledge Machines.
   The Study of Law and Informatics

   Prof. P. Seipel (ed.), Prof. J. Bing, P. Blume, Prof. B. Brodda, H. Burkert, S.E. Colman, Prof. D.H. Flaherty, Prof. em. J. Hellner, C. Magnusson, Prof. K. Selmer, P. Wahlgren

6. Transborder Flow of Personal Data within the EC

   A.C.M. Nugter

7. Nordic Studies in Information Technology and Law

   P. Blume (ed.), M.Andersen, H. Bender, J. Bing, M. Börjesson, J. Kiuru, A. Saarenpää, P. Seipel, L. Skuterud

8. Amongst Friends in Computers and Law.
   A Collection of Essays in Remembrance of Guy Vandenberghe

   H.W.K. Kasperen and A. Oskamp (eds.), G.P.V. Vandenberghe †, P.H. van den Berg, J.M.A. Berkvens, J. Bing, E.J. Dommering, H. Franken, J.A. Keustermans, W. Kilian, A.W. Koers, D. Kracht, F. Kuitenbrouwer, A. Martino, A.P. Meijboom, G-J van Opdorp, Y. Poullet, S. Saxby, U. Seiber, M. Smith, J.M. Smits, J.H. Spoor, C. Stuurman, R.E. Susskind, M. Vivant, H.H. de Vries, M.C.M. Weusten, R.F. Walker

9. The Law of Information Technology in Europe 1992.
   A comparison with the USA

   A.P. Meijboom and C. Prins (eds.), J-F. Bellis, D. Bender, S.E. Colman, P. L'Ecluse, N.S. Ende, H.W. Hanneman, T. Hoeren, R.S. Laurie, E.C. Nooteboom, P. Samuelson, J. Scherer, M.D. Scott, H. Stern, C. Stuurman, M. Vivant, C.M. Wissels

10. Computer Program Protection in the USSR.
    A new era for socialist copyright law

    C. Prins

11. Automation of Legal Reasoning.
    A Study on Artificial Intelligence

    P. Wahlgren